HISTORICAL SOCIOLOGY

HISTORICAL SOCIOLOGY

PHILIP ABRAMS

Cornell University Press
Ithaca, New York

First published 1982 by Cornell University Press.
First printing, Cornell Paperbacks, 1982.
Third printing 1993.

International Standard Book Number (paper) 0–8014–9243–2
International Standard Book Number (cloth) 0–8014–1578–0
Library of Congress Catalog Card Number 82–61210

Printed in the United States of America

⊗ The paper in this book meets the minimum requirements of the American National Standard for Information Sciences—Permanence of Paper for Printed Library Materials, ANSI Z39.48-1984.

Publisher's note

Philip Abrams died after completing his final revision of this book. The publishers are most grateful to Professor Abrams's colleague Mr Richard Brown, of the University of Durham, who was most helpful in the preparation of the manuscript for press.

Contents

Preface

The chapters in this book try to do two things. They argue that many of the most serious problems faced by sociologists need to be solved historically. And they suggest that many of the supposed differences between sociology and history as disciplines do not really stand in the way of such solutions. Taken as a whole they propose that there might be much to be gained by reconstituting history and sociology as historical sociology. I am not talking about the need to give historical work more 'social context', nor about the need to give sociological work more 'historical background', nor even about the desirability of each field of work being 'informed' by work in the other. What I have in mind is a more radical recasting of problems, a deeper and subtler modification of styles of analysis, a more open and thorough-going recognition of the extent to which in some fundamental respects the two disciplines are trying to do the same thing and are employing the same logic of explanation to do so. The argument rests on the claim that at the heart of both disciplines is a common project: a sustained, diverse attempt to deal with what I shall call the problematic of structuring.

In the past thirty years the gap between history and sociology appears to have narrowed dramatically. The rise of quantitative history; a shift of interest among sociologists to problems of social transition; a growing concern among historians to understand the 'mentalities' of past societies and to explore the history of such unconventional matters as oppression, class-formation, lunacy, crime, magic, domestic social relations and generally, people in the mass; the publication of a series of very ambitious and ostensibly sociological works dealing with the processes involved in the formation of twentieth-century democracy and dictatorship, the great modern revolutions and even 'the modern world system'; a profound crisis in marxist thought over the nature of historical materialism and the passages between modes of production; a widespread borrowing of categories between the disciplines; all this has served to make earlier efforts to maintain strict distinctions and boundaries between history and sociology seem increasingly quaint, contrived and unnecessary. A few diehards on either side have held out for the old separations. Some radical critics have deplored the rather ill-considered and opportunistic nature of much of the recent convergence. Yet as Stedman Jones has noted (1976) the general consensus is plain enough: sociology as a theoretical discipline and history as an empirical discipline have been happily drifting towards one another for several years; a fruitful and contented marriage may now be envisaged.

With Stedman Jones I am not altogether happy about this image of confluence. But whereas his reservations have to do with the poverty of the theory he sees sociology as likely to bring to history – history needs theory but not sociological theory – mine relate to the whole conception of the disciplines as somehow different in principle in the first place. My argument in this book is that in important ways the conventional debate on the relationship between history and sociology, both on the side of those who welcome convergence and on the side of those who deplore it, is essentially misconceived. In my understanding of history and sociology there can be no relationship *between* them because, in terms of their fundamental preoccupations, history and sociology are and always have been the same thing. Both seek to understand the puzzle of human agency and both seek to do so in terms of the process of social structuring. Both are impelled to conceive of that process chronologically; at the end of the debate the diachrony-synchrony distinction is absurd. Sociology must be concerned with eventuation, because that is how structuring happens. History must be theoretical, because that is how structuring is apprehended. History has no privileged access to the empirical evidence relevant to the common explanatory project. And sociology has no privileged theoretical access. Moreover it is the task that commands attention not the disciplines. That, in any event, is what I shall be arguing.

There have, undeniably, been many digressions, deviations, fantasies and false starts. Much of the inter-disciplinary flag-waving and territorial wrangling between historians and sociologists has been focused on these lapses rather than on the central concerns of the disciplines as such. Admittedly, boundary disputes still persist. But I shall suggest that many of them rest on a confusion between principle and practice, a failure to distinguish clearly between what history and sociology require historians and sociologists to do and what for a variety of fortuitous reasons some historians and sociologists actually do, a failure to separate the logic of explanation from the rhetoric of academic interests. Indeed, much of the claimed difference between the disciplines is hardly more than a series of attempts by the authors concerned to appropriate the sort of work they happen to do for the discipline they happen to profess. Conversely, to the extent that one directs attention to problems rather than to practices, and the more single-mindedly one does so, the harder it proves to establish credible boundaries. If one attends seriously to the problematic of structuring as a way of formulating fundamental issues of social analysis all the proposed boundaries seem to me to collapse.

Some familiar contributions to the debate by Edward Thompson may serve briefly to illustrate my argument at this point. On a number of occasions and in a number of widely-quoted statements Edward Thompson has sought to advance the claim that class is to be understood as a relationship and not as a thing; specifically, as an historical relationship, an event not a structure or object. Sociologists in general and some marxists in particular are singled-out by him as typical purveyors of the contrary view. Mistaken marxists, Thompson has argued, try to discover class as a thing; sociologists, equally mistaken, claim that class does not exist because they cannot discover it as a thing. Against both versions of the heresy Thompson (1963:9) maintains the thesis that 'the notion of class entails the notion of historical relationship'. And so, like any relationship, 'it is a fluency which evades analysis if we attempt to stop it dead at any given moment and anatomise its structure'. Hence, 'the finest-meshed sociological net cannot give us a pure specimen of class ... the relationship must always be embodied in real people and in a real context'. Many sociologists might have to be forgiven for being puzzled to know just what Thompson expects them to find controversial in such a statement. But let us leave them puzzling for a moment and consider the fuller and more famous version of his argument (1965:357). Here again the 'placing' of sociology is achieved in quite blanket terms, as a gracious condescension:

> Sociologists who have stopped the time-machine and, with a good deal of conceptual huffing and puffing, have gone down to the engine-room to look, tell us that nowhere at all have they been able to locate and classify a class. They can find only a multitude of people with different occupations, incomes, status-hierarchies, and the rest. Of course they are right, since class is not this or that part of the machine, but *the way the machine works* once it is set in motion – not this interest and that interest, but the friction of interests – the movement itself, the heat, the thundering noise. Class is a social and cultural formation (often finding institutional expression) which cannot be defined abstractly or in isolation, but only in terms of relationship with other classes; and ultimately the definition can only be made in the medium of time – that is, action and reaction, change and conflict ... class itself is not a thing, it is a happening.

In his main argument here Thompson is of course also quite right – and I would extend his argument from class to most other supposed social entities. But it is not an argument which divides sociologists from historians in any generic way. Some sociologists, but also some historians, have indeed tried to treat class as a bit of the machine (and despite Thompson some of them have actually emerged from the engine-room waving what they claimed was the relevant bit). And some sociologists, as well as some historians, have insisted that as a social relationship class must be understood historically, in action. Weber's analysis, elaborated by Parkin (1974), of the transparency and closure of classes is just such a treatment as Thompson favours. So surely is the work done by Lockwood in *The Black-Coated Worker* (1958), by Willis in *Learning to*

Labour (1977), by Mallet in *The New Working Class* (1975), by
Sennett and Cobb in *The Hidden Injuries of Class* (1977),
Westergaard and Resler in *Class in a Capitalist Society* (1975),
by Barrington Moore Jnr. in *Injustice* (1978), by Wolf in
Peasant Wars of the Twentieth Century (1971) and of course,
triumphantly by Marx in *The 18th Brumaire of Louis
Bonaparte* (1962). Appreciation of the historicity of class, of
class as a relationship enacted in time (with equal stress on all
four of those words) is simply not a form of wisdom private to
the historian. Nor are the larger insights that time exists in
motion and that society is the time-machine working.
Sociologists and historians *alike* need to understand how that
maddeningly non-mechanical machine works if the puzzle of
human agency is to be resolved.

The paradox of human agency is hardly a new discovery,
although from Hobbes onwards many people have unveiled it
as solemnly as though it were. In effect it is the empirical common
denominator of a vast body of social analysis which has always
obstinately refused to be relegated or confined to any single formal
academic discipline. We find it at the very origins of historical
materialism in the work of Vico, pervasively in the writings of
Marx and Engels. It is Schiller's problem of alienation, Hegel's
problem of estrangement and Lukacs' problem of reification.
It is celebrated as the intellectual pivot of sociology by Herbert
Spencer. It is a recurrent nightmare in the work of Max Weber.
We find it tamed as the problem of unintended consequences
and latent functions by R. K. Merton (1957), re-invigorated as
the 'awesome' heart of the social construction of reality by
Berger and Luckmann (1967), strenuously wrestled with by
Alvin Gouldner (1970) and Alan Dawe (1979), claimed as the
defining concern of historians by Edward Thompson (1978).
The problem of agency is the problem of finding a way of
accounting for human experience which recognises simultaneously and in equal measure that history and society are
made by constant and more or less purposeful individual
action *and* that individual action, however purposeful, is made
by history and society. How do we, as active subjects make a
world of objects which then, as it were, become subjects
making us their objects? It is the problem of individual and
society, consciousness and being, action and structure; a

problem to which the voices of everyday life speak as loudly as those of scholars. It is easily and endlessly formulated but, it seems, stupefyingly difficult to resolve. People make their own history – but only under definite circumstances and conditions: we act through a world of rules which our action creates, breaks and renews – we are creatures of rules, the rules are our creations: we make our own world – the world confronts us as an implacable and autonomous system of social facts. The variations on the theme are innumerable; and the failure of the human sciences to work the theme to a satisfactory conclusion is inscribed on page after page of the literature of each of those sciences, as it is in the babbling echoes of the theme constantly thrown up from our ordinary experience of ordinary social relations. The estranged symbiosis of action and structure is both a commonplace of everyday life and the unbudgeable fulcrum of social analysis.

In sociology the distinctive product of the puzzle of agency is 'the two sociologies', the coexistence of a sociology of action and a sociology of social system which never manage to meet to settle their residual problems of system and action. More especially, as Dawe (1979) has stressed, the history of sociology is a history of repeated attempts to give the idea of action a central and active place in interpretations of the relationship of individual and society which repeatedly end up negating themselves and producing a sociology in which action is subordinated to system. Just as in the practice of life action succumbs to powers and constraints which are themselves the products of action, so in sociology attempts to theorise the patterning of experience from the perspective of action have ended up as theories in which the explanation of agency succumbs to the logic of social system. By many devious routes sociology seems to have spent its time rediscovering the dismal paradox Dawe (1979:398) ascribes to Weber, 'human agency becomes human bondage because of the very nature of human agency'.

Insofar as the dilemma of agency is a practical dilemma of individuals in society we should not expect it to be resolved by the human sciences. Marx was surely right when he maintained that practical dilemmas of that sort, the contrived dualities of consciousness and being, are to be resolved, if at all, in practice and not in thought. What thought, or at least knowledge, can do, however, is to help us to understand the terms and conditions of our dilemmas by filling-out their form and content. And the most promising move I can envisage from that point of view so far as the dilemma of human agency is concerned is to insist on the need to conceive of that dilemma historically: to insist on the ways in which and the extent to which the relationship of action and structure is to be understood as a matter of process in time. I would almost say that it is a question of trying to build a sociology of process as an alternative to our tried, worn and inadequate sociologies of action and system. And that is where the problematic of structuring comes in. It re-unites sociology with the other human sciences, especially history. And it does so, not by way of a casual marriage of defective theory to an unprincipled empiricism, but through the re-discovery of an authentic and fundamental common interest. Whatever the apparent pre-occupations of historians and sociologists, whatever excesses of self-indulgent fact-grubbing or zealous theory-construction may have distracted them, it is the common and inescapable problematic of structuring which gives their work its final seriousness.

I hope the term problematic is not regarded as esoteric or sectarian. Although the word has become a term of art in some quarters its reference is really quite straightforward. A problematic is a rudimentary organisation of a field of phenomena which yields problems for investigation. The organisation occurs on the basis of some more or less explicitly theoretical presuppositions – it is an application of assumptions and principles to phenomena in order to constitute a range of enquiry. Johnson (1979:201) speaks of a problematic as 'a definite theoretical structure', a 'field of concepts which organises a particular science or individual text by making it possible to ask some kinds of questions and by suppressing others'. In other words one's problematic is the sense of significance and coherence one brings to the world in general in order to make sense of it in particular. The fact that one is moving within 'a field of concepts' may or may not be overtly conceded and understood. Some disciplines are more forth-coming than others. Some seek to persuade through the rhetoric of a seemingly artless empiricism. Thus, as Johnson aptly continues: 'In works of history the organising ideas and presuppositions may lie very deep. They none the less exist.' And once that is granted the common centrality of the problematic of structuring surfaces swiftly enough. On the side of history the starting point for a recognition of the fact that that is the problematic within which one has been working is perhaps no more than a, possibly startled, realisation that the stories one has worked so hard to tell are not after all self-explanatory – that one has in fact oneself been structuring, not just 'telling'. In that respect the self-consciousness of works such as *The Making of the English Working Class* or *Injustice* represents a vital revolution in the writing of history. On the side of sociology things are, of course, slightly more complicated. It was not so much the relevance of history that sociologists failed to see as the relevance of time. Even when interest in the sociology of past societies and in problems such as the transition to industrialism was at its highest, and even among those who were themselves working on such historical questions, sociologists retained an impressive ability to ignore the fact that history happens in time. Accordingly, they also managed not to see either the possibility or the need to reconstitute the action and structure antimony as a matter of process in time, to re-organise their investigations in terms of the dialectics of structuring.

There were indeed some general calls for a recognition of the importance of historical time in social analysis and some adumbrations of how the re-thinking of sociology on the basis of that recognition might proceed. Such encouragements came, moreover, from quite diverse sources. C. W. Mills (1959) regularly insisted on the inseparability of history and sociology. E. A. Shils (1975) more than once urged his colleagues to see that 'time is also a constitutive property of society'. John Barnes (1971) valuably directed attention to issues of duration and succession. Pierre Bourdieu (1973, 1977) forcefully established the power of the notion of reproduction as a way of conceiving the social processes mediating structure and practice. The problematic of structuring was, slowly and piecemeal, being formulated as an alternative to the problematic of action and structure. Yet the most ambitious, wide-ranging and sustained attempt to identify that alternative, the work of Norbert Elias (1978b), was to remain largely neglected for years. It seems that the emptiness of the old answers had to be appreciated ad nauseam before sociologists would seriously consider the possibility of asking different questions. Perhaps, although it is too soon to tell, the break came in 1979 when Dawe demonstrated the exhaustion of the old programmes and almost at the same moment Giddens published a manifesto for a new, time-centred enterprise.

Central Problems in Social Theory is the first work in which the problematic of action *and* structure, in all its forms, is directly repudiated and replaced as a basis for general theory by the problematic of structuring – although Giddens himself does not use that term. What he does do of course is to present the essential terms and relations of a complex formal theory of 'structuration', a theory built round the idea of the 'fundamentally recursive character of social life' and designed precisely to to express 'the mutual dependence of structure and agency' in terms of process in time. Here, the necessity of appropriating time as well as history is at last fully seized:

> The exclusion of time on the level of the duree of human agency has its counterpart in the repression of the temporality of social institutions in social theory – a repression effected largely by means of the division of synchrony from diachrony. On the basis of this division, sociologists have been content to leave the succession of events in time to the historians, some of whom as their part of the bargain have been prepared to relinquish the structural properties of social systems to the sociologists. But this kind of separation has no rational justification: with the recovery of temporality as integral to social theory history and sociology become methodologically indistinguishable. (Giddens, 1979:8)

Giddens's attempt at a formal general theory is of course only one of many tasks that invite attention within the framework of the problematic of structuring. Indeed, the formal general theory he elaborates is only one of many such theories which the problematic could sustain and between which dialogue might be frutiful. Another obvious but perhaps less glamorous task would be to investigate the implications of the notion of society as structuring for what might be called 'concrete historical studies'. It is to the clearing of the ground for that task that this book is addressed. In successive chapters I shall explore some ways in which a fairly mundane working apprehension of the problematic of structuring has emerged from successive attempts by sociologists to explain relatively specific historical transitions and master specific problems within the traditional domain of the historian. Failure has been as instructive as success in this respect and I shall not neglect a number of spectacular sociological mis-apprehensions of history. But there have been spectacular successes, too. And I hope by the end to have established, admittedly with less panache than Giddens, that a long collective tussle with immediate matters of historical explanation has also been a way of discovering the problematic of structuring and realising its capacity to integrate history and sociology as a single unified programme of analysis.

For Giddens (1979:230): 'What history is, or should be, cannot be analysed in separation from what the social sciences are, or should be ... There simply are no logical or even methodological distinctions between the social sciences and history – appropriately conceived.' And the appropriate conception is that of the process of structuring. In that sense Edward Thompson (1978:276) is both absolutely right and absolutely mistaken when he rules that: 'In the last analysis the logic of process can only be described in terms of historical analysis.' He is right in that the analysis must be through and through an analysis of structuring situated in process in time. He is mistaken in that, once that is conceded the separation of history from sociology ceases to have meaning. The chapters that follow hope to demonstrate and celebrate the meaningless of that separation.

1

Introduction:
sociology as history

Three types of historical sociology

Try asking serious questions about the contemporary world
and see if you can do without historical answers. Whether it is a
matter of conflict in the Middle East or in Northern Ireland, or
racism in urban ghettoes, of poverty and social problems on
the Clyde or the Tyne, or of the fall of governments in Italy or
Chile, we tend to assume that an adequate answer, one that
satisfactorily explains whatever it is that puzzles us, will be one
that is couched in historical terms. This appeal to history is not
a natural human inclination but it has become almost natural
to the modern western mind. The idea that 'in my beginning is
my end', that the present needs to be understood as a product
of the past, is one we have come to take for granted. And in
taking it for granted we achieve, perhaps unconsciously, an
important sociological insight. For it is indeed not the
'problem families' living in west Newcastle or south Chicago
today who explain the concentration of social ills in those
areas, but the long term workings of housing markets and job
markets of which those families are the present victims. It is not
the intransigence of the present governments of Israel or Syria
that explains the persistent risk of war in Palestine, but the
meaning and depth of that intransigence in the setting of
centuries of cultural and religious struggle, imperialism and
mistrust. It is not the incompetence or opportunism of
contemporary Italian politicians that accounts for Italy's
endless crisis of government, but the problems resulting from
attempts throughout the past century to make a unified nation

state out of a deeply divided and fragmented society. Insofar as we reject explanations of the present that deal with the present, insofar as we turn to history for more satisfactory explanations, we are turning towards a deeper and more realistic understanding. And we are also turning towards sociology.

Sociological explanation is necessarily historical. Historical sociology is thus not some special kind of sociology; rather, it is the essence of the discipline. All varieties of sociology stress the so-called 'two-sidedness' of the social world, presenting it as a world of which we are both the creators and the creatures, both makers and prisoners; a world which our actions construct and a world that powerfully constrains us. The distinctive quality of the social world for the sociologist is, accordingly, its *facticity* – the way in which society is experienced by individuals as a fact-like system, external, given, coercive, even while individuals are busy making and re-making it through their own imagination, communication and action. Thus the central issue for sociological analysis can be said, by Berger and Luckmann (1967), to be the resolution of the 'awesome paradox' discovered in turn by each of the founding fathers of sociology: 'how is it possible that human activity should produce a world of things?' And increasingly sociologists have come to affirm the wisdom of their founding fathers in concluding that there is only one way in which that paradox can be resolved: namely, historically. The two-sidedness of society, the fact that social action is both something we choose to do and something we have to do, is inseparably bound up with the further fact that whatever reality society has is an historical reality, a reality in time. When we refer to the two-sidedness of society we are referring to the ways in which, in time, actions become institutions and institutions are in turn changed by action. Taking and selling prisoners becomes the institution of slavery. Offering one's services to a soldier in return for his protection becomes feudalism. Organising the control of an enlarged labour force on the basis of standardised rules becomes bureaucracy. And slavery, feudalism and bureaucracy become the fixed, external settings in which struggles for prosperity or survival or freedom are then pursued. By substituting cash payments for labour services the lord and peasant jointly embark on the dismantling of the feudal order their great-grandparents had constructed.

In both its aspects, then, the social world is essentially historical. Process is the link between action and structure. The idea of process and the study of process are the tools to unlock Berger and Luckmann's 'awesome paradox'. What we choose to do and what we have to do are shaped by the historically given possibilities among which we find ourselves. But history is not a force in its own right any more than society is. Rather, as the French historical sociologist Roland Mousnier puts it (1973:145): 'History has no direction of its own accord, for it is shaped by the will of men and the choices they make. Yet with every second that passes, men are making their choice by their behaviour.' And how we behave now – whether we throw a bomb or go on a peace march, whether we protest about inequality or thrive on it – is very largely a matter of what previous experience has made possible and meaningful for us. The conscientious exam candidate and the truant are both dominated by the historically established weight of the institutions of education; the meaning of their activity derives from the reality of those institutions. We can construct new worlds but only on the basis and within the framework of what our predecessors have constructed for us. On that basis and within that framework the content of our activity may re-make or un-make the institutions that surround us. This shaping of action by structure and transforming of structure by action both occur as processes in time. It is by seizing on that idea that history and sociology merge and that sociology becomes capable of answering our urgent questions about why the world is as it is; about why particular men and women make the particular choices they do and why they succeed or fail in their projects.

In this sense historical sociology has always been a core element of sociology as a whole. The idea of process is crucial to the way sociological work is done. But sociology became historical in more specific ways, too. As a distinct way of thought sociology came into being in the face of momentous historical changes and from the first was shaped by the experience of those changes. By the 1840s, when systematic social analysis first became widespread in Europe, it was a common feeling that the pace and range of change associated with the political and industrial revolutions of the previous two generations had left the social world an incomprehensible chaos in which only the fact of change itself was certain. In the words of the poet Lamartine 'the world had jumbled its catalogue' (cit., Burrow, 1966:94). Faced with the prospect of intellectual and social anarchy the early sociologists sought an ordered understanding of the processes of social change and above all of the changes involved in the transition to industrialism. Marx, Weber and Durkheim, the three founding fathers whose influence is greatest today, all made the nature of the transition to industrialism the basic organising concern of their work and sought through understanding that particular transition to move to a larger understanding of social process, or history, in general. So, too, did their contemporaries Comte, Spencer and Hobhouse. All were sharply aware of living in a world that was changing dramatically from year to year and in which the relationships between the changes people wanted and the changes that actually occurred were mysterious, frustrating and obscure. Why did the pursuit of wealth seem to generate poverty on an unprecedented scale? Why did the triumph of the principles of liberty and equality appear to go hand in hand with monstrous new forms of oppression? Was what was happening to social relationships in the course of industrialisation a matter of chance, of choice or of necessity? How far was industrialism an unavoidable destiny? Which of its characteristics could be altered by human action, and how. Such questions could be answered in many different ways. What the early sociologists agreed about was that these were the important questions to ask. The transition to industrialism compelled the imagination. From the analysis of that transition one could move to a more general but no less historical sociology.

Thus Max Weber emphasised the ever increasing bureaucratisation of the social world which he saw as a dominant tendency of industrialisation. And he sought to relate that tendency to other characteristic tendencies of the same transition: changes in the scale of organisation, in the forms of the division of labour and its complexity, in the nature of legitimate authority and in the social bases of power. But his interest went beyond identifying the tendency to bureaucracy and relating it to its causes and correlates. He was also concerned with the strength of the tendency to bureacracy, with the extent to which it was a necessity of industrial society and with the extent to which and the ways in which it could be resisted or eluded. The study of bureaucratisation was thus at a deeper level a study of the relationship between individuals and institutions, a study of the *possible* ways of living in industrial society. In much the same manner Karl Marx's emphasis on the formation of classes and the structuring of class conflict was also an interest in identifying ways in which men could act within a powerfully given social setting to bring about desired results, a study of the relationship of social action and social structure in general. And the same can be said of Emile Durkheim's exploration of the relationship between the division of labour and the moral disorder he termed anomie. At the heart of each of these formidable contributions to sociology was the simple question: to what extent does the world have to be the way it is? It was the decision to seek an historical answer to that question that made each of these men sociologists.

We shall look in some detail at the answers offered by Marx, Weber and Durkheim both to the problem of the transition to industrialism and to the more general problem of grasping the relationship of social action and social structure as a matter of historical process. But there were of course many less successful attempts to deal with those problems and although we no longer need to spend time on them in any detail it is worth saying here something about the general way in which they went wrong. Modelling social science firmly on the natural sciences it was tempting to look for social laws that could claim the force of natural laws. Above all it was tempting to try to reduce the actual chaos of social change to intellectual order by postulating what one English social scientist called 'laws of tendency' (Buckle, 1857:27). The most ambitious versions of this attempt were those that evoked the idea of evolution and sought to identify laws of evolution underlying and governing the process of historical change. But while theories of evolution seemed to give a very strong and clear answer to questions about the nature of the transition to industrialism, spelling out in emphatic detail just where society was headed, they did so, paradoxically, by suppressing and denying the more profound concern of historical sociology, the concern to explain the relationship of social action and social structure as a genuinely two-sided relationship. Instead, these theories imposed on that relationship the notion of necessary laws of evolution, of a logic of evolution and of a goal that had to be reached. Willy-nilly, society was moving in a certain direction, through states of development and according to laws of growth. The only realistic action available to the individual in such an analysis is to adjust his behaviour to bring it into line with the tendencies which the laws of evolution will in any case realise. In such an approach the meanings and actions of individuals which should be half the subject matter of sociology simply cease to be interesting or important. At most one might, as Herbert Spencer did (1961), aloofly note the folly and perversity that led men blindly to defy their destiny. One modern and modified version of this type of spurious historical sociology, the argument that has come to be known as the 'convergence thesis', is discussed later in this book. For the rest it must suffice to say that when ideas of evolution and development occur in social analysis they usually do so now as they did in the 19th century as metaphors that lead one away from a genuine historical sociology rather than towards it.

There is, however, another type of sociology which is genuinely historical in my sense even though it does not concern itself at all with issues of the transition to industrialism or even with any other type of large-scale social transform-ations. Indeed, it might be called micro-history. History, the interaction of structure and action, is not of course something that happens only on the large stage of whole societies or civilisations. It occurs also in prisons, factories and schools, in families, firms and friendships. Any relationship that persists in time has a history if we choose to think of it in those terms; action in even the most restricted setting can be treated historically because it has a history. The state of childhood is also the process of growing up. The condition of being ill is also the process of becoming cured. And even in these small-scale social settings teasing out historical processes, the sociology of *becoming*, is for the sociologist the best way of discovering the real relationship of structure and action, the structural conditioning of action and the effects of action on structure. It is simply the most fruitful way of doing sociology. What we discover when we treat small scale social settings in this way is merely a history in which ordinary individuals loom larger than usual and in which the detailed interdependence of the personal and the social is accordingly that much more easily seen. The fact that we are talking about personal careers rather than about social revolutions, about, say, the child in the family rather than the working class under capitalism, or individuals becoming deviant rather than societies becoming industrial does not call for a different type of analysis. If anything the study of small scale interaction makes the necessarily historical nature of good sociology more rather than less apparent. What B does now can only be explained in terms of its relationship to what A did before in such settings; we have to see it as a moment in a sequence. We are forced to recognise here that it is not social structure as a timeless world of facts or social action as a timeless world of meanings but history that is the proper subject matter of sociology – that structure and meaning are related through action in time. Later on I shall examine some of the work of Erving Goffman and of David Matza as examples of this type of powerful but small scale historical sociology.

Meanwhile, we have three types of concern which can be said to constitute historical sociology. First, the specific concern with the transition to industrialism – to which we might add a concern that has emerged in recent years about what industrialism in its turn is turning into. Second, a concern to trace the pattern of freedom and constraint involved in the careers of life-histories of individuals in the immediate personal worlds of everyday social life – families, hospitals, churches, work-places. And third, the underlying insistence that what sociology is ultimately about is the relation of the individual as an agent with purposes, expectations and motives to society as a constraining environment of institutions, values and norms – and that that relationship is one which has its real existence not in some abstract world of concepts, theories and jargon but in the immediate world of history, of sequences of action and reaction in time. By contrast, theories about the relation of past, present and future which rule out the need for detailed examination of the action of individuals on social structure and vice versa by proposing laws and stages of evolution and development with a necessity of their own may be dismissed as something less than serious sociology. (I am not going to digress here to discuss evolutionary and developmentalist arguments in detail; definitive criticisms of them can be found in the works of Popper (1959), Nisbet (1969) and Hirst (1976).) And by the same token it should be clear that what is being advocated when we speak of historical sociology as the central element of sociology as a whole is a great deal more than a request for more 'historical background'. Most sociology books do have a chapter or so setting out the historical background of whatever is going to be discussed in the body of the book. Such chapters typically give an account of 'significant' events which provide the context for present experience – thus, slavery is often presented as part of the background to the contemporary situation of blacks in the United States of America, or the development of contraceptive techniques as an important background factor in understanding the modern family. But too often the rest of the analysis is quite a-historical – the black ghetto is not treated as something that is constantly being constructed and coped with; the modern family is not analysed as something that people receive and transform in the course of living their personal relationships. Doing justice to the reality of history is not a matter of noting the way in which the past provides a background to the present; it is a matter of treating what people do in the present as a struggle to create a future *out of* the past, of seeing that the past is not just the womb of the present but the only raw material out of which the present can be constructed. An example may help at this stage to bring this rather general argument to earth. Consider the question of the welfare state.

Making sense of social welfare

By the welfare state I mean the measures a government takes to protect the standard of living of its subjects in circumstances where the ordinary workings of the market are judged incapable of doing so adequately. Such circumstances typically include old age, childhood, motherhood, illness, disability, unemployment and low wage employment. And the measures taken will typically include pension schemes, child benefit or family allowance schemes, insurance protection against unemployment, industrial accidents and sickness and some degree of public control of health and education services. But while there might be fairly wide agreement about a minimal definition such as this of what the welfare state is, the larger problems of interpreting what any particular welfare system is and how it works have always been controversial. In Britain for example we find wide ranging controversy over both the effects and the purposes of social welfare. And behind those debates lies a much deeper controversy about the way in which the welfare system as a whole should be understood in the analysis of modern British society. These issues in turn link up with other disputes about why it is that our welfare system seems so persistently to fail to achieve its purposes – why for example in 1968 a fairly conservative analysis could conclude that despite all our welfare provisions 'around 5 million people are living below the standard which the Government feels to be the national minimum' (Atkinson, 1968).

So far as the effects of social welfare are concerned arguments range from the view at one extreme that welfare is an 'idler's charter' which shelters the irresponsible from the need to work, to the claim at the other extreme that it is a huge confidence trick in which working people are gulled into paying while they are working for the inadequate 'benefits' the state appears graciously to bestow on them when they are unable to work. There is a similar diversity of view about the purposes of welfare (Marshall, 1970). Some take the view that the purpose of the welfare state is simply to eliminate poverty, to achieve a national minimum standard of life below which no one is allowed to fall. Others hold, more ambitiously, that welfare schemes should seek as Marshall puts it, to 'maximise welfare', to develop services that will continuously improve the whole quality of life of the entire community centred on the idea not of a minimum standard for some but of an optimum standard for all. And then, more radically, there are those who hold that the purpose of social welfare measures is to advance the pursuit of social equality by redistributing real income from the wealthy to the less wealthy sections of society. Arguments about the merits or demerits of what welfare services actually do are of course closely bound up with these differing views as to what welfare should do. At the same time in a country such as Britain it is fairly clear that while some services have been organised on the basis of one conception of the purpose of social welfare, others seem to embody quite different purposes: thus, while the Supplementary Benefit system can at best be thought of as an attempt to eliminate poverty the Health Service is presumably an attempt to maximise welfare and the introduction of comprehensive education is at least often seen as a move in pursuit of equality. So what are we to make of our welfare system as a whole?

Strictly contemporary, a-historical, studies can of course tell us what the welfare state does. They would reveal, for example, that it actually does very little to redistribute income, that its failure to redistribute income means that its ability to maximise welfare is quite severely limited and that in recent years it has even failed quite spectacularly to eliminate poverty. But once we have that picture further questions arise if we try to pursue a sociological explanation of *why* the system works as it does. And as we move from what questions to why questions our sociology has to become historical. We find we increasingly want information about the ways in which the welfare state was constructed. Not that history provides an unambiguous answer. Far from it. But it is through historical analysis that we can begin to piece together what feels like a sociologically adequate understanding of why our present welfare state is the curiously mixed and often ineffectual creature we have found it to be. What we are after is an account in terms of action and structure, of social process, of how our welfare system came to be put together in this particular way.

Four such accounts are suggested in the available literature (Goldthorpe, 1964a, Parkin, 1972, Gilbert, 1973). By comparing them from the point of view of their adequacy as explanations of the welfare state we can get some idea of what is involved in good historical sociology. For convenience we can, by seizing on the main idea each of them advances in explaining the development of social welfare, label them respectively as the 'enlightenment' theory, the 'necessity' theory, the 'action' theory and the 'power' theory of social welfare.

The *enlightenment theory* proposes that welfare measures are introduced primarily as a result of the influence of informed and concerned public opinion and that it is the nature of that opinion that determines the nature of the measures. Such a view would emphasise the role of enlightened thinkers such as T. H. Green lecturing on the social responsibilities of the state in Oxford in the 1870s, and of social scientists such as Charles Booth and Sir William Beveridge producing research that demonstrated the need for welfare measures in later years, in creating a consciousness among politicians and legislators of reforms that could be introduced as well as a commitment to introduce them. Many of Green's pupils did indeed go into public life and were to testify later to the importance of his ideas in shaping their conduct. And few would deny the impact of Booth on the reconstruction of the Poor Law after 1905 or the direct influence of Beveridge on the character of the social security measures introduced in the 1940s. Nor can one altogether reject the more general argument found in such studies as A. V. Dicey's *Law and Public Opinion in England* (1905) that there are 'currents of opinion' in society, that such currents vary in strength at different periods and that when any one such current is particularly strong it will eventually impinge on legislators and find expression in legislation: thus, the introduction of welfare measures after 1895 is explained by Dicey in terms of the prior rise to dominance of a 'collectivist' current of opinion. Yet this approach surely leaves some vital questions unanswered, indeed unasked. Where, for example, do currents of opinion come from? Why is one, rather than another dominant at any particular time? And how precisely do such currents become embodied in legislation? For the sociologist, in other words, the enlightenment theory is too one-dimensional to be altogether satisfactory. It recognises, one might say, that men make their own history but not the equally important fact that they do not make it just as they please. Of course men act on the basis of ideas but the ideas they have at any particular time and still more the influence of these ideas is not just an intellectual matter. Many good ideas never get a hearing; many bad ideas flourish for generations. Their success or failure has to be understood in a more social way than the enlightenment theory allows – as matter of the social conditions in which they exist and of the resistance or welcome they find among people with the power to act.

By contrast the *necessity theory* of social welfare goes almost to an opposite extreme in emphasising the role of social conditions regardless of ideas and opinions in bringing about social reform. In this view attention is concentrated upon the existence of circumstances – poverty, unemployment, disease, illiteracy and the waste of life and resources associated with them – about which something has to be done. Social reform is seen as the unavoidable response to those compelling social problems. Thus, in his *Essays on the Welfare State* R. M. Titmuss (1958) appears to see many of our contemporary social services as a necessary response to the weakening of the family unavoidably brought about by industrialisation. In the same way he argues that modern warfare, especially after 1939, creates a need for welfare measures through its 'requirement' for a physically healthy population (to man the armed services), for the organisation and care of the city populations evacuated to the countryside and for the maintenance of a huge number of dependants – women, children and the injured. Such arguments, again, find a general expression in studies which treat the whole development of the welfare state as the inevitable solution to social problems inevitably created by the chaotic workings of the market in the course of the development of urban, industrial societies. A modified version of the argument from necessity can also be found in the view, adopted aggressively by Bismarck in Germany and slightly less openly by Lloyd George in Britain, that social welfare measures must be introduced if socialism is to be avoided; welfare is the necessary ransom capital has to pay to labour to avoid something worse. To my mind this is the strongest version of the necessity argument. But even this version is, once more, strangely one dimensional. It usually forces us to pay attention to the ways in which social facts and conditions constrain and impel men to act in certain ways and it corrects the bland tendency of the enlightenment theory to detach ideas from their social context. But at the same time it tends to deny the equally important fact that what men do in the face of even the most constraining social conditions is indeed something that they *choose to do*. In the seventeenth century people accepted poverty, in the nineteenth they were outraged by it – even though it is arguable that the conditions of life of the poor were actually worse in the seventeenth century than in the nineteenth. But then in the nineteenth century many middle class people took the view that the real problem of the poor was not their wages but their addiction to alcohol; that too was a choice, an interpretation of social conditions not just an inevitable response to social conditions. And if social welfare is a necessary response to the problems of industrialisation how was it that the Germans were the first to recognise the necessity or that the Americans managed to avoid doing so virtually until the 1960s? The necessity theory makes too much of social structure and too little of social action to be acceptable as an adequate historical sociology.

The *action theory* of the history of social welfare is a deliberate attempt to redress that imbalance. It seeks to deal with the specific, detailed features of historical change in a way that both the enlightenment and the necessity approaches fail to do; to explain why the problem of old age is met by contributory pension schemes in one country and by non-contributory schemes in another, or why welfare is treated as a right of the citizen in one period and as a gift of the state in another. It fills the gap between the ideas of great men and the problems of society by concentrating on the diverse ways in which problems are experienced by actual members of society and on the ways in which members of society turn their experience into competing and alternative proposals for dealing with problems and struggle to secure one solution rather than another. Thus, Goldthorpe in his important essay, 'The Development of Social Policy in England' (1964a), concludes that, 'the course of development followed must be interpreted as in large part the outcome of successive encounters between various sectional groups pursuing different and often conflicting objectives'. From such a point of view the analysis of the welfare state becomes a matter of seeing how the particular measures introduced in this country, rather than any others came to be introduced in the course of debates, campaigns and struggles between many different social groups – employers' organisations, the labour movement, religious groups, statisticians, doctors of medicine – each advocating different measures and proposing the solutions that made the best sense from their particular point of view. Legislation is a sort of net product of that process. The rivalry between the Church of England and the Nonconformist churches is built into early English educational policy. The views and interests of the medical profession and the private insurance societies dominate the early history of the health service. What matters in every context is to treat the explanation of social change in terms of 'cleavages and tension' and of 'the purposive action of individuals and groups in pursuit of their ends'.

In other words we do here have a serious attempt to understand history as a nexus of action and structure; an attempt to treat the task of sociological explanation as a matter of showing how people's action is shaped by the historically given social structures within which they find themselves and how their action becomes a process through which those structures are in turn changed. Yet the action theory has its own difficulties. The history of social policy is full of purposive action which fails to achieve its purpose, of groups pursuing ends which do not get realised. The measures that are introduced are not just a net result of the play of forces and groups in society; they seem rather to be a certain sort of result, a result in which some groups get rather more of what they want and some rather less. Some measures prove 'possible'; others do not. British Ministers of Housing after 1918 found themselves regularly unable to introduce the policies they favoured because they could not control either the building industry or the Building Societies. More generally the pattern of policy seems invariably to be shaped not just by the play and interaction of social interests and groups but by the fact that some interests and groups prove persistently more influential than others.

It is this aspect of social process that the *power theory* of social welfare seeks to take up. In contrast to the action theory it emphasises the extent to which action does after all take place within a social structure and that one of the things we mean by social structure is power – the fact that what any particular group of people get is not just a matter of what they choose to want but of what they can force or persuade other groups to let them have. Thus Parkin in *Class Inequality and Political Order* (1972) treats the welfare state not simply as the outcome of pressure on the part of groups of reformers but rather as an expression of what powerful opponents of reform chose to concede to that pressure. Demands for measures that would redistribute income between groups in society did not succeed. Rather, the measures that were introduced provided benefits for the poor by transferring income within the life cycle of the poor themselves. The point about such measures is not that they were preferable to the reformers but that they were *acceptable* to their opponents; and the powerfulness of those opponents was the decisive factor. Without denying the role of theorists in formulating reform ideas, or the relevance of social conditions in providing contexts in which reform of some sort can be made to seem necessary and urgent, and while recognising purposive action as the dynamic element of social change, the power theory thus achieves a more balanced and realistic sense of the relation of action and structure than any of its rivals – one in which the forcefulness of both is recognised. It is better history and better sociology. It answers questions which other approaches leave unresolved. And it gives us a framework within which we can understand both the pattern and the detail of the particular social process – the making of the welfare state – with which we are concerned.

Welfare in this view comes to be seen not only as an alternative to the uncontrolled workings of the market but also as an alternative to the greater control involved in the demand for socialism. One can thus trace, as Parkin does, a number of ways in which the welfare state as an alternative to *both* capitalism and socialism was constructed partly by design and partly by default as the most the weak could obtain and the most the strong would allow. It is action in the context of that sort of power not just action alone that explains why we ended up with, for example, a social security system based on flat rate contributions rather than on direct taxation proportional to income – a system in other words that imposes a relatively greater burden on lower income groups. More generally it explains why we have ended up with a welfare state rather than with either socialism or social equality. As Parkin puts it (1972:43):

> The attempt to remedy inequality by the welfare approach brings about relatively little disturbance of the stratification system. As a result it is much more palatable to the dominant class than certain other solutions would be. The reasons why socialists advance proposals for dealing with inequality are no doubt very different from the reasons which make such proposals acceptable to the dominant class. For socialists the attack on inequality contained in educational reforms and welfare measures springs from an ideological commitment to improve the lot of the under-class. But their eventual acceptance by the dominant political class rests on quite different grounds. Without too much exaggeration we could say that whether or not socialist approaches to inequality become politically viable or acceptable depends on whether or not they confer advantages on the dominant class or at least on important sections of it. Welfare and meritocratic reforms do carry such advantages ... Egalitarian reforms designed to change the rules of distribution and ownership do not. It is not surprising then that the former interpretation of socialism is accepted as politically legitimate while the latter is regarded as irresponsible or utopian.

Seen thus the making of the welfare state becomes an authentic record of the encounter of social activity and social structure.

Summary

Historical sociology is not, then, a matter of imposing grand schemes of evolutionary development on the relationship of the past to the present. Nor is it merely a matter of recognising the historical background to the present. It is the attempt to understand the relationship of personal activity and experience on the one hand and social organisation on the other as something that is continuously constructed in time. It makes the continuous process of construction the focal concern of social analysis. That process may be studied in many different contexts: in personal biographies and careers; in the rise and fall of whole civilisations; in the setting of particular events such as a revolution or an election, or of particular developments such as the making of the welfare state or the formation of the working class. The particular context to which sociologists have chosen to pay most attention is the one I have called the transition to industrialism. But in the end historical sociology is more a matter of how one interprets the world than of what bit of it one chooses to study. And on that basis one can say firstly, that there is no necessary difference between the sociologist and the historian, and secondly that sociology which takes itself seriously must be historical sociology. As C. Wright Mills (1959) put it, the whole 'intellectual promise' of the discipline is 'to enable men ... to become aware of historical structures and of their own place within them'.

2

The transition to industrialism: anomie

One cannot do historical sociology in a vacuum. Before you begin you must make some assumptions about what is worth studying. Living and acting within the social structures of industrialism sociologists have easily assumed that the construction of those structures, the transition to industrialism, is the one thing especially worth studying. Sociology as a whole is about that transition more than about any other historical process. The distinctive categories and concepts of the discipline, its critical problems and theories, are all coloured by the underlying assumption that industrialisation is the general historical process we most need to understand. It is not surprising, then, that the early sociologists we find most impressive and influential today are all writers who concerned themselves directly with the task of explaining industrialisation.

But just as to begin one must make assumptions about what the significant problems are, so one must at the outset also make assumption about what *sort* of problems the significant problems are. The raw materials of history are vast, endlessly complicated and in themselves no more than details in a chaotic flux of events. To make sense of that chaos we must start by attributing some provisional meaning to it; bringing to it some ideas of our own about the patterns that might exist within the flux and about how such patterns are produced and changed. The ancient historians for example tended to assume that history was made by great men; thus, the significant pattern they identified as the rise and fall of the Roman Empire was for them shaped almost entirely by the actions and characters of emperors, generals and kings. In his novel *I Claudius*, based on the work of those historians, Robert Graves at one point has his hero note that the explanation of the story of Rome is thus reduced to a matter of the lives of two or three hundred people. For those people the reign of Tiberius was an experience of brutal and horrific imperial absolutism; but for the other five million citizens of Rome the same period was one of peace and prosperity, the establishment of good government and flourishing trade. Most modern historians would certainly feel that the experience of the five million was at least as important as that of the three hundred in any account of the growth and decline of Rome that they could take seriously. But that is not quite the point I want to make here. It is not just that the sense of significance modern historians bring to the study of the past and to the interpretation of historical processes differs from that of the ancient historians. Rather it is that modern historians no less than ancient ones cannot but bring some sense of significance with them to their work. They, too, have to start with an idea of what sort of analysis will satisfy them – and once more that is something they bring to history not something history imposes on them.

One result of this is that there can be many differing or conflicting historical interpretations of the same episodes, events and experiences. And another is that in trying to decide between such conflicting or alternative accounts we must not simply 'appeal to the evidence' – what we will accept as evidence is after all a matter of what we in turn think is significant – but must also examine the assumptions underpinning the different accounts and ask how far the evidence marshalled in any particular account is, from our point of view, limited or distorted by those assumptions and how far on the other hand the whole package of assumptions and evidence strikes us as an adequate treatment of a significant problem.

This becomes an immediate challenge when we turn to consider the historical sociology of industrialisation. Agreed as they were about the significance of the problem of industrialisation, the founding fathers of sociology had very little in common when it came to the point of working out an initial sense of what industrialisation involved. They all started, as one must, with some notion of how action and structure were related, some idea, hypothesis, model or theory that indicated to them the sort of process they could expect to find emerging from that relationship. But fortunately the assumptions they made in that respect were strikingly dissimilar – fortunately because the resulting debate has been a fruitful and creative one for sociology as a whole. In this and the next two chapters, therefore, we shall examine the principal contributions to the explanation of industrialisation made by Emile Durkheim, Karl Marx, Max Weber and the groups of later writers who can be associated with them. At the beginning of chapter 5 I shall summarise the state of the debate between these three types of account of the transition to industrialism noting some emerging agreements as well as some continuing disagreements.

In each case the analysis will be found to have two principal elements. We may call these 'contrasts of type' and 'theories of tendency'. Each account offers us a contrast between industrial society as a general type of society and pre-industrial society as an alternative general type. In effect models are proposed identifying what are thought to be the essential characteristics of industrial society (or the present) and doing so by contrasting them with the essential characteristics of another model identified as pre-industrialism (or the past). In many cases these contrasts of type are based on variations of a single master trait: Ferdinand Toennies' most famous contribution to sociology (1955) is the contrast he drew between industrial society as a type of social system organised in terms of the impersonal links of 'association', and pre-industrial society as a system organised in terms of the closer, tighter links of 'community'; Sir Henry Maine (1954) drew a similar master distinction between present and past by emphasising the substitution of 'contract' for 'status' as the basis of social action in industrial society. The analyses we shall examine are more complex than these but all of them also proceed within the framework of a contrast of type. Similarly, all of them, having identified the difference between the present and the past in terms of a contrast of type, develop theories as to how the present was constructed out of the past by focusing attention on ways in which the historical interaction of social action and social structure can be seen to be *tending towards* the substitution of the industrial type for the pre-industrial. In some cases the tendency is treated as a strong, almost unavoidable one; in others it is much weaker, much more variable and much more actively constructed by the immediate activity of actual individuals – and such differences will prove very important when we come to judge the adequacy of different theories of this kind as good historical sociology. For the moment it must suffice to say that the organising features of all varieties of historical sociology concerned with the transition to industrialism do appear to be the contrast of type and the theory of tendency elaborated within it.

All approaches to the sociology of industrialisation also seem to agree on the broad nature of the fundamental empirical changes involved in the transition. As Faunce and Form (1969) put it, there is a general agreement that 'among the hallmarks of industrial society are a complex division of labour, an occupationally based stratification system and rationalised procedures for achieving social intergration' and that these attributes in some sense 'are the basic structural characteristics of industrial societies'. Given that agreement about the core elements of industrial society as a type of society, there has also been a measure of common ground in identifying the processes through which industrialism is created. Thus, to quote Faunce and Form again (1969:3)

> The processes with which we are primarily concerned are economic growth or increasing income per capita, mechanisation of production and increasing size of production organisations. The consequences of these processes in combination are important changes in patterns of division of labour, bases of social stratification and mechanisms of social integration.

Without necessarily accepting the particular cause and effect relationship – economic change leading to social change – suggested in this passage we can certainly accept the claim that the transition to industrialism has been identified by sociologists almost unanimously as a matter of the three types of social structural change Faunce and Form specify: in the division of labour, in the nature and sources of inequality and in the ways societies are integrated or held together. Taken together these changes have been said to constitute an overall process of 'structural differentiation'. Structural differentiation is a process in which different tasks or functions are increasingly separated out from one another and attached to specific social positions or roles. It is assumed that in pre-industrial society the whole of life is encompassed within a relatively limited array of social roles. Everyone is either a peasant, a lord, a merchant or a monarch, a child, a man or a woman, a believer or a heretic, and these few basic social positions govern and contain everything else that one is or does: peasants serve their lords and the whole process of production is contained in that relationship: the social standing of one's family determines one's occupation and whom one marries; children are reared within the family and perpetuate it by taking on the economic functions and social positions of their parents. But in the course of industrialisation the range of occupations enormously increases and the strong connection between family background and occupational task is broken; government, administration, the educational training of children all become specialised tasks performed by people specifically recruited for that purpose. From the point of view of the individual, life becomes much more fragmented: being a child in the family is something different from being a pupil in a school; one's own occupational destiny is not necessarily that of one's parents; being a wife ceases to be a status that determines the whole of one's working life; family life is separated from the life of work and may also be separated from the world of leisure activities; there are different religions within the same society, different ways of life, different bits of one's own life are governed by quite different moralities – at home you are expected to treat a few people as though they were unique, at work you are expected to treat everyone as though they were the same; try reversing the moralities and you are in trouble. The social world has become diverse and differentiated; it is, as Herbert Spencer put it, a world of 'complex heterogeneity'.

All that is, of course, a caricature. The pre-industrial world has its own complexities. And the industrial world is often simpler than it looks – family background for example still does determine occupational destiny for most people in a remarkably powerful way. Nevertheless, the caricature is not altogether absurd. It points, however unsubtly, towards the most immediately striking difference between industrial and pre-industrial societies, a difference that seems to be empirically undeniable. The range and degree of specialisation of occupations really are vastly increased; the moral separation of the various roles an individual takes or plays really does occur; industrial society is that sort of new social world. The emphasis on the transition to industrialism as a process of structural differentiation is thus not misplaced. But to emphasise that aspect of the transition gives rise to a rather special problem. If industrialisation is seen as above all a process of differentiation, specialisation, separation-out, fragmentation and the creation of distinct worlds in which different individuals, or worse, the bits of individuals involved in particular roles, live, then the problem that especially calls for explanation when one thinks about industrialism is obviously the problem of social integration. How on earth does the newly differentiated, diversified social system hold together? It is this problem which particularly dominates the historical sociology of the school inspired by Emile Durkheim.

Durkheim: the transition to chaos

The problem of social integration is the central concern of the whole of Durkheim's work. It is in his first major study, *The Division of Labour in Society* (1933) that it is treated most specifically in the context of the transition to industrialism and by way of a contrast of type between industrial and pre-industrial societies. For Durkheim social integration was primarily a matter of morality – of the coordination of individual activity within a social system on the basis of personal commitment to collective standards and rules. From the point of view of that assumption what was problematic about industrialisation as a process of structural differentiation was the way it broke up the shared universe of standards and rules within which all the members of pre-industrial societies seemed to have lived. The tendency of industrialisation was to make people increasingly different from one another and morally to encourage them to emphasise differences rather than similarities. Given a powerful tendency in that direction how could society continue to cohere?

Durkheim finds his answer in the workings of the process of structural differentiation itself. For him the dominant and dynamic element of that process is the march of the division of labour and his argument is that as labour becomes more and more minutely divided and specialised the foundations of the fairly simple forms of integration of earlier societies are undermined but at the same time the basis for a new and more complex form of integration is created. The progress of the division of labour dissolves one type of society and constitutes another. The contrast is captured in Durkheim's famous distinction between mechanical solidarity and organic solidarity.

In common with most other social analysts of his time Durkheim experienced the present as a perplexing and disorderly reality sharply contrasted to a past which he believed to have been orderly and understandable. With the English writer G. H. Lewes (cit., Burrow, 1966:94) he could have said: 'In this plight we may hope for the future but we can cling only to the past; that alone is secure, well-grounded. The past must form the basis of certainty and the materials for speculation'. And so, with the great majority of his contemporaries he set about understanding the present through a lens which he believed to represent the past. The past he took to be a social world decisively different from the present in being marked by a very low level of division of labour and a very high degree of social solidarity, a world that was structurally undifferentiated and morally cohesive. Compared to that model of the past the social world of the present was marked both by a dramatic increase in the division of labour and by a dramatic decline of social solidarity: 'we repeatedly insist', he wrote, 'upon the state of juridical and moral anomie in which economic life actually is found' (1933:1); and again: 'functional diversity induces a moral diversity that nothing can prevent', 'disturbances are naturally more frequent as functions are more specialised' (1933:361). The two distinctive features of the world produced by industrialisation, in other words, go hand in hand. What precisely, then, does the advance of the division of labour do to social solidarity; and how?

Because solidarity is what Durkheim calls a 'moral fact' it cannot be observed directly; it is a matter of the dispositions within the minds of individuals. One must therefore, he argues, be content to observe it only indirectly through the study of social arrangements and practices which can be treated as indicators of moral facts – such as law, religion and folk custom. The particular indicator on which he seizes in *The Division of Labour in Society* is law. And what the law characteristic of past, pre-industrial or as he sometimes says, simple societies indicates to him is the condition of mechanical solidarity. Law in such societies is above all penal law, concerned with the repression of crime and imposed across the board on criminal acts without regard to individual circumstances and cases; it indicates the participation of all the members of society in a strong, uniform and inclusive moral order. By contrast, as the division of labour advances legal systems come more and more to consist of laws concerned to regulate the exercise of particular functions or maintain particular relationships; civil, commerical, administrative and domestic law rather than penal law now constitute the bulk of the legal system and give it its distintive character. And in this kind of law individual circumstances and functions are precisely what matter. In Durkheim's own terms repressive law is replaced by restitutive law. And what that change indicates is the increasing extent to which individuals participate in society not just as members of a single dominant moral order but genuinely as individuals with specialised roles and distinct identities.

The type of solidarity expressed by repressive law Durkheim calls mechanical solidarity. Its hallmark is the way in which individuality is contained within and limited by a 'strong and defined ... common conscience'; everyone is caught up in a single moral system and that system is brought to bear forcefully on all infractions and deviations. Such solidarity is possible only because, given the low level of the division of labour all individuals experience the world in very much the same way; it is a solidarity based on likenesses. Given those likenesses that part of the personality that is shaped by society completely dominates that part that we shape for ourselves and which expresses truly individual qualities. In the extreme case Durkheim suggest, 'individuality is nil'; a peasant is a peasant is a peasant. Obviously such a type of solidarity cannot survive a dramatic development of the division of labour; for as labour is divided people become different; each person now finds 'a sphere of action that is peculiar to him; that is, a personality' (1933:131).

The division of labour itself is seen as springing from the struggle of individuals to exist more fully as individuals in the face of an increasing volume and density of population and consequent pressure on resources. The first step is the creation of monarchy – chiefs and kings are the first individuals, the first people to acquire a sphere of action peculiar to themselves in which their own personalities can flourish independently of the common morality. Perhaps the ancient historians were not so mistaken in thinking that in their own societies history was the history of kings. Anyway, the process of dividing labour is driven on by the increasing intensity of the struggle of individuals to exist – specialisation of production, then of other kinds of work, is seen as the decisive form that struggle takes so far as the transition to industrialism is concerned. And as it proceeds the dominance of the common conscience is steadily eroded and counteracted by advancing individuality. In the extreme case a society is achieved in which the only really common moral imperative is the requirement experienced by every individual that he or she should truly be an individual, should be someone unlike everyone else, a unique self. In such a society mechanical solidarity has clearly become impossible. What takes its place?

At this point Durkheim seems undecided. On the one hand he observes that in practice nothing seems to have taken its place; that the actual condition of industrial society is one of unfettered egoism, confusion, disintegration and chronic anomie. On the other hand he argues that in principle the division of labour does in itself generate a new basis for solidarity – as the emergence of restitutive law indicates. Restitutive law expresses the way in which in becoming more specialised people also become more elaborately, precisely involved with and dependent on one another; the producer of motor cars is not also a producer of clothes; the employer is not also an employee; the bureaucrat is not also a farmer. The division of labour differentiates people but it does so in a way that impels them powerfully to cooperate with one another. In making themselves more specialised as individuals people also increase their interdependence as members of a society. As the common conscience succumbs to individuality in the face of the division of labour so the division of labour generates a new basis for solidarity rooted in the recognition of interdependence between specialised occupations. The solidarity based upon this interdependence is what Durkheim means by organic solidarity. And because he sees the development of the division of labour as itself a natural outcome of the struggle for existence he can conclude that: 'it is an historical law that mechanical solidarity which first stands alone, or nearly so, progressively loses ground, and that organic solidarity becomes, little by little, preponderant' (1933:174).

But here we must note that as an exercise in historical sociology Durkheim's treatment of the division of labour is notably unhistorical. Not only is there nothing in the way of careful historical documentation of the processes he describes anywhere in the book – he is not interested in anchoring his argument in any sort of demonstration of what actually happened – but it is clear that although he talks of historical laws he is in fact much more interested in the logical connection between the two types of society he has constructed than in their historical connection. The logical relation is one in which the division of labour solves the problems it creates. Thus: 'the division of labour is, then, a result of the struggle for existence, but it is a mellowed denouement'; it emancipates the individual from the common conscience but re-integrates society on the basis of occupational interdependence and a system of occupational moralities; it triumphantly resolves the paradox of enabling the individual to be 'at once more individual and more solidary'. But the historical relation is quite different. The actual record of the workings of the division of labour in the transition to industrialism is recognised by Durkheim in three chapters at the very end of his book devoted to what he calls 'abnormal forms' of the division of labour. But the point about the abnormal forms is that they are also the actual ones. It seems that there is more to historical sociology than the construction of contrasts of type and the derivation from them of theories of tendency. The third crucial ingredient, so remarkably neglected by Durkheim, is the critique of models and theories on the basis of close historical analysis – and beyond that the rejection, modification or reconstruction of models and theories grounded in whatever close historical analysis reveals. Durkheim's discussion of the abnormal forms of the division of labour is a sort of appendix to his main argument in which the relevance of this third dimension of historical sociology is recognised – although the problem it presented him with is not resolved.

He recognises three abnormal forms of the division of labour, three ways in which instead of producing the social harmony and integration it should produce occupational specialisation leads to conflict and social fragmentation. There is the inefficient division of labour, the anomic division of labour and the forced division of labour. The trouble in the first case is that the historical reorganisation of work results, as labour is progressively divided and sub-divided, in a great deal of waste; large numbers of people have too little to do, too much to do or jobs that are badly defined or fail to fit in with the work of others. The actual history of the division of labour gives rise at any given moment to a pool of people whose activities are simply not coordinated with those of the rest of society – small shopkeepers might be a case in point at the present time. The anomic division of labour, which is the abnormal form that most concerned him, is again a specifically historical product of the way the division of labour actually occurs. The speed and discontinuity of social change create situations in which in entering new occupations or embarking on new enterprises, people simply do not know where they are; the whole context of their activity is socially unregulated; there are no taken-for-granted ground rules for the conduct of the new social practices and relationships. In a sense anything goes and every contact with other people is treated on the basis of self-interest, as an occasion for suspicion, competition or conflict. Relationships are conducted on the basis of an egoistic 'groping' (a word Durkheim uses several times), rather than on the basis of an appreciation of interdependence. Durkheim finds examples of this historical outcome in economic and commerical crises and above all in industrial conflict; the whole world of economic activity turns out to have developed towards a condition marked by the complete absence of mutually approved and functionally relevant regulation: the 'new conditions of industrial life naturally demand a new organisation, but as these changes have been accomplished with extreme rapidity, the interests in conflict have not yet had the time to be equilibrated' (1933:370). The third abnormal form, the forced division of labour, is equally a matter of the specific historical context in which the division of labour occurs. But here it is a question of the context for industrialisation set by the actual social arrangements of the past rather than of the outcome of the activities of those living in the present. The division of labour does not occur in a context of equality of opportunity in which each individual can specialise as he chooses on the basis of his own abilities and preferences. Rather, it takes place against the background of an established system of inequalities in which some start out with great masses of wealth, property and other advantages at their disposal while others have nothing but the labour they can sell in an unfavourable market. In these circumstances the division of labour instead of taking its 'natural' course is forced or coerced into patterns of caste and class. Because the logic of the division of labour presupposes equality of opportunity this forcing of the historical division of labour into persistent patterns of inequality becomes a further source of social division and conflict. As well as an absence of regulation the history of the division of labour thus proceeds on the basis of the wrong sort of regulation; such regulation as there is, the regulation forcibly imposed by class, thus further distorts the process as a whole.

We are left, then, with a situation in which actual history in at least one sphere of activity, the sphere of work, departs drastically from the ideal or possible history Durkheim had extracted from the idea of the division of labour. And because in the transition to industrialism that sphere comes to colour and dominate all other spheres the transition as a whole has to be seen not as a reintegration of society on a new basis but as a disintegration, a transition to endemic conflict, division and anomie. In his Preface to the second edition of *The Division of Labour in Society*, Durkheim acknowledges the gap between his ideal history and actual history quite frankly (1933:3):

> What brings about the exceptional gravity of this state (of anomie), nowadays particularly, is the heretofore unknown development that economic functions have experienced for about two centuries. Whereas formerly they played only a secondary role, they are now of the first importance. In the face of the economic, the administrative, military and religious functions become steadily less important. That is why it can be said, with some justice, that society is, or tends to be, essentially industrial. A form of activity which has assumed such a place in social life evidently cannot remain in this unruly state without resulting in the most profound disasters. It is a notable source of general demoralisation.

He goes on to propose two kinds of deliberate action which he thinks will free the division of labour in industry from its abnormalities: the abolition of inherited property and wealth as a means of counteracting the forced division of labour; and the creation of self-conscious occupational and professional organisations and occupational moralities as a means of cultivating an awareness of interdependence and hence of substituting regulation for anomie. We need not follow him into these arguments, however. Instead, we can ask at this point what we should make of Durkheim's type of historical sociology. At first sight it seems to have been something of a failure. By concentrating on spelling out the logic of a process derived from his contrasts of type and his initial assumptions about the nature of the division of labour Durkheim appears to have got the actual history of industrialisation terribly wrong. His 'mellow denouement' is just what does not take place. Nevertheless, schematic and unhistorical as his work is, it is I think ultimately also a considerable achievement and a success. Just because the approach is so schematic, because it outlines a clearly defined possible process of transition and does so in terms that are tightly controlled by the logic of the idea of the division of labour it ends up by bringing to light and focusing attention on crucial features of the actual historical process of industrialisation of which Durkheim had been unaware at the outset and which his theory alone could not have predicted. It forces us to recognise, as Durkheim himself does, that alongside the division of labour anomie and class inequalities are fundamental influences in the historical construction of industrialism. To that extent Durkheim and his readers are further forward at the end of *The Division of Labour in Society* than they were at the start. Used in an essentially open-minded way as a tool of enquiry rather than a dogma the treatment of the transition to industrialism in terms of the logically probable history of the division of labour proves to be a fruitful and constructive contribution to historical sociology. It points out in a quite specific way why the theoretically probable course of events did not occur. In doing so it suggests the next questions we might ask and indicates what a more adequate interpretation of industrialisation would have to include.

Durkheim's heirs

But Durkheim's achievement was not just a negative one. Mistaken as he may have been about the tendency of the division of labour to produce social cohesion his underlying sense of the sort of process involved in the transition to industrialism has been accepted as correct by most contemporary sociologists. Most contemporary studies of industrialisation start from the assumption that what has to be explained is a process – identified by Durkheim – in which societies become at one and the same time more differentiated and more complexly interdependent. That is to say, the problem is not just to identify and account for the ways in which the process of structural differentiation is offset and counteracted by a concurrent process of growing and increasingly complex interdependency within society as a whole. This is the process which Szymon Chodak (1973) refers to as 'growing societal systemness' and Neil Smelser (1968) calls 'a contrapuntal interplay between differentiation (which is divisive of established society) and integration (which unites differentiated structures on a new basis)'. Chodak and Smelser are perhaps the two contemporary sociologists who have worked most effectively within this Durkheimian framework and we shall return to their work in chapter 5. But as Chodak observes almost all recent studies of industrialisation have built explicitly or implicitly on Durkheim's assumptions; his general framework has become the common framework within which the nature of the problem of industrialisation is specified.

It is of course an extremely general framework. The overall assumption is that in the course of the transition of industrialism societies acquire an enormously increased and varied array of distinct component parts – an expanded population, plus the distribution of that population into many more separate and independent activities and occupations, plus the appearance of many new and functionally specific social institutions (firms, bureaucracies, political parties, professional organisations and so forth) – and that those component elements come to be coordinated with one another and into society as a whole in increasingly varied and elaborate ways. That assumption gives one a clear sense of what to look for. But at the same time it does not pre-judge the question of what we shall find. It does not tell us how differentiation or integration are actually brought about or how they are related to one another – it does not for example tell us anything about the relative importance of the division of labour as a source of differentiation and of social stratification as a source of integration. It leaves us free to make our own judgements about such more specific processes in the light of our own historical inquiries. That lack of specificity is perhaps the strength of the approach rather than a weakness. It sets us a sociologically interesting problem without prescribing any particular historical answer. One might nevertheless feel that the trouble Durkheim got himself into by concentrating so exclusively on the division of labour and almost ignoring the concomitant development of anomie and inequality does give us a clue as to where we might look next in seeking to improve on Durkheim's own contribution to historical sociology.

3

The transition to industrialism:
class formation and class struggle

If one were to criticise Durkheim's treatment of history one would do so, I think, mainly on the ground that he grossly exaggerates the sense in which history is a social process independent of the individuals who, historically, enact it. Apart from two or three short passages in which he refers to the role of the struggle for existence as the source of the development of the division of labour there is really nothing in his historical analysis which even implicitly does justice to the fact that history, whatever its general patterns and outcomes, is from day-to-day made by individuals. The division of labour does not just develop or evolve in some sort of automatic or reflex response to the struggle for existence. It is always socially constructed, taking one form rather than another because some particular people have acted in one way rather than another – have within the given terms of the struggle for existence chosen to pursue the struggle by, say, specialising as merchants or masons rather than continuing as peasant jack-of-all-trades. It is not just the abstract logic of the division of labour that produces that result, however. It occurs within some historically constructed setting of opportunity and constraint – a setting in which many are obliged to be peasants or unskilled workers while a few can choose to be masons or merchants. The difficulty is especially clear in Durkheim's discussion of the 'forced' division of labour. But the problem he faces there, that some people have the power in any actual historical situation to determine how labour is divided for others while many more find that their labour must be divided in ways over which they have little or no control, is surely not

some sort of specially odd or as Durkheim called it 'abnormal'
case but rather what normally happens in most societies most
of the time. What proportion of any given group of school-
leavers in contemporary Britain have any real range of choice
about the way in which their labour will be divided?

In other words the division of labour occurs historically
within some context of structured inequality. It is this issue of
the way in which historically constructed power creates a
framework for the choices of actors in any particular present
that lies at the heart of the type of social analysis pioneered by
Karl Marx and Friedrich Engels. Unlike Durkheim, Marx and
Engels constantly insist on the two-sidedness of history – on
the ways in which history is at one and the same time a product
of both the chosen action of individuals and the forceful
constraint of social structure. My own experience suggests that
in this respect at least Marx and Engels were more perceptive
sociologists than Durkheim. As Marx puts it at the start of his
most subtle and sustained essay in historical sociology, *The
18th Brumaire of Louis Bonaparte*, 'Men make their own
history, but they do not make it just as they please; they do not
make it under circumstances chosen by themselves, but under
circumstances directly encountered, given and transmitted
from the past' (1962:i,252). History is made by the action of
individuals in pursuit of their intentions; but the variety and
conflict of those intentions and the weight of the past in the
form of ideas and institutions shaping and setting limits to the
possibilities of action ensure that in practice history becomes a
record of the *unintended* consequences of individual action. As
Engels puts it, 'Men make their own history, whatever its
outcome may be, in that each person follows his own
consciously desired end, and it is precisely the resultant of these
many wills operating in different directions and of their
manifold effects upon the outer world that constitutes history'
(1962:ii,391).

For Marx and Engels the problem of unintended consequences thus becomes the essential problem of historical
sociology: 'the many individual wills active in history for the
most part produce results quite other than those intended –
often quite the opposite'. The task is to understand the
relationship between what people intend their actions to

achieve and what the historical record shows them to have achieved. The failure to understand that relationship is responsible for the widespread illusion that history – since it seems unrelated to human intentions – is either governed by immutable and independent laws of its own, a matter of necessity, or a meaningless record of random events, a chaos of chance and accident. The type of analysis which Marx and Engels term historical materialism was an attempt to increase the possibility of effective action in the present by revealing just how present action is contained by the structures of the past. Through grasping the real relationship of present to past they aimed to overcome the sense of the futility of present action that sprang from the belief that history was either a meaningless flux or an inexorably and externally determined evolutionary process.

They identified their work as *historical* materialism because they saw human societies as embedded in their own past and thus regarded history as the necessary method for any adequate understanding of one's own world. And they identified it as historical *materialism* because they regarded the processes and relationships of production as the essential and defining processes and relationships in the creation of human societies. In *The German Ideology* where the nature of historical materialism is most directly and extensively discussed by Marx and Engels, production is treated as 'the first historical act' and the production and reproduction of material life is seen as the 'fundamental condition of all history, which today, as thousands of years ago, must daily and hourly be fulfilled merely in order to sustain human life' (1965:28). Earlier (1959:121) Marx had declared that 'the whole of what is called world history is nothing but the creation of man by human labour', and in a later work Engels (1962:ii,136) was to say even more emphatically: 'the materialist conception of history starts from the proposition that the production of the means to support human life – and next to production the exchange of things produced – is the basis of all social structure'. Such a starting point for social analysis was not especially uncommon in the mid-19th century. It led Marx and Engels much as it was to lead Durkheim to a sociology centred on the study of the history of the division of labour. And it was at this second stage rather than in their initial assumptions and propositions that Marx and Engels really diverged from other social theorists of their time. For them, the division of labour is also a division of men and of society. The process of production entails relationships which both create society and separate individuals from one another. And the core of both aspects of the division of labour is not the interdependence of functions as it was for Durkheim, but inequality; specifically, the division of society into classes.

Marx and Engels speak constantly of the 'definite relations' involved in all processes of production. Thus (1962:i,89):

> In production men not only act on nature but also on one another. They produce only by cooperating in a certain way and mutually exchanging their activities. In order to produce, they enter into definite connections and relations with one another and only within these social connections and relations does their action on nature, does production, take place.

And again (1962:ii,488), 'we make our history ourselves, but under very definite assumptions and conditions'; or (1965:46), 'the fact is, therefore, that definite individuals who are productively active in a definite way enter into ... definite social and political relations'. The relations entailed by the division of labour are seen as 'definite' in three ways. They constitute a specific 'mode' of production. Each mode of production is also a specific mode of power. And in turn each mode of power is a defining context for action, a definite way in which the past imposes itself on the present. The division of labour, the necessary means of satisfying human needs and creating human society, separates individuals from one another and produces a conflict between private and common interests. The specific form of this separation and conflict, this mode of production, is at any historical moment a question of power, of the ways in which the division of labour is made to work to the advantage of some and the disadvantage of others; the simplest form of the division of labour it is suggested is that embedded in the relationships of the family and based on the power of men over women and of parents over children. And the power created through the division of labour at any one moment of history is at the next moment presented to individuals as a system of independent and external constraints – the state, religion, law, custom, how things are – in terms of which their own future action must be shaped. Thus (1962:i,362-3) 'In the social production which men carry on they enter into definite relations that are indispensable and independent of their will; these relations of production correspond to a definite stage of development of their material powers of production. The sum total of these relations of production constitutes the economic structure of society – the real foundation, on which rise legal and political super-structures'.

Here Marx has introduced several new ideas. They all, however, follow strictly from his understanding of the dynamic and divisive nature of the division of labour. The division of labour permits economic development because it represents an every more efficient way of satisfying human needs, generating new needs and then satisfying them. At the same time, insofar as the way in which labour is divided gives some people power in relation to others through their ability to appropriate a privileged share of what is produced and use it to their own advantage a contradiction develops between the *forces* of production on the one hand and the *relations* of production on the other. Relationships brought into being to advance the satisfaction of common needs become, as a result of the appropriation of surplus produce by some, an obstacle to the further satisfaction of those very needs. Ironically, it is the mere fact that the division of labour does generate a surplus over and above what is immediately needed for the subsistence of the producers that permits the development of this sort of contradiction. Labour begets property; the separation of individuals is turned into the inequality of individuals. The most rudimentary form of this development is, Marx and Engels suggest, found within the family (1965:52):

The nucleus, the first form of [property] lies in the family where wife and children are the slaves of the husband. This latent slavery in the family, though still very crude, is the first property, but even at this early stage it corresponds perfectly to the definition of modern economists who call it the power of disposing of the labour-power of others. Division of labour and private property are, moreover, identical expressions: in the one the same thing is affirmed with reference to activity as is affirmed in the other with reference to the produce of the activity.

Increasingly, therefore the division of labour is experienced by the individual not as a means of realising common human interests in which he or she participates but as a remote, external system standing over against the individual and which he or she is compelled to enter (1965:54):

> The social power, i.e. the multiplied productive force, which arises through the cooperation of different individuals as it is determined within the division of labour appears to these individuals, since their cooperation is not voluntary ... not as their own united power but as an alien force existing outside them, of the origin and end of which they are ignorant, which they cannot control, which, on the contrary, passes through a peculiar series of phases and stages independent of the will and action of men.

Somehow the most distinctive and fundamental of human creations, the relations of production, comes to appear as a power existing independently of human beings. The purpose of historical sociology for Marx and Engels was to unmask the ways in which this apparent independence of economic history from human will had been, historically, brought about. In that unmasking exercise the crucial element was as they saw it an understanding of the significance of class – an understanding that within any mode of production the division of labour did not separate individuals randomly into isolated social atoms, but systematically into social classes.

Marx and Engels were at one with Durkheim in seeing the division of labour as the means by which human beings acquire individuality; it is through the division of labour that humanity progresses from the sheep-like existence of the tribe to the enormously varied individuality of the modern world. But for Marx and Engels the division of labour is even more forcefully the source of inequality. The appropriation of surplus gives the appropriators an interest in common and against other members of their society. They emerge as a class in open or latent conflict with other classes. The division of labour separates individual interests from the common interest; but it also re-groups interests along the lines of class. And in doing so it gives the powerful classes the means of consolidating their power: the surplus they have appropriated can be used to create legal, political, religious and cultural institutions in which class domination is legitimated and enforced. In place of the old common interest which class has shattered a new 'illusory common interest' which is really an account of the world legitimating class domination, is brought into being. The distinctive and principal form of this illusory common interest was, for Marx and Engels, the state. Class power and political power are two sides of the same historical coin.

Through the division of labour individuals take up definite roles in relation to one another, and to the means of production: man and woman, master and slave, merchant and peasant related to one another not only through the economic nexus of production but also through the social nexus of ownership and non-ownership (1965:43): the various stages of development of the division of labour are just so many different forms of ownership; that is, the existing stage in the division of labour determines also the relations of individuals to one another with reference to the material, instrument and product of labour. Yet, although the world of the division of labour appears to be a field of external power from the point of view of each new individual who enters it there is in fact nothing rigidly deterministic about the process of class formation as Marx and Engels understand it. Here the twosidedness of their sense of history is very apparent. Classes are made by people in certain circumstances; the definite, externally given nature of the circumstances does not at all diminish the importance of purposeful human action. The forms of the division of labour and of ownership and inequality do not march blindly through history with a momentum of their own. Specific modes of production and specific forms of inequality are actively made or not made by specific historical actors in specific historical settings. Consider this example offered by Marx and Engels in *The German Ideology* (1965:82):

In the Middle Ages the citizens in each town were compelled to unite against the landed nobility to save their skins. The extension of trade, the establishment of communications, led the separate towns to get to know other towns, which had asserted the same interests in the struggle with the same antagonist. Out of the many local corporations of burghers there arose only gradually the *burgher* class. The conditions of life of the individual burghers became, on account of their contradiction to the existing relationships and of the mode of labour determined by these, conditions which were common to them all and independent of each individual. The burghers had created the conditions insofar as they had torn themselves free from feudal ties, and they were created by them insofar as they were determined by their antagonism to the feudal system which they found in existence. When the individual towns began to enter into associations, these common conditions developed into class conditions. The same conditions, the same contradiction, the same interests necessarily called forth on the whole similar customs everywhere.

Or more generally in the same work: 'Separate individuals form a class only insofar as they have to carry on a common battle against another class; otherwise they are on hostile terms with each other as competitors'. Classes are formed as a structuring of individual action in the course of what Durkheim saw as the general struggle for existence. Once formed, however, 'the class in its turn achieves an independent existence over against individuals so that the latter find their conditions of existence predestined, and hence have their position in life and their personal development assigned to them by their class'. Class becomes the decisive setting for the next round of the struggle for existence; the struggle for existence is primarily, once it is social, a class struggle. Or as Marx and Engels put it in the famous opening passage of the *Communist Manifesto* (1962:i,34): 'The history of all hitherto existing society is the history of class struggles.'

Free man and slave, patrician and plebeian, lord and serf, guild master and journeyman, in a word oppressors and oppressed, stood in constant opposition to one another, carried on an uninterrupted, now hidden, now open fight, a fight that each time ended either in a revolutionary reconstitution of society at large or in the common ruin of the contending classes.

From the point of view of understanding marxism as a form of historical sociology the essential elements of the thought of Marx and Engels would seem to be: i) their sense of the constantly two-sided interaction of action and structure, purpose and constraint, through time as the basic form of history, ii) their sense of the dynamism of the division of labour as a source of both new forms of individuality and new forms of inequality, iii) their sense of the way in which the contradiction between the forces of production and the relations of production hardens into systems of class relationships and class domination – because the division of labour in all its forms is also a division of appropriation and ownership, and iv) their sense of the way in which class domination legitimates itself in the form of an illusory common interest embodied in religion, philosophy, law and above all the state – so that at any given moment in history the reality of class relationships is more or less thoroughly masked by an illusory world which the individual encounters as given, as the obvious and necessary context for his or her life.

The central concern of Marx and Engels was of course to unmask that illusory world as it existed in their own time. For them the nineteenth-century end-product of the history of the division of labour was not just industrialism but a distinctive class structuring of industrialism in the form of bourgeois society, capitalism. The hallmark of capitalism as a form of the division of labour, or the division of ownership, is the emergence of a class of producers who can own nothing but their own labour-power which they are forced to sell in return for wages paid to them by a class who for their part own the whole array of the means of production. Large scale industry is the distinctive form of production associated with this relationship; and the commodity, the standardised exchange-able object, is its distinctive product. The life work of Marx and Engels was above all an analysis of the real relationships of inequality hidden within the apparently natural market laws and political arrangements associated with capitalism; an attempt to unmask the facts of man-made exploitation behind the illusion of an externally given economy.

The identification of European industrialism as capitalism and the broad account of the essential relationships of capitalism advanced by Marx and Engels are hardly controversial any longer. There is still of course violent controversy as to whether the benefits of this mode of production in terms of economic growth (the dynamism of the forces of production) do or do not justify or outweigh its disadvantages in terms of human values (the oppressiveness of the relations of production). But that need not concern us here. From the point of view of understanding marxism as a form of historical sociology it is not the general analysis of the nature of capitalism so much as the more specific treatment of questions of historical transition, especially of the transition from feudalism to capitalism, that commands attention. Given that capitalism as the dominant mode of production of modern times emerged uniquely in a particular part of the world (Western Europe and North America) and in a particular era (broadly the 'early-modern' period between, say 1500 and 1800), the acid test for the force and adequacy of marxism as a type of historical sociology might well seem to be its ability to explain just why and how capitalism rose to dominance just when and where it did and not elsewhere or at another time. It is to that issue that marxist discussions of the 'transition from feudalism to capitalism' are addressed.

In practice, however, Marx and Engels as well as later marxists offer us three kinds of historical writing and we shall need to look at least briefly at all three. First of all there are discussions of historical method, of the way in which historical argument and analysis should proceed, of the problems with which it should be concerned and of the sort of explanations the historian should try to achieve. Good examples of this sort of work are found in *The German Ideology* and in many of the letters Engels wrote towards the end of his life to sympathisers or critics who, he thought, had failed to understand the real nature of historical materialism. Then there are a large number of historical case studies of particular situations, episodes or events. Typically, these are intended to bring out in detail the nature of the interaction of social structure and individual action within some specific historical setting. They emphasise the complexity, subtlety and pervasiveness of the ways in which class relationships set the scene for individual life and trace, too, the ways in which the forms of belief, politics, law, culture peculiar to given modes of production, societies and epochs come to be settings for action in their own right over and above the constraints of class. In the works of Marx and Engels two outstanding examples of such case studies are Marx's *The 18th Brumaire of Louis Bonaparte* and Engels' *The Peasant War in Germany*. And finally we find a set of major attempts to unravel the whole process of historical genesis involved in the transition from one mode of production to another, especially in the transition from feudalism to capitalism in the West. Interesting modern examples of this type of work are found in the famous debate that occurred in the 1950s following the publication of *Studies in the Development of Capitalism* by Maurice Dobb (1946), and in ambitious synthetic studies such as *Lineages of the Absolutist State* by Perry Anderson (1974).

Marxist historical method

We have already touched on the basic underpinnings of the marxist approach to history. Engels summarised it in a Preface he wrote for an English edition of *The Communist Manifesto* in 1888 (1962:i,28). Its 'fundamental proposition' he held was:

> That in every historical epoch the prevailing mode of economic production and exchange and the social organisation necessarily following from it form the basis upon which is built up, and from which alone can be explained the political and intellectual history of that epoch; that consequently the whole history of mankind (since the dissolution of primitive tribal society, holding land in common ownership) has been a history of class struggles, contests between exploiting and exploited, ruling and oppressed classes.

At the very least such a proposition tells one unambiguously what to look for and what to take seriously and what sort of explanation to attempt in history. Put in a strong form like this, however, it does appear to make marxist history a type of economic determinism and to invite a crude reduction of everything else in history to questions of class. Both Marx and Engels spent a good deal of effort repudiating that sort of interpretation of their work. The repudiation has resulted in a great deal of debate as to just what they did mean and many critics have argued that the position they seem to have adopted, the view that economic relations determine history 'in the last resort', with a great deal happening in between, is an unacceptable evasion of the real issue of whether marxism is or is not a form of economic determinism. Nevertheless, that really does seem to be the position they took, both in their statements of principle and, more importantly, in the practical way in which they actually wrote history. So far as statements of principle are concerned a letter written by Engels to Heinz Starkenberg in 1894 is representative (1962:ii,503):

> What we understand by the economic relations which we regard as the determining basis of the history of society, is the manner and method by which man in a given society produce their means of subsistence and exchange their products among themselves.
>
> Political, juridical, philosophical, religious, literary, artistic, etc., development is based on economic development. But all these react upon one another and also upon the economic basis. It is not that the economic situation is *cause, solely active*, while everything else is only passive effect. There is rather, interaction on the basis of economic necessity, which *ultimately* always asserts itself.
>
> So it is not, as people try here and there conveniently to imagine, that the economic situation produces an automatic effect. No. Men make their history themselves, only they do so in a given environment, which conditions it, and on the basis of actual relations already existing, among which the economic relations, however much they may be influenced by the other, the political and ideological relations, are still ultimately the decisive ones, forming the keynote which runs through them and alone leads to understanding.

Whatever the philosophical flaws and methodological evasions in this sort of statement – and there is a whole literature devoted to pointing them out – it does seem that the point of view it expresses can in practice support a very distinctive and on the whole rather rich and convincing approach to the study of history. Glimpses of this effectiveness are constantly provided in the way Marx and Engels themselves open out their discussions of historical transitions from the economic sphere towards politics and culture, constantly allowing politics and culture to be at least the immediately determining factors in the historical record. Engels (who, generally speaking was much more interested in and shrewder about historical analysis than Marx), again provides many striking demonstrations. Thus, in an Introduction he wrote in 1892 to the essay 'Socialism: Utopian and Scientific' he defends historical materialism by showing how it can be used to explain, for example, the religious bigotry of the English middle class in the mid-19th century. He begins with the class conflicts of the Middle Ages when the rising middle class of the towns, 'had conquered a recognised position within medieval feudal organisation, but this position, also, had become too narrow for its expansive power' (1962:ii, 102–3). He then offers what at first looks like a crudely deterministic comment: 'the development of the middle class, the bourgeoisie, became incompatible with the maintenance of the feudal system; the feudal system, therefore, had to fall'. But the falling of feudalism turns out to have been a remarkably devious, roundabout matter; not a question of direct class conflict, but something achieved, and only achieved, by way of religion, politics and culture. The Catholic Church and the history of science become key factors in the explanation (1962:ii,103):

> The great international centre of feudalism was the Roman Catholic church. It united the whole of feudalised Western Europe, in spite of all internal wars, into one grand political system ... It surrounded feudal institutions with the halo of divine consecration. It had organised its own hierarchy on the feudal model and, lastly, it was itself by far the most powerful feudal lord, holding as it did one third of the soil of the Catholic world. Before profane feudalism could be successfully attacked in each country and in detail, this, its sacred central organisation, had to be destroyed.

But there was another detour, too. Alongside the development of the urban middle class occurred a dramatic development of natural science and mechanics; and 'the bourgeoisie, for the development of its industrial production, required a science which ascertained the physical properties of natural objects and the modes of action of the forces of nature'. There developed accordingly an affinity between the middle class and science which meant that as scientists gradually withdrew from the protective intellectual umbrella of religion and became critics of the church in their drive to ask questions outside the limits prescribed by faith the middle class were drawn, indirectly, into an attack on organised religion: 'Science rebelled against the Church; the bourgeoisie could not do without science, and, therefore, had to join the rebellion'. From these arguments Engels derives the conclusion of the first stage of his analysis (1962:ii,103):

> The above, though touching only two of the points where the rising middle class was bound to come into collision with the established religion, will be sufficient to show, first that the class most directly interested in the struggle against the pretensions of the Roman Church was the bourgeoisie, and, second, that every struggle against feudalism, at that time, had to take on a religious disguise, had to be directed against the Church in the first instance. But if the universities and the traders of the cities started the cry, it was sure to find, and did find, a strong echo in the masses of the country people, who everywhere had to struggle for their very existence with their feudal lords, spiritual and temporal.

So a compelling connection between class conflict and a religious form of action has been established. But that is only the first step in the explanation. Some varieties of the religious struggle against feudalism led to dead ends; only one particular variety permitted the sort of middle class break-through that was achieved in England. The Lutheran attack on the church was, for example, a calamitous dead end. Involving as it did a rallying of religious opposition under the leadership of the German princes, it was undermined by the panic of the urban middle classes in the face of the demands of their peasant and artisan allies. Rather than stand by those allies the bourgeois group surrendered themselves into the hands of the princes. And (1962:ii,104):

> From that moment the struggle degenerated into a fight between the local princes and the central power, and ended by blotting out Germany for two hundred years from the politically active nations of Europe. The Lutheran reformation produced a new creed indeed, a religion adapted to absolute monarchy. No sooner were the peasants of northeast Germany converted to Lutheranism than they were from free men reduced to serfs.

Calvinism by contrast made possible an attack on organised feudalism much more conducive to the advancement of bourgeois interests. We shall have to look at Calvinism in detail in the next chapter as it provided a crucial element in Max Weber's analysis of the rise of capitalism. For the moment we may note that it managed to combine intense individualism, with ruthless spiritual elitism and both with a commitment to democratic or republican forms of organisation among the elite. Thus inspired, a much more confident middle class leadership could engage in a much less compromising assault on its enemies. At this point, however, a number of special features of the setting in which Calvinists found themselves acting in the particular case of England became important. The great feudal lords had extensively destroyed or emasculated each other in the Wars of the Roses; their successors had maintained their social position by moving away from exclusively feudal forms of exploitation toward an increasing involvement with money, trade and commodity production. The assault of the Tudor monarchs on the Catholic Church further emphasised this tendency by creating 'new bourgeois landlords wholesale', as Engels puts it. As a result when the middle classes launched their own attack on feudalism significant proportions of the aristocracy were themselves already 'bourgeoisified' to a significant degree. The conflict did not become an unambiguous class struggle and at the end of it the aristocracy and bourgeoisie were able to strike a compromise based on coexistence, Calvinism and the joint suppression of the lower classes (1962:ii,105–6):

> The compromise of 1689 was, therefore, easily accomplished. The political spoils of 'pelf and place' were left to the great landowning families, provided the economic interests of the financial, manufacturing and commercial middle classes were sufficiently attended to. From that time the bourgeoisie was a humble but still a recognised component of the ruling classes of England.

But as the bourgeoisie themselves saw it their new and privileged position had been won by and under the banner of Calvinism and it was increasingly on that basis that they sought to maintain it (1962:ii,106)

The merchant or manufacturer himself stood in the position of master, or, as it was until lately called, of 'natural superior' to his clerks, his workpeople, his domestic servants. His interest was to get as much and as good work out of them as he could; for this end they had to be trained to a proper submission. He was himself religious; his religion had supplied the standard under which he had fought the king and lords; he was not long in discovering the opportunities this same religion offered him for working upon the minds of his natural inferiors and making them submissive to the behests of the masters it had pleased God to place over them.

Intense and rigid religious commitment thus became the distinctive form of class relationships in this period of English history. And the commitment tended to be intensified within the middle class with every internal or external threat to the established balance of those relationships. The rise of free-thinking and of materialism and their association with revolution and a general turbulence among the lower classes from 1789 through to the risings throughout Europe in 1848, combined with the enormously increased size and much more visible presence of a partially organised working class in the wake of industrialisation all impelled the English middle class therefore towards a compulsive re-affirmation of their religious principles in the middle years of the century (1962:ii,113):

> Thus if materialism became the creed of the French Revolution, the God-fearing English bourgeois held all the faster to his religion. If the British bourgeois had been convinced before of the necessity of maintaining the common people in a religious mood, how much more must he feel that necessity after all these experiences? Regardless of the sneers of his Continental compeers, he continued to spend thousands and tens of thousands, year after year, upon the evangelization of the lower orders. Hence the parsons' majorities on the school board, hence the increasing self-taxation of the bourgeoisie for the support of all sorts of revivalism, from ritualism to the Salvation Army.

Whatever one may think of the accuracy or adequacy of this sort of explanation it can hardly be called economic determinism. Rather, it is just what Engels called it, a flexible and comprehensive 'historical materialism' (1962:ii,488):

The economic situation is the basis, but the various elements of the superstructure – political forms of the class struggle and its results, to wit: constitutions established by the victorious class after a successful battle, etc., juridical forms and even the reflections of all these actual struggles in the brains of the participants, political, juristic, philosophical theories, religious views and their further development into systems of dogmas – also exercise their influence upon the course of the historical struggles and in many cases preponderate in determining their *form*. There is an interaction of all these elements in which amidst all the endless host of accidents (that is of things and events whose inner connection is remote or so impossible of proof that we can regard it as non-existent, as negligible), the economic movement finally asserts itself as necessary. Otherwise the application of the theory to any period of history would be easier than the solution of a simple equation of the first degree.

The real difficulty with a method such as this does not, then, lie in the rigidity of its determinism but rather in its very flexibility. The problem is not that it too crudely explains all historical events and developments in terms of the relations of production, ownership and class, but that it makes such generous provision for the *mediation* of those influences by political, cultural and ideological factors that the causal connections between economic relationships and historical change become extremely difficult to trace. What really makes the marxist method hard to pin down is, paradoxically, the recognition it demands of the historical importance of ideological influences, of belief, perception and ideas. In Engels's treatment of the religious dogmatism of the English middle class in the 1850s it became clear that so far as the middle classes themselves were concerned class interest had come to be hidden behind a screen of religious commitment. More generally, the way ideology works is to make people unaware of what from a marxist point of view are the 'real' reasons for their actions. How then does one work back from what people believe they are doing to the 'real' meaning of what they are doing? In the absence of statements from Calvinist employers to the effect that they are engaged in disciplining the lower orders how is one to get behind the statements they do offer to the effect that they are engaged in promoting Christianity to show that despite their own beliefs the real historical significance of their religiosity is as a form of class discipline?

To my mind this is the fundamental dilemma of marxist historical sociology. Until some means of solving it is achieved marxism cannot (and indeed usually does not) claim to offer a scientific *demonstration* of the ultimate economic determination of history. Rather, it offers a more or less convincing *interpretation* of history as ultimately determined by economic relationships. How convincing such interpretations can be is a matter that must be decided by looking at the best examples of such treatments of history. The challenge for marxist historical sociology is to penetrate the 'veil of illusion' in which marxist analysis sees people in class society living their everyday lives and to reveal the ulterior, real, meaning of what they do. Particular historical case studies, investigations of specific historical problems, not general statements of principle, are the real test of how well that can be done.

Case studies: the failure of revolutions

Marx's two long essays, 'The Class Struggles in France' (1962:i,139–246) and 'The 18th Brumaire of Louis Bonaparte' (1962:i,247–344) are the more remarkable in that they were written not as armchair reflections on the remote past but as an immediate response to contemporary events. They are studies of the historical process not in retrospect but as it was being made. They are an attempt to explain the failure of a revolution. In February 1848 a great popular uprising overthrew the French monarchy and proclaimed a democratic republic; within four years, in December 1851, a furtive coup d'etat enabled Louis Bonaparte to destroy the republic and, a year later, establish himself as Emperor. Why had the attempt to create a republic ended by producing an empire – above all, an empire embodied in the uniquely paltry and inept figure of Napoleon's nephew? In his two essays Marx seeks to answer this question through an analysis on two levels: those of political action on the one hand and of social structure on the other. The argument moves constantly and with breathtaking agility from one level to the other; detailing a sequence of events, then placing it in the context of some structured balance of social forces; interpreting the balance of social forces and then tracing a new sequence of events through which that balance expressed itself. The overall purpose is to bring historical materialism to life through a vivid demonstration of the dynamic energy with which action and structure interact to constitute history.

The study opens with a crisp statement of its central theme; from February 1848 onwards almost everything that was done in the name of the revolution in fact contributed to the defeat of the revolution – men make their own history but not just as they please. The various groups that united briefly to create the republic went on to act separately to make the republic impossible. The base-line for the analysis is Marx's under-standing of the nature of the regime that was overthrown in February 1848 – a regime of bankers. The fact that we are to be offered a class analysis is established at once; but so is the fact that it is not going to be a simplistic class analysis (1962:i,139): 'it was not the French bourgeoisie that ruled under Louis-Philippe but one fraction of it – bankers, stock-exchange kings, railway kings, owners of coal and iron mines and forests – the so-called finance aristocracy'. That being so, the February revolution embodied an alliance of *all* the social interests frustrated or oppressed by the ascendancy of the finance aristocracy: industrial bourgeoisie, petty bourgeoisie, peasantry and proletariat rose together in an improbable but momentarily coherent common protest against that regime. 'The Class Struggles in France' opens with a careful analysis of the several ways in which the power of finance capital made the constitutional monarchy of Louis-Philippe intolerable to each of these groups. But Marx then recognises that oppression alone is not a sufficient cause of revolution. Rather oppression has to be *made* intolerable by actions and events. In this case the two crucial precipitating events were both 'external' to the French political system: the crop failures of the later 1840s combined with a general collapse of the Euopean money market initiated in England. The ensuing panic among the French aristocracy of finance led to demands from the industrial bourgeoisie for a share in political power and that demand, once voiced, became a focus for the opposition of all the other classes and fragments of classes in French society. Hence arose a general 'popular' agitation for reform, universal suffrage, the devolution of power.

But at this point another curiously 'accidental' factor proved all-important. This was the fact that the government was in Paris, and so was the French working class. The isolation of Paris from the rest of France meant that the action of the Parisian workers, playing their distinctive part in the general agitation, was decisive in shaping the initial character of the revolution. The workers set up barricades in the streets, defended them with arms and demanded a republic. Alone in the face of this demand, echoing as it did the events of 1789, Louis-Phillipe and his ministers lost their nerve, vacated their offices and made room for a Provisional Government. The mass of armed workers in Paris insisted that this equally isolated regime proclaim the republic. For one brief moment the revolution had been made by the working-class. But instantly the other elements of the alliance against Louis-Phillipe reappeared (1962:i,144): 'The Provisional Government which emerged from the barricades necessarily mirrored in its composition the different parties which shared in the victory. It could not be anything but a compromise between the different classes which together had overturned the throne, but whose interests were mutually antagonistic'. The unrealistic, fantastic nature of the alliance, Marx suggests, was captured in the way in which the leading personality of this phase of the revolution became the poet Lamartine: 'this was the February Revolution itself, the common uprising with its illusions, its poetry, its visionary content and its phrases'.

But at once the realities of conflict behind the symbols of unity began to make themselves felt. Ironically, the very demand of the workers for a republic based on universal suffrage was, in its effects, to prove the means of undermining the power of the workers. It opened the door to entry to the political stage for all social groups throughout French society – including the re-entry of the very finance aristocracy and monarchist landlords who had so recently been expelled. Most decisively, however, universal suffrage brought the French peasantry into French politics, through the constitutional arrangements of the republic they became the ultimate 'arbiters of the fate of France'. Their arbitration was, however delayed by the fact that, dispersed throughout the French countryside the peasants could not act directly and took time to realise and express their common interests. Meanwhile, the centre of the stage was occupied by other groups, the workers, great landowners and financiers and above all by the various fractions of the bourgeoisie who, happily unaware that the real power was in the wings, proceeded to enact the 'tragi-comedy' of the republic destroying itself. The rest of 'The Class Struggles in France' traces the unfolding of the drama these groups played out.

The Parisian working class proved unable to maintain the control of the direction of the revolution which it had seized in February once the nation as a whole had been drawn into the republic because the working class did not in fact exist as a self-conscious, organised class in France as a whole. The development of the working-class Marx argues is historically dependent on the development of the bourgeoisie; the former is brought into being by and in opposition to the emergence of the latter. And because the bourgeoisie, especially the industrial bourgeoisie had not yet established a general dominance in French social relations the French proletariat itself remained, half-formed, unselfconscious, unorganised. Its power in Paris misrepresented the pattern of class formation and the balance of class power as a whole. And as soon as the Parisian workers began to make demands which were at odds with the interests of their revolutionary allies their own isolation and weakness became apparent. And as that happened the middle-class leaders of the revolution increasingly felt able to act independently of and then against the workers. The critical issue from their point of view, Marx argues, was financial – a matter of establishing the economic credibility of the republic, of stabilising its credit: 'credit became a condition of life for the Provisional Government, and the concessions to the proletariat, the promises made to it became so many fetters which had to be struck off'; the costs of social policies for the working classes were seen as incompatible with the need for the government to honour its debts. Having first tried to solve the problem by taxing the peasants, the advocates of the restoration of credit gradually came to see that only one other solution was available to them; namely, 'to have done with the workers'.

There followed, Marx suggests, a period in which the bourgeoisie carefully tested its strength in relation to the workers, skirmishes and manoeuvres in which its power was secured and consolidated and the workers isolated from other social groups; the forming of a new militia, the meeting of the National Assembly following nationwide elections in May, a piecemeal assault on the workshops set up in the first days of the revolution served to separate the workers from the republic. Universal suffrage, he argues, 'unchained the class struggle' and accordingly 'in the National Assembly all France sat in judgement upon the Paris proletariat'. The republic now officially repudiated the workers both for the irresponsible costs of the policies they urged and for the unconstitutional dangerousness of their constant direct action in the streets. Finally in June the skirmishes erupted into war, 'the first great battle was fought between the two classes that split modern society'. The workers took to the streets again and after five days of fighting they were, in the name of the republic savagely suppressed. The illusion of class harmony created in February collapsed into the reality of civil war. The lesson of the defeat of the workers in June 1848 to Marx was clear: working class interests had to be obtained *against* the bourgeoisie not alongside them.

Yet this first act of republican self-destruction did not provide a stable basis for a subsequent middle-class republican regime. Rather, the same process repeated itself again and again as different groups within the remaining republican alliance sought to establish their own ascendancy and get rid of their troublesome allies. The June battle had been fought by the National Assembly in the name of the republic but also for the protection of property and the constitution; the banner in which all these themes were united was that of Order. And in each ensuing round of the drama the cry of Order served to shift the political centre of the republic further to the right. And in each case the essence of Marx's analysis is to try to reveal behind the political facade of successive conflicts a steadily clarified class reality. Thus the next round involved the parliamentary defeat of a group of radical democrats within the

Assembly; a defeat embodied in measures such as revival of controls over the press, a restriction of rights of association and ruthless enforcement of the rights of property. Behind the parliamentary battle Marx discerns a further narrowing of the social base of the republic. What was really happening he argues was the expulsion from the revolutionary alliance of the petty bourgeoisie, the small shopkeepers and traders and handicraftsmen who had played their own crucial role in the February rising as well as in the suppression of the workers in June. It was from this group above all that demands for freedom and the rights of the individual had come. But this group, too, had since February borne much of the immediate burden of the financial crises of the republic; it had become a group of debtors. And the real meaning of the measures of the autumn of 1848 lay in that fact (1962:i,168), in 'the petty bourgeois as debtors being handed over to the bourgeois as creditors'.

Increasingly, then, under the banner of order the republican parliamentary regime moved towards the creation of a legal and political framework for the enforcement of the sort of social relationships needed for the full development of the bourgeoisie as a class against all other classes. But increasingly, too, as an actually rather weak bourgeoisie moved in that direction the parliamentarians felt the need for strong government; as the social alliance behind the republic was stripped down, the republic had increasingly to be imposed by some on many others. Successive attempts at constitution-making thus gave progressively more power to an increasingly independent executive arm of government in relation to the unreliable legislative arm. It is this development that Marx documents, emphasising at each stage the accumulating self-destructive contradictions which he sees being produced by each new attempt to stabilise the republic. Together, he argues, they reveal a central contradiction which the republic could not resolve (1962:i,172):

> The comprehensive contradiction of this constitution ... consists in the following: the classes whose social slavery the constitution is to perpetuate, proletariat, peasantry, petty bourgeoisie, it puts in possession of political power through universal suffrage; and from

the class whose social power it sanctions, the bourgeoisie, it withdraws the political guarantee of this power.

In other words, the politicians of the bourgeoisie, committed to republicanism, could not give the bourgeoisie a constitution that would ensure their power; but, because they were committed to the bourgeoisie, neither could they produce measures and policies acceptable to the rest of France. Lurching from one expedient to another they gradually solved their problem by settling for what was more and more a presidential rather than a republican regime; for a means of effectively imposing order at whatever cost to the principles of republicanism.

This analysis, pursued in detail through the 'Class Struggles', explains, insofar as we think it succesful, why the republic was short-lived. It does not of course explain why the specific way in which it died was the establishment of the empire of Napoleon III. It is to that task that the '18th Brumaire' is addressed. And it is in this context that the full force of Marx's earlier observation of the role of the peasantry in this period of French history is made clear. The first Presidential elections were held on December 10th 1848 and in those elections Louis Napoleon was swept into office with a majority of five million votes over his main rival. The Presidency, instrument of order, was, Marx argues, the distinctive creation of the bourgeois politicians of the republic; the filling of the Presidency with Louis Napoleon was the no less distinctive achievement of the French peasantry. But why? If December 10th 1848 was indeed 'the day of the peasant insurrection', why did their insurrection take this particular form? Alienated from the republic by the tax burdens it had imposed on them the peasantry might have been expected to protest against the republic sooner or later. The presidential elections based on universal suffrage gave them a means of making their views known in a concentrated form; of expressing a peasant view in a way that had national significance. But even so, why Louis Napoleon?

Marx is at pains to reject any view of history which emphasizes the role of 'great men'. In its place he constantly tries to stress the ways in which individuals become historically significant as a result of opportunities for action given them by the unfolding of more general social relationships; individuals become 'great' through their meaning to and for others not by virtue of their own special properties. In the case of Louis Napoleon Marx argues that it was his meaning for the French peasantry that made him historically significant. In himself he was in Marx's eyes anything but great: 'clumsily cunning, knavishly naive, doltishly sublime, a calculated superstition, a pathetic burlesque, a cleverly stupid anachronism, a world-historic piece of buffoonery' – this is if anything one of the milder views of the Prince-President that Marx offers us. Yet these very qualities were also, to Marx, critical in ensuring Louis Napoleon's success. His ludicrous campaigns to present himself as the true political heir of his uncle were no less ludicrous because they had the effect of making available to the peasants a symbolic focus for their interests which had substantial meaning to them: 'Napoleon was to the peasants not a person but a programme. The republic had announced itself to the peasants with the tax collector; they announced themselves to the republic with the emperor'. And 'Behind the emperor was hidden the peasant war. The republic that they voted down was the republic of the rich'. The first Napoleon, as Marx saw him had indeed 'represented the interests of the peasant class'; and in that sense the peasants made Louis Napoleon his uncle's heir.

However, Louis Napoleon also meant other things to other groups. A generalised discontent with the republic had been created in the course of 1848 and he alone among the presidential candidates was able to catch-up all its distinct elements; much as the idea of the republic had served as a unification of opposition to the monarchy so the idea of Napoleon now served as a unification of opposition to the republic (1962:i,175):

> To the proletariat the election of Napoleon meant the ... dismissal of bourgeois republicanism. To the petty bourgeoisie, Napoleon meant the rule of the debtor over the creditor. For the majority of the big bourgeoisie Napoleon meant an open breach with the [constitutionalist] faction of which it had had to make use, for a moment, against the revolution ... Lastly, the army voted for a Napoleon against the Mobile Guard, against the peace idyll, for war ... Thus it happened ... that the most simple-minded man in France acquired the most multifarious significance. Just because he was nothing he could signify everything.

At that same time Napoleon stood in a curiously one-sided relationship to each of these groups and especially to the peasantry. Although he meant things to them he was not in any real sense committed to them. This was made brutally clear in the case of the peasantry by the fact that seven days after he took up office his government announced that the salt tax, the abolition of which had previously been decreed and had been especially demanded by the peasants, would be retained. 'With the salt tax, Bonaparte lost his revolutionary salt', says Marx; the notion of any real tie between him and the peasantry as a class was smashed. Thus, while peasant enthusiasm for the idea of Napoleon can explain Louis Napoleon's initial election it cannot alone account for his subsequent restoration of the empire. The empire was anything but the class rule of the peasantry. To understand the final destruction of the republic we must therefore, Marx argues, return to the groups more actively involved in republican politics.

The vital factor in Marx's ensuing analysis becomes the fear among the spokesmen of credit, property and the existing social hierarchy, the party of order, of the risks inherent in political arrangements which allowed the proletariat, peasants or petty bourgeoisie any significant participation in government. Haunted by this fear on the one hand and by the fear of a Bonapartist restoration on the other the politicians of the republic created an impossible situation for themselves. Having created a strong presidency they then decreed that no president could serve for more than one term of four years – thereby ensuring that Louis Napoleon and any one else who saw benefits in his government would have a vital interest in overthrowing the constitution. But at the same time they failed or refused to adopt policies which could give any social groups other than the still-emerging bourgeoisie any reason to support the republic. They created an unavoidable conflict between the executive and legislative branches of the republic while also making it clear that the legislature would be used to favour the interests of one narrow and as yet insecure social class. Because that interest had no mass basis they needed the executive to secure it. Hence, in the end their political struggle against the executive proved a fantasy. They had to surrender the republic to the executive once it became clear that the executive was the only force capable of guaranteeing the interests of their class. The body of the '18th Brumaire' is an attempt to provide detailed documentation for this thesis.

To my mind, Marx's analysis succeeds. Long before Louis Napoleon's coup d'etat the republican politicians had *implicitly* reached the conclusion that they would rather have the sort of society they favoured enforced by an authoritarian regime than have any other sort of society encouraged by the political system they professed. In that context the coup d'etat was a mere formality. In his close analysis of the political history of the last years of the republic Marx again and again moves through three distinct levels of action and experience. He starts with the short-term, day-to-day phenomena of politics – the speeches, debates, appointment and dismissal of ministers, arrests, proclamations, the level of events. And within the chaos of action and reaction at that level he discerns a steady move towards the concentration of power among the parliamentary groups in the hands of the party of order and at the same time towards the increasingly explicit recognition within that party of their weakness in relation to the president. This patterning of political action is in turn explained by Marx in terms of a major structural contradiction in the politics of the republic – the fact that the republican constitution was both the expression of the political power of the bourgeoisie and directly subversive of that power. Hence, the emergence of the party of order and hence that party's persistent dismantling of the republic in the very name of the republic. In effect the party of order 'declared the political rule of the bourgeoisie to be incompatible with the safety and existence of the bourgeoisie, by destroying with its own hands in the struggle against the other classes of society all the conditions for its own regime, the parliamentary regime'. Hence in turn the culminating paradox of a constitution providing for a strong but temporary president alongside a weak but permanent legislature. But from this second level, the level of the underlying structure of politics one can move both back to the first level, the level of political events or to a third, deeper level of explanation, that of the social structure as a whole. It is this last move that had to be made in Marx's view if explanation is to be complete. If we want really to account for events, or really to account for the general structure of politics, it is finally to social relations in society as a whole that we must turn. In this particular case the feature of the social relations of French society on which Marx seizes to explain both the general crisis of the republic and the specific seizure of power by Louis Napoleon is the peculiar balance of class power between the bourgeoisie and the peasantry. The bourgeoisie had appropriated the political stage; but in a crucial sense real power was still in the wings. Within the republic neither of these classes could either dominate or cooperate with the other. For Marx the heart of the problem lay in the peculiar nature of the peasantry as a class. His historical analysis thus brings him to his famous discussion of the sense in which peasants both are and are not a class (1962:i,334):

> The small holding peasants form a vast mass, the members of which live in similar conditions but without entering into manifold relations with one another. Their mode of production isolates them from one another instead of bringing them into mutual intercourse ... Their field of production, the small holding, permits of no division of labour in its cultivation, no application of science and therefore no diversity of development, no variety of talent, no wealth of social relationships. Each individual peasant family is almost self-sufficient; it directly produces the major part of its consumption and thus acquires its means of life more through exchange with nature than in intercourse with society. A small holding, a peasant and his family; alongside them another small holding, another peasant and another family. A few score of these make up a village and a few score of villages make up a Department. In this way the great mass of French society is formed by simple addition of homologous magnitudes, much as potatoes in a sack form a sack of potatoes.

And:

> Insofar as millions of families live under economic conditions of existence that separate their mode of life, their interests and their culture from those of other classes and put them in hostile opposition to the latter, they form a class. Insofar as there is merely a local interconnection among these small-holding peasants and the identity of their interests begets no community, no national bond and no political organisation among them, they do not form

a class. They are consequently incapable of enforcing their class interest in their own name, whether through a parliament or through a convention. They cannot represent themselves, they must be represented.

Universal suffrage enabled this real but otherwise impotent social interest to express itself; as separate individuals millions of peasants went to the ballot box and voted for Louis Napoleon. Yet the sense in which the prince-president was their representative was a curious one. In no way was he of the peasantry; nor had the peasantry any means of controlling him once they had elected him. Their distinctive lack of cohesion and organisation as a class meant that if he was to be effective it had to be on the basis of a power other than the power of peasants. At the same time the fragmentation of the peasantry meant that their political representation if it was to exist at all had to exist as government not as a party. Thus (1962:i,334): 'their representative must appear as an authority over them, as an unlimited governmental power that protects them against the other classes ... the political influence of the small-holding peasants therefore finds its final expression in the executive power subordinating society to itself'. Conversely, once Louis Napoleon had been placed firmly on the political stage by the peasantry his special relationship to them left him free to be cast as the representative of anyone else who needed him. As the party of order and the bourgeoisie at large edged slowly towards the realisation that the political system they had created was at odds with their social interest – as they came to understand that what they most needed was not politics but the state – Louis Napoleon became in their eyes increasingly eligible as the representative of their interests, too.

The final sections of 'The 18th Brumaire' trace the way in which the French bourgeoisie recognised the logic of their situation. Perhaps recognised is too strong a word for the process Marx describes (1962:i,323):

Picture to yourself the French bourgeois, how in the throes of ... business panic his trade-crazy brain is tortured, set in a whirl and stunned by rumours of coups d'etat and the restoration of universal suffrage, by the struggle between parliament and the executive power, by the ... war between Orleanists and Legitimists, by the communist conspiracies in the south of France, by alleged Jacqueries in the Departments of Nièvre and Cher, by the advertisements of the different candidates for the presidency, by the cheap-jack slogans of the journals ... think of all this and you will comprehend why in this unspeakable, deafening chaos of fusion, revision, prorogation, constitution, conspiration, coalition, emigration, usurpation and revolution the Bourgeois madly snorts at his parliamentary republic: 'Rather an end with terror than terror without end'.

Louis Napoleon, as Marx adds 'understood this cry'. The peasantry and bourgeoisie could not collaborate with one another; but they could coexist on the basis of the abolition of politics and the substitution of government; Louis Napoleon became the symbol and means for such a coexistence. It only remained for him to bribe the army, arrest the few remaining troublesome politicians at dead of night and bring down the curtain on the drama of the republic; the play had been over for some time before the curtain fell.

The ensuing regime of Louis Napoleon was not of course able to overcome the contradictions from which it sprang. But for eighteen years it put those contradictions on ice. Elsewhere (1965:53) Marx and Engels had already observed that the distinctive function of the modern state is to provide an 'illusory common interest' overarching and obscuring real conflicts of interest. And the distinctive feature of the Second Empire was in Marx's view precisely the way in which it constructed and elaborated 'the state' as an alternative to politics (1962:i,333): 'only under the second Bonaparte does the state seem to have made itself completely independent'. In place of the impossible politics of the republic in which the various classes acted out their powerlessness and hostility the new regime provided an administrative apparatus and an ideology of common interest; both were imposed on France under the guise of the state. But of course there was no common interest: the destiny of Louis Napoleon after 1851 was to seek desperately to be all things to all interests and to succeed in being nothing to anyone (1962:i,641): 'the contradictory task of the man explains the contradictions of his government, the confused groping which seeks now to win, now to humiliate first one class and then another and arrays them all uniformly against him.' The way in which the empire had come into being meant that the class struggles in France had been suspended, not that they could be settled. Political history is social history writ large.

Arguably Marx's studies of the political history of France between 1848 and 1852 are not the best available example of a marxist historical case study. I would myself rank Engels's analysis of another failed revolution, the peasant rising in Germany in the early years of the reformation (*The Peasant War in Germany*) as more impressive in terms of both historical scholarship and subtlety of interpretation. But the two essays I have discussed are probably more important than any others as a test of marxism's historical method. After all, the central issue for marxism is the analysis of the development and destiny of capitalism. And it is to the problem of historical explanation at a particular and crucial moment in the formation of capitalism that these studies are addressed. Any assessment of the adequacy of marxism as a form of historical sociology must therefore take them into account. My own feeling is that whatever one thinks of Marx's particular interpretations and conclusions one cannot but be convinced by the power of his method. There are many things in these writings of which conventional standards of scholarship are bound to make one suspicious – his delighted and obvious contempt for Louis Napoleon as a person, his equally obvious readiness to use any evidence that will serve his argument with no attempt to weigh its standing, his often elusive use of terms such as 'bourgeoisie', 'party of order', 'proletariat', with little or no attempt to specify just what groups are being referred to on any particular occasion. Yet underlying all that there is a conception of what historical-sociological explanation should be which remains, to my mind, very powerful. I hope this feeling will become clearer when we examine the way in which marxists have treated their most important general historical problem: the transition from feudalism to capitalism.

The transition from feudalism to capitalism

A difficulty sometimes experienced in reading the historical case studies of Marx and Engels is that they do not at any point make the *design* of their argument explicit. In the last section I argued that these works do have a specific and coherent method which involves the to-and-fro analysis of three levels of reality: events and appearances, the subjective world of action; political structure, the institutions, causes and ideologies created immediately out of the world of action; and class structure, the underlying formations within which action is contained. This method in turn follows from their general understanding of the nature of history and society and is strictly and efficiently applied in each of their main historical studies. But because they do not at any point within these works spell out just how they are arguing the effect on the reader can be confusing. Although their purpose is to show how the flux of day-to-day events is embedded in and shapes both political structure and social structure, the reader can easily find himself, like the French bourgeoisie in 1849 lost if not panic-stricken in the chaos of events.

This is a particular pity as it is especially their method, rather than their theory that is of importance for historical sociology. It is not the dialectic of class conflict but the dialectic of action and structure and process in terms of which the workings of class conflict are explored that makes these works valuable models of historical sociology. We may reject Marx's view of the significance of the relations of production and we may deplore his cavalier handling of the detail of history and still be impressed by the *way* in which he develops his historical analysis of the relation between events and the relations of production. It is not the specific claim that the relevant levels of analysis are those of events, political structure and class structure that matters in this context but the realisation that somehow the task is to analyse society in a way that recognises the two-sided dynamism of the relationship of action and structure and the consequent necessity of understanding that relationship historically. The one theoretical claim that is made explicit in Marx's case studies is to do with the weight with which the past bears on the present. It was the weight of the past that led the French in 1848 to seek emancipation in the form of a republic and then to escape from the consequences of emancipation through the form of Napoleon.

When we turn to the marxist analysis of the transition from feudalism to capitalism, the problem raised by Marx and Engels is almost the exact opposite. What we find in their writing are several very clear statements of how, in principle, the rise of capitalism must have occurred – and therefore of how it should be studied historically – but hardly anything that seeks to implement these guidelines in detail. Marx himself provides us with an account of what is *logically necessary* for the development of capitalism. For capitalism to become a dominant mode of production, labourers must be free to sell their labour power for wages, capitalists must be able to accumulate the means of buying the labour power of others, and the production and exchange of commodities must have developed to a point where the accumulation of capital and the selling of labour power for wages can be primarily related to each other through commodity production. Since these are the prerequisites for the transition to capitalism, and since capitalism did indeed develop, it follows that there must have been historical processes through which the prerequisite conditions were fulfilled. But although an enormous range of historical evidence is discussed in Marx's various writings on this subject, and especially in *Capital*, his interest is not really in closely tracing or identifying such actual processes of transition. Rather it is in elaborating and clarifying an argument about what *had* to happen for capitalism to emerge and thereby in emphasising the distinctive nature of capitalism as a social system. For example, since the accumulation of surplus is a precondition for capitalism there plainly had to be a process of previous or as Marx calls it 'primitive' accumulation prior to capitalistic accumulation itself. So Marx's chapter in *Capital* on 'The Secret of Primitive Accumulation' (1970:i,713) tells us what to look for in history but it is not in any real sense an attempt to demonstrate that the sort of process predicted by Marx's theory actually occurred.

Marx's analysis of the nature of capitalism involves seeing some of the most essential features of that system as the direct opposites of the most essential features of the system that preceded it as a dominant mode of production in European history, feudalism. Thus, feudalism rests on social relations in which the labourer is not in immediate control of his own labour power, is not free to sell it to others but specifically 'un-free'. Capitalism, by contrast, turns on the 'freedom' of the immediate producer in that crucial respect. And this is but one of a set of oppositions which mark capitalism as the logical antithesis of feudalism. Yet capitalism grew out of feudalism and did not grow out of any of the other types of pre-capitalist modes of production which Marx identified and briefly examined in preparing to write *Capital*. How, then, can a social system give rise to its opposite? Plainly, for Marx, this has to be a matter of the working out of the contradictions built into the basic relationships, the structure, of the initial social system. However, it is one thing to produce this sort of answer as a matter of principle or theory and to give a generalised, abstract account of what one had in mind – 'the historical movement which changes the producers into wage-workers' – but quite another thing to show that the historical process actually was like that, that the transition from feudalism to capitalism was *made* in ways that can truly be described in the terms required by the theory.

Marx thus left his heirs with two main historical problems. How to explain the failure of pre-capitalist systems other than feudalism to provide a historical 'womb' for capitalism? And how to explain the fact that capitalism did grow out of European feudalism? In practice, these questions implied for marxists an attempt to discover how far and in what ways the growth of capitalism was indeed 'intrinsic' to feudalism, in the sense of being the product of the working-out of feudalism's own contradictions, rather than a product of more general, accidental or external forces and action. There is no room here to discuss the full range of ambitious, meticulous and in many ways definitive historical studies that have been produced since the death of Marx in the attempt to answer the questions he raised. But one or two themes and features of the debate on those questions can perhaps exemplify both the type of answers towards which marxist historical sociology seems to be moving and the range of further problems which those answers have produced.

So far as English marxist historians are concerned the non-marxist Belgian historian Henri Pirenne (1936, 1939) must be credited with the unravelling of an exceptionally important strand of debate. In a series of deeply researched studies Pirenne argued that the development of capitalism in Europe occurred not within the relationships of feudalism but from without and through the erosion and transformation of the marginal, least feudal, aspects of feudal society. Specifically, he argued that the decisive influence in developing an economy of production for exchange alongside the feudal economy of production for use was provided by trade and commerce and especially long-distance trade practised by merchants who were intruders into the feudal world rather than products of it. The juxtaposition of the two economies, a feudal countryside and capitalistic towns, began to dissolve feudal social relations once the feudal lords and princes had come to want the commodities the merchants could offer them. In this view commerce invaded the essentially stable world of the feudal manor and conquered it; the explanation of the rise of capitalism lies, ultimately, outside feudalism. Plainly, such a view poses a serious challenge to the marxist conception of the historical importance of the inner contradictions of social systems as the decisive sources of change. Not surprisingly it was strongly resisted by marxist scholars.

A particularly authoritative statement of the marxist answer to Pirenne was provided in 1946 by Maurice Dobb. In *Studies in the Development of Capitalism*, Dobb argued that feudal social relations were inherently unstable and that trade and commerce became significant only after that instability within feudalism had made itself felt. To pursue that argument, let alone to explore in historical detail and with any real precision the question of the transition from feudalism to capitalism, it is obviously necessary to have a clear idea of just what feudalism was. For Dobb (1946:35) feudalism was not just any mode of production based on unfree labour but more specifically a mode of production based on serfdom – a condition under which the direct producer is at once in immediate possession of the means of production and at the same time forcibly coerced into fulfilling 'certain economic demands of an overlord'; he is, as it were, the unfree possessor of the means of production. In various forms this system became generally established in Europe in the 11th century. Thereafter signs of its dissolution – the reorganisation of production on the basis of contractual wage-labour – become increasingly evident. The question at the heart of the problem is how was this dissolution brought about.

Dobb finds an answer in what he calls (1946:42) the 'inefficiency of feudalism as a system of production, coupled with the growing needs of the ruling class for revenue'. These factors, strictly internal to feudalism, produced in his view a constant 'pressure on the producer to a point where this pressure became literally unendurable'. The feudal ruling class had to derive its income from the surplus it could extract from the servile class; to increase its income it had to put pressure on that class to surrender ever larger proportions of its product or its labour. Given that productivity was strictly limited by available technology and the lack of any reinvestment of the surplus extracted by the lords in technical development, while the needs of the lords were constantly inflated by the costs of their typical activities, war and politics, there was a built-in instability within the feudal relationship which drove both parties, lord and serf, to seek non-feudal solutions and alternatives to their feudal predicament. The first part of Dobb's *Studies* is devoted to tracing the ways in which this instability worked itself out – in emigration from the manors, in peasant risings and riots, in ventures by lords into commerce and by peasants into small-scale commodity production for non-feudal markets; in the sale to serfs of their freedom, the substitution of cash payments for labour services, the leasing of estates, the hiring of wage-labourers. At periods when labour was cheap and productivity high these expedients could work to the advantage of the lords but when labour was scarce and productivity low, the typical state of affairs in medieval Europe, they aggravated rather than solved the basic problem. By the fourteenth century the feudal economy had thus in Dobb's view reached a condition of general crisis. To that crisis two solutions were available for the feudal rulers; they could intensify traditional forms of feudal exploitation through coercion of the producers; or they could on a massive scale substitute rents and the external marketing of estate produce for direct services as the basis of their income. Where they could do the former, in most of eastern Europe for example, they did. Where they could not, they seized if they could the opportunity to do the latter. And it was at this point that the relatively independent prior development of trade and markets became important.

But the inner crisis of feudalism is seen as preceding the exploitation of commercial opportunities. And the long term effect of the way lords and peasants responded to that crisis was, in Dobb's phrase, that the producer was 'shaken loose' from feudal dependence by a combination of his own resistance to feudal exploitation and his lord's driving need to increase his revenues even by non-feudal means. The producer was at once 'freed' and detached from immediate possession of the crucial means of production, the land. Once shaken loose in these ways, however, producers had to enter new types of relationship; the free landless labourer must sell his labour-power for wages; the rent-paying tenant can begin to increase his own surplus through commodity production and market transactions. The demand for new levels of surplus arose within the feudal relationship; the realisation of the demand through new types of relationship blew feudalism apart.

Dobb's analysis of the passage from feudalism to capitalism is noticeably more historically detailed and specific than that of Marx. It moves more readily between a theoretical sense of what had to happen and an empirical discussion of what actually did happen. But for that very reason it also raised many new issues and difficulties and gave rise to a vigorous and continuing debate among marxist historians as to just how capitalism developed. Was serfdom really the essence of feudalism? At what point in time can one identify the high noon of feudalism as a mode of production? In what detailed ways did the inner contradictions of feudalism really work themselves out? What was the relative contribution of different types of fugitives from feudal relationships (small scale producers on the one hand, great merchant financiers on the other) to the destruction of the feudal grip on production? What sort of social system filled the gap between the high noon of feudalism and the decisive emergence of capitalism three or four centuries later? The marxist analysis of the transition to capitalism requires answers to all these and to a host of more specific questions and the debate between Dobb and Pirenne has been carried forward in terms of ever more specific research intended to answer them.

The remarkable thing about this debate (both among marxists and between marxists and non-marxists) is that it has not as yet undermined the basic marxian conception of the relationship between feudalism and capitalism. Increasingly detailed historical research has led to a recognition of the many varieties of the feudal relationship from region to region and of the range of outcomes other than capitalism that resulted in actual past time from the inner crises of feudalism (absolute monarchy being the conspicuous example). The problem of explaining the rise of capitalism has thus become steadily more sharply specified – a matter of one particular solution in one particular area to one particular version of the crisis of feudalism. But within that narrowing of the problem, that increasingly precise understanding of its context, has gone an increasingly confident ability to demonstrate that the making of capitalism was indeed a matter of the creating of a particular solution to the problems of feudalism by particular human beings in a particular historically structured situation. Marxist history has become steadily more impressive the more it has moved away from the assertion of vast historical necessities towards closely researched studies of the ways in which those necessities were realised in the lives of specific individuals in specific places and at specific times. The debate launched by Maurice Dobb (Hilton, 1976) has made the task of the marxist scholar much more complex, much more a matter of minute historical investigations; but it has also strikingly vindicated the general marxist understanding of how history happens. To read Hilton (1973, 1974, 1975) or Duby (1974) on the way their new freedom was used by emancipated serfs in medieval Europe or Porchnev (1963) on the desperate efforts of the seventeenth-century nobility to stave off the crisis of their class by the creation of absolute monarchy is to be vividly impressed by the force of marxist historical sociology once it moves down from the logic of general social evolution to the analysis of the way history is made within defined structural settings at particular moments in time.

Historical sociology, at least of this variety, does not, it seems, lend itself to strong statements of generalised theories of social development. What it does do is to provide some very powerful tools for understanding why certain things happened at given times. From that sort of understanding, established case by case, one might hope eventually to move back towards some sort of general statement about such general processes as the transition from feudalism to capitalism. Meanwhile the case studies serve as indications of the possible credibility of the approach as a whole. More generally, the problem and danger facing marxist historical sociology is evidently one of balance. Marx at his best and the best marxist historians such as Maurice Dobb, achieve a complex balance of experience and abstraction, of explanation in terms of individual meaning and action and of explanation in terms of structure and process. Ideally, such a mode of historical sociology envisages the integration of highly abstract analysis at the level of the structure and logic of modes of production (theory) and very specific, concrete analysis at the level of the practical being and relationships of classes (history). The agenda of marxist historical sociology calls for analysis which accounts for class experience and action in terms of the logical formation of modes of production and simultaneously accounts for modes of production in terms of the historical formation of class experience and action. Such an analysis can be glimpsed as a possibility in *Studies in the Development of Capitalism* and in some of the work of Marx and especially of Engels. But in 'The 18th Brumaire' Marx himself tended to upset the balance by attending one-sidedly to experience and action, just as in *Capital* he tended to upset it in the opposite direction by using action and experience merely to illustrate or exemplify the logically required workings and contradictions of his abstractly conceived and elaborated model of capitalism as a mode of production. Contemporary marxists have, if anything, found the balance of experience and abstraction which their historical sociology properly requires even harder to strike. I suspect that in different ways it is achieved in the work of Rodney Hilton and Perry Anderson. But Edward Thompson, perhaps the most famous and respected of modern marxist historians, is accused of evicting theory from history and in turn criticises his critics, among them the most famous and respected of modern marxist theorists, for evicting history from theory. Both sides rightly claim that the other had abandoned an essential component of marxist social analysis.

The debate is representative of the condition of contemporary western marxism. Its respective extreme positions indicate a characteristic splintering in practice of a project which in principle has to conceive of history and theory as inseparable.

4

The transition to industrialism: rationalisation

A criticism often made of marxist historical sociology is that it tends to side-step the issue of why individuals choose to act in the ways they do, to ignore the problem of what their action means to them subjectively and to overlook the ways in which meaning is rooted in culture. That people who can subsist only by selling their labour-power for wages should indeed sell their labour-power for wages does not perhaps invite explanation at the level of meaning; for them life is governed by structural necessities. But that people who can subsist perfectly well without accumulating capital should nevertheless compulsively accumulate capital surely does raise a problem of choice, of subjective meaning and of the cultural contexts of meaning; here the sociologist has something to explain which cannot be explained simply by reference to the structure of social relationships. Indeed in practice the pressure of structural necessity seems never to be absolute. Even in concentration camps and slave plantations action is shaped by the meanings people bring to their predicaments or can wring out of them. An adequate sociology of such predicaments surely has to offer an analysis not only of the observable relationships of power and powerlessness within them but equally of what is made of those relationships by those involved in them; an analysis of the complex of meaning within which the relationships are enacted.

In much of his work Marx was, of course, well aware of this problem. After all, 'The 18th Brumaire' does end with a detailed discussion of just what the napoleonic idea meant to the different social groups in France and of the crucial importance of those meanings in bringing about Louis Bonaparte's peculiar political success. Yet there is, in fact, a sense in which the criticism is justified – especially if we turn from the marxist historical case studies to marxist treatments of large scale and long term historical processes such as the transition from feudalism to capitalism. Here the drive to establish class formation and class struggle as the prime movers of historical change and thence to identify the relationships within which those processes are embedded and realised does often seem to make consideration of the subjective worlds in which class formation and class struggle occur something of an unnecessary luxury. Capitalism could only be produced out of the contradictions of feudalism and when all the detours and dead-ends have been allowed for, one way of working-out the contradictions of feudalism had to produce capitalism. Given such an underlying sense of necessary, law-like connections between past structure, present action and future structure it is perhaps understandable that the subjective meaning of action to the individual should be treated as a possibly interesting but essentially secondary, background matter in historical analysis. Certainly a good deal of marxist historical sociology gives this impression.

From this point of view one could also argue that the historical sociology of Marx and his heirs is not very unlike that of Durkheim and his school. For both, the subjective world of the individual is the least important problem to be investigated. Both recognise that the relationship between social structure and events are *mediated* by the subjective interpretations of the individual. Durkheim allows that although the suicide rate is caused socially, by the general properties of social environments, it is immediately enacted by individual suicides who have interpreted their sufferings as intolerable. Marx allows that if capitalism emerges from the contradictions of feudalism it does so through the emergence on the historical stage of individuals who are not just driven by necessity but able and ready to seize new opportunities contained within those contradictions. But in the end, for both schools, the problem of the meaningfulness of action is by-passed because, at what is believed to be a more fundamental level, action is held to be determined, or at least adequately explained, by the larger structural predicaments, crises and contradictions in which individuals find themselves and in which they have to act. The meaning of action is inferred from the structural setting not studied directly. And there is to that extent a vital sense in which the problem of meaning, of the cultural contexts of action, remains a missing link in the chain of both marxist and durkheimian historical explanation. This missing link is in turn the distinctive concern of the historical sociology of Max Weber.

Indeed, it was the particular task of explaining action in terms of its meaning for the actor that was for Weber the justification for sociology as a distinct intellectual discipline. As against the other socio-economic cultural sciences 'the specific task of sociological analysis' in Weber's eyes was precisely 'The interpretation of action in its subjective meaning' (1968:i,4). The whole of Weber's work can be read as a massive attempt to establish sociology in that sense on an objective basis, to find the grounds for an objective account of subjective worlds. At the same time he never seems to have believed, as Durkheim appears to have done, that sociology in his special sense of the discipline should or could supplant or even dominate the other social sciences. Rather, he urges the need, if adequate explanations are to achieved, to add sociological analysis to other sorts of analysis. In particular, in relation to the study of historical problems, he nowhere suggests that the 'interpretation of action in terms of its subjective meaning' should be substituted for, say, the economic interpretation of history. His argument is, rather, that the one must be united with and balanced by the other; that the missing link should be discovered, not that it should replace the chain. One has only to look at representative examples of his historical work, such as the discussion of medieval towns in *Economy and Society* (1968:ii, 1266), or his essay on 'The Social Causes of the Decline of Ancient Civilisation' (1976:387), to see how far Weber was from giving the world of subjective meaning, which he believed to be the special province of sociology, any preponderant importance among the causes of historical change. Thus, his analysis of the decay of Roman civilisation is developed in terms of the interdependence and interaction of the following factors: the urban nature of ancient civilisation; the development of slave labour as a means of supplying the essentially non-productive town-dwellers with the consumables that made up the material elements of ancient civilisation; the disappearance in the face of slave labour of the more expensive and less productive forms of free labour; the failure of the slave population to reproduce itself naturally at a rate that kept pace with the demands of an ever-growing class of parasitic free citizens; the creation of standing armies as a means of increasing the slave population unnaturally, through war; the further augmentation of the pressure on slave production resulting from the need to maintain these armies; the eventual inability of the armies to produce new supplies of slaves – that is, to conquer new territories; the gradual flight from the towns and the construction of small-scale manorial economic units of a self-sufficient nature in the face of that predicament; *and* the inability of Roman emperors, generals and landowners to conceive of any alternative to more taxes, more soldiers and more slaves as a way of solving the problems created for them by slaves, soldiers and taxation. In terms of the objective economic possibilities within the world of ancient civilisation the estates could have been turned into military units for the defence of the empire. Surplus could then have been returned to production instead of being taxed out of the economy to sustain unproductive mercenary armies. But within the mental world available to ancient civilisation such solutions were unthinkable; the Romans were trapped by the culture they had created; ancient civilisation had to die as a state of mind before the middle ages could begin. The subjective, in other words, is crucial to the explanation as a whole; but it is also only a very small part of it. In Weber's own words (1930:183): 'it is, of course, not my aim to substitute for a one-sided materialistic an equally one-sided spiritualistic causal interpretation of culture and history. Each is equally possible, but each ... accomplishes equally little in the interest of historical truth.'

Weber's historical method

Three things are important about the passage just quoted: The firm rejection of any sort of one-sided sociological knowledge;

the emphasis Weber places on *causal* explanation as the object of historical sociology; and the words that I omitted. The missing words are 'if it does not serve as the preparation, but as the conclusion of an investigation.' That concession to one-sidedness in the preparation of social inquiry commands attention because a peculiar feature of Weber's sociology is his determined attempt to overcome the one-sidedness of knowledge by the use of a deliberately one-sided method of research.

To Weber all knowledge of the social world was in the last resort irretrievably one-sided. He saw the world as an infinite flux of events all equally meaningful or meaningless. In that chaos, meaning is created by a one-sided accentuation of the point of view of particular actors, a selection and patterning which imposes itself on the chaos. Both the 'absolute infinitude' of the flux of events and the one-sidedness of social knowledge as an imputation of meaning within the flux were for Weber inescapable properties of the human predicament. 'As soon as we attempt to reflect about the way in which life confronts us in immediate concrete situations, it presents an infinite multiplicity of successively and coexistently emerging and disappearing events both within and outside ourselves.' (1949:72). And since, in the face of that multiplicity the social scientist enjoys nothing in the way of a special, privileged status, since the sociologist can no more stand outside the flux of history than any other human being, social science can never hope to grasp the whole truth about society; there can be 'no absolutely "objective" scientific analysis of ... social phenomena independent of special and "one-sided" viewpoints.' (1949:72).

If sociological analysis is limited by the fact that sociologists are unfortunately also human, it is nevertheless an attempt to make the most that can be made of the human predicament. It is an attempt to understand how meaning comes to be effectively imputed to chaos; to explain how culture is hammered out of the flux; to see how one-sidedness works. The sociologist has the peculiar task of struggling against the human predicament while knowing that sociologists, too, are trapped within it. We can only see the world at all, Weber argued, by seeing a part of it. We can proceed towards social knowledge only on the basis of some culturally-shaped sense of significance. Conversely, the demand that the historian or sociologist should do work that is 'relevant', 'meaningful' and concerned with 'important' rather than 'trivial' matters is no more than a demand for an explanation in terms of 'relationships that are significant for us.' (1949:73). Works of social science are judged significant because they contribute to a larger configuration of meaning in which the social scientist and the audience for social science both exist. Turned round again, what we select for study is not something objectively given and observed by us in a 'presuppositionless' way; our objects of study are selected and constructed out of the infinity of phenomena by being first defined as meaningful within our sense of cultural significance. We study what is significant for us and we explain the problems we study in terms of their significance for us.

For Weber the recognition of this cultural one-sidedness was nevertheless a crucial first step towards sociological knowledge. The only way to overcome – or at least minimise – the one-sidedness of one's vision of the social world is to begin by being self-conscious about the fact that one's vision *is* one-sided. The difference between social science and naive observation does not lie in the social scientist's special mastery of laws or general theories about social development or social organisation but, on the contrary, in the understanding of the partial and imaginative nature of such ideas. In a powerful image Weber suggests that the essence of social science, methodologically, is the creation of *utopias*. What one does is to reconstruct and reorganise reality imaginatively; one creates 'ideas' of reality, conceptual patterns which 'bring together certain relationships and events of historical life into a complex, which is conceived of as an internally consistent pattern.' (1949:90). Through 'the analytical accentuation of certain elements of reality' the social scientist creates models of the world in which the necessary or possible relationships between different factors are specified with a high degree of logical clarity and precision. And by thus carrying one-sidedness to an extreme the social scientist acquires a tool with which reality can be very fruitfully examined. Just as the moralist can judge the actual world by comparing it to a utopia so the social scientist can apprehend the actual world by relating it to an 'ideal type', a unified analytical construct.

Ideal types are neither typical nor ideal. They are not constructed to represent what actually exists or what should exist. Rather, they are logically and formally precise statements of possible relationships. Weber's examples are the city economy, the handicraft system, capitalism, the church, the sect, the essence of Christianity, the state. In each case he argues that what social scientists do is to construct an unreality which is unambiguous, exact and wholly abstract in order to perceive through it a reality which is ambiguous, volatile and elusively concrete. Thus (1949:97):

> All expositions for example of the 'essence' of Christianity are ideal types enjoying only a necessarily very relative and problematic validity when they are intended to be regarded as the historical portrayal of empirically existing facts. On the other hand, such presentations are of great value for research and of high systematic value for expository purposes when they are used as conceptual instruments for comparison with and the measurement of reality. They are indispensable for this purpose.

Social science thus turns commonsense knowledge into an instrument for the creation of its own quite different kind of knowledge. The ideal type so exaggerates the one-sidedness of commonsense that it becomes impossible – or at least it ought to become impossible – to equate one's ideas with reality: 'in its conceptual purity this mental construct cannot be found empirically anywhere in reality.' (1949:90). Our ideas of the world can then be used as tools, noticeably unlike the actuality of the world and which we can employ as measures or lenses to analyse actuality in a serious, potentially objective, way.

From the point of view of historical sociology – and most of Weber's own empirical work can be identified as historical sociology – the particularly relevant part of his discussion of this methodological issue is perhaps that concerned with the use of what he calls 'developmental' ideal types. It is here, too, that his reservations about marxism as well as his respect for Marx are probably most evident. One begins, in his view, by creating ideal-typical constructs of particular historical social systems. Then (1949:90), 'historical research faces the task of determining in each individual case, the extent to which this ideal construct approximates to or diverges from reality, to what extent for example, the economic structure of a certain city is to be classified as a "city economy". When carefully applied these concepts are particularly useful in research' – precisely as a preliminary, orienting device. In dealing with the problem of the transition to capitalism one can for example, 'work the "idea" of "handicraft" into a utopia by arranging certain traits, actually found in an unclear, confused state in the industrial enterprises of the most diverse epochs and countries, into a consistent ideal construct by an accentuation of their essential tendencies.' Thence one can proceed to the elaboration of a pure model of a total 'handicraft system'. Simultaneously and in the same manner one can construct an 'ideal-typical capitalistic productive system' and thence the utopia of a capitalistic culture – 'one in which the governing principle is the investment of private capital.' But, as Weber himself immediately asks, what is the significance of such ideal-typical constructs for an empirical social science concerned for example with the causes of the development of capitalism? Do these models help us to grasp empirically adequate causal explanations or are we simply playing a fanciful 'conceptual game'? There is, Weber maintains, only one criterion relevant to the resolution of that issue, 'namely, that of success in revealing concrete cultural phenomena in their interdependence, their causal conditions and their significance.'(1949:92). Accordingly, 'the construction of abstract ideal types recommends itself not as an end but as a means' – a means, however, which we *must* use if we wish to understand the cultural significance of events as distinct from merely recording their incidence.

To refer to capitalism or feudalism or to any of a host of similar categories regularly used by historians and sociologists is not, Weber insists, to refer to states of affairs that have been objectively found to exist in the real world. We are not invoking a 'presuppositionless description of some concrete phenomenon'. Rather, we are making reference to a more synthetic concept abstracted from the observable multiplicity of concrete phenomena. And that is what we have to do if we are to hope to make sense of the phenomena. It follows that since we must use such synthetic concepts it is best that we should both know that that is what we are doing and that we should make the synthetic concepts we use as precise and coherent as possible. Ideal types are no more than extremely precise and coherent synthetic concepts. Both the analytical value of such conceptions and the great difficulty of not confusing them with reality become especially apparent, however, when we begin to construct ideal types of developmental historical sequences – such as the transition from feudalism to capitalism. It is above all the temptation to impose accounts of the law-like relationships between concepts on the empirical study of historical events, and then to claim that one has. identified real laws of historical development which is seductive and must be resisted. By contrast Weber provides a helpful illustration of what can properly be done (1949:101):

> One can, for example, arrive at the theoretical conclusion that in a society which is organised on strict 'handicraft' principles, the only source of capital accumulation can be ground rent. From this perhaps one can ... construct a pure ideal picture of the shift, conditioned by certain specific factors e.g., limited land, increasing population, influx of precious metals, rationalisation of the conduct of life – from a handicraft to a capitalistic economic organisation. Whether the empirical-historical course of development was actually identical with the constructed one, can be investigated only by using this construct as a heuristic device for the comparison of the ideal type and the 'facts'. If the ideal type were 'correctly' constructed and the actual course of events did *not* correspond to that predicted by the ideal type, the hypothesis that medieval society was *not* in certain respects a strictly 'handicraft' type of society would be proved. And if the ideal type were constructed in a heuristically 'ideal' way ... it will guide the investigation into a path leading to a more precise understanding of the non-handicraft components of medieval society in their peculiar characteristics and their historical significance. *If* it leads to this result, it fulfils its logical purpose, even though, in doing so, it demonstrates its divergence from reality.

Ideal typical developmental constructs must in other words be sharply distinguished from historical reality and so long as that is done such constructs become a crucial *means* of 'explicitly

and validly imputing an historical event to its real causes.'
Marxism, Weber goes on to suggest, is a uniquely rich source
of developmental constructs. (1949:103): 'the eminent ...
heuristic significance of these ideal types when they are used for
the *assessment* of reality' is, he claims, 'known to everyone'.
But by the same token marxist developmental constructs are
uniquely prone to being treated not as ideal types but as
empirically valid, real laws, tendencies and necessities. And as
soon as they are treated in that way they become as pernicious
as they are valuable when treated as unreal ideal types.

Methodologically disciplined in this way, Weber believed
that it was possible for the historian and the sociologist to move
towards 'an empirical science of concrete reality.' The self-
conscious 'confrontation of empirical reality with the ideal
type' was, moreover, not in his eyes simply a recipe for academic
exercises; it was the basis for a practical, this-worldly
knowledge, an understanding of 'how we have come to be as we
are today.' (1949:72):

> Our aim is the understanding of the characteristic uniqueness of
> the reality in which we move. We wish to understand on the one
> hand the relationship and the cultural significance of individual
> events in their contemporary manifestations, and on the other
> hand the causes of their being historically so and not otherwise.

The purpose of the method Weber advocated was to enable the
historical sociologist to resolve that sort of problem.

Weber's historical problem

For Weber the 'characteristic uniqueness of the reality' in
which he moved was, as it had been for Marx, caught in the
notion of capitalism rather than in the broader and vaguer idea
of industrialism. He also agreed with Marx, as several writers
have pointed out, in his account of the main socio-economic
characteristics of capitalism. But his distinctive sense of the task
of sociological analysis led him to take up for particular
examination just that dimension of the rise of capitalism which
Marx had tended to ignore – to focus his attention on the ways

in which the activities that were conducive to the rise of capitalism came to be positively meaningful to some particular people in some particular historical circumstances. For Weber the mere availability of capital and labour power, necessary as both were as preconditions for capitalism, could not in itself explain the actual growth of capitalism into a dominant economic and cultural order. It was essentially necessary, too, to understand why those resources were given significance and used in early modern Europe in ways in which they had not been elsewhere. The sociological problem of the rise of capitalism was specifically to identify the meanings that enabled people to make something, on a massively and socially fateful scale, of the resources available to them. And conversely, to identify the meanings that in other periods and cultures prevented other people from making the same thing of the same resources. Much of Weber's work accordingly pursues a problem noted but never fully explored by Marx – that of the failure of capitalism to develop outside modern western Europe despite the frequent existence of many of the structural and material conditions for it. Exploring the problem of the rise of capitalism in Europe led Weber unavoidably to the problem of the failure of capitalism to mature in classical antiquity or India or China or Islam.

Weber's sense of the cultural significance of capitalism – which provided the basis for his perspective in analysing it – was itself bound up with his more general understanding of the whole movement of modern history. For him modern society was above all a society pervaded by rationalism; and its history was a history of rationalisation, of an ever-growing involvement in a rationalistic culture and of ever-growing commitment to rationalistic forms of action. In turn, the peculiar hall-mark of this peculiarly modern rationalism was, as he saw it, a calculating, amoral approach to human problems which progressively invaded all apects of life. It was in this sense that rationality was the peculiar historical 'fate' of the world in which he lived. As Dennis Wrong puts it (1970:26):

By 'rationalisation' Weber meant the process by which explicit, abstract, intellectually calculable rules and procedures are increasingly substituted for sentiment, tradition and rule of thumb in all spheres of activity. Rationalisation leads to the displacement of religion by specialised science as the major source of intellectual authority; the substitution of the trained expert for the cultivated man of letters; the ousting of the skilled handworker by machine technology; the replacement of traditional judicial wisdom by abstract, systematic statutory codes. Rationalisation demystifies and instrumentalises life. It means that ... there are no mysterious, incalculable forces that come into play, but rather that one can, in principle, master all things by calculation. This means that the world is disenchanted.

This special kind of rationalism, the rationalism of fine calculation of means to ends regardless of the value of the ends, the celebration of efficiency and the cult of technique, had come in Weber's eyes to be the dominant cultural force, the pervasive meaning of all modern social life. In economic relationships the drive to this type of rationalism was embodied in the rise of capitalism – and as he saw it contemporary visions of socialism only prefigured a further rationalisation. Politically, the same impetus works itself out in the elaboration of ever more detailed systems of impersonal, bureaucratic organisation and administration. Culturally, it finds its expression in a general demystifying of the world and in the specific rise of technology and science, including social science, in the place of magic, imagination and religion.

Yet just as the structure of the modern world was contradictory in Marx's eyes, built as it was merely on the substitution of capitalist relationships for feudal class relationships, so for Weber the culture of the modern world was profoundly contradictory since it embodied a rationalisation which was at odds with reason. In his own terms a gulf is opened between 'formal' and 'substantive' rationality. More and more, people orient their lives to the idea of doing things efficiently, of achieving their ends by the most economical, precisely calculated means. But as they become more and more rationalistic in this sense their actions progressively cease to be oriented to values over and above that sort of rationality. The means becomes an end. Secularisation gives rise to a science-dominated culture in which whatever is 'scientific' is valued regardless of its social effects, and only what is scientific is accepted and esteemed as knowledge. The rationalisation of politics gives rise to vast structures of formal law and bureaucratic administration within which officials cling compulsively to the routines of their offices regardless of the political, moral or social ends served by their official activity. Economically, the rise of capitalism sees a shift of orientation from accumulation for the reasonable purposes of subsistence, self-preservation and comfort to the irrationality of meticulously calculated accumulation for accumulation's own sake. Thus in the end in every field of experience 'every radical rationalisation creates irrationalities with the necessity of a fate.' But not only are rationalistic means of action increasingly treated as independent ends of action so that other reasons for action are lost sight of; increasingly, too, devotion to rationalistic action for its own sake creates a world of institutions, procedures and norms which stands over against individuals and blocks their pursuit of values other than rationalistic action. Karl Loewith seems to catch Weber's meaning well in this respect (1970:114):

> As that which was originally merely a means (to an otherwise valuable end) becomes an end or an end-in-itself, actions intended as a means become independent rather than goal-oriented and precisely thereby lose their original meaning or end, that is, their goal-oriented rationality based on man and his needs. This reversal however, marks all modern culture; its establishments, institutions and enterprises are rationalised in such a way that it is these structures originally set up by man which now encompass and determine him like an iron cage.

Rationalism as the central mode of meaning, the distinctive orientation to action of the modern world is, then, problematic for Weber because it is the source of irrationalities, unfreedom and the retreat of ultimate values from practical life. The cultural significance of the historical making of the modern world thus resides, for him, in the ways in which it is a history of rationalisation. That history is embedded in economic action (the rise of capitalism), political action (the rise of bureaucratic administration, law and the state) and cultural action (the decline of magic and religion and the rise of science and technique). The analysis of rationalisation thus provides the unifying theme of Weber's excursions into all fields of historical sociology. Conversely, although the transition to capitalism is seen by him as the most momentous, significant and analytically crucial form of rationalisation, that transition was not, in his view, something that could be understood in isolation, merely as economic history. However one-sidedly one might have to approach history for methodological reasons, the reality of history was one in which economic action, political action and cultural action are entangled in a single social whole. Weber's studies of the problem of the rise of capitalism are therefore invariably, and often predominantly, also studies in religious history and in political history as well as in economic history. Indeed, his sense of the specific task of the sociologist as being that of pursuing causal explanations at the level of meaning impelled him not just to try to place the history of economic action in its cultural and political context but to a much more radical confrontation of economic history and cultural and political history. Sociologically, the problem of the rise of capitalism had to be defined as a problem of the world of meaning in which capitalistic economic action was enabled to grow. It was a matter of understanding and then explaining not capitalism as such but the *spirit* of capitalism. The explosion and diffusion of capitalistic activity had to involve, whatever else it might have involved and pre-supposed a complex of meaning, an ethic or spirit within which the historically extraordinary practices and relationships of capitalism could be understood as proper or even necessary. The work of the historical sociologist of capitalism is therefore first to understand just what the ethical medium in which capitalism grew was and secondly to explain how such an ethos could have come to exist.

The spirit of capitalism

In a series of lectures delivered in 1919 just a year before his death, Weber tried to crystallise his sense of the general historical problem that had concerned him for at least the last fifteen years. What is striking in these lectures (1961), reconstructed from his students' notes and published as his *General Economic History*, is the way in which they renew and elaborate themes first presented in essays he wrote in 1904 exploring the relationship between the spirit of capitalism and the ethos of protestantism in the 16th century and themselves published as *The Protestant Ethic and the Spirit of Capitalism* (1930). In both works his particular concern is to explain how the state of mind which he identifies as the spirit of capitalism was enabled and encouraged to flourish in western Europe and nowhere else, in the modern era and at no other time. It is not that the spirit of capitalism is held to be the unique or even the decisive cause of the rise of capitalism; it is simply that it is the peculiarly problematic cause from a sociological point of view.

Capitalism develops, Weber argues, amid a general rationalisation of life which the rise of capitalism itself both expresses and sustains just as it is sustained by it. Capitalistic activity is found in some measure in almost all civilisations and periods. What is required for the emergence of capitalism as a dominant mode of economic action is a general rationalisation of all aspects of economic action. What was important in western Europe was that the application of rationality to economic life occurred in the midst of a much more inclusive rationalisation affecting politics and culture as much as the forms, forces and relations of production (1961:260):

> In the last resort the factor which produced capitalism is the rational permanent enterprise, rational accounting, rational technology and rational law, but again not these alone. Necessary complementary factors were the rational spirit, the rationalisation of the conduct of life in general and a rationalistic economic ethic.

The Protestant Ethic and the Spirit of Capitalism opens with an account of this diffuse, all-encompassing rationalisation within which capitalism constitutes the 'most fateful force'. What has happened in the western European case is not that the pursuit of profit has been generalised but that the pursuit of profit has come to be organised in a distinctive way – resting primarily on the rational enterprise and the rationalised relations of production embodied in the sale and purchase of the labour power of legally free labourers. The problem therefore (1930:24) 'is not ... the development of capitalist activity as such [but] rather the origin of this sober bourgeois capitalism with its rational organisation' of all the forces and relations of production. And to deal with that problem forces us, or at least it forced Weber, to consider in turn the general problem of rationalisation 'peculiar to the Occident'. The sober bourgeois capitalism of the west is seen as being informed by a spirit, the spirit of capitalism, peculiar to it and absent elsewhere; the spirit of capitalism itself is, however, part and parcel of a much more general rationalising spirit: 'it is a question of the specific and peculiar rationalism of Western culture.' Weber's analysis centres on the ways in which that type of rationalism creates opportunities for capitalism and on the ways in which in its absence obstacles to capitalism cannot be overcome (1930:26).

> It is hence our first concern to work out and explain genetically the special peculiarity of Occidental rationalism and within this field that of the modern Occidental form. Every such attempt at explanation must, recognising the fundamental importance of the economic factor, above all take account of the economic conditions. But at the same time the opposite correlation must not be left out of consideration. For though the development of economic rationalism is partly dependent on rational technique and law, it is at the same time determined by the ability and disposition of men to adopt certain types of practical rational conduct. When these types have been obstructed by spiritual obstacles the development of rational economic conduct has also met serious inner resistance.

The idea of the spirit of capitalism as used by Weber is, of course, a striking example of his conception of an ideal type; it is the classical illustration, too, of his method of historical explanation through the construction of ideal types. The spirit of capitalism is indeed a 'one-sided accentuation' of reality designed to allow historical relationships to be more clearly seen by the historian as well as to enable their significance to be assessed. It is a conception 'gradually put together out of the individual parts which are taken from historical reality to make it up', and serving to focus analysis on relationships which the analyst has already presumed to be of crucial causal significance. It postulates a particular bridge between the rise of capitalism and the earlier historical condition which Weber (ideal-typically) identified as 'traditionalism'. Only by building the bridge in theory can one tell whether the passage from traditionalism to capitalism was made in that sort of way in reality. At the same time the bridge is conceived of as carrying both a broad and a narrow track: the broad path of rationalisation and the narrow central path arising within it of the spirit of capitalism, a particular rationalisation of economic life.

A difficulty in reading much of Weber's work on the rise of capitalism is precisely the difficulty of recognising that he is, in this sense, doing three things at once. He is developing an ideal type, the spirit of capitalism, which is itself a special mode of a larger ideal type, western rationalism. At the same time he is trying to determine how well the notion of the spirit of capitalism will serve as an explanatory bridge, itself carried by the process of rationalisation, between traditionalism and the rise of capitalism. And thirdly, if the idea of the spirit of capitalism looks like a strong explanatory bridge in principle there is the problem of explaining the existence of something like that spirit in historical reality.

Although the notion of the spirit of capitalism as a specific bridge to capitalism is generally seen as Weber's most distinctive contribution to historical sociology it is probably sensible to say something about the nature of each of the banks he saw that bridge as spanning before considering his account of the bridge itself – not least because his analysis of the historical nature and functions of the spirit of capitalism is in the end so subtle and elusive that the metaphor of the bridge will probably have to be abandoned!

Capitalism, then, is defined for Weber in terms of distinct economic practices embodying a distinct complex of meaning. Whereas for Marx capitalism is a type of relationship, a particular form of exploitation, for Weber it is a type of practice, a particular way of organising and giving meaning to economic action, a way expressed most clearly in the firm or enterprise (1961:207):

Capitalism is present wherever the industrial provision for the needs of a human group is carried out by the method of enterprise, irrespective of what need is involved. More specifically, a rational capitalistic enterprise is one with capital accounting, that is, an establishment which determines its income-yielding power by calculation according to the methods of modern bookkeeping and the striking of a balance.

Capitalism may be more or less developed and extensive in different social systems but a whole social system can be called capitalistic when – as in modern Europe – this mode of economic action has become so widespread that were it taken away, 'the whole economic system must collapse'. However, if the enterprise as an instrument of rational capital accounting functioning as the normal means of providing for everyday wants is the immediately visible form in which capitalism becomes dominant, that development itself depends on and is bound up with a number of conditions which must be satisfied. Here the structures and relationships which characterise capitalism for Marx reappear in Weber's analysis. He sees the rise of the rational enterprise as involving six such conditions (1961:208): 'first, the appropriation of all physical means of production ... as disposable property of autonomous private enterprises'; second, 'the freedom of the market, that is, the absence of irrational limitations on trading' such as those imposed by guilds and privileged social groups legally appropriating labour and commodities to their own use; third, 'capitalistic accounting presupposes rational technology, that is, one reduced to calculation to the largest possible degree' – which, of course, is what is achieved by mechanisation and bureaucratic organisation. Fourth, and closely related to rational technology is 'calculable law' – that is, a legal and political environment operating according to known, universalistic rules in which the advantages of economic calculation can be fully realised; fifth is the requirement for labour power to be turned into a commodity by the introduction of 'free labour', workers 'who are not only legally in the position, but are also economically compelled, to sell their labour on the market without restriction'. Weber's emphasis (1961:208–9) on this feature of capitalism is as strong, and as integral to his whole account of capitalism, as that of Marx:

It is in contradiction to the essence of capitalism, and the development of capitalism is impossible, if such a propertyless stratum is absent, a class compelled to sell its services to live; and it is likewise impossible if only unfree labour is at hand. Rational capitalistic calculation is possible only on the basis of free labour; only where in consequence of the existence of workers who in the formal sense voluntarily, but actually under the compulsion of the whip of hunger, offer themselves, the costs of products may be unambiguously determined by agreement in advance.

And finally, capitalism as a generally dominant mode of economic action presupposes 'the commercialisation of economic life', that is, 'the general use of commercial instruments to represent share rights in enterprise and also in property ownership'. Property thus takes on 'the form of negotiable paper' and the door is fully opened to capitalistic speculation in an unfettered market.

Weber's account of capitalism is in many respects thus very similar to that of Marx. But in some important respects the similarity is deceptive. At bottom Weber's attention is directed at a quite different problem. While we could perhaps say that he agrees with Marx about the structure of the social relations of capitalism his constant concern is to emphasise an aspect of the cultural character of those relations which was of only secondary interest to Marx; their driving and ultimately irrational, rationalism; the all-pervading demand for a calculable world that informs and unifies them.

And, of course, it was precisely in terms of that aspect of social action that Weber saw capitalism as being most sharply at odds with the traditional world out of which capitalism had grown. By contrast to his endless, explicit insistence on the cultural and structural concomitants of capitalism he pays rather little direct attention to the nature of traditionalism *except* insofar as he needed to identify those properties of traditionalism that served as obstacles to the rationalisation of economic, political and cultural action. Thus, his analysis of traditional authority is concerned with the ways in which different combinations of two main features of traditionalism – the insistence that everything be done now as it was done in the past, and the engrained privileges of elders, monarchs and nobles, together with the use of arbitrary political action and highly personalised power to subordinate economic life to the

needs and interests of those groups – all work to block the
realisation of the conditions necessary to capitalism.

Traditionalism can take many forms but from Weber's point
of view the important thing about all of them is that they
effectively resist the rationalisation of law, administration,
production, distribution and all other social relations and thus
effectively prevent the growth of capitalism. Such capitalistic
activity as exists in traditional societies is firmly contained
within terms set by the needs of the traditionally dominant
social groups. For example, where such needs are met by
forced contributions in kind or forced services 'the development of markets is obstructed, the use of money is primarily
oriented to consumption and the development of capitalism is
impossible' (1968:i,238). In more sophisticated and extended
forms of traditional rule certain types of capitalism associated
with commerce and tax-farming and the provisioning of
armies 'often reach a very high degree of development'; but not
only are such capitalistic activities themselves definitely
subordinated to political control and exploitation by traditional
interests, other kinds of capitalism are emphatically prevented
from developing: this is especially 'true of the type of profit-
making enterprise with heavy investments in fixed capital and
a rational organisation of free labour which is oriented to the
market purchase of private consumers'. That, crucial, form of
capitalism Weber sees as 'altogether too sensitive to all sorts of
irrationalities in the administration of justice, in other forms of
administration and in taxation', all of which are inherent in
traditionalism and all of which 'upset the basis of calculability'
in everyday economic life.

Again, of the more arbitrary forms of traditionalism which
he calls 'Sultanism' he remarks (1968:i,238): 'two fundamental
bases of the rationalisation of economic activity are entirely
lacking; namely a basis for the calculability of obligations and
of the extent of freedom which will be allowed to private
acquisitive activity'. Of all forms of traditional administration
– the family of elders, the noble household, royal favourites,
coalitions of great feudal vassals and so forth – he notes,
similarly: 'traditionalism places serious obstacles in the way of
formally rational regulations, which can be depended upon to
remain stable and hence are calculable in their economic

implications and exploitability'. And his analysis of the distinctive cultural features of traditionalism follows essentially the same pattern. The traditional world is stamped by a unique and curious combination of properties that defies rationalisation: it is at once unchanging and arbitrary. Life must follow the ways of the past; and at the same time life cannot be planned. Traditional religions are thus characterised both by inviolable sacred rules handed down from time immemorial, and by magic. The patterns of life are fixed in ways that cannot, must not, be broken just because they are traditional; at the same time life is unpredictable, unreliable, miraculous. The state of mind typically produced in such cultures is one of 'naive piety' and superstitious acceptance; of the surrender of human destinies to an enigmatic providence. Economically, from the point of view of individuals in such a world, there is simply *no point* to the sorts of activities required to sustain capitalism even if they were otherwise possible. For example (1961:260):

> At the beginning of all ethics and the economic relations which result, is traditionalism, the sanctity of tradition, the exclusive reliance upon such trade and industry as have come down from the fathers. This traditionalism survives far down into the present; only a human lifetime in the past it was futile to double the wages of an agricultural labourer in Silesia who mowed a certain tract of land on a contract in the hope of inducing him to increase his exertions. He would simply have reduced by half the work expended because with this half he would have been able to earn ... as much as before. This general incapacity and indisposition to depart from the beaten paths is the motive for the maintenance of tradition.

Traditionalism, then, is the historical source of the rise of capitalism but traditionalism tends systematically and in principle to obstruct the development of all the conditions necessary to capitalism. What happened? How did capitalism break out of the cage of tradition? It is axiomatic for Weber that the escape was not merely a result of wanting to escape; 'traditional obstructions are not to be overcome by the economic impulse alone'. The inhabitants of early modern Europe were not noticeably more acquisitive than the inhabitants of other traditional societies from which capitalism did not emerge. On the contrary (1961:261):

> The notion that our rationalistic and capitalistic age is characterised by a stronger economic interest than other periods is childish. The moving spirits of modern capitalism are not possessed of a stronger economic impulse than, for example, an oriental trader. The unchaining of the economic interest merely as such has produced only irrational results; such men as Cortes and Pizarro, who were perhaps its strongest embodiments were far from having an idea of a rationalistic economic life. If the economic impulse in itself is universal, [however], it is an interesting question as to the relations under which it becomes rationalised and rationally tempered in such a fashion as to produce rational institutions of the character of capitalistic enterprise.

It was not by merely *wanting* profit that people broke the barriers to rational economic action embedded in traditionalism. How, then, was it done?

Weber's answer, and it is surely a unique and masterly sociological contribution to the solution of a compelling historical problem, centres on the suggestion of a peculiar, unintended but momentous conjunction between the protestant ethic and the spirit of capitalism. At a particular historical moment the former provided a basis on which the rational conduct of life should be legitimised in the face of traditionalism while the latter injected rationalisation into economic action. Weber's analysis moves backwards in time however. From the point of view of explaining the rise of capitalism the spirit of capitalism logically precedes the protestant ethic. That is to say, the spirit of capitalism emerges first in the train of enquiry. We are led to postulate the spirit of capitalism in order to explain capitalism. Only after that do we have to face the question of where the spirit of capitalism itself came from, of 'whose intellectual child' it was. The first thing that must be understood is simply that capitalism could only have been hammered out of traditionalism if economic action was supported by *some* ethos that defined as necessary, possible and proper social relations and social practices which the whole ethos of traditionalism stamped as either inconceivable or obnoxious.

The ethical pivot of the spirit of capitalism, Weber then suggests (1961:269; 1930:180), is the conception of individual life as a 'calling', a vocation in which the individual has a compelling duty to labour. The moral value of work in this conception does not lie in the possibility of enjoying the fruits of one's labour; it lies in the possibility of labouring strenuously. And that applies to the work of acquiring wealth as much as to any other kind of work. Moral attention is focused not on spending but on getting. Self-indulgence and adventure are as alien to this ethos as idleness; the whole point is to use one's life meticulously following a calculated regime. Satisfaction is found not in spending lavishly but in earning diligently: 'labour must be performed as if it were an absolute end in itself, a calling.' What is new and distinctive in such an ethos is not greed or unscrupulousness but the subjection of greed and unscrupulousness to the idea that life is a tool to be rationally and methodically used. Rational economic action according to a calculated plan is not natural; if it is to become normal it must be strongly legitimated; the rise of capitalism presupposes that it does become normal; the concept of life as a calling is the specific way in which it is legitimated. Thus (1930:54) 'this peculiar idea ... is what is most characteristic of the social ethic of capitalistic culture and is in a sense the fundamental basis of it.'

Agreeing with Marx that capitalism had to break through the objective social relations of the feudal, traditional world, Weber goes on to insist that historically its decisive achievement was its ability to break through and transform the *meaning* of the traditional world and substitute a morally charged conception of the overriding obligation of the individual towards 'the content of his professional activity, no matter ... whether it appears on the surface as a utilization of his personal powers, or only of his material possessions (as capital)' (1930:54). He finds in the diaries of Benjamin Franklin a striking expression of the way in which the spirit of capitalism could reconstruct the meaning and value of economic life (1930:48):

Remember that time is money. He that can earn ten shillings a day by his labour, and goes abroad, or sits idle, one half of that day, though he spends but sixpence during his diversion or idleness, ought not to reckon that his only expense; he has really spent, or rather thrown away, five shillings besides. Remember that credit is money... Remember that money is of the prolific, generating nature. Money can beget money and its offspring can beget more, and so on. Five shillings turned is six, turned again is seven and threepence, and so on until it becomes a hundred pounds. The more there is of it, the more it produces at every turning, so that the profits rise quicker and quicker. He that kills a breeding sow destroys all her offspring to the thousandth generation. He that murders a crown, destroys all that it might have produced, even scores of pounds ... He that is diligent in his business shall stand before kings.

Such statements are the antithesis of traditionalism. In them the possibility and the morality of calculated economic action for its own sake are rampant. Not only is the individual 'dominated by the making of money, by acquisition as the ultimate purpose of life', but particular procedures and ways of acquisition have come to be seen as the height of virtue, social value and personal worth. A way has been found of giving the often brutal, unnatural and unreasonable activities essential to capitalistic development a measure of necessity, legitimacy and reasonableness.

Weber thus argues both that something like the spirit of capitalism was in principle a necessary precondition for the growth of capitalism and that something like the spirit of capitalism did indeed exist in historical reality at an appropriate moment in western history. His next problem is to explain how that, logically necessary, development was in practice brought about. How did such a preposterous view of life actually acquire legitimacy and moral force? His answer is prefaced by two important warnings, both of which are designed to stress the historically specific nature of the problem he is addressing. First, he emphasises that the spirit of capitalism is not to be understood as a state of mind that is necessarily always associated with capitalism or indeed only associated with capitalism. His argument is only that it was one among several necessary conditions for the rise of capitalism at a certain time and in a certain place. It can be found in antiquity when it does not prove sufficient to sustain the growth of a dominant capitalistic mode of economic action. And conversely, once capitalism has become the dominant mode of economic action it can survive quite well without the support of the spirit of capitalism. Thus (1930:54):

> The capitalistic economy of the present day is an immense cosmos into which the individual is born, and which presents itself to him, at least as an individual, as an unalterable order of things in which he must live. It forces the individual, insofar as he is involved in the system of market relationships, to conform to capitalistic rules of action. The manufacturer who in the long run acts counter to these norms, will just as inevitably be eliminated from the economic scene as the worker who cannot or will not adapt himself to them will be thrown into the streets without a job.

What is to be explained is, then, the specific contribution of the spirit of capitalism at a specific time and in conjunction with other specific factors. Secondly, he insists that the explanation of the appearance of the spirit of capitalism as a 'way of life common to whole groups of men' cannot simply be absorbed into some general history of the 'development of rationalism as a whole'. Still less is it acceptable simply to deduce it from such a history. The general history of rationalism is varied, erratic and manifold, full of false starts, dead ends and isolated advances. The rationalisation of private law, for example, was achieved to a high degree within the Roman empire. There is no even march forward, and once again historical sociology is a matter of identifying a specific conjunction of causes – the conjunction which in this case produced the specific form of rationalisation associated with the 'idea of a calling and the devotion to labour in the calling.'

Having defined and narrowed his problem in this way Weber finds the solution to it in the particular relationship between the spirit of capitalism and the ethic of protestantism brought into being in Europe in the 16th and 17th centuries. Culturally, traditionalism is saturated by religion. Any escape from traditionalism that called for human action from within the world of tradition had therefore to be itself grounded in religious meaning. Unintentionally, and uniquely among the great world religions, Christianity contained, in Weber's view, the possibility of such an escape – or more precisely and significantly of an escape by way of a process of rationalisation. The overt ethics of almost all varieties of Christianity were, of course, unfavourable to capitalistic activity; economic action generally and commercial activities in particular, above all those involving credit transactions and loans at interest, were regarded as being at best morally dubious and more probably as reprehensible. Yet buried within Christianity Weber found a drive towards rationalism which in due course and indirectly was to make a vital contribution to the rise of capitalism – and so, ironically and at last, to the undermining of all religions including Christianity. Paradoxically 'the germs of modern capitalism must be sought in a religion where officially a theory was dominant which was ... in principle strongly hostile to capitalism' (1961: 262).

The 'secret' of Christianity among the wold religions, that is, among the various belief systems generated within traditional society, was, Weber argued, twofold. Its peculiar ability to provide a moral escape-route from traditionalism lay partly in its antipathy to magic and partly in its commitment to the idea of a planned achievement of salvation. The antipathy to magic was itself inherited from Judaism but was coupled in Christianity with a principled statement of the idea of human destiny as a rational design. Certainly the design is that of God not of man; nevertheless, human existence is understood in Christianity as governed by a calculated intention. Christianity is in Weber's word a 'great rational prophecy'. It builds on an account of a plan for the achievement of salvation which human beings can in principle apprehend and to which they can accordingly adjust their lives. It proclaims the subjection of fate to intelligence (1961:265).

> In all times there has been but one means of breaking down the power of magic and establishing a rational conduct of life; this means is great rational prophecy. Not every prophecy by any means destroys the power of magic; but it is possible for a prophet who furnishes credentials in the shape of miracles and otherwise, to break down the traditional sacred rules. Prophecies have released the world from magic and in doing so have created the basis for our modern science and technology and for capitalism.

Prophecy asserts the possibility of successfully realising intentions; appropriate modes of action will bring the prophecy true. Within Christianity as well as within all prophetic religions the appropriate mode of life is, once more in Weber's words, that of 'asceticism'; a self-denying, meticulously ordered discipline that subjects every detail of life to the rationality of the (divine) plan.

Weber – sensibly – does not regress to consider the problem of explaining the origins of Christianity, but, accepting the invention of a rational religion as more or less historically given, turns his attention to the ways in which the unavoidable tension between rationalism and faith within Christianity worked itself out. For centuries, of course, the tension was kept in the background of religious life by certain distinctive compromises which the Christian churches were able or were required to make as Christianity established itself as a dominant religion. The separation of church and state was one such compromise, crucial not only in the general recognition it implied of the existence of fields of action governed by distinct even if closely related moralities, but more specifically in the way in which within the post-Roman world it permitted a variety of secular activities, both economic and political, which would have been condemned within the internal ethos of Christianity to coexist with Christianity and pursue their own history. A similar pattern marks the relationship of Christianity to magic. For Weber (1961:265) 'the dominance of magic outside the sphere in which Christianity has prevailed is one of the most serious obstacles to the rationalisation of economic life.' Chinese engineers could build roads only in places where there were no spirits to be disturbed by their activities. Indian workmen refused contact with others whose impurity might defile them. Ancient Egyptians placed scarabs on the hearts of the dead in order to hide their sins from the deities and enable them to slip by subterfuge into paradise. 'Obviously capitalism could not develop in [groups] thus bound hand and foot in magical beliefs.' Yet, Christianity, while insisting that life is governed by its great rational prophecy and not by magic and that human beings are accordingly uniquely responsible for their own progress towards salvation, never in the long centuries of Catholic ascendancy in the west imposed the full burden of that responsibility on the mass of believers. Elements of magic were, in fact, smuggled back into Christianity in the 'sublimated' form of the Eucharist. And still more importantly, the priest as confessor with power to forgive sins was placed between the individual and the ruthless commitment to rational responsibility for one's own destiny which Christianity strictly implied. Thus (1961:268):

> For the men of the middle ages the possibility of unburdening themselves through the channel of the confessional, when they had rendered themselves liable to punishment, meant a release from the consciousness of sin which the teachings of the church had called into being. The unity and strength of the methodological conduct of life were thus, in fact, broken up.

And finally, for those Christians who found intolerable such compromises with nature, superstition and irrationality, and who felt impelled to live wholly in terms of the overt teachings of the church, Christianity invented its most brilliant compromise with the world – the monastery. In the monastery the ideal Christian life was visibly held up as a model to the world; at the same time the actual practice of such a life was safely insulated from the world. For Weber the essence of 'monk ethics' was the self-denying, rationalistic discipline of asceticism; 'which signifies the carrying out of a definite methodological conduct of life.' Asceticism embodied the full rationalistic potential of Christianity; but the ascetic life was as yet, institutionalised as an ideal, not as a practice required of all believers. Rather (1961:267), 'the most worthy individuals in the religious sense withdrew from the world and established a separate community.' The monk, then, was within Christianity, 'the first human being who lived rationally, who worked methodically and by rational means towards a goal, namely the future life.'

> Only for him did the clock strike, only for him were the hours of the day divided – for prayer. The economic life of the monastic communities was also rational. The monks in part furnished the officialdom of the early middle ages; the power of the doges of Venice collapsed when the investiture crisis deprived them of the possibility of employing churchmen for overseas enterprise. But

the rational mode of life remained restricted to the monastic circles.

The achievement of the Reformation unintended again to be sure, was to unleash asceticism on to the world at large. The abolition of the monasteries and the withering away of the confessional left Protestant Christians face to face with those responsibilities for the rational organisation of their own destinies always imposed on them in principle by Christian doctrine. The 'other-worldly' asceticism of the monasteries was brought to an end only to be replaced by a driving demand for asceticism in the world; 'You think you have escaped from the monastery, but everyone must now be a monk throughout life.' The new conception of individual life was, Weber argues, expressed most clearly and brutally in the Protestant, above all the Calvinist, conception of life as a calling. In their onslaught on the protective, privileged institution of the Catholic church and in their struggle to win the right to live directly in accordance with their own understanding of the divine will, free of the mediation of priests, Protestants emphatically reasserted as a duty of all Christians *in* the world the very asceticism which had previously inspired the monastic withdrawal *from* the world. In the Calvinist account of Christian doctrine all are called to live a strenuous, orderly, sober and planned life in the world and directly under the eyes of God and for His glory. Only a few are saved; none can have certain knowledge of salvation; and works cannot alter the destiny decreed for the individual. But the life of all is part of the minutely-determined, all-pervading divine plan and one distinguishing feature of the saved is the remorseless, thorough-going confidence with which they live their own lives *as though* they knew they were saved and in accordance with that plan. The intense individualism of Protestantism gave Christians a new dilemma which became more acute the more radically Protestants insisted on the freedom and duty of the individual to live in direct relationship with God. No guarantee of salvation can now be found outside the individual. How then is the individual to live with the potentially terrifying burden of ignorance now thrust upon his or her shoulders? Calvinist pastoral teaching made two distinctive proposals to enable the individual Christian to cope with this predicament. 'On the one hand it is held to be an absolute duty to consider oneself chosen and to combat all doubts as temptations of the devil.' And 'on the other hand, in order to attain that self-confidence intense worldly activity is recommended as the most suitable means.' One is, as it were, instructed to *use* one's life as a calculated means of at once fulfilling God's plan, and assuaging one's own inner panic. A driving and driven existence is proposed (1930:115, 117):

> Thus the Calvinist, as it is sometimes put, himself creates his own salvation, or, as would be more correct, the conviction of it. But this creation cannot, as in Catholicism, consist in a gradual accumulation of good works to one's credit, but rather in a systematic self-control which at every moment stands before the inexorable alternative, chosen or damned ... The God of Calvinism demanded of his believers not single good works but a life of good works combined into a unified system.

It was naturally no part of the intention of the early Protestant divines to provide moral legitimation for a way of life so well suited to the energetic and single-minded pursuit of rational economic activity. Many of the Protestant pioneers were indeed deeply hostile to all commercial and materialistic occupations. Yet Protestantism – especially in those intensely individualistic forms which developed in England, Scotland and the Netherlands – did in a unique way do just that. 'The drain of asceticism from everyday worldly life had been stopped by a dam and those passionately spiritual natures which had formerly supplied the highest type of monk were now forced to pursue their ascetic ideals within mundane occupations.' Indirectly, but in a quite compelling way, the Protestant programme for the salvation of the soul made a rationalistic devotion to the efficient conduct of worldly tasks not only a proper but an imperative basis for action. It is not that Protestantism was in any way specifically oriented *towards* capitalism. Yet there was a powerful, unintended congruence, an 'elective affinity' in Weber's own term, between the understanding of life demanded by Protestantism and the comprehensive rationalisation of all social action and relationships implicit in capitalistic practice. The 'idea of the necessity of proving one's faith in worldly activity' could thus, deviously but forcefully, provide a legitimating context for the otherwise outrageous relationships and ways of life that capitalism entails. Put crudely (1961:269):

> This development of the concept of the calling quickly gave to the modern entrepreneur a fabulously clear conscience – and also industrious workers; he gave to his employees as the wages of their ascetic devotion to the calling and of cooperation in his ruthless exploitation of them through capitalism the prospect of eternal salvation ... Such a powerful, unconsciously refined organisation for the production of capitalistic individuals has never existed in any other church or religion.

The Protestant Ethic and the Spirit of Capitalism traces the ways in which this organisation of meaning so strangely conducive to unleashing the spirit and thence the practice of capitalism was purveyed into the mundane world through the development of the protestant sects. Weber's argument is that the history of religion in the seventeenth century is thus also the history of the piecing together of a possible context for the growth of a 'specifically bourgeois economic ethic'. The struggle to emancipate the believer from the church has served also to create a world of meaning in which it was possible to free the capitalist from tradition.

The causes of capitalism

What sort of explanation of the rise of capitalism does Weber then offer us? What sort of argument and analysis is he really advancing? It is certainly *not*, as he himself insists, an argument that turns on any sort of general claim about the causal primacy of ideas or beliefs in historical change. Nor is it an argument about how capitalism *had* to develop. He is not claiming that capitalism could only have developed in a context permeated by the Protestant ethic, or that the Protestant ethic must be seen as a necessary condition for the rise of capitalism in general terms. In effect, he hardly offers us an explanation of the rise of capitalism at all but only of the rise of capitalism in western Europe in a particular historical epoch and setting. His argument is that within that setting and only within that setting the contribution of the Protestant ethic was indispensable to the rise of capitalism; had the Protestant ethic not created a favourable context of meaning the possibility of capitalism within early modern Europe could not have been realised when and as it was. In that sense only can the Protestant ethic be regarded as the cause of the rise of capitalism. If one removes the role of the Protestant ethic the rest of that particular historical story could not have been the same.

This is at once a strong and a highly specific claim. And it takes us to the heart of Weber's understanding of historical sociology as an exercise in cumulative explanation. Causality in history does not for him imply intention; nor does it imply a social world governed by abstract general laws. Causal importance is a matter of the contribution of any specific factor in a given historical complex to the construction of that complex as a whole. If one can show that a particular complex, say modern western capitalism, could not have come into being if factor 'x', say the Protestant ethic, had not been present, then factor 'x' can be identified as a cause of the complex as a whole. But only in that specific conjunction of factors. And only as *a* cause among others. And Weber does quite freely identify several other causes of capitalism. In the *General Economic History*, for example, the creation of a rational ethos for the conduct of economic action is but one strand of a process of historical construction which has equally important economic, technological and administrative strands (1961:208). Indeed, one could argue, viewing Weber's work as a whole, that it was the administrative strand, associated with the formation of the state, law and bureaucracy that most deeply engaged his attention (1961:249).

Thus, alongside the familiar 'Weber thesis' about the religious origins of capitalism it would be quite easy to set another about its political origins. If the Protestant ethic gave capitalistic activity a meaning it had never before achieved it was the nation state, and above all an international system of warring nation states, that provided the crucial opportunities for capitalistic activity to bear fruit; it was (1961:250) 'the closed national state which afforded to capitalism its chance for development', both by creating a demand for capital and by establishing the legal and administrative framework within which capital could be most effectively accumulated. For many modern sociologists, therefore, Weber's decisive contribution to historical sociology is not found in the way he teases out the complex affinity between the Protestant ethic and the spirit of capitalism but in his analysis of the role of formal law and bureaucratic administration as facilitating frameworks for capitalistic practice. Talcott Parsons, for example (1960), taking Weber's work as the principal point of reference for his own sociology of industrialisation, emphasises not so much Weber's 'essentially correct' discussion of the ethic of ascetic Protestantism as the 'major keynote' struck by his analysis of bureaucracy, especially 'bureaucracy in the business enterprise ... one of the major bases on which he distinguished the rational bourgeois capitalism which he felt to be the central modern Western phenomenon, from the many other types which he discussed.' Just as the rise of capitalism in Europe involved an ethical rationalisation it also involved an administrative rationalisation. The question of the sources and nature of that rationalisation had, therefore, also to command Weber's attention; he saw it as a second crucial 'cause' of the rise of capitalism and his analysis of its causal significance follows essentially the same path as his analysis of the causal significance of ascetic protestantism.

As the methodological practice of formal rationality capitalism plainly 'pre-supposes' an orderly, calculable environment. The construction – on the basis of political rather than economic power – of the 'rational state', that is, of political domination based on formal, universalistic law, administration by professional officials and the systematic definition of procedures of control, was, like the Protestant ethic, an indispensable but indirect occasion for the discovery of a critical opportunity for capitalism to break out of its traditionalistic constraints. Once again, we are confronted with a long chain of specific historical causes leading, in conjunction with others no less specific, to a momentous and unintended result. It was, Weber argues, not just law and officialdom but a particular type of law and officaldom – legal-rational domination – developed uniquely in the West that was important. Once again, Weber offers an illuminating contrast between European experience and that of classical China. In Confucianism China achieved a religion no less rational than Protestant Christianity but whereas the rationality of the latter was a 'formal' rationality oriented to mastering human destiny, that of the former was a substantive rationality oriented to acceptance. Similarly Chinese civilisation developed an apparatus of officials but that officialdom never took root as administrators of a body of formal law independent of substantive considerations attached to cases, magical beliefs and the whims of the Imperial household; the practice of regular bureaucratic administration as a procedure in its own right never broke free.

> Very different is the rational state in which alone modern capitalism can flourish. Its basis is an expert officaldom and rational law. The Chinese state changed over to administration through trained officials in the place of humanistically cultured persons as early as the 7th and 11th centuries but the change could be only temporarily maintained; then the usual eclipse of the moon arrived and arrangements were transformed in reverse order (1961:250).

And again (1961:252):

> In China it may happen that a man who has sold a house to another may later come to him and ask to be taken in because in the meantime he has been impoverished. If the purchaser refuses to heed the ancient Chinese command to help a brother, the spirits will be disturbed; hence the impoverished seller comes into the house as a renter who pays no rent. Capitalism cannot operate on the basis of a law so constituted. What it requires is law which can be counted upon, like a machine; ritualistic-religious and magical considerations must be excluded.

Formal law covering all relevant actions and transactions and administered by a trained body of specialists who are themselves predictable in the sense of being servants of the law they administer is the administrative context most favourable to capitalism; and such a context was indeed created historically in early-modern Europe. The Roman empire gave

Europe the idea of formal law and the power struggles of church and state, of states with one another and of rulers with their subjects then encouraged the growth of bureaucracy as the most technically efficient means of administering and implementing formal law and maintaining it as a form of domination separated from all substantive considerations.

Weber does not trace the detail, or even seek to identify the significant moments of the historical creation of bureaucracy in the way he had traced the actual conjunction of the protestant ethic and the spirit of capitalism. Yet it is clear that his sense of the role of bureaucracy as a 'cause' of the rise of capitalism is identical to his sense of the role of ascetic protestantism. Without the 'input' at an appropriate historical moment of bureaucratic administration and formal law the possibility of capitalism latent in early modern Europe could not have been realised. Its realisation pre-supposed rational administration just as it pre-supposed a rationalistic ethic – and just as it pre-supposed also the private appropriation of the means of production, free labour and so forth. The rise of capitalism is to be understood as a specific historical event with multiple and cumulative causes acting in a specific structural conjunction. Whether or not the 'Weber thesis' stands up to empirical scrutiny – and there have been powerful suggestions that it does not (Green, 1959; George and George, 1961; Samuelsson, 1961; Elton, 1963) – its strategy of explanation would seem to be of fundamental importance for historical sociology.

5

The problem of tendency: functional historical sociology and the convergence thesis

Historical sociology, we can now say, treats history as the way social action and social structure create and contain one another. Its method is necessarily dialectical, reflecting the endlessly moving interplay of fact and meaning that constitutes, decomposes and reconstitutes social experience. The work of Durkheim, Marx and Weber can be seen as a struggle to achieve the flexible, many-sided vision that historical sociology demands. The hazard which above all faces their modern intellectual successors is that of lapsing into the one-sidedness from which they themselves in different ways and to different degrees had managed to escape. The temptation to move from the discovery (or construction) of pattern and probability within given historical configurations of action and structure to the assertion of supra-historical causal sequence or destiny is very strong. The task of the historical sociologist, however, is to discern the specifically *historical structuring* of action without falling into the trap of separating structure from action or postulating a theory of history in which a succession of structural types – like the parade of ghostly kings in Macbeth – has an existence independent of the creation of structure through action. Durkheim, Marx and Weber each broke with the evolutionary theories of their contemporaries in their effort to develop an analysis of history which could identify pattern and tendency in this way without spilling over into a trans-historical teleology which discovered possibility and probability in the interaction of purpose and structure without transforming the structuring of action into a supra-historical developmental process governing both structure and action with law-like necessities independent of human agency. They all had great difficulty in achieving such an analysis; in moving, one might say, away from historical theology and towards historical sociology. Weber could not resist the temptation to speak of bureaucratisation as the inexorable fate of the industrial world. Marx urged the inevitability of socialism; Durkheim insisted on the forceful logic of the division of labour. Yet all three were – on any close and open-minded reading of their work – really talking about more or less compelling *options* within the configuration of the industrial revolution and not about imperatives of development controlling it externally. Durkheim's best empirical work is concerned with egoistic and anomic forms of action produced by the division of labour and systematically undermining the logic of the division of labour. The point of writing the *Communist Manifesto* and of all the other polemical and directly political activities in which Marx and Engels engaged, was precisely that the transition to socialism was not an inevitable necessity of capitalism but a possibility within it which could be realised through appropriate action. Whenever Weber spoke of the rationalisation of industrial culture and its drive to formal bureaucratic organisation he also insisted on the ambiguities of rationalism and on the real possibility of mastering formal rationality through action based on deliberately chosen principles of a quite different nature. For Weber rationalisation was a fate only if people chose to be inactive in a certain way, just as for Marx socialism was a fate only if people chose to engage in definite activities. Yet if Durkheim, Marx and Weber had such difficulty in steering a course towards historical sociology it is perhaps not surprising that many of their successors have surrendered once again to the easy charms of historical theology, and that modern sociology has seen the appearance of 'neo-evolutionism' and of trans-historical theories centred on ideas of the 'logic of industrialism'.

Modern sociology has carried the imprint of its three great intellectual progenitors in very much the ways one might have expected. Durkheim's concern with the problem of individualism and social solidarity, of the possibility of cohesion in the face of an explosion of egoism, has been formative in shaping studies of deviance and social control – in the sociology of religion, education and crime. Marx's insistence on the need to root social analysis in the processes of class formation and class struggle has increasingly dominated modern work on social inequality and the state; his strong sense of the specifically historical nature of the social world has proved a decisive influence in all fields of sociology where attention has been directed to issues of conflict, oppression and resistance. Weber's compelling arguments for the multiple and contingent causation of every historical present, combined with his emphasis on rationalisation as the cultural master-theme of our particular present, have given a distinctive colouring to the sociology of science, knowledge and religion, to the analysis of formal organisations and to work on the 'modernisation' of underdeveloped countries. And most fruitfully, these influences have not remained isolated in distinct fields of study. Much of the vitality of contemporary sociology springs from the way in which in every field of sociological work a debate has developed between Durkheimian, Weberian and Marxist conceptions of social process and social structure. Thus, the sociology of education is caught up in an encounter between Marxist and Durkheimian understandings of the functions of schooling and the conditions of educability; the analysis of social inequality is in the throes of a long-standing dispute between Marxist and Weberian conceptions of the forms and dynamics of social stratification; the sociology of religion thrives on unresolved differences between Weberian and Durkheimian accounts of the nature of religious practices, beliefs and organisation. And of course quite separate influences have also been felt to further complicate and diversify sociological work as a whole – for example, the development from psychology and literary studies of a sociology of private life, building on the close analysis of small-scale interactions and the relationship of individual identity and social structure. This work, too, has come to have significance for historical sociology in recent years.

Nevertheless, in the field of large scale historical sociology modern work has been influenced primarily by the achievements of Max Weber, and by a vigorous and more or less explicitly Marxist assault on what modern sociologists have made of the work of Weber. The pivot of this assault is the claim that in extending and applying Weber's ideas about the nature of industrialisation modern scholars, captivated by the possibility of imposing various elegant conceptual schemes on the vast untidiness of history, have managed to abandon Weber's own insistence on the open-ended and many-sided nature of historical causality and to re-introduce just those properties of developmental teleology and one-sided determinism which Weber himself was above all anxious to avoid. The debate has resolved around two closely related issues, although it has found echoes across whole ranges of recent sociological work. There is the issue of the extent to which analysis of the historical structuring of industrialisation in the past can support the elaboration of a general model of 'industrialism' which can in turn be held to embody the future destiny of countries at low levels of industrialisation in the present. And there is the issue of the extent to which the analysis of social change within highly industrialised societies since, say, 1920, the historical sociology of industrialism as it were, indicates the emergence from industrialism of a new and no less culturally significant type of social system or stage of history. Briefly, there is the debate about 'convergence', and there is the debate about 'post-industrialism'. Is there an industrial destiny to which all pre-industrial or industrialising nations will have to bow? And is there in prospect a post-industrial destiny discernible in the changes occurring within industrial societies to which in their turn all industrial societies will have to bow? The affirmative answer to both questions has been strongly argued by eminent sociologists. And it has been as strongly repudiated by others as a profound vulgarisation, indeed a travesty, of what historical sociology can properly hope to achieve. This chapter will be mainly devoted to following the course of the first of those debates in the hope that we can indeed learn something from it about the scope and limits, of historical sociology sensibly understood.

The critical influential link between the ideas of Durkheim, Marx and Weber and these modern debates is provided by the work of Talcott Parsons and to understand what modern sociology has made of its founding fathers it is essential to begin by considering Parsons's own highly creative synthesis of this intellectual heritage. Before doing that, though, it is right to emphasise again the extent to which Marx, Weber and even Durkheim were not themselves doing the sort of thing (transforming tendency into teleology) commonly attributed to modern advocates of the convergence thesis and to modern proponents of the idea of post-industrialism by their various critics. They did all engage in the derivation from historical analysis of conceptions of 'stages' or 'configurations', types of social system, modes of production, distinct structures or orders in history. Such work is an essential heuristic measure in historical sociology. And they did all attempt to identify empirically certain probabilities and possibilities of action contained within given configurations, a restrospective analysis of tendency or potential. Such work is the distinctive feature of historical sociology – at least substantively – as a form of explanation. What they all carefully did *not* do was to infer or postulate the existence – as the evolutionists before them had done – of meta-historical laws of development binding successive stages or configurations of history in inevitable genetic sequence. It is that third step, which grows so easily out of the first two, is so easily confused with them by critics and which Durkheim, Marx and Weber struggled so resolutely to avoid, that is manifestly beyond the reach of historical sociology, lapsing instead into a peculiarly a-historical historicism. The fact that both Marx and Durkheim have been charged with taking that third step, coupled with the fact that neither of them, on what I have argued is the true reading of their work, really did take it, should at least make us a little cautious when faced with the claim that modern sociologists, both marxist and non-marxist, have done so. The boundary between the legitimate analysis of tendency and the illegitimate postulate of teleology is at once crucial for historical sociology and one that seems to be dangerously unfixed – or perhaps, more readily fixed in the eye of the beholder than in reality.

The work of Talcott Parsons, decisive as it has been in setting the terms in which modern sociology has absorbed and elaborated the ideas of Durkheim, Marx and Weber, always hovered uneasily around this uncertain boundary. On the one hand (1966) he took up a frankly 'evolutionary perspective', asserting the existence of a process of 'directional' development from a single, western origin and culminating at present in an

international system of 'modern' industrialism, with modernity
most fully achieved (perhaps one should not be surprised to
learn) in the United States of America. Moreover (1971), in
many passages the process of development as Parsons
described it often seemed to be driven forward by the logic of
development itself in the form of functional necessities of the
modernising social system: analytically, attention is directed to
a dialectic of functional problems and solutions to those
problems through which social systems evolve towards ever
higher levels of social organisation. For example (1949), the
transformation of family relationships during and after the
industrial revolution – the separation of home and work and
the structural isolation of the conjugal family unit – is presented
as a change demanded by the irresistible requirements of the
modernising occupational system, a fate which spouses,
parents and children simply *had* to acknowledge. Conversely,
'the producing organisation must develop an authority system
which is not embedded in kinship'. Such statements surely
imply a view of history in which functional necessities govern
structural changes in society and do so in advance of the events
through which social structure is constituted. More fundamentally, his identification of the United States as the special
bearer of modernity, the lead nation to which others will
increasingly approximate, surely depends more on his prior
theoretical commitment to the view that the direction of
modernisation is necessarily towards pluralism, decentralisation
and individualism than on any sort of historical demonstration
that that is the direction change has actually taken in the
United States, let alone on any empirical evidence that the
functional advantages of modernity can only be realised by
way of the particular structural and cultural characteristics he
attributes to the United States. In arguments of this sort is not
Parsons falling into the worst kind of a-historical historicism,
into just the sort of error for which he himself once brusquely
dismissed Herbert Spencer from the community of serious
sociologists?

On the other hand Parsons, perhaps more than anyone else,
always saw himself as taking up Weber's insistence that the
distinctive object of study of sociology is action (1937). He
always argued that social systems are to be understood as the

abstract forms in which action in the sense of concrete social interaction is integrated. More specifically, for all his emphasis on the logical necessity of solving functional problems – if a system becomes more differentiated, for example, it is bound to face problems of integration which must be solved if the system is to persist – he was usually very careful to recognise that logical necessity is not at all the same thing as historical necessity. Thus (1971:38), he acknowledges that many societies have collapsed precisely because they did not recognise let alone solve the problems of integration brought on by structural differentiation. Where then does Parsons really stand? Does he successfully combine functional analysis with historical sociology, or is he merely imposing a functionalist teleology on historical experience? Plainly, his argument needs closer consideration. Three of his many writings may serve for this purpose: the essay, 'Some Reflections on the Institutional Framework of Economic Development' (1960), and the two short books, *Societies: Evolutionary and Comparative Perspectives* (1966) and *The System of Modern Societies* (1971). It is in these works that Parsons most explicitly presents his theory or 'paradigm' of evolutionary change derived from his general analysis of the dynamics of systems of action, and seeks to validate the theory empirically – the end product of that exercise being the claim that the United States may be regarded as the world's leading society from the point of view of modernisation.

Despite its adventurous conclusion Parsons's analysis begins in a quite traditional manner, finding the hallmark of the uniqueness of industrialism as a type of social system in the degree and elaborateness of the structural differentiation it embodies and treating the process of structural differentiation as the principal form in which industrialism is created historically (1960:102). With Weber he emphasises the importance of the separation of political and religious authority in western Christianity in creating social space, 'a sphere of immunity', in which economic action could be pursued (1960:105). And he places particular emphasis on the way in which the separation of property rights from central political domination achieved within western feudalism, and the concomitant association of property rights with kinship, created both a distinctive opportunity and a distinctive necessity in the early history of capitalism – the initial formation of capitalist industry on the basis of the family firm: 'the decisive thing about the family firm, seen in our present perspective, was its "emancipation" in the sense of *structural differentiation*, from the political system' (1960:108). The differentiation already achieved meant that entrepreneurs *could* capitalise industry by means of the family firm: it also meant that if capitalisation was to occur at all at that time in those societies it would have to occur in that form. And finally, the fact that it did initially occur in that way carried the structural differentiation of economic and political action, organisation and power to new heights, making it indeed the essential structural characteristic of capitalist industrialism.

However, his analysis now enters more difficult territory. Two strands of his argument are especially relevant and worth following here. One concerns the further history of the process of structural differentiation. The other is the way in which he then deals with the much larger problem of identifying the overall direction of social evolution as a process of 'modernisation'.

The creation of the family firm as a focus of economic activity was associated, Parsons next argues, with a further and in some ways even more profound process of differentiation, that 'between the household and the organisation in which the members of the household perform occupational roles' (1960:110). He notes that this segregation of home and work began at the bottom of the social hierarchy as, in effect, a condition imposed on their workforce by the way the new entrepreneurs chose to organise production. In other words he does here give us not only a sense of process and structure but also at least an implicit sense of agency, an indication as to how the process of restructuring in question might have been actively made by particular human agents. As he proceeds, however, it is just this sense of agency which is increasingly hard to discern in his writing. His next argument concerns the way in which the differentiation of domestic and economic roles crept up the social hierarchy, gradually transforming even top management and the whole organisation of production. In a revealing passage he describes this further change as something that *had* to occur as the appropriate structural solution to a distinctive functional problem of the mid-nineteenth century economy. Thus (1960:111): 'there was a fundamental structural asymmetry in the firm, between the achieved-occupational component at the bottom, and the ascribed-kinship component at the top ... from a sociological point of view this was a temporary and unstable structure, further development was bound to challenge the status of the ascriptive lineage component in the upper reaches of the organisation'. The remainder of 'Reflections' traces the general extension of 'the principle that the firm is a structure of occupational roles' through all levels of economic activity, a thoroughgoing separation of control from ownership and a bureaucratisation of production which leads Parsons to suggest that capitalism is no longer an appropriate name for the advanced western ecnomomies which should instead be identified as 'bureaucratic industrialism': 'it is this new bureaucratic industrialism, not the classical capitalism of a century ago', moreover, 'which is the essential reference point for analysing the problems of economic development in the non-European world' (1960:116). Increasingly, as one follows Parsons through this argument, one is aware that this exposition is in terms of structural change divorced from historical action; it is a catalogue of effects without causes; and one cannot help suspecting that his indiffernece to causes (in the sense of specific human agency) has much to do with the fact that the functionality of the effects, their role in the process of development, is itself sufficient explanation of them for this author. The transformation of top management, for example, is seen as coming about in part 'as a function of the increasing complexity of technology' which required the employment of highly trained professional staff at higher and higher levels of responsibility, and in part as a function of the development of a market for capital which meant that 'access to capital ... no longer required the commitment of personal property by the owning-managing kinship units and the automatic flow of all proceeds back to these units' (1960:112).

This sort of explanation is perfectly legitimate and useful so far as it goes. But already we can see that as historical sociology it really does not go very far. No doubt family control did come to seem both anomalous and inefficient to some people as technical criteria for authority were advanced and as alternative means of capitalising production and extracting surplus were devised. Historically, however, the elimination of the family firm was brought about not by structural asymmetries or changing functional requirements but by the active use of new management systems and the vigorous exploiting of new forms of capitalisation to render the old forms progressively less profitable. In the face of enhanced competition the family firm either transformed itself into something else or was driven off the market. The precise way in which this happened also varied dramatically from industry to industry and from society to society according to varying entrepreneurial strategies and the opportunities and constraints of different cultures and historical situations. The kind of analysis pursued by Parsons seems to predispose the analyst to lose sight of this type and level of activity. It is not that explanation in terms of agency is in principle incompatible with explanation in terms of functional problems, or that the latter cannot in principle be made to accommodate detailed variations. But there clearly is a tendency, evident in the work of Parsons, to allow the elegant logic of functional analysis to lead one to ignore the fact that, to whatever extent history can in retrospect be seen as a matter of the varying resolution or non-resolution of functional problems history is made not by functions but by people. The level of abstraction at which Parsons, quite deliberately, casts his analysis in order to grasp the relationships of function and structure does tend to mean that his treatment of social evolution is also quite brutally abstracted from the concrete and specific enactment of history by historical actors. The test of the validity of an attempt to integrate functional analysis and historical sociology has to be the extent to which it achieves explanations which are adequate both in terms of functional requirements and in terms of agency. The difficulties of that task are already evident in Parsons's discussion of the rise of bureaucratic industrialism. They are much more apparent in his larger treatment of the dynamics and direction of social evolution as a whole.

When Parsons is attending to history, to what actually happened, his concern is primarily with the process of structural differentiation. When, by contrast, his interest turns from history to evolution, to the problem of the direction of change and the nature of 'modernity', a different process which he calls 'adaptive up-grading' dominates the analysis (1966:22). He presents evolution as a fourfold development in which differentiation is, as it were, the driving force and adaptive upgrading, or the 'enhancement of adaptive capacity', is the distinctive evolutionary pay-off, the product. Differentiation, the 'division of a unit or structure in a social system into two or more units or structures that differ in their characteristics and functional significance for the system', only gives rise to a 'more evolved' system when 'each newly differentiated component has greater adaptive capacity than the component that previously performed its primary function'. What, then, are we to understand by 'greater adaptive capacity'? With disconcerting banality Parsons appears whenever he is relatively explicit and concrete, rather than elusive and abstract, by this to mean something like increased productivity: 'the participating people ... must become more productive than before, as measured by some kind of output-cost relationship' (1966:22). In those cases where adaptive upgrading follows the differentiation of home and workplace we might, for example, find the family becoming more loving and caring while the factory produces a wider range of goods more economically – resulting in both happier children and bigger profits. More generally adaptive upgrading plainly implies an increased capacity on the part of the society in question to master a wide range of environmental hazards – war, plague, protest, floods – without significant structural change. The two other processes which must occur for evolution to be present concern the integration of the system in question and the pattern of its values. Specifically in the case of 'modernisation' the processes are those of 'inclusion' and of 'value-generalisation': membership of the system is extended to previously excluded groups; and values are redefined so that an ever greater diversity of members, ways of life and functions can be legitimated and contained within the system as a whole. Evolution, then, is the creation of social systems of ever-higher adaptive capacity. Adaptive upgrading presupposes structural and functional differentiation which in turn raises problems of integration and values which must be solved if the system as a system is to reap the benefits of adaptive upgrading.

How does Parsons move from this model of the process of evolution to his conclusion that the most evolved nation in the contemporary world is the United States of America (1971:86)? The definition itself, with its primary emphasis on the differentiation (above all on the differentiation of economic and political structures and functions as in capitalism) rather than on fusion (as in socialism), obviously helps. More particularly, the assumption that adaptive upgrading is the crucial measure of evolution is, especially if upgrading is really to be understood as mainly a matter of increased productivity by way of increased differentiation, one that gives the whole analysis a remarkably ethnocentric bias. It claims to find an objective and universal criterion of evolution in what is manifestly an especially American characteristic and an especially American value. Many critics would no doubt insist that it is not at all clear that adaptive upgrading does have any objective evolutionary significance apart from the fact that it is what the United States has been notably good at for the last hundred years. Members of many societies might well regard evolution as a matter of quite other sorts of collective achievement, including some of those stigmatised by Parsons as evolutionary failures – for example, the plainly non-adaptive, indeed suicidal, insistence on cherished cultural values in the face of overwhelming hostile external power. Some of the societies Parsons somewhat unhelpfully identifies as 'dead ends', such as classical Athens and ancient Israel, could surely be held in terms of other criteria to have been a good deal more evolved than many of those he sees as lead societies of the future – including even the United States of America. Then again, one could reasonably point out that the mere use of the idea of evolution – at least in Parsons's sense of adaptive advancement – commits one at the outset to a treatment of history which has got to culminate in the discovery of a peak of advancement, normally in one's own immediate milieu. While we must agree with Weber that any study of the past will be constructed in terms of significance for the present we can also agree that the ruthless and brutally selective ranking of past societies in terms of their success or failure as steps towards the present which the idea of evolution seems to encourage makes nonsense of any attempt to know the past empirically. The point of the concept of evolution one might say is to legitimate the present not to understand history. It is very noticeable that Weber, whom Parsons constantly cites as his principal inspiration, nowhere invokes the notion of evolution in his own attempts to explain the historical construction of society.

However, despite the parochialism and tendentiousness of his model of social evolution, Parsons does not in fact seek to establish the modernity of the United States as a matter of definition or by formal inference from the model; rather, he argues that while the leading status of the U.S.A. does indeed follow from his theoretical analysis that analysis is in turn validated by empirical, specifically historical fact. Accordingly, a large part of *The System of Modern Societies* is devoted to an analysis of the way in which a social structure uniquely endowed with adaptive capacity was constructed, historically, in the United States. In other words the argument proceeds on two fronts. On the one hand the theory requires that whichever society has solved the problems of differentiation, integration and value generalisation most successfully and so achieved the highest level of adaptive upgrading must be recognised as standing at a peak of modernity. On the other hand empirical historical analysis shows that structures uniquely conducive to that achievement have been uniquely produced in the U.S.A. So if we agree to accept adaptive upgrading as an appropriate criterion of modernity – and it is not at all clear that we should – can we then accept Parsons's version of history as establishing the special modernity of his own society? For the historical sociologist the answer to that question must depend on whether Parsons turns out to be arguing from history to functions or, as one might fear, from functions to history.

Maddeningly, he appears to do both. There are certainly passages where his argument seems to be governed by the simple teleological question 'what does adaptive upgrading require?' For example, having established that the two crucial 'bridges' from classical antiquity to the modern world were Christianity and Roman law he then faces the problem of accounting for the discontinuity of development between the fourth and the ninth centuries and deals with it as follows: 'a deep societal "regression" was necessary before the religion could *grow with* the structure of a new society, before its legitimizing and regulating potential could fully develop' (1966:93). So much for the collapse of Rome and the Dark Ages. Then again, when he insists on the unique integration of American society achieved on the basis of equality of opportunity is his account not shaped more by the needs of his model of modernity than by close historical observation – of, for example the pit of intractable poverty, exclusion and victimisation to which whole sections of the American population have chronically been relegated? On the other hand much of his analysis, drastically selective as it is, abridged and generalised as it inclines to be, plainly rests on a much more direct appeal to evidence of historical action. For example when he tells us (1971:91) that: 'American society ... abandoned the tradition of aristocracy with only a mild revolutionary disturbance. It also lacked the heritage of Europe's peasant classes. As an industrial working class developed the typical European level of class consciousness never emerged, largely because of the absence of aristocratic and peasant elements', he is obviously advancing a claim with important functional implications but it is one which is primarily to be accepted or rejected on the basis of identifiable historical evidence. Again, his analysis of England in the sixteenth and seventeenth centuries emphasising as it does not the familiar theses of constitutional revolution, religious crisis and economic growth but rather the dramatic differentiation of religion, government and economy from one another and from the 'societal community' is at once what one would have to find in order to account for the enormous leap in adaptive capacity achieved by England in that period in the terms of Parsons's model of evolutionary process *and* a finding directly rooted in and referring to historical evidence. The form of argument in such passages is the proposition: 'as a result of particular processes of historical construction realised in given societies in given epochs those societies acquired in those epochs social structures better suited than any others currently existing to solving the functional problems involved in adaptive upgrading'. Whatever one thinks about the value of adaptive capacity as a yardstick of evolution such an argument is hardly invalid in principle, nor is it necessarily a-historical; on the contrary it invites elaboration, grounding and validation in terms of quite specific historical and comparative research. It is that sort of argument that Parsons again attempts in his chapter on the United States.

The result reveals startlingly the extreme difficulty in integrating functional explanation and explanation in terms of agency in historical sociology. The thesis of the chapter is that, seizing the historical opportunities given to them by the fragmentary structures of the 'first new nation' the inhabitants of the United States contrived to create a social system in which differentiation has been carried to an unprecedented level while at the same time the functional problems posed by differentiation (for social systems) have been solved with unprecedented success. But the presentation constantly evades consideration of, or even reference to, actual historical practice and experience. What Parsons is interested in are the functional effects of American social structure; the issue of how those effects were actively produced, the problem of the historical creation of social structure, is really quite secondary for him and tends to be by-passed. For example (1971:91):

> The societal community must be articulated not only with the religious and political systems but also with the economy. In the United States the factors of production, including land and labour, have been relatively free of ascriptive ties, and the Federal Constitution has guaranteed their free movement among different states. This freedom has encouraged a high degree of division of labour and the development of an extensive market system. Locally oriented and traditionally directed economic activity and the ascriptive community structures in which they were embedded have thus been undermined, which has had important consequences for the stratification system; to the extent that the latter was rooted in occupational structure it was pushed toward universalism and an open class structure but not toward radical egalitarianism.

Here the attempt to fuse historical analysis and functional analysis really does not work at all; vast ranges of action and experience are implied and we are asked to take them all on trust. Elsewhere (1971:93), although still dogged by the same difficulty of finding a form of presentation which will allow him to show at one and the same time that people make their own history and that the way in which they do so constitutes the required solutions to functional problems, Parsons is slightly more successful:

> A highly developed legal system is central to a stable societal community that has dispensed with religious and ethnic uniformity as radically as has American society. The Puritan tradition and the Enlightenment fostered a strong predilection for a written Constitution with its echoes of covenant and social contract. An individualistic fear of authoritarianism had much to do with the separation of government powers. A federal structure was practically necessitated by the legal separation of the colonies. All three circumstances placed a premium on legal forms and on agencies charged with legal functions. Also many of the framers of the Constitution had legal training. Even though they provided for only one Supreme Court, without specifying membership qualifications and with very little specification of its powers, they did lay the foundations for an especially strong emphasis on the legal order.

Although the treatment of history in passages such as this is still firmly controlled by the author's prior sense of functional requirements, at least some effort is being made to recognise that requirements are met not because they are requirements but because specific historical actors in definite social relationships and structures do things which intentionally or unintentionally have appropriate effects. One gets the impression that functionalist historical sociology could, if only the meshing of action and function were explored in more detail and with rather more awareness of the incidence of conflict, deviance, failure and irrelevance (as opposed to successful problem-solving), achieve quite powerul and convincing analysis. However, in Parsons's own work this remains more a matter of promise than of performance.

Two themes are central to his analysis of American history: the claim that the distinctive structuring of American society has taken an 'associational' rather than a market or a bureaucratic form: and a great emphasis on the role of the 'educational revolution' in solving problems of integration and value-generalisation in the most recent phase of adaptive upgrading (1971:96). In marked contrast to his earlier argument about the emergence of 'bureaucratic industrialism' out of market industrialism Parsons now discovers 'a third main type of structuring that modern societal collectivities make possible', namely 'associationism' (1971:92). Associational structuring, whether in the form of the proliferation of voluntary associations, interest groups and community organisations, or in the appearance of 'fiduciary' boards of directors in firms and corporations, competitive political parties and trade unions or in the extensive professionalisation of work, has come, he argues, to provide the characteristic structural device in terms of which American society is both differentiated and integrated: 'the main trend is ... not toward increased bureaucracy ... but rather toward associationism'. - And insofar as the adaptive capacity of this form of structuring is enormously greater than that of either market or bureaucratic structures a door is opened for treating associationally structured societies (the U.S.A. today) as more evolved than either market structured societies (the U.S.A. a century ago) or bureaucratically structured societies (the U.S.S.R.). Unfortunately, although this claim has undeniable plausibility on theoretical grounds two kinds of empirical work needed to give it substance are almost entirely neglected by Parsons. He asserts (1971:114) that 'the American societal community that emerged was primarily *associational*'. But the historical work of demonstrating the emergence and primacy of associationism as a distinct form of structuring remains undone. Those who believe in the primacy of bureaucratic structuring, or of monopolistic capitalism for that matter, are simply told that they are mistaken. And the comparative demonstration of the superior adaptive capacity of associationism as against bureaucracy, for all societies as opposed to those initially structured on the basis of radical differentiation, is no less blandly ignored. At best Parsons here gives us a programme for functionalist historical sociology, not the thing itself.

The educational revolution receives rather closer and more satisfactory attention. Empirically, the extent of that revolution in the United States (40% of youth in higher education), and its origins and momentum in the struggle of new immigrant groups to secure inclusion in American society and of the older groups to control the terms of inclusion for the newcomers are persuasively indicated. Its effects in terms of integration, value-consensus, a general up-grading of occupations, a positive valuation of 'science' and 'knowledge' and the diffusion of an ideology of equality of opportunity are documented rather than merely asserted, with the result that their functionality in terms of the adaptive upgrading of the American system becomes a relatively plausible conclusion. Indeed, here, where Parsons might well have used a strong functionalist argument – centred on the technical requirement of the American economy for an ever more skilled labour force in order to maintain a general productive dynamism – he concentrates instead on the subjective meaning of education for the educated and not on its objective meaning for the system. By contrast, the system requirement for education *is* pointed out when he comes to discuss the Soviet Union (1971:122). Coupled with certain awkward difficulties lurking in his account of the educational revolution in the United States – such as his rather noticeable failure to account for the persistent exclusion of most American blacks from the overall up-grading of their compatriots – this sort of imbalance of emphasis must make one wonder just how far Parsons has any sort of serious scholarly interest in history as distinct from his obviously very serious commitment to celebrating his own society.

In stressing the general movement of industrial societies towards common forms of organisation, whether bueaucratic or associational, Parsons sets the scene for the debate on 'convergence'. And in envisaging a future for industrial society centred on the completion of the educational revolution and more generally 'of the type of society we have called "modern",' he no less emphatically sets the scene for the discussion of 'post-industrialism'. Yet a very visible feature of the way in which both of these issues have been taken up is that almost all of the authors concerned have retained Parsons functionalist strategy of explanation but abandoned his own attempt to set the analysis of the historical tendency of the history of industrial societies in the framework of a general functionalist theory of social evolution. Before turning to the recent debate on convergence we should obviously ask whether the apparent rejection of Parsons's larger strategy of analysis – the emphasis on what is happening within a single historical epoch rather than on the evolutionary design of history as a whole – is or is not response to the difficulties implicit in the much more ambitious work attempted by Parsons himself.

Teleology is the view that developments are due to the purpose or design that is served by them. Parsons and other functionalist evolutionists obviously come extraordinarily close to teleology in this sense. The argument that the late nineteenth century bureaucratisation of economy and government or the isolation of the conjugal family *had* to occur in the face of system requirements for differentiation and integration would certainly seem to be claiming that system design governs history. The conclusion that modernisation in the next century or so may be expected to follow the American lead and see a completion of that pattern in other societies surely rests on the idea that adaptive upgrading in its modern phase involves a distinctive design, that is a system, which will powerfully shape the history of those societies. Evolution is conceived of as the unfolding of successive patterns of adaptive upgrading and there is clearly at least a formal and abstract sense in which the design requirements of those patterns are held to account for actual historical developments. But what matters is whether that type of teleological explanation is held to apply in a concrete, substantive sense as well. Unfortunately that is something very difficult to determine, especially in the case of Parsons. There certainly are occasions on which he gives the impression of believing that people will if they can do the things that are conducive to adaptive upgrading and will do so without necessarily realising that that is what they are doing – strains and tensions occur, indeed, when they cannot find such ways of acting. The urban middle classes may have created a new type of family in the name of love but what they were *really* doing – the explanation is offered as definitely more fundamental – was segregating the ascriptive world of kinship from the achievement-oriented occupational world, which somehow *had* to be done if the adaptive capacity of the system as a whole was to be enhanced. But the important word there is 'if'. Parsons nowhere commits himself to the view that evolution is bound to occur. His argument is, implicitly anyway, always that adaptive upgrading is a possibility of certain historical situations; but a possibility that can be realised only in certain ways; functional requirements are required historically only if upgrading is to occur; they are not requirements in the sense that upgrading has to occur. He is a teleologist in the weak sense of proposing that the achievement of certain purposes entails particular courses of action; not in the strong sense of arguing that those purposes are bound to be achieved.

He gives the impression of going further than this for a number of reasons. Basically, his argument is of the 'if ..., then ...' form: if adaptive upgrading is to occur, then certain system requirements will have to be met. When writing about history, however, that form of argument is, unless one is very careful, easily allowed to fall into the form, 'because ..., then ...', with the 'then' acquiring a temporal as well as a logical meaning: because adaptive upgrading requires differentiation and so forth, differentiation and so forth then occurred. Parsons does not succeed in keeping historical and functional explanations distinct from one another let alone in effectively combining them in a unified historical sociology. Largely this seems to be because his a priori 'knowledge' of functional requirements makes him quite excessively impatient when it comes to the business of establishing historical relationships. If the effects were produced and the functions performed, some sort of appropriate relationships must have existed – Parsons does not seem to see the point of identifying them. His treatment of history becomes breathtakingly and very misleadingly, selective. Agency is treated as a trivial or distracting detail. Digressions and deviations from the sequence of adaptive upgrading, historical structures within which action did not generate the particular effects in which Parsons is interested, are categorised as failures or dead-ends. Choice, conflict and coercion as contexts of action are neglected because only the effects of action are of real analytical significance. To the extent that the structures appropriate to modernisation are known theoretically by their functions, they need not – Parsons seems to feel – be known empirically by their relationships. His history tends accordingly to become a presentation of a succession of structures dissociated from action. Another way of putting it would be to suggest that for functionalists the identification of function explains *why* things happen with such power that examining *how* they happen comes to seem quite unimportant. Historical analysis, by contrast proceeds on the assumption that the explanation of why things happen is inextricably contained within accounts of how things happen. Functionalist historical sociology cannot simply impose the former procedure on the latter but has to coordinate and combine them. It seems to me that it is Parsons's failure to see the need genuinely to combine historical explanation with functional explanation, rather than a commitment to teleology or even to an interest in long-range social evolution, that makes him an unsatisfactory historical sociologist. Conversely, it is of course the formal and over-persuasive teleology of functional analysis as such, rather than Parsons's specific interest in global evolution or merely a fortuitous lack of interest in 'what happened', that must explain his failure to see that need.

But can the work be done more successfully? If functionalism is not inherently incompatible with historical sociology can the integration envisaged but palpably not accomplished by Parsons be achieved by others? The formal teleology in functionalism does not entail a substantive teleology and should therefore be amenable in principle to integration with explanation in terms of agency. Indeed, the most striking feature of the most famous exposition of the convergency thesis, *Industrialism and Industrial Man* (Kerr *et al.*:1960) is the degree to which the authors centre their work on the actions and strategies of industrialising elites while seeking to develop a functional analysis of industrialisation. By contrast, however, restriction of interest to a single historical epoch or transition is not in itself going to be any guarantee of greater success in the practical coordination of function, structure and agency in historical analysis. That is not a problem of scope but of procedure.

Kerr, Dunlop, Harbison and Myers advance in *Industrialism and Industrial Man* not only the best known but in many ways the strongest version of the argument that the history of industrialisation converges in all industrialising societies on a common structural form. Their argument is centred on the notion of a 'logic of industrialism', in the sense of structural requirements for industrialisation, to which historical process, whatever its point of departure and whatever the particular purpose of its agents, must succumb. And they concentrate their analysis on politicians, managers and workers as agents of industrialisation precisely in order to elucidate the ways in which the logic of industrialism overcomes purpose, practice and relationships in every type of industrialising society. In other words, for all its restriction of scope to the single historical transition of industrialisation, it is in every analytical respect a much more aggressive version of the interpretation of history advanced by Parsons. Not only is industrialisation an 'invincible' process it is one that poses a more or less unalterable destiny for those who live through it (1960:19).

> Although industrialisation follows widely differing patterns in different countries, some characteristics of the industrialisation process are common to all. These are the prerequisites and the concomitants of industrial evolution. Once under way the logic of industrialisation sets in motion many trends which do more or less violence to the traditional pre-industrial society.

Eventually, 'social systems will be reasonably uniform around the world as compared with today's situation'. While 'no two cases of industrialisation can be expected to be identical', it is emphatically the case that 'the inherent features of industrialisation tend to create the pure industrial society whose major characteristics' can be inferred from the analysis of industrialisation; and 'this pattern of abstractions constitutes the logic of industrialism' (1960:46).

Before considering their argument, the difficulties it raises and the debate that has revolved around it in more detail it is perhaps worth remarking that this type of historical sociology has never been merely an academic exercise but has had for most of the authors concerned its own compelling and quite practical historical interest. The classical sociological accounts of the transition to industrialism were all more or less explicitly concerned with capitalist industrialisation. That was after all the only mode in which industrialisation had, historically, occurred. It was widely argued that that was the mode in which it had to occur so far as the initial transition was concerned and whatever socialist or bureaucratic structures might eventually be formed out of it. Durkheim, Marx and Weber were also agreed in envisaging a fairly radical eventual further transformation of industrialism springing from the strains and contradictions generated by the capitalist mode: for Durkheim this was a matter of a corporatist re-integration of society effected by the state, for Marx of the victory of socialism, and for Weber of an increasingly pervasive bureaucratic restructuring. The existence after 1917 and more dramatically after 1945 of a number of societies proposing a directly socialist transition to industrialism, the Soviet demonstration of the dramatic viability of such non-capitalist industrialisation, at least in the sense of spectacularly rapid economic growth, and the presence on the stage of world politics of a host of countries manifestly about to industrialise and for which the question of the correct, efficient, just mode of industrialisation was of urgent concern, all transformed the earlier terms of the debate on the destiny of industrialism. The preponderant influence among academic sociologists of Max Weber meant that most western sociologists who had thought about the direction of change within capitalist industrialisation had, much in the manner of Parsons in 'Some Reflections' (1960), come to the conclusion that rather extensive bureaucratisation with increasingly strong integration of bureaucratic industry and bureaucratic government would be the way in which the conflicts, inefficiencies and strains of capitalist industrialism would be solved. In other words the emergence of something like 'bureaucratic industrialism' as the structural type distinguishing the modern phase of the history of industrial society was widely envisaged. Bendix documented a formidable trend towards bureaucratisation as measured by the number working in 'administrative' as against 'productive' occupations for the United States, France, Britain, Germany and Sweden from 1895 to 1950 (1956:211). Eisenstadt produced perhaps the most cogent of a number of analyses of the functionality of bureaucracy as a regulative mechanism for industrial societies (1965:183–212). On the other hand the obvious empirical example of bureaucratic industrialism was the Soviet Union. If, as Faunce and Form (1969:17) contend having reviewed the literature on the historical experience of industrialisation: 'the problems confronting rapidly industrialising societies cannot be met by traditional institutions or by haphazard organisational innovations ... purposive formal organisations must be forged to define new goals, rationally select the most appropriate means to meet those goals and marshal the necessary resources ... [and the] organisational form best designed to do these things is the bureaucracy' – if all that is the real lesson of history, capitalism would appear to be something of a red herring. The bureaucratic socialist societies might seem to have solved in advance the problems of a phase of industrialisation the capitalist societies had painfully to live through.

Without making the links too precise it seems fairly clear that the convergence debate was in large measure a response to the practical as well as to the intellectual consequences of this dilemma. Marx, Weber and others had shown that the tendency of the earliest phase of industrialisation, for both historical and functional reasons, had to be capitalistic. But they had also suggested that capitalism was itself only the configuration of a particular historical moment. Given the creation of non-capitalist varieties of bureaucratic industrialism and a world-wide clamour for recipes for economic growth the question of the tendency of industrialisation became urgent in a quite new way. Was there, indeed, *a* tendency any longer? If so, where did it lie? Here, perhaps, was a privileged opportunity for historical sociology to demonstrate its practical usefulness while renewing its traditional intellectual vigour.

Rather crudely, four positions have been taken up in the resulting debate. It is suggested that industrialisation reveals a pattern of convergence towards an essentially *associational* social structure – with something like the United States emerging as an exemplar of what it is everyone else is converging towards. Conversely it is held that the direction of industrialisation is indeed convergent but that the convergence is towards a structural type that is essentially *bureaucratic* – in which case the Soviet Union may be seen as exemplifying the destiny of industrialism. A third view is that while there is certainly directionality within the history of industrialising societies the direction is not convergent but *divergent*: there are many different modes of industrialism and industrialisation involves options between different modes. And finally, it is argued that there is *no direction*; or rather, that the degree of common structure entailed by industrialisation is so minimal that it is nonsense to speak of any sort of logic of industrialism or direction of industrialisation; the history of industrialisation in different societies suggests that industrialisation is a process subordinated to and shaped by other structural properties of each society, not one that imposes itself on them. It is noticeable that Talcott Parsons has in different writings (1960, 1971) espoused both of the first two points of view. I hope it will be agreed, too, that his uncertainty in this respect is very largely a consequence of his failure to examine industrialisation historically; functional theory permits either of the two interpretations; only empirical historical investigation can determine which of the functionally acceptable possibilities is actually being realised. Fortunately most of the participants in the convergence debate apart from Parsons have recognised that necessity. The great merit of Kerr and his co-authors is that they not only recognise it but recognise it as a problem of relating function to agency.

Industrialism and Industrial Man was one product of a large programme of research studies of 'human agents in the industrialisation process'. The particular project it attempts is to relate what various agents of industrialisation actually did to an abstract conception of what industrialisation could be thought to require deduced from generalisations about the common structural properties of societies already at a fairly advanced level of industrialisation. The book is written in terms of a dialectic between the logic of industrialism and the actions of political elites, workers and managers in different societies in the course of industrialisation. Despite the authors' strong statements about the force of the logic of industrialism in the book's opening chapters the work as a whole is remarkably undogmatic and flexible in the way it relates the requirements of industrialism to concrete historical action. The logic of industrialism is treated as only one of three structuring contexts within which industrialisation actually proceeds. The other two being the purposive actions of industrialising elites and the specific pre-industrial structural and cultural characteristics of each industrialising society. The history of industrialisation in any given country is held to be determined within these three contexts together in a process in which each contains and acts on each of the others. The functional requirements of industrialism constitute, abstractedly, a pressure for all industrialising societies to build similar social relationships and institutions. But concretely that pressure is felt, chanelled, counteracted by pre-existing relationships and institutions in each country and by the intentions, under-standings and powers of those who actively introduce industrialisation. The *universal* tendency towards a single industrial destiny is off-set by tendencies specific to each society and embedded in its historically given circumstances and also by tendencies relative to the type of leading group that constitutes the driving force of industrialisation in any context. The real issue therefore is to ascertain how far the logic of industrialism imposes itself on industrialisation in all cases – recognising that the answer may well be, 'not very far at all'. The probability that that will be the answer is increased by the fact that the authors' account of the logic of industrialism, their model of what, deductively, industrialisation can be held to require, is a fairly modest one which leaves room for a great deal of variation between cases. They see the logic of industrialism as expressing itself in four main ways: in the nature of the work force, in the scale of social organisation, in the types of values through which social cohesion is sought and in a distinctive expansiveness. The work force has to become more skilled; the range of skills has to increase; occupational and geographical mobility have to increase; the work force must be more highly educated and education must be oriented to technique; and the overall structure of the work force has to become highly differentiated, mainly stratified in terms of occupational skill. The centre of gravity of social organisation comes to reside in the town rather than the countryside and in government rather than in economic relationships; government must expand and social organisation takes the form of an extended and complex 'web of rules'. Values centred on science, technology, progress and production must replace those centred on magic, religion and tradition as the basis of ideological consensus. And local and national entities will tend to crumble in the face of the universal availability and manifest power of industrial technology.

Even if necessities of that order were not diluted and diverted by human purposes and by the constraints and possibilities of specific pre-industrial relationships – as Kerr and his co-authors recognise them to be – the sense in which they demand a common industrial outcome is hardly overpowering. The logic of industrialism seems to leave ample room for indefinite diversity: Japan is not required to become more like France, nor the Soviet Union more like the U.S.A. It seems clear that so far as the logic of industrialism is concerned there may well be senses in which all industrial countries will be more like each other than any of them will be like any pre-industrial society, but that that is about as far as the requirements go. Moreover, the strategies, powers and dilemmas of each of the five different types of leading groups they identify (dynastic elites, middle classes, revolutionary intellectuals, colonial rulers and nationalist leaders), do alter the pace, extent, structural forms and relational consequences of industrialisation as do the historical settings in which they act. In relation to topic after topic the authors of *Industrialism and Industrial Man* thus recognise that their logic of industrialism sets only 'a general direction', one which contains 'several roads' and 'diverse routes'. For example (1960:263):

> Industrialisation universally creates industrial relations systems which establish a web of rules relating the managers and the managed. In all systems managers share rule making functions, in varying ways and degrees, with workers and the state. In the course of industrialisation rule-making tends to become more formal. There have been pointed out many common features to the substantive rules which are derived from the logic of industrialis-ation and the common features of technology and market constraints. But there is also diversity in these rules derived from the policies of industrialising elites ... It is essential to see how the inner logic and implications of industrialisation are given diverse form by the policies and ideologies of particular elites.

Since the diversity in question here ranges from worker

cooperatives to multi-national corporations, across the whole range of varieties of trade unionism, from collective bargaining to non-negotiable state wage policies, from systems based on the right to strike to those in which striking is a criminal offence it seems difficult to contend that the logic of industrialism is really the predominant force in the history of industrialisation. Can one really insist that the creation of *some* sort of rule-bound industrial relations system is somehow of more consequence and significance than the extreme diversity, contrast and polarisation of the systems actually historically produced? Surprisingly, Kerr and his fellow authors go on, regardless of their own observations of diversity, to do just that. From their analysis of the ways in which the logic of industrialism makes itself felt as different groups with different strategies industrialise different societies they derive both a strong general conclusion about the weight of the logic of industrialism relative to their other two elements – 'the logic of industrialisation prevails eventually, and such similarities as it decrees will penetrate the outermost points of its universal sphere of influence' – and the specific discovery of an overall convergence on a single, quite specifically defined, structural type of industrialism, pluralistic industrialism, which constitutes 'the road ahead' (1960:265).

If this leap from diversity to convergence is not called-for by their own account of the logic of industrialism, how and why is it made? The obvious answers would seem to be either that the other factors in their analysis have for contingent reasons worked with rather than against the logic of industrialism to produce a convergence not required by the logic of in-dustrialism; or they may have made an empirical mistake, either not observing crucial details or more probably misjudging vital evidence in ways that overstate the convergence effect. The possibility of empirical, more especially historical, error is a little difficult to determine, however, since along with most other contributors to the convergence debate the authors of *Industrialism and Industrial Man* manage to be remarkably parsimonious about appealing to anything that might pass as hard evidence. Nevertheless in a well-known and trenchant critique Goldthorpe (1964b) does seem to me to have shown that in at least one major respect, the question of changes in stratification and social mobility, they do both ignore important matters of fact and misjudge the meaning of the facts they report in a rather serious way. He points out that the case for convergence towards a pattern of increasing mobility depends on focusing on inter-generational mobility and on mass mobility across the blue-collar/white-collar divide and on ignoring career mobility and elite mobility where the evidence suggests either that mobility diminishes or at least that traditional immobilities persist in certain versions of industrialisation. Not only is the true picture a good deal more diverse than Kerr and his colleagues allow, but just because it is diverse it is hard to see how it can be explained in terms of any inherent properties of industrialism. Goldthorpe goes on to suggest that quite apart from the diversities which the historical record obliges one to recognise as the actual, and often carefully constructed, outcome of industrialisation, a more principled objection should also be advanced against the way in which these authors treat the history of inequality. Basically, his point is that the very conception of industrialism as a unitary type of social system is mistaken – because over-generalised. In systems of the Soviet type industrialisation occurs in a milieu that is primarily institutionalised on the basis of political power, whereas in systems of the British or American type the decisive structuring of power is economic and institu-tionalised on the basis of a definite differentiation of economic from political relationships. This obvious difference is, Gold-thorpe argues, so fundamental in its implications for the course of industrialisation that it makes nonsense of any single model of industrialism and imposes the recognition of a basic generic difference between at least two types of structural setting for industrialisation. Whether or not the direction of change in, say, patterns of social mobility appears to be the same, the funda-mental structural contexts are so different that it is absurd to think of them as involved in a single set of functional necessities or subject to a common logic. Thus (1964b:114):

> In Soviet society hierarchical differentiation is an instrument of the regime. To a significant degree stratification is *organised* in order to suit the political needs of the regime; and as these needs change, so too may the particular structure of inequality. In other words the Soviet system of stratification is characterised by an important

element of 'deliberateness', and it is this which basically distinguishes it from the Western system, in spite of many apparent similarities ... Soviet society is not, in the same way as Western society, *class* stratified ... It follows that the arguments [of Kerr *et al.*] on the development of stratification systems can have no general validity. Their underlying rationale, in terms of the exigencies of an advanced industrial technology and economy, is destroyed. The experience of Soviet society can be taken as indicating that the structural and functional imperatives of an industrial order are not so stringent as to prevent quite wide variations in patterns of social stratification, nor to prohibit the systematic manipulation of social inequalities by a regime commanding modern administrative resources and under no constraints from an organised opposition or the rule of law.

Much of this criticism could of course be taken on board by Kerr and his co-authors without too much trouble. Arguably all Goldthorpe is saying is that they have slightly under-estimated the capacity of a certain type of industrialising elite, the revolutionary intellectuals, to impose their own will on the history of industrialisation. He is pointing to an instance in which their account of the relationships between socio-cultural factors and elite strategies and the logic of industrialism needs to be modified slightly to recognise rather greater current diversity or a slower pace of convergence than they had allowed. The crucial issue is whether in the face of such qualifications there is or is not still an overall, long term tendency to convergence, *a* road ahead, the road of pluralism. It is just at this point, however, that the full force of Goldthorpe's argument becomes clear. It is precisely in relation to the development of pluralism that the initial structuring of industrialisation, doggedly reinforced by powerful groups thereafter, proves more forceful historically than the logic of industrialism. The tendency towards pluralism, associationism and so forth makes sense historically within the framework of capitalist industrialisation as a possible, acceptable and achievable way of resolving or managing certain problems. It is just the sort of development that does not make sense on such grounds within the framework of Communist industrialisation. In such systems problems are defined, faced and solved in systematically different terms (1964b:115):

It may be said that no serious gounds exist for believing that within Soviet society any such diffusion of power is taking place, or, at least, not so far as the key decision-making processes are concerned. The regime may be compelled to give more consideration to the effects of its decisions on popular morale and to rely increasingly on the expertise of scientists, technicians and professionals of various kinds; it may also find it desirable to decentralise administration and to encourage a high degree of participation in the conduct of public affairs at a local level. But the important point is that all these things can be done, and in recent years *have* been done, without the Party leadership in any way yielding up its position of ultimate authority and control. Indeed, it is far more arguable that since the end of the period of 'collective' rule, the power of the Party leadership has become still more absolute and unrivalled.

In other words the argument from the logic of industrialism to pluralistic convergence depends on an underlying assumption about the relationship of economic and political power – their separation and the ultimate primacy of the former – which is no longer justified; which has, indeed, been falsified by the history of industrialisation itself since 1917.

Very similar objections could be advanced in relation to the arguments urged in *Industrialism and Industrial Man* about the decline of protest among workers, about the liberating and egalitarian effects of education and about the powerfulness of professional associations. In these contexts too, one would find that significant empirical variations had been overlooked and that apparent similarities had been overemphasised at the cost of ignoring more profound differences of meaning. And throughout the book one finds the same central and distorting tendency for the authors, despite their own reservations, to be carried away by the idea of the logic of industrialism into postulating convergence as a tendency bound (just because it is a matter of logic and not of mere practice) to outweigh all tendencies to diversity, sooner or later. And the same readiness to emphasise formal convergence (the existence of a web of rules everywhere, for example) while playing down substantive variation (the radically different content of the webs of rules from case to case). One might also discern a worrying ethnocentrism: although these authors never overtly identify the present structure of their own society as the future of other people's societies in the way Parsons does, it is obvious that their model of industrialism does build on the fundamental structural characteristics of a fairly pure capitalism just as it obviously does not build on, or even allow for, the basic structural features of any sort of socialism.

Yet none of these criticisms necessarily undermines the *type* of analysis attempted in these and other main contributions to the convergence debate. The organising functionalist strategy, the use of a conception of the logic of industrialism, exploration of the relationship between the functional requirements implied by that model and historical structure and action, the empirical demonstration within that framework of convergence or divergence, all of this *could* be rescued from the sort of objections we have been considering. None of them establishes that the prodedure as such is flawed – only that it has been less than perfectly deployed. The issue between Kerr, Dunlop, Harbison and Myers and their critics is not quite so clear-cut in this respect as I think it is in others. Goldthorpe for example, speaks for several critics who have taken the view that the form of argument involved in reference to notions such as the logic of industrialism is inherently vicious (1964b:117):

> In the first place, there is the exaggeration of the degree of determinism which is exercised upon social structures by 'material' exigencies, and, concomitantly with this, the underestimation of the extent to which a social order may be shaped through purposive action within the limits of such exigencies. Secondly, and relatedly, there is the further underestimation of the diversity of values and ideologies which may underlie purposive action; and thus, from these two things together, there results the tendency to envisage a future in which the complex patterns of past development will become increasingly orderly and aligned – the tendency, in fact to think in terms of the road ahead rather than in terms of a variety of roads.

But although cast in more general terms these objections are still really to the conduct of the enquiry not to the principles of its design. Indeed Kerr and his co-authors are fully aware in principle of the issues of action and purpose on which Goldthorpe insists. They may have failed in practice to recognise the influence of action and purpose as against the influence of the logic of industrialism as fully as the historical evidence suggests they should have done. But it is not at all clear that that failure is a necessary consequence of introducing the notion of the logic of industrialism. Against Goldthorpe they themselves cite Alexander Gerschenkron and before him Karl Marx as advocates and exemplars of the successful use of deductive models in historical sociology. They might also of course have cited Max Weber – indeed, doing so might have helped them insofar as it would have alerted them to the problem of one-sidedness involved in the use of such models. And surely the experience and achievement of Marx and Weber do legitimate Gerschenkron's claim (1957) that we cannot, as sociologists, 'approach historical reality except through a search for regularities and deviations from regularities, that is to say, by conceiving it in terms of constructs of our mind, of patterns, or models'. Yet *Industrialism and Industrial Man* is manifestly not a work that stands comparison with either the work of Weber or that of Marx. If the shared strategy of explanation is not a fault, what is?

The way that Kerr and his colleagues relate their own work to that of Marx is revealing in this context. Empirically they present their analysis as 'turning Marx on his head', as a demonstration of the ways in which the history of industrialisation has taken – and has had to take – courses contrary to those anticipated by Marx: the decline of protest on the part of the working class, the vanguard role of managers not of proletarians, the growth of pluralism rather than of polarisation. But methodologically they see themselves as grasping an essentially sound method of analysis previously employed by Marx and pioneered by his immediate predecessors, the classical political economists. This is the method of confrontation between the historical record and the 'long-run deductive model of the industrialisation process'. Thus (1960:22):

Marx applied deductive methods to long-run economic and social processes. The preface to *Capital* states that it is the '... ultimate aim of this work, to lay bare the economic law of motion of modern society'. He was concerned to develop the logical implications inherent in the 'capitalist mode of production'. Marx's thought was thus concerned with long-run developments, '... it tries to uncover the mechanism that, by its mere working and without the aid of external factors turns any given state of society into another'. A recognition of the long-term tendencies inherent in early in-dustrialisation *under capitalist or bourgeois leadership*, regardless of whether the particular deductions have always proved historically valid in restrospect, was a considerable intellectual achievement ... In applying deductive methods to long-run economic and social processes, he illustrated the potentialities of a powerful tool of analysis. The method compels attention to the inner logic and necessities of the industrialisation process.

Yet there are two respects, both of profound importance, in which it is clear that they have in fact quite misunderstood Marx's method. Consider first the words I have italicised in this passage from *Industrialism and Industrial Man*: 'under capitalist or bougeois leadership'. What they recognise there but quite fail to incorporate in their own analysis is the substantive theoretical, as opposed to formal methodological, design of the work of Marx: *Capital*, like all his other major works is concerned with the long-run tendencies of a configuration specified as a concrete structural type not as an abstract process. Marx's law of motion dealt with the working out of distinct and historically specified relations of power, not with the logic of a model abstracted from all structural milieux. By contrast, Kerr and his co-authors organise their analysis in terms of a model which is drastically diluted so far as any sort of substantive specification is concerned. The dilution, the construction of the model at a level of abstraction which frees it from reference to any particular structural type looks like a great gain in terms of the range of systems the authors can discuss. In reality it is a great loss in terms of their ability to say anything precise or substantial about any particular system. And secondly, as we saw in chapter 3 Marx regarded analysis of the 'logical implications' inherent in abstractedly conceived modes of production as at best only one half of an adequate analysis. The other half, to which he devoted himself no less whole-heartedly, was a matter of very close, detailed, exhaustive study of the practical making of history. Invariably, Marx advances his arguments in terms of massive empirical documentation, moving with great subtlety and speed from evidence to interpretation and back again in an attempt to reveal his laws of motion in motion. He understood that long-run deductive models are essential tools of investigation but that what has to be investigated is history; and they are not tools for disposing of history. By contrast, most contributions to the convergence debate are again conspicuously impoverished so far as both historical depth and the tight, detailed integration of interpretative model and historical evidence are concerned.

I would not, then, agree with those who argue that the procedure employed in works like *Industrialism and Industrial Man* is invalid in principle. On the contrary it seems to be an essential device of historical sociology but one that has to be complemented by both substantive theory and close empirical research. Unless models of process are contained and counteracted in that way their tendency to absorb rather than to explain history will be almost irresistible – with the sort of results considered in this chapter. If they are not used at all, history as a relation of present and past will remain baffling. One sociologist who has made a determined and relatively successful attempt to use analytical models in this more open and three-dimensional manner is N. J. Smelser (1959, 1963b); some of the general features of his approach to historical sociology deserve consideration here. To begin with it is noticeable that his substantive concern is appreciably more specific than that of either Kerr and his co-authors or Parsons; for example, he sets himself the problem of analysing the relationships between social structure and economic development (in the sense of growth of output per head of population), in a particular period and place rather than the conditions for general societal evolution or the nature of 'the road ahead'. Then he goes on to specify what economic growth entails for the social structures in which it occurs in terms which are at once very generalised so far as universals are concerned and very specific at the level of concrete variations. The common requirements imposed on social structure by economic growth are in his view a matter of increased complexity experienced in three very broad forms: differentiation, integration and 'social disturbances ... which reflect the uneven advances of differentiation and integration, respectively' (1963:33). By contrast, the variations in specific historical experience permitted within a framework of functional necessities as generalised as this are obviously very great indeed. The problem that Smelser has to face is accordingly not one of possibly imposing an over-determining, over-specified logic of development on social and economic history – in that sense the advance in commonsense represented by his model is considerable – but the opposite one of showing that a model as thoroughly diluted as this can do any explanatory work at all. Does it not leave the explanation of the course of history in different societies so wide open and susceptible to variations induced by local structural conditions and purposive action as to be a virtually blind guide so far as any sort of empirically grounded generalising comparative historical sociology is concerned? In many respects that would be a fair criticism but in one very important sense it is not. Much of Smelser's subsequent analysis is little more than a shopping list of what actually happened in different countries in the course of economic growth loosely cast within the all-embracing net of the differentiation-integration concept. But it is a different matter when he turns to the analysis of 'disturbances'. The idea of disturbance is of course strongly logically entailed by the ideas of differentiation and integration. More importantly disturbance is a highly plausible practical historical correlate of differentiation and counteracting efforts at integration. Differentiation messes people around, making them dis-satisfied, disoriented and with urgent problems to solve. Integrative measures solve some of those problems but not necessarily in the ways people feel appropriate. Furthermore the processes of differentiation and integration are not normally in phase with one another. Historically we are not talking about a smooth flow of functional requirements but about highly discontinuous, provoking, disturbing experience. The disturbance of people's lives and their more or less disturbing responses to such disturbance is on both theoretical and empirical grounds a highly appropriate focus of attention if one wishes to bring down to earth historically the functionalist paradigm of differentiation and integration. It is one basic way in which the law of motion gets enacted. To that extent at least Smelser has moved functionalism towards history.

Meanwhile the debate on convergence has remained unresolved. The proponents of post-industrialism – above all, Bell (1974) – have renewed the argument for convergence towards a model of which the United States still provides the conspicuous real instance. Writers such as Feldman and Moore (1969) have meticulously documented the astounding diversity of every element of structure and culture in the course of industrialisation in different actual societies. Chodak (1973:66) and others have attempted a compromise based on the argument that while there is convergence in the sense of an irreversible growth of complexity in all industrialising societies, a growing 'systemness' to use his own term, there is no convergence in the sense of approximation to a single structural type of system. Rather, there are distinct and perhaps incompatible varieties of complex systemness each pursuing their own historical courses. The attraction of this sort of argument is that it at once recognises the force of certain minimal functional requirements of industrialism – the growth of structural complexity – while at the same time accepting that empirically, as a matter of what has happened, those requirements can be and are met in fundamentally different ways by actors with diverse purposes and powers in diverse structural settings. Unfortunately, this rather sensible way of disposing of the grander functionalist ambitions and returning to a practise-oriented historical sociology has not found general acceptance. Controversy persists.

There is, however, perhaps one basic issue involed in the earlier debates which has largely been settled by agreement: namely the question of the sense in which one can properly invoke the idea of inevitability in historical sociology. Clearly, the ability of Marx and Engels to make a case for the inevitable growth of capitalism out of feudalism did not enable them either to make a case for an inevitable transition from capitalism to socialism or, what is more puzzling, to demonstrate that feudalism had to give rise to capitalism. In the same way much of the ambiguity readers have found in the work of Weber seems to result from the fact that he argues both that capitalism had to arise from the conjunction of structural and cultural conditions that existed in 16th-century Europe and, emphatically, that that conjunction did not have to give rise to capitalism. Parsons's ability to show, for example, that a higher level of adaptive capacity necessarily arose from the structural-functional balance of pre-industrial American society is not matched by an ability to show that that balance had to generate higher adaptive capacity. Historical sociology seems both to have and to want the power to make statements about inevitable development – and this of course has been a besetting problem for the convergence debate: on the one hand it can be shown that industrialism had to arise out of pre-industrialism, but on the other hand it seems it cannot be shown that anything particular has to arise out of industrialism. The difficulty is easily resolved as soon as it is appreciated that two quite different types of inevitability statement, only one of them properly historical, are involved in the different claims. And it is precisely this appreciation which has emerged from the convergence debate; possibly as its most important conclusion.

The relevant distinction has been drawn in a discussion of just this problem by Elias (1978a). It is the distinction between that which is inevitable in the sense that all conditions necessary for its existence have been met and that which is inevitable in the sense that all other possibilities have been ruled out. Retrospective analysis of change, which historical sociology has to be, can hope to achieve the former even when it has no hope at all of achieving the latter. Elias puts it as follows (1978a:160):

> A development may be represented schematically as a series of vectors A→B→C→D. Here the letters represent various figurations of people, each figuration flowing from the previous one as the development takes its course from A to D. Retrospective study will often clearly show not only that the figuration at C is a necessary precondition for D, and likewise B for C and A for B, but also why this is so. Yet, looking into the future, from whatever point in the figuration flow, we are usually able to establish only that the figurational at B is one possible transformation of A, and similarly, C of B and D of C. In other words, in studying the flow of figurations there are two possible perspectives on the connection between one figuration chosen from the continuing flow and

another, later, figuration. From the viewpoint of the earlier figuration the later is – in most if not all cases – only one of several possibilities for change. From the viewpoint of the later figuration, the earlier one is usually a necessary condition for the formation of the later.

In other words it is quite within the bounds of historical sociology to show that capitalism had to arise out of feudalism or even bureaucratic industrialism out of capitalist industrialism if historical analysis reveals that the former in each case contained all the conditions required for the latter to be brought into existence. It does not at all follow that one can claim that feudalism had to give rise to capitalism or capitalist industrialism to bureaucratic industrialism. Such claims presuppose a quite different order of knowledge, one not normally available either to the historian or to the sociologist. Historical sociology can hope to show everything is inevitable once it has happened. But it is constrained to assume that nothing is inevitable till then.

6

The problem of design: the formation of states

A major attraction of the types of historical sociology I have looked at so far has lain in the promise they held out of the possibility of long-range theorising. In their different ways each proposed a means of generalising about the direction, dynamics and design of history on a grand scale. On the basis of more or less careful attention to historical details they advanced theories of the socio-genesis of whole social, economic or cultural systems over long periods of time. They were attempts to analyse structuring. Whatever their hazards and difficulties the appeal of such projects – the prospect of grasping the shape of human destiny which they imply – is plainly profound and persistent. And such projects have indeed persisted in contemporary social analysis. So before turning to some quite different, and at first sight considerably less ambitious, kinds of historical sociology I want in this chapter to look at a few of the more powerful recent attempts to renew historical sociology as a form of long-range empirical social theory – a theory of social structuring. I have chosen a group of studies which, although very diverse in their theoretical inclinations, are united by a common substantive interest: the problem of the formation of political systems or states. The studies in question are Anderson's *Lineages of the Absolutist State* (1974), the anthology *Party Systems and Voter Alignments* (1967) edited by Lipset and Rokkan, Eisenstadt's *The Political Systems of Empires* (1963) and Barrington Moore's *The Social Origins of Dictatorship and Democracy* (1966).

Whatever their differences these works share not only a

common interest in the historical construction of political systems but, more significantly from my point of view, a common ambition to *theorise* history, to achieve a reasoned interpretation of the design of long-term historical change and to do so on the basis of arguments which integrate general social theory and detailed historical documentation rather than asserting the claims of either against the other. The most forceful statement of this shared ambition is provided by Anderson (1974:8):

> The premise of this work is that there is no plumb-line between necessity and contingency in historical explanation, dividing separate types of enquiry – 'long-run' versus 'short-run', or 'abstract' versus 'concrete' from each other. There is merely that which is known – established by historical research – and that which is not known: the latter may be either the mechanism of single events or the laws of motion of whole structures. Both are equally amenable, in principle, to adequate knowledge of their causality. One of the main purposes of the study undertaken here is thus to hold together in tension two orders of reflection which have often been unwarrantably divorced ... weakening [our] capacity for rational and controllable theory in the domain of history.

Such an ambition may be pursued on varying scales and with very different immediate points of reference: Barrington Moore and Lipset and Rokkan are concerned with the conditions permitting or preventing the construction of 'democracy' in the course of industrialisation; Anderson and Eisenstadt with the 'conditions under which the political systems of historical bureaucratic empires became institutionalised'; in an earlier essay Anderson (1964) addressed himself to the 'differential formation and development of British capitalist society since the seventeenth century'; and a later study by Moore (1978) examines the 'social bases of obedience and revolt' with reference to the historical formation of the German working class between 1848 and 1920. Similarly long-range interpretive historical sociology may involve varying theoretical perspectives and very different types of evidence. But however it is pursued, its underlying inspiration is the belief that the problems of apprehending the design of history, of analysing history as a comprehensive process of structuring, are not in principle different from those of any other task of historical explanation. There are differences of scale, of conceptualisation and of the availability of relevant evidence. But beyond that the historical explanation of general forms or trajectories is seen as involving the same sort of work as the historical explanation of specific events or particular relationships. 'Feudalism' is a construct, and problem, on a different scale from, say, 'the field systems of East Anglia in the eleventh century', analysis of 'the democratic state' demands an order of evidence over and above anything needed in considering 'the redistributive effects of social insurance in Wilhelmine Germany' or 'tax resistance in Massachusetts before 1770'. But the theoretical construction of knowledge involved in the more concrete studies is in fact just as much a matter of the *imputation of significance*; the problem and its resolution are no less theoretically constructed. And conversely, in both types of case whether or not the problem can be solved, the knowledge achieved, is a question of 'that which is known' and 'that which is not known'. The problem of evidence is one of access in practice not of availability in principle. And this group of authors proceed on the basis of the assumption that what is known includes the evidence necessary to establish long-range historical generalisations, the extended analyses of process which are for them the most important mode of historical work. Important problems demand audacious measures. Alternatively, as Anderson puts it: 'the limits of our sociology reflect the nervelessness of our historiography'. At least these authors are well endowed with historiographical nerve.

The problems with which they are concerned are sometimes presented with deceptive simplicity. Seemingly quite straightforward questions are raised about the 'genesis' of political conflicts, or the 'social nature' of absolutism. Or we are faced with issues which appear to invite quite conventional narrative treatment – as in the case of Barrington Moore's opening puzzle (1966:3): 'why did the process of industrialisation in England culminate in the establishment of a relatively free society?' But for these authors the answers to such questions are embedded in complex and far-reaching theories of history; their problems take their meaning from theory and are to be answered in terms of theory. Their resolution is found not in a story but through comparison. In every case the project is theory-governed; a well-planned voyage of discovery not a naive exploration.

Anderson, for example, is taking up a long-standing and quite sharply-defined problem in marxist theory – the problem of the social nature of absolutism is in effect that of accounting for an awkward disjuncture in the transition from feudalism to capitalism. As a formal theory of the laws of motion of modes of production marxism does not require absolutism or any other political formation to mediate the passage from feudalism to capitalism. Nor does it easily allow for such mediation. Yet in the exemplary case the long absolutist interregnum manifestly occurred. A world was constructed which was for a long period neither unambiguously feudal nor unambiguously capitalist. The logical moment of transition turned out historically, in the event, to be a matter of several centuries. Somehow or other these centuries, the epoch of the absolutist state, have to be accounted for since history is the this-wordly reality in which the truth of theories, according to Marx, is proved or disproved. Specifically, the problem is to make clear the relationship of the absolutist state to feudalism and capitalism as modes of production and class power. Marx and Engels themselves had both recognised the problem and aggravated it by the uncertainty of their own responses to it. In different passages of their works they can be found treating absolutism as, variously, a feudal political form, a form of relatively independent state built out of the balance of feudal and capitalist class forces, and a capitalist political form. A resolution was plainly called-for.

Similarly, Moore is not just seeking 'to explain the varied political roles played by the landed upper classes and the peasantry in the transformation from agrarian societies ... to modern industrial ones' (1966:xi), but to do so in terms of a quite systematic theoretical understanding of the relationship between the history of lord and peasant on the one hand and the political outcomes – democracy, communism or fascism – of industrialisation on the other. And Lipset and Rokkan, again, are not just asking the string of naive empirical questions with which their book opens but seeking to theorise the relationship between the political organisation of social conflict as a long term historical process and the achievement of stable and effective 'democratic' regimes – to identify a common design underlying and accounting for the superficial diversity of the political systems of modern capitalist societies. And Eisenstadt for his part, in choosing to examine the formation and dynamics of the 'bureaucratic empires' is in fact addressing a fundamental problem of functionalist social theory – that of 'the relationship between the political system and social structure'; or more precisely, of the annoyingly untidy relationship between imputed functions and observed structures. In sum, however specific the apparent empirical point of entry of these studies may appear, their major concern is to establish, as economically as possible, theoretically powerful generalisations about long-term historical processes. In Barrington Moore's words they seek 'a large scale map of an extended terrain' – an analysis of structuring.

Feudalism, capitalism and the absolute state

Anderson resolves the ambivalence of Marx and Engels about the social meaning of the absolutist monarchies of early modern Europe by opting firmly for the view that these regimes are to be understood as political crystallisations of feudal social power. Just as Marx and Engels (1962:36) identified the modern democratic state as an 'executive committee for the management of the common affairs of the whole bourgeoisie', so Anderson in effect sees the absolute monarchies as executives for the last ditch defence of the common interests of the whole class of feudal nobility. And just as the democratic state may in its generalised defense of capitalism have to discipline, thwart or even destroy individual capitalists or indeed whole sections of the class, so the absolutist state in its coercive assertion of a feudal system of exploitation sometimes had to discipline, thwart and even destroy some individual lords, or even whole sections of the dominant feudal class. In neither case is the social meaning and identity of the political system undermined by such actions; the common and long term interests of the class as a whole are superimposed, however forcibly, on the wayward and ephemeral interests of some of its members by the larger and more comprehensive intelligence of government. In other words, a crucial feature of Anderson's argument is the claim that the fact that absolutist monarchs often appeared to be waging war on the feudal nobility cannot in itself be treated as evidence of the non-feudal nature of absolutism. Rather, the political order of absolutism enshrined the essential structures and relationships of feudal exploitation – even against the wishes of the feudatories. Such a claim obviously raises rather urgently the question of just what sort of evidence could be regarded as conclusive in any attempt to coordinate and integrate actually available historical evidence (the evidence of action) with theories of the nature of historical forms (theories of structures and structuring). In this instance the argument is plainly about the functions of absolutist regimes and not about the purposes, beliefs or dispositions of those who constructed or experienced them. For Anderson the problem of the social nature of absolutism turns out to be a matter of discovering what absolutism did for different social classes. His is a sociology in which meaning is revealed by function. The task of the historical sociologist in this sort of enterprise is to demonstrate functions. We shall see that that is in fact the challenge that most doggedly besets each of our exercises in long-range theorising. And I shall argue that at its best this sort of 'soft' functionalism, a functionalism stripped of teleology and recast as a properly historical mode of analysis is really rather formidable; a serious basis for a serious historical sociology.

Meanwhile, the substance of Anderson's interpretation is complicated by his recognition that, at least in Western Europe, the absolutist states while being essentially feudal political systems – 'a redeployed and recharged apparatus of feudal domination' (1974:18) – were at the same time also positively functional for the emergent forces and relationships of capitalism. The uncertainty of earlier writers is thus made understandable through the suggestion that these regimes had a genuinely dual character – at once enforcing feudalism in essential matters (essential from a feudal point of view that is), such as the relation of the lord and master and the political and cultural privileges of aristocrats, *and* permitting the expansion of capitalist practices and relationships elsewhere. The secret of the formation and persistence of this type of state system is found by Anderson precisely in this duality of function which made the world of absolutism in its Western European version at once politically feudal and socially not-feudal: 'the apparent paradox of Absolutism in Western Europe was that it fundamentally represented an apparatus for the protection of aristocratic property and privileges, yet at the same time the means whereby this protection was promoted could simultaneously ensure the basic interests of the nascent mercantile and manufacturing classes' (1974:40). Or as Engels had put it more succinctly (1947:126): 'the political order remained feudal while society became more and more bourgeois'.

The system as a whole was thus doubly functional, or in Anderson's term 'determined': 'fundamentally ... by the feudal re-groupment against the peasantry after the dissolution of serfdom; but ... secondarily by the rise of an urban bourgeoisie' (1974:22). In other words the state systems of the absolute monarchies were brought into being on the basis of a temporary compatibility of class interests between feudal nobilities and an emergent bourgeoisie at a moment of profound feudal crisis. They arose one might say on the basis of a determined *in*determinacy in the relationship of feudal and bourgeois interests – both of which could find satisfaction in the elaboration of wide-ranging and well-policed systems of property law. But their fundamentally feudal nature was revealed in the way in which when feudal and bourgeois interests did clash they finally and decisively committed themselves to the former. They were states 'founded on the social supremacy of the aristocracy and confined by the imperatives of landed property.' Accordingly, we find not only that 'no political derogation of the noble class ever occurred in the Absolutist state', but more conclusively perhaps that 'its feudal character constantly ended by frustrating and falsifying its promises for capital' (1974:41). The authentic symbol of such regimes one could suggest was thus the bank bankrupted by a royal repudiation of debts incurred in efforts to appropriate land through war.

The analysis is logically well-turned. But logical elegance is no guarantee of historical accuracy. Indeed, many historians would argue that it is a guarantee of inaccuracy. How is a significant fit between the record and its interpretation to be demonstrated? By the standards of, say, the *American Sociological Review* Anderson appears remarkably unself-conscious in tackling this problem. He adopts the comparative method but gives the impression of being largely indifferent to the formal requirements of that method. The comparative method is indeed the necessary strategy of long-range historical theory and from Mill (1843) and Durkheim (1938) by way of Radcliffe-Brown (1951) and Nadel (1951) to M. J. Levy (1952) and R. M. Marsh (1967) social scientists have laboured to articulate its proper rules. From these efforts something like a textbook recipe for good comparative analysis has emerged in which above all the following ingredients are stressed: the need to define one's empirical units of study in a way which separates them cleanly both from one another and from one's hypotheses about their significance; the need for crisp and exact formulations of all postulated relationships of interdependence between the primary units of study and whatever factors are presumed to stand in significant cause or effect relationship to them; the importance of establishing equivalence of meaning between phenomena treated as indicating significant similarity or variation between units of study and their cause or effects – thus, the 'totally different meaning' of divorce in Christian and Islamic societies is commonly cited as vitiating comparative studies of the family; the importance of meticulous sampling, specification of indicators, measurement, analysis of correlation. The comparative method is, as Durkheim put it, the method of 'the indirect experiment', and sociologists have incessantly urged one another to observe its procedures with appropriate rigour. Yet where we do indeed find authors such as Lipset and Rokkan minutely concerned with such matters in setting-up their studies of the making of modern political democracies, Anderson appears to go to work with an almost wilful disregard for the approved forms and rules.

He never, for example, gives us a definition of the absolutist state which is dissociated from his principal theoretical claim (hypothesis) that absolutism was a form of state characterised by its functional commitment to the defence of feudalism. In other words, his definition of absolutism solves in advance the problem his book as a whole is supposed to be investigating. State forms which failed to perform the crucial function, however far they might have shared the strictly political attributes of absolutist regimes such as extensive armies, bureaucratic administration, formalised and comprehensive systems of taxation and law, were *ipso facto* so far as Anderson is concerned, not absolutist states. Then again, his unit of analysis is one which, historically, is quite notoriously not independent of other units of the same type: whatever else one might say about the nation state its history manifestly is entangled with that of other nation states – a fact Anderson is quite happy to recognise and exploit when it suits him to do so. Nor is any effort made to establish the equivalence of such crucial matters as, say, Spanish *corregidores*, French *officiers* and English magistrates – crucial forms of absolutist bureaucracy in supposedly similar absolutist regimes. Nowhere is any attempt made to specify the tightness of fit of the relationship between state form and social function in terms of precise correlations or consistent co-variance. In sum, from the point of view of the sociological methodologist the whole enterprise is easily identified as thoroughly cavalier and probably reprehensible.

Yet such formal, methodological worries seem to me both to miss the substantive point and to misunderstand the analytical design of *Lineages of the Absolutist State*. Rather, in a curious way the very methodological looseness of Anderson's study can be understood as evidence of its sensitivity and power as historical sociology. Let us start the appraisal again, this time in terms of what the author does, his own implicit canon of rules, rather than in terms of what some sociologists might have wanted him to do, the explicit canon of good comparative method. The work is addressed to the oldest and most fundamental of all themes in historical sociology: the problem of capitalism. Like Weber, Anderson seeks to explain the genesis of capitalism in terms of the historical realisation of conditions theoretically necessary for its existence. It would have been highly disingenuous for him, as a serious marxist, to have written as though he did not know what he was looking for. His own thinking seems, in fact, to have started from the theoretically reasonable assumption that since capitalism established itself first and indigenously only in western Europe, western European history must have contained a series of unique filters to capitalism. So he quite correctly confronts us not with an open-ended empirical investigation of the correlates of a given political form but with the thesis that the absolutist states were such a filter – a passage found consistently where capitalism did emerge and consistently not found where it did not emerge. This fairly high degree of theoretical specification of his problem does not, however, preclude quite thoroughgoing comparative analysis thereafter. On the contrary, his book can be read as a quite exceptionally exhaustive working of an intellectually serious problem in terms of the strategies of comparative analysis as classically formulated by John Stuart Mill.

For Mill, as is well known, comparative analysis ivolved two distinct and complementary modes of argument (1843: 3 ch. 8): the Method of Agreement and the Method of Difference. Taken together he saw these methods as providing a strong design for the establishmentof law-like connections of cause and effect between any given phenomenon and 'the circumstances which precede or follow' it. The Method of Agreement compares different instances in which the phenomenon occurs in order to eliminate the causal significance of antecedent or consequent circumstances which are not invariably associated with the phenomenon. The Method of Difference compares instances in which the phenomenon does occur with 'instances similar in other respects in which it does not', with a view to isolating the source of difference. Thus: 'If an instance in which the phenomenon under investigation occurs, and an instance in which it does not occur, have every circumstance in common save one, that one occurring only in the former; the circumstance in which alone the two instances differ, is the effect, or the cause, or an indispensable part of the cause, of the phenomenon'. Both methods proceed by elimination: 'The Method of Agreement stands on the ground that whatever can be eliminated is not connected with the phenomenon by any law. The Method of Difference has for its foundation, that whatever can not be eliminated, is connected with the phenomenon by a law'. The Method of Difference is thus plainly the stronger form of argument so far as the determination of causal relationships is concerned and as Mill recognised, is at once the crux of proof in the natural sciences and exceptionally difficult to implement in most fields of social science – the sharply defined and tightly controlled conditions of similarity and variation it requires (experimental conditions, that is) simply not being attainable from the data of human history. Mill therefore went on to consider a variety of modifications and approximations to the ideal method which one might realistically hope to use in the social sciences. The remarkable thing about the group of historical sociologists I am interested in here, and especially about Anderson, is the degree to which – while the methodologists cry for the moon – they have successfully adopted Mill's second-best strategies.

Lineages of the Absolutist State opens by comparing a number of western European countries in each of which a feudal crisis marked by the irretrievable collapse of serfdom was followed by the construction of a centralised monarchical regime equipped with an apparatus of elaborate military, administrative and fiscal and legal control. Each of these state systems, the comparison reveals, was built on the combination of the absolute public authority of the state with the absolute private rights of (noble and incidentally other) property. And each succumbed to the emergence within it of capitalist interests, receiving its quietus in the throes of a bourgeois revolution. This group of states is then compared with a further group in Eastern Europe in which the feudal crisis and the centralised monarchical regime appear, in which the feudal function of the regime is no less evident, but in which the bourgeois denouement is missing. A further comparison with a centralised monarchical regime unaccompanied by either feudal functions or bourgeois outcome (the Ottoman Empire) is then introduced and followed by another involving a feudal social order succeeded by a bourgeois social order without the bridge of political absolutism (Japan). Plainly any attempt to apply Mill's approved modes of analysis in their strict form to this range of variation would eliminate any systematic relationship between absolutism and either feudalism or capitalism. That Anderson manages to tease a plausible case for such systematic relationships out of the mess of evidence confronting him is a result of the fact that the modifications to good method which he introduces are specifically historical – embodying the importance of the word 'lineages' in his title. It is the historical location of these systems in relation to one another and to their own pasts that is the crucial explanatory variable in his analysis and not any of the formal, structural or even rational properties of the systems as such.

Absolutism, Anderson argues, acquired significance as a filter to capitalism when, and only when, it was constructed within a particular sequence of interactions and social relations – those of the western European 'lineage', in which it functioned as 'the redeployed political apparatus of a feudal class which had accepted the commutation of dues ... a *compensation* for the disappearance of serfdom'. In the absence of that phasing absolutism either did not emerge or was not a significant condition for the formation of capitalism. Thus, in the eastern European 'lineage' the largely similar institutions of political absolutism served 'as the repressive machine of a feudal class that had just erased the traditional communal freedoms of the poor ... a device for the *consolidation* of serfdom, in a landscape scoured of autonomous urban life or resistance'. (1974:195). The feudal pivot is there in both cases but the machine does different work at different times in the history of the class. Where capitalism emerged from feudalism without the shell of absolutism first nurturing it on the other hand, as in Japan, the lineage is distinctively different again; in this case essentially discontinuous and contrived, a gently dissolving feudalism transformed into self-destruction by 'the exogenous impact of Western imperialism'; a forced and forceful encounter between two distinct historical times. Where, again, the political machine, or something very like it, existed without the feudal connection (as in Islam and China), not only did it not serve as a filter to capitalism but the formal similarity of political structures belies a radical difference in the real nature, meaning and historical significance of the state system; in effect it was a different machine – not absolutism. But this is not just a point of formal definition; it is indeed a theoretically necessary claim but one which, Anderson is at pains to show, is also sustained empirically in terms of the historical performances of the regimes in question. Its force springs simultaneously from the fact that it is theoretically required and from the fact that it was historically so. In theory absolutism is a political system rooted in private property in land; in history 'the bedrock of Osmanli despotism was the virtually complete absence of private property in land'. On that bedrock the House of Islam could no more build an absolutist state than the eastern European absolutisms in their social landscapes 'scoured' of all non-feudal features could synchronise the preservation of feudalism with the growth of capital. In both cases the lineages were inappropriate.

I cannot here re-capitulate or digest much of the complexity and detail with which these central arguments are deployed and elaborated. What is important is that Anderson's treatment *is* both complex and detailed – and that in both its complexity and its detail it is thoroughly historical. Thus, the eastern European growth of absolutism is, for example, not treated as a mere product of 'the definitive enserfment of the peasantry' – although to do so would satisfy the formal requirement of the comparative method. Rather, Anderson recognises that historically the establishment of the 'second serfdom' cannot suffice to account for eastern European absolutism and in order to do that methodological canons must be violated by the introduction of a specifically historical, exogenous, even contingent factor: the political impact of the feudalism of western Europe, already re-organised under the panoply of absolutism, on a still highly localised feudalism in the east: 'To explain the subsequent ascent of Absolutism it is necessary first of all to reinsert the whole process of the second serfdom into the *international* system of late feudal Europe'. Localised feudal power could enforce serfdom: what it could not do, additionally, was to co-exist with much more powerful, centralised systems of feudal power – just because the normal object of feudal international policy was land and the normal media of feudal international relations were either war (the aristocratic appropriation of land by violence) or a peculiarly extortionate diplomacy (the aristocratic appropriation of land by intimidation, bribery or at best, marriage). It was, in this view, precisely the peculiar historical culture of feudalism that impelled feudatories in the east to concentrate their resources in at least 'equivalently centralised state machines' to those in the west. *Lineages of the Absolutist State* is full of such concessions to the deviousness of history. And it is precisely these concessions, this sort of readiness to take history on board over and above the requirements of theory, that give the book its power.

The most striking instance of this two-sideness, and it will have to serve to indicate the persistent depth of Anderson's analysis, appears in the general conclusions he advances. Again and again he repudiates the possibility of restricting his argument to the discovery and assertion of the sort of 'laws of connection' which for Mill were the proper purpose of comparative analysis. His argument is indeed centred on the demonstration of a cluster of law-like connections between feudalism, absolutism and capitalism. But it is also constantly complicated by recognition upon recognition of the specifically historical detours taken by such connections. Thus (1974:420):

> What, then, was the specificity of European history which separated it so deeply from Japanese history, despite the common cycle of feudalism which otherwise so closely united the two? The answer surely lies in the perdurable inheritance of classical antiquity ... What rendered the unique passage of capitalism possible in Europe was the *concatenation of antiquity and feudalism* ... The 'advantage' of Europe over Japan lay in its classical antecedence, which even after the Dark Ages did not disappear 'behind' it, but survived in certain basic respects 'in front' of it.

A complicated understanding of historical time is being proposed here. But again the important feature of the argument for historical sociology is that it is precisely in the complicated social organisation of time that the structuring of this or that 'present' is unearthed. In this sense history ultimately explains itself:

> The real historical temporality governing the three great modes of production that have dominated Europe up to the present century was radically distinct from the continuum of evolutionary

chronology. Contrary to all historicist assumptions, time was as if at certain levels inverted between the first two, to release the critical shift to the last. Contrary to all structuralist assumptions there was no self-moving mechanism of displacement from the feudal mode of production to the capitalist mode of production, as contiguous and closed systems. The *concatenation* of the ancient and feudal modes of production was necessary to yield the capitalist mode of production in Europe – a relationship that was not merely one of diachronic sequence, but also at a certain stage of synchronic articulation. (1974:421–2).

This 'collocation' of times, the overlay of antiquity and feudalism which gave western Europe its special historical dynamism and, specifically, concentrated that dynamism for a time in the structures of absolutism, is found concretely by Anderson in the relationship of town and country, in the intellectual terms of reference of art and science, in the relationship of church and state and above all in the superb framework for the refinement of property rights provided by Roman law – so far 'in advance' of the murky contracts of feudalism. The revival and re-enforcement of Roman law was the distinctive mechanism which allowed the absolutist regimes to consolidate simultaneously, public authority and private property. Its historical availability was a crucial condition for the absolutist solution to the crises of feudalism in western Europe – alone. In this sort of argument of course Anderson is once again in exceptionally close agreement with his outstanding precursor in historical sociology: Max Weber.

Does the project succeed? Does the attempt to generate a knowledge of the historical structuring of absolutism – or anything else – by holding generalisation and detail in tension, by steering a zig-zag course between historicism and structuralism and between fact and theory, actually deliver that sort of knowledge? Or does it merely hand us a mish-mash of bad history and bad sociology? Is historical sociology really no more than bad history plus bad sociology? Or can the type of balancing act attempted by Anderson attain its own substantial mode of knowledge through the synthetic transformation of history and sociology? The enterprise is certainly vulnerable to criticism from both sides. I have tended to dwell on the sorts of criticism likely to be urged from the side of sociology – worries about the dereliction of method that results from excessive sensitivity to detail. But it is no less susceptible to the criticisms of historians – worries about the dereliction of scholarship that results from excessive attachment to theoretical generalisation. Anderson's erudition is formidable but by the standards of, say, the *English Historical Review* his work must appear remarkably shallow – an interpretive sweep across a very wide range of secondary authorities, taking on trust far too much that the truly professional historian would insist on researching. Without essaying a direct answer to such challenges at this stage I would concede that if historical sociology as a brand of social analysis of substance and value in its own right can be achieved by relaxing and counter-balancing the requirements of good sociology and good history, the task of integration, of creating and holding the tension, is one that must call for special and considerable skills. It presents problems of technique as well as problems of epistemology. Just how serious those problems are, and how well on the whole Anderson masters them, become clear if we pause to consider some other recent attempts at comparative historical sociology.

The genesis of democracy

In different ways both Barrington Moore and Lipset and Rokkan demonstrate the ease with which the balance can be upset. And oddly, in each case what goes wrong is the opposite of what one might have expected from the overt style of the work. Lipset and Rokkan confront us with a cumbersome, outrageously elaborate apparatus of formal classification and analysis, but their real problem is the recalcitrant untidiness of the empirical detail they assemble. Moore plunges into his historical case studies with little apparent concern for the requirements of theory, but in the end the disabling flaw in his work is the subordination of historical evidence to the terms of a rigid interpretive theory. They thus illustrate much better than some more successful essays in this genre, such as Reinhard Bendix's *Nation Building and Citizenship* (1964), how very delicate an exercise large scale historical sociology needs to be.

Representing the fruit of twenty years of sustained effort in political sociology 'Cleavage Structures, Party Systems and Voter Alignments', the long essay with which Lipset and Rokkan introduce their anthology, is concerned with the relationship between social divisions, interests and conflicts on the one hand ('cleavage structures') and the organisation of political alliances and oppositions on the other ('party systems and voter alignments'). They treat parties and party systems as embodying a selective representation, repression and ordering of social conflicts, and assume that there is some systematic connection to be found between different forms of this selective political institutionalisation of social divisions and various general qualities of the ensuing political systems – such as democracy, stability, range and type of parties and party systems, effectiveness in relation to given policy objectives and so forth. And in seeking to understand that connection they formulate their problem as a matter of historical structuring: a question of the phased articulation of the history of social conflict with the history of political organisation. In this sense, insofar as they construct their problem in terms of a complex and extended process of structuring, with certain forms of the process hypothetically resulting in certain forms of political system, the project is plainly an authentic exercise in historical sociology.

They go on, however, to set this problem in the context of a highly generalised, many-layered framework of theory and classification which in its very generality seems to me to lack clear and usable guidelines for the interpretation of actual historical evidence. They begin with the notion of the four basic functions of social systems proposed by Talcott Parsons (1951): integration, adaptation, goal attainment and latent pattern maintenance. And they suggest that the performance of these functions (each by its own distinctive functional subsystem), and the 'interchanges' between subsystems which that involves, will generate distinct types of 'cleavage bases within national political communities.' Quite apart from its highly dubious implication that people come into conflict with one another because they are performing different functions for social systems, or because they are seeking to perform the same function in different ways rather than because they have irreconcilable values, beliefs, purposes, interests and expectations (to say nothing of differential power), this approach immediately causes trouble. The range of 'cleavage bases' permitted by the model is both unspecific and enormous. And the model itself contains no way of identifying those 'cleavage bases' likely to be historically consequential or theoretically significant in any given context. So all one can do is to pick on those which for extraneous, or commonsense, reasons happen to seem consequential and significant to oneself. And that, in a manner characteristic of their whole procedure is just what Lipset and Rokkan do. They want to explore the relationship between different patterns of social conflict and the emergence of different types of party and party system in the course of 'modernisation'. So without wasting much time on a consideration of the sorts of conflicts their model of functions and functional subsystems might yield in principle they at once turn to a discussion of those which seem empirically interesting to them. Given that their proposed theoretical framework is in fact no more than an idle taxonomy this is a quite sensible, indeed unavoidable, step for them to take. But it is the first of many in which they reveal that their analysis is actually controlled not by a strong interpretive theory but by a more or less uneasy awareness of the empirical diversity of historical action, combined with a shrewd instinct to keep things as simple as possible. What is odd is that they themselves see their work as a *theoretical* analysis.

The cleavages which they in effect then assume and assert to be significant in pre-modernised societies for the shaping of the politics of modernisation are of four kinds (1967:7): conflicts centred on the defence of local territories or cultures against the claims of central government; conflicts over the control of the society as a whole; conflicts over the allocation of resources and benefits between interest groups formed primarily by the division of labour; and conflicts of an 'ideological' nature between groups committed to mutually exclusive systems of beliefs or values. In an obscure and theoretically vacuous attempt to link this plausible account of the historical world to their initial functional model these conflicts are identified as 'the internal structure of the I (integration) quadrant'. The cleavages themselves are next organised in terms of two cross-cutting axes – the axis of centre-periphery conflict and the axis of functional conflict – although how one would locate, say, the Tudor coup d'état against Richard III, the expulsion of James II, the revolutions in 1848 in terms of these axes is not made clear. And this exercise is described as transforming 'the Parsonian dichotomies ... into continuous coordinates' (1976:10). Once again one is struck by the absence of purposeful links between the quite cogent empirical questions these authors want to ask and the formal models of social process they insist on abstracting from, or weaving around, these questions. Because they have no theory of empirical causation – as distinct from a theory of social forms – their assignments of significance tend to seem quite wilful. Just *why* (1967:9) should 'the locus for the formation of parties and party constellations in mass democracies' be 'the I quadrangle' of their functional model (leaving aside the fact that 'quadrangle' is plainly not the word they want)? In what possible sense are the origins of the main British political parties for example more firmly located, or more usefully understood as located, in the integrative subsystem than anywhere else? To emphasize the territorial and religious themes in the French revolution is reasonable enough; but to wholly disregard the extent to which that revolution was also about taxes, incomes, property rights and bread or about estates, classes and political power, and the extent to which the locus of formation of subsequent French politics lay in those conflicts (all A-G interchanges in the terms of their model) is surely wayward not to say historically incorrect? If one purports to have a comprehensive theoretical framework one is duty bound to frame the empirical world comprehensively. Still, it could be urged that the important thing from the point of view of historical sociology is not so much the arbitrariness or inadequacy with which empirical problems are tied to theoretical frameworks as what happens when, pushing models and frameworks quietly into the background, one sets out to explore the empirical problems.

Unfortunately the answer in this case is that one is given another model. In fact the essay consists of a succession of eight separate models introduced successively as the authors move steadily closer to actual variations in actual political systems. At the juncture we have reached their model of the inner structure of the integrative system is joined by a model of what might be called the early formation of social frameworks for political systems, 'a simple three-phase model of the process of nation building' (1967:9). In what appears to be a period immediately prior to the appearance of mass suffrage, organised parties and party systems they see the conflicts springing from their cross-cutting axes of cleavage being, in three analytically distinct steps, more sharply articulated, consolidated in a variety of relatively stable alliances and increasingly politicised in the form of demands for reform and the building of political parties. The process as a whole constitutes an even firmer mould for the subsequent organisation of political activity. The question then is, what sorts of early alliance create what sorts of mould? Alas, the enthusiasm one might feel for the relative historical concreteness of this part of their analysis has to be restrained on three counts. First, the conceptual pivot of their model, the idea of 'nation-building' proves alarmingly slippery. Second, it becomes clear that the point of their conception of the three-phase process of nation-building is to enable them to exemplify patterns of movement within their more abstract model of the social system rather than to discover patterns of movement in history. And third, in the event they do not produce either an empirical or a theoretical answer to their own crucial question about the ways in which 'socio-cultural conflict' pre-structures party systems but merely elaborate a typology of ways in which the question might be answered and factors anyone attempting an answer would need to consider.

The problem with the concept of nation-building is that it pre-judges without actually specifying the historical significance of certain powerful people and groups. It confuses function and outcome with relationship and action. The term refers to the processes by which the energies, resources and conflicts of a population are mobilised in the agencies of a nation state. Nation-building is the function of those processes; but it tends to slide into being a description of the action of *some* participants in the processes: 'the active nation-building elite'. And the trouble with that shift is that it is at once too exclusive and too inclusive. Nation-builders pop up everywhere (Napoleon and Metternich and Mazzini and Talleyrand), or wherever you want them (Metternich and Talleyrand but *not* Napoleon or Mazzini). Unlike the practice of absolutism, the practice of nation-building is curiously elusive, the work of vaguely specified 'nation-builder alliances', or a still vaguer 'central nation-building culture'. Sometimes the difficulties of giving such terms any clear empirical reference are such that Lipset and Rokkan slip quietly into talking about dominant and subordinate groups instead; but not often.

However, one advantage of the concept of nation-building, an important one for these authors, is that it provides an easy bridge back from the world of history to the abstract world of their functional model. Thus (1967:9): in the second phase of nation-building 'local oppositions to centralisation produce a variety of alliances across the communities of the nation: the commonalities of family fates in the L quadrangle generate associations and organisations in the I quadrangle.' And later still, 'the alliances in the I quadrangle will enter the G quadrangle.' More substantially, in their attempt to order the phase of alliance building, the early transformation of cleavages into structural moulds for later party politics, they invoke the idea of two major revolutions, the Industrial and the National, as sources of what became in 19th century Europe four decisive and simplifying lines of conflict. The Industrial Revolution produced conflicts between land and industry and between employers and workers; and the National Revolution produced conflicts between 'the central nation-building culture' and an array of peripheral cultures and interests and between state and church. The previous diversity of cleavages was, one way or another, progressively crystallised and institutionalised around these four major lines. Once again a heartening move towards empirical analysis seems to be being made. But once again, instead of going on to consider why some of the basic cleavages were critically influential in some countries and others elsewhere Lipset and Rokkan are content simply to exemplify the possible variations and to do so in ways which are often glaringly indifferent to historical evidence however well they serve to fill out the boxes of their model. As they say (1967:40), 'We are less concerned with the specifics of the degrees of fit in each national case than with the overall structure of the model'. Thus, the National Revolution was 'triggered in France' and the 'decisive battle' of the French Revolution 'came to stand between the aspirations of the mobilizing nation-state and the corporate claims of the churches,' a battle in which 'the fundamental issue between Church and State focused on the control of education' (1967:15). No iota of evidence is offered to support this highly original reading of French history but the importance of the church-state struggle over education, required by the model, is amply illustrated from the political history of the Netherlands. In Britain, of course, the fundamental issue between the churches and the state was the control of alcohol. But that is another history.

My third objection to this style of historical sociology, that it fails to generate substantive answers to its own serious substantive questions, could perhaps be thought unfair so far as Lipset and Rokkan are concerned. After all 'Cleavage Structures, Party Systems and Voter Alignments' is an introductory essay and introductions are a proper place to ask questions without providing answers. Is it not enough to formulate a cluster of important questions and to propose a framework in which they could be answered? Especially if, as they suggest, much of the information needed for adequate answers has not yet been assembled? Two reasons persuade me that the objection is nevertheless justified. First, Lipset and Rokkan do in fact advance highly concrete and specific historical explanations of 'variations in cleavage structures and party constellations' whenever they can – as in their treatment of agrarian and local separatist parties for example. In other words, the framework is productive of *some* answers now and the question of its relative unproductiveness is therefore that much more compelling. And secondly, because it seems to me that the relative unproductiveness of this type of approach is a matter of principle not of choice; that is, it is built-into the type of approach and therefore has important implications for how historical sociology should, and should not, be practiced. These authors are eminent and sophisticated sociologists who are making a powerful appeal for a more historical, indeed a distinctively historical, sociology. At the very least they deserve criticism.

If one follows this essay through its remaining stages – the two revolutions and four resulting cleavage bases, the three phases of nation-building, the four thresholds of political mobilisation, the eight types of basic political opposition and alliance (plus two exceptions), the three (or four) stages of party and party-system formation – to its conclusion (1967:50) that 'the party systems of the 1960s reflect ... the cleavage structures of the 1920s' with, awkwardly, the 'few but significant exceptions' of France, Italy, Spain, Germany, the whole of eastern Europe and perhaps Portugal, although that excessively peripheral area is not actually considered, one can only end up sharing Lipset and Rokkan's own sense of the 'bewildering variety' of the empirical world. Yet the point of the essay was to reduce that variety to some sort of order for the purpose of explaining its variations (1967:37): 'the model not only offers a grid for the mapping of parallels and contrasts among national developments, it also represents an attempt to establish an explanatory paradigm of the simplest possible structure to account for a wide range of empirical variations'. So one is fully entitled to ask what, then, is explained by the 'paradigm' and, conversely, why some things seem to remain unexplained.

In effect two major explanatory claims are made. First, it is claimed that the party systems of Europe were pre-structured by, or more strongly 'can be interpreted as products of' sequential interactions between a limited range of cultural and economic oppositions and alliances. And secondly it is urged that these systems were accordingly 'set' in important respects before the appearance of mass parties of the working class and in turn therefore decisively pre-structured the destiny of such parties. The second of these claims is advanced in terms of a quite clear conception of causality: specific variations in party systems prior to the advent of organised labour have specific consequences for what happens during the advent of organised labour. The party system constitutes a clearly defined independent variable in terms of which the postulated cause and effect variations can be explored in an orderly way. In this sort of exercise, as Stinchcombe had remarked (1968:129): 'the elegance and power of an explanation can only be as good as the casual connections among variables allow it to be. An exact conceptual representation of the operative causal forces is of great importance.' The briefly sketched discussion of the impact of working class parties on western party systems at the end of Lipset and Rokkan's essay could quite plainly be filled out to meet these requirements. It is not nearly so clear that the earlier explanatory claim, which dominates the essay as a whole, also meets them. What we find there, under the umbrella of the general, and redundant, model of system functions and functional interchanges, is an ultimately ill-defined statement of co-variance in which possible causal connections are notably hard to grasp – *except* within the context of the singular history of particular countries.

Eight types of party system (or perhaps ten, or maybe more) are held to have emerged from eight (or possibly more) distinct sequences in the historical structuring of social conflicts between the Reformation and the appearance of organised mass parties. Each sequence, of course, has its own internal causal design, a logic of cumulative probabilities: an early alliance in power of landed interests and an established church gives non-conformists, industrialists and town-dwellers a possible basis for concerted political action which they might well not have had had the ruling group consisted of some other constellation. And each sequence can be shown to be at least an approximately adequate description of the political history of at least one actual nation. The difficulty is that the terms of the paradigm are set in such a way that there are almost certainly as many theoretical sequences as there are actual sequences: each theoretical sequence covers only the case that exemplifies it; and each case exemplifies a different sequence among the multitude of possible arrangements of the relevant variables. History is its own cause; but in this instance in a thoroughly mystifying way. An over-generalised, over-abstracted conception of the key variables of the paradigm results in acute difficulties in establishing analytical control of the empirical diversity of the historical world. In the end, and very sensibly, torn between the highly disciplined but theoretically unfocused and undynamic categories of their general functional model of social process and the chaos of detail in the empirical evidence available to them, Lipset and Rokkan effectively abandon the former and succumb to the latter.

This is not to deny that in the middle ground some important and innovative historical sociology is accomplished. My point is that it could have been accomplished with a good deal less theoretical fuss and a good deal more empirical punch if the project had been attempted in a rather different way. The cleavage structure/party systems model which they elaborate does allow one to explain the political history of each country studied in a relatively economical way – *given* the weighting of relevant variables found to exist in that country. It also points to common, if rather diffuse, junctures in the history of the whole range of societies studied at which, one way or another, episodes of structuring crucial to the history of each occurred – again, *given* the weighting of relevant variables that happened to exist in each case. What it does not do is either to postulate, let alone demonstrate, clearly defined causal connections between variables, or explain the weighting of relevant variables in any given country at any given time. At this vital point history is taken for granted. The chain of causality snaps. The cases just happened as it were. Thus (1967:20):

> A similar *rapprochement* took place between the east Elbian agricultural interests and the western business bourgeoisie in Germany, but there, significantly, the bulk of the Liberals sided with the Conservatives and did not try to rally the working class electorate to their side in the way the British party did.

Just like that. Or again (1967:21):

> The conflict between landed and urban interests was centred in the commodity market. The peasants wanted to sell their wares at the best possible prices and to buy what they needed from the industrial and urban producers at low cost. Such conflicts did not invariably prove party-forming.

Sometimes they did and sometimes they didn't. Historically, commentaries of this sort are entirely sound. But their effect is to relax the grip of the supposedly explanatory model to a quite disconcerting degree. 'In Britain and the Scandinavian countries', to take a final example (1967:22), 'the attitudes of the elites tended to be open and pragmatic'; so those countries ended up with relatively 'domesticated' labour movements. But did the elite attitudes just happen? Quite consistently in observations such as these analytical definition and control of key historical variations is lost. History eludes theory; causality resides in unexpected intervening variables. On some occasions the rural-urban cleavage structured party systems decisively; on other occasions it did not. Some elites were open others closed. Behind everything that Lipset and Rokkan explain fundamental matters remain unexplained. Their explanations always begin in effect with the term 'given' – given an open elite, given a strong Roman Catholic minority, given in fact some variation on which the whole explanation hinges. They identify some of the essential components of the historical sociology of party systems – the cleavage structures and above all the idea of the structuring effects of the phased articulation of cleavages with one another. But they fail to theorise, as distinct from formalising, the relationships between these components and so fail to account for, as distinct from describing, the empirical variations that interest them. Because they have no theoretical answer, however tentative, to their question when will one type of cleavage prove more salient than another they can achieve no empirical answer other than, when it was salient in the past. While such an answer is an important assertion of the indispensable contribution of historical analysis to sociology it is hardly satisfactory as an explanatory response to the question posed. Indeed, it is highly unsatisfactory because it tends to substitute historical regression for historical explanation.

To turn from Lipset and Rokkan to Barrington Moore is, at first sight, to enter a completely different world. A sharply crystallised statement of causal connection is presented at the outset. The selection and treatment of cases is firmly controlled by the theoretical terms of that statement. Admittedly Moore's focal empirical concern is with the political consequences of the history of two of the cleavages identified by Lipset and Rokkan (land-industry and employer-worker), but where their effort seems always to be to keep their categories as general and abstract as possible, the problems of *The Social Origins of*

Dictatorship and Democracy are invariably couched in terms which purport to have highly specific empirical reference (lord and peasant, bourgeois revolution, capitalist democracy, fascism, communism). 'We seek to understand the role of the landed upper classes and the peasants in the bourgeois revolutions leading to capitalist democracy, the abortive bourgeois revolutions leading to fascism, and the peasant revolutions leading to communism' (1966:xvii). And by contrast to the plethora of vaguely related or unrelated variables which Lipset and Rokkan allow to enter their framework of analysis Moore concentrates attention remorselessly on a single dimension of variation: 'The ways in which the landed upper classes and the peasants reacted to the challenge of commercial agriculture were decisive factors in determining the political outcome' (1966:xvii). Three systematically varied reactions are postulated each hypothetically structuring in decisive ways a distinct political denouement. In Stinchcombe's sense one could hardly ask for anything more elegant.

But does elegance go hand in hand with explanatory power in the way Stinchcombe seems to imply? A very striking feature of Moore's book is the shift that occurs within it from a deterministic to a probabilistic tone and mode of argument. As the relationship of class and state is explored progressively in the case studies of England, France, the United States, China and Japan it becomes progressively more nuanced, more finely varied, more susceptible to extraneous influences. In the very first pages of the study of England it is made clear that in that instance the shift to capitalist democracy was governed and permitted historically not only by the turn to commercial agriculture on the part of the landed upper classes but by a persistent and radical violence which served both to dispossess the feudal peasantry and to decimate the upper classes themselves. The shift to commercial agriculture was effected in the course of class struggles between lord and peasant in which the classes were not only pitted against each other but divided among themselves. A generalised violence was both the means and the condition for the move to commercial agriculture. And as case follows case it emerges that in each of them the class relations which are Moore's central concern were mediated and shaped by local historical factors of this sort and not simply driven forward by their own momentum. Whether or not Moore had got his history right – and some distinguished historians have argued that he has not – the mode of argument is certainly historical in its insistence on the importance of both location in time and phasing over and above the logic of relationships in determining outcomes. The effective thesis is that certain resolutions of the relationship of lord and peasant led to certain political systems but *only* at certain, not repeatable, historical moments and in each case under certain, not reproducible, historical conditions. Thus (1966: 413–4):

> To a very limited extent these three types – bourgeois revolutions culminating in the Western form of democracy, conservative revolutions from above ending in fascism and peasant revolutions leading to communism – may constitute alternative routes and choices. They are much more clearly successive historical stages. As such they display a limited determinate relation to each other ... Without the prior democratic modernisation of England, the reactionary methods adopted in Germany and Japan would scarcely have been possible. Without both the capitalist and reactionary experiences, the communist method would have been something entirely different if it had come into existence at all.

The terms of the analysis thus become appreciably more relaxed as the study proceeds. Not only do 'the historical preconditions of each major political species differ sharply from those of the others' – which is, of course, quite compatible with the original strong form of the thesis – but, 'within each major type there are also striking differences' and when closely examined those differences are so bound up with specific, local historical circumstances that generalisations about the role of an 'independent' variable such as the relation of lord and peasant can only sensibly be cast as statements of probability. What saves Moore's study from a retreat to eclecticism in the face of this discovery is his firm insistence on sticking to his original, narrowly defined empirical terms of reference; on pursuing a comparative analysis of the role of the specific relationship of lord and peasant in the political history of modernisation rather than lapsing into a study of the causes of modernisation in general. Ironically perhaps, it is the determined narrowness of empirical reference in that sense which saves the book as an important contribution to large-scale historical sociology. Of course, some enlargement of the empirical terms of the argument does occur – that is precisely why the form of argument is progressively relaxed. Most noticeably the urban commercial and industrial bourgeoisie make their appearance as a third crucial class formation in the passage to democracy, fascism or communism. Increasingly the case studies appear to drive their author to talk in terms of a three-way relationship between landlords, peasants and 'the urban upper classes' as the real matrix of each society's political destiny. An alliance of equals between a commercially-oriented landed class and an urban bourgeoisie seems finally to be as important as the actual commercialisation of agriculture in the genesis of political democracy; and conversely, 'the fateful coalition of a strong landed elite and weak bourgeoisie', rather than just the persistence of a dominant class of landlords, 'has been the social origin of rightist authoritarian regimes and movements' (1966:431).

Should Moore perhaps have gone still further in opening his analysis to new empirical variables? How far would that have driven him towards a general indeterminacy? Already the expansion he does permit impels a move away from the strict 'if A, then B' form of argument initially hinted at towards the much less stringent pursuit of 'tentative general hypotheses about the conditions under which (A) could be favourable to the growth of (B)'. And even that with the rider that, 'all these things can happen it seems only at [a particular historical moment and therefore] that they will be repeated anywhere in the twentieth century ... seems highly unlikely' (1966:425). Clearly there is an acute problem in large-scale historical sociology of finding objects of study and terms of explanation which are sufficiently restricted to permit the analysis of theoretically pertinent propositions and at the same time sufficiently inclusive to save one from the charge of blatant one-sidedness. Would *The Social Origins of Dictatorship and Democracy* have been a more historically adequate study if Moore had posed his problem in terms of class relationships in general instead of trying to concentrate on the relationship of lord and peasant? Or would not Lipset and Rokkan have been able to argue more cogently if they had concentrated on a single relational variation within their vast framework of variations – say, the relationship between churches – rather than trying to identify the parameters of possible variation across the whole range of possibly relevant variables? But perhaps voyages of discovery such as Moore's are only possible when people like Lipset and Rokkan have first made maps, however fanciful later explorers may show the maps to have been? And perhaps accurate maps can only be drawn when single-minded explorers such as Moore have beaten a sufficent number of tracks through a previously impenetrable terrain?

Be that as it may, we should note that the sort of analysis with which Moore concludes is very much closer to the sort of analysis Lipset and Rokkan seem to be looking for than one would initially have expected. The problem itself is recast in terms which plainly echo those of 'Social Cleavages, Party Systems and Voter Alignments' (1966:423): 'In very broad terms, our problem becomes one ... of trying to identify those situations in the relationship between the landed upper classes and the town dwellers that have contributed to the development of a relatively free society in modern times'. And the echoes are heard again in the sort of formula through which in the end Moore characterises such situations. Consider his statement of the conditions for democratic development (1966:430): 'the development of a balance to avoid too strong a crown or too independent a landed aristocracy ... a turn toward an appropriate form of landed aristocracy ... a weakening of the landed aristocracy and the prevention of an aristocratic-bourgeois coalition against the peasants and workers ... a revolutionary break with the past.' And at this stage the commercialisation of agriculture appears as no more than 'among the most decisive determinants influencing the course of subsequent political evolution'.

While the surrender of any conception of very strict causal determination in such conclusions is obvious enough it is also true that these carefully qualified propositions are, albeit of the same type as those of Lipset and Rokkan, still very much more specific – and therefore useful – in their empirical connotations. The cluster of conditions found to be conducive to the growth of capitalist democracy is after all quite different from, say, those proposed as conducive to the authoritarian mode which Moore (mistakenly in my view) identifies as fascism: labour repressive agriculture, a centralised bureaucratic state and 'a commercial and industrial class which is too weak and dependent to take power and rule in its own right and which therefore throws itself into the arms of the landed aristocracy and royal bureaucracy' – and which is welcomed by them because weak as it is it is still strong enough to be a worthwhile ally against peasants and workers. Something concrete, serious and testable *has* been said here about the genesis of democracy and dictatorship in mid-twentieth century Europe even if it has not been said with the sort of causal closure some ideals of social science might require or some of both Moore's admirers and his critics might have wished. And come to that, even if it is wrong. The extraordinary success of *Social Origins of Dictatorship and Democracy* surely owes a great deal to just this ability on Moore's part to provide such *relatively* specific answers to broad and general questions. In his journey of exploration (to use the metaphor he himself favours for this sort of work), he does trample down some rare and fragile historical plants – his theory-derived attachment to the term fascism, his insistence on the *peculiar* violence of countries travelling the democratic path, his willingness for the sake of a neat theory to lump together as instances of a common type countries in which aristocracies took to commerce and countries in which they were virtually destroyed, all betray the weight of his boots. But at least he does cut a path through the forest of empirical detail; and he does so without using the sort of theoretical and taxonomic bulldozer favoured by Lipset and Rokkan.

Purpose, function and persistence: absolutism revisited

A noticeable feature of the studies I have discussed so far has been their relative indifference to the intentions, dispositions and purposes of the individuals whose lives made up the historical processes in which the authors were interested. Attention was centred firmly on structural conditions and functional effects, on the institutional consequences of relationships, whether intended or unintended but in either case with the *actual* intentions of the parties to the relationships treated as a factor of quite minor explanatory importance. One of the two great merits of S. N. Eisenstadt's *The Political Systems of Empires* (1963) is – ironically, since he more explicitly than any of the other authors is an avowed structural-functionalist – that he makes motive a principle determinant in the historical construction of political regimes. The second is that whereas the other authors are mainly concerned to explain change – the coming into being of democracy or dictatorship, passages from feudalism to capitalism, the rise of new types of party political organisation – Eisenstadt's main interest is in the phenomenon, and problem, of persistence. The heart of his book is an analysis of the dynamics of stability. It is built on a salutary understanding of the fact that the formation of states has a present as well as a past; that historical time is a medium of continuity as well as of change.

The book (incidentally, from the point of view of the comparative method it is much the most carefully designed and successfully executed of these four works) is a study of twenty states which Eisenstadt identifies as belonging to the type of 'historical bureaucratic empires': pre-industrial regimes marked by a high degree of centralised political power operating through an extensive system of impersonal administration. The category obviously includes Anderson's absolutist states of early modern Europe but also includes many instances which, lacking the specifically feudal context of absolutism in Anderson's sense are placed cleanly outside that grouping in *Lineages of the Absolutist State*: the Arab caliphates from the Abbasids to the Ottoman empire, successive dynasties of the Chinese empire, the Inca and Aztec states, the Mogul empire and its Hindu predecessors, Sassanid Persia, the Hellenistic, Roman and Byzantine empires, the regimes of ancient Egypt and such 'conquest empires' as those of Spain in South America and of Britain in India. Disregarding their diverse historical origins and diverse historical destinies Eisenstadt groups them as a phenomenon for explanation on the basis of their specifically political characteristics. What all these regimes have in common, he argues, the feature that justifies one in treating them all as instances of a type, is precisely a form of politics not found elsewhere and found in all of them. Whatever internal variations between them may be found they all share certain common political characteristics which distinguish them from other regimes no matter what overlaps and parallels there might be in other respects. Using a number of control cases of other types of political system – feudal, patrimonial, modern and so forth – to confirm the cogency of this basic classification he identifies the common characteristics of the historical bureaucratic empires as follows (1963:19): '*a limited autonomy*' of the political sphere manifested by (i) 'the development of autonomous political goals' by the rulers and to a lesser degree by others, (ii) 'a limited differentiation of political activities and roles' from other activities and roles expressed especially in the emergence of a process of specifically 'political struggle', (iii) attempts to 'organise the political community into a centralised unit' and (iv) the 'development of specific organisations of administration and political struggle.'

Most distinctive of all, however, was what might be called the organising contradiction at the heart of these political systems in their historical actuality. Insofar as regimes of the specified type existed historically they did not do so as exemplifications of the abstract type Eisenstadt postulates but in specific contexts which structured them quite concretely. The limited nature of their differentiation, autonomy, centralisation and so on was not just a formal matter. Concretely, it was imposed by the nature of the traditional social worlds in which the bureaucratic empires were constructed and of which the rulers themselves were an integral part and within which their legitimacy was firmly located and defined. The regimes embodied a break with tradition manifested intellectually in the idea of a specifically political sphere of action and specifically political goals, and manifested structurally in the actual albeit limited differentiation of political institutions, roles and projects. But they were also bound to tradition both culturally in the rulers' commitment to traditional legitimations and structurally in their commitment to received systems of social stratification, hierarchy and privilege. The acute contradiction between the goals of the rulers and their commitments is, for Eisenstadt, the analytical pivot of the historical bureaucratic empires. It is in the light of that conception of their organisation that he examines how they came into being, how most of them persisted for quite long periods of time and how they eventually turned some into more and some into less differentiated systems.

This way of conceptualising his field of study is, of course, highly generalised and relatively abstract – plainly the 'limited autonomy' of the political sphere can take many different concrete forms. At first sight the relatively narrow terms of reference of a study such as Anderson's would seem to admit a much firmer grasp of actual historical structures and processes. The question is whether the comparative abstractness of Eisenstadt's conception of the historical bureaucratic empires has off-setting advantages in identifying important sources of variation in the structuring and destiny of particular states. I shall follow his argument briefly with that question in mind.

Because his point of departure is the goals of the rulers – their common pursuit of political autonomy – Eisenstadt has in fact a quite precise central point of reference to guide his analysis of the vast body of empirical evidence relevant to his problem: under what conditions could such goals be institutionalised in the particular, partially successful, form of the historical bureaucratic empires? But although the goals of the rulers provide the focus of his argument in this sense the argument itself is not a voluntaristic one. As the negative cases of Charlemagne and Genghis Khan testify, rulers cannot institutionalise empires just by wanting to do so – however strong their will, however clear their purpose and however great their power. Both the drive to create autonomous political and administrative structures and the (partially) successful creation of such structures occur, Eisenstadt insists, only under certain quite definite social conditions of possibility (1963:30). These conditions provide the second essential variable in his theory of the formation of the imperial regimes. Specifically, the objective of political autonomy and centralisation emerges and has some prospect of success only when a limited measure of general structural differentiation exists in the non-political spheres of society as well; when some people have escaped from the rigid statuses and roles of traditional agrarian social relationships; when religious, cultural and economic activities and resources have to some extent been 'disembedded', when commercial and urban and even professional ways of life have a certain substance and independence within the society as a whole. The net effects of this state of affairs in Eisenstadt's eyes are twofold: firstly, a reservoir of what he terms 'free-floating resources' comes to exist in the society, 'manpower, economic resources, political support and cultural identifications not ... committed beforehand to any primary particularistic-ascriptive groups'; and secondly problems of regulation and control are generated in the form of competition and conflict over the allocation, exploitation and use of these resources. The distinctive political goals of the rulers are a response to these problems. And the free-floating resources themselves are the key to the rulers' ability to realise their goals. The institutionalisation of the regimes was made possible by the capacity of the rulers to mobilise and appropriate the resources generated by structural differentiation in order to settle the issues created by the existence of those resources – issues which existing non-political mechanisms could not resolve to the satisfaction of some or all of the parties concerned. The issues created the political drive; the drive expressed itself in political machinery to control the resources; the resources sustained the growth of the machinery. It was the *interaction* of the statemaking purposes and activities of rulers and the resources produced by limited structural differentiation that provided the basis for the historical bureaucratic empires as a distinct state form.

This piece of theorisation is sufficiently sharp and substantial for Eisenstadt to be able to deploy, as the next stage of his argument, a whole series of predictive hypotheses about the destinies of particular empires and to validate them to varying degrees in terms of the relevant historical evidence. Clearly, for example, the extent and level of the bureaucratic institutional development could be expected to co-vary with the two basic components of the systems specified in the theory, the autonomy of the ruler's goals and the structural differentiation of the society. Conversely the institutional-isation of the political systems could be expected to precipitate crises of various kinds to the extent that it either exhausted the supply of free-floating resources in the society (the index of structural differentiation) or inhibited the autonomy of the ruler's goals by tying government too tightly to this or that group in the general political struggle. Those were in fact two of the commonest ways in which the historic bureaucratic empires collapsed. But although Eisenstadt devotes a great deal of his effort to the elaboration and confirmation of such hypotheses the heart of his analysis is elsewhere. The real point of his initial theorisation of the bureaucratic empires is that they were not just products of conjunction – of the coincidence of certain sorts of social differentiation and certain kinds of political goals. Much more fundamentally they were products of contradiction, edifices which were only possible if founded on contradiction.

The rulers had to be bound up to the traditional social order in commitments of a cultural, an economic, a social and political nature. Yet their state-making enterprises were premised upon the curtailment if not the sustained erosion of that order. They contrived to enact their goals despite their commitments by developing political apparatuses which could mobilise and exploit the modest free-floating resources of the societies they ruled. But in so doing they also aggravated the contradiction by advancing the very social differentiation – if only in the form of new channels of political control and struggle – which gave them their opportunity, and their problem, in the first place. At the same time they sought to encourage those groups which provided the society's free floating resources but, irreducibly committed to traditional values of all sorts, they realised their political goals by controlling and exploiting those resources to degrees which effectively stifled, alienated or obliterated the very groups most likely to generate them. In such circumstances, given such a double commitment to both tradition and change, the persistence of the historical bureaucratic empires obviously becomes highly puzzling – especially as many of them persisted for century upon century. It is this puzzle of the persistence of an absurd state of affairs which provides the central concern of *The Political Systems of Empires* (1963:111).

Here too, however, Eisenstadt's analysis rests on a hypothesis derived from his prior treatment of the formation of

the regimes: namely, that the conditions for their persistence
are to be found in the ability of the rulers to sustain a political
process (of administration, struggle, exaction and decision)
which served, in effect, to perpetuate the specific conditions
that brought the regimes into being in the first place – that is,
'the constant co-existence of certain levels of autonomous
political goals and orientations and of limited but pervasive
differentiation of the social structure' (1963:11). In sum, the
historical bureaucratic empires were a balancing act. An
outcome of struggle taking the form of a machine for the
articulation and regulation of struggle, they survived by
sustaining a dialectic of struggle between the rulers' goals and a
diversified opposition to those goals. The secret of their success
(or failure) Eisenstadt finds, in what could be considered the
most important empirical product of his study, in the
functioning of the bureaucratic apparatus which was their
peculiar institutional hallmark. To a greater or lesser extent the
bureaucracies, meshed into both the traditional and non-
traditional groups as an instrument of exaction and control,
functioned also as a medium of struggle. Functionaries
represented the groups they regulated as it were. The
persistence of the empires was critically dependent upon the
capacity of the bureaucracies to act as channels of struggle as
well as of control – which is one reason why the sale of office
and subsequent 'aristocratisation' of incumbents was always
such a vital matter for these regimes. But this maintenance of a
bureaucracy open to the interests of the ruled population,
although it could often be accomplished with great skill for
long periods, was in the end governed by the balance of the
basic conditions of existence of the empires. It was not just a
matter of chanelling the struggle of social groups vis-a-vis one
another and the rulers, but of producing outcomes to that
process which left the fundamental patterns of social
differentiation between social groups and between them and
the, marginally autonomous, rulers in their original delicate
oscillation, that is, undisturbed. And here the fundamental
inner contradictions of the systems became decisive.

Overtly the rulers were faced with the problem of
circumventing 'traditional' opposition to their policies. To a
greater or lesser extent their efforts to mobilise resources

through taxation, law, military ventures, bureaucratic control, fiscal, monetary and commercial policies, *even* when these measures were conceived as strategies for the defence of a traditional world of ascribed statuses, values and privileges, constituted an implicit onslaught on such statuses, values and privileges. They had to enhance the statuses, values and even privileges of non-traditional groups which generated the crucial resources which permitted the existence of the political structures which could alone resolve the various struggles between traditional and non-traditional interests. In the face of opposition the onslaught had either to be abandoned – with a resulting loss of political autonomy and hence effective collapse of one of the essential conditions of existence of this type of political system – or made explicit. Commonly, the rulers met this oppostion by adopting policies which sought both to strengthen the supply of free-floating resources in the society, and thence available to them, thus side-stepping direct resistance from traditional (usually aristocratic but often also peasant) sources, and directly curtailing the political powers of traditional interest, above all aristocratic interests, in order to make room for these non-traditional initiatives. The defence of tradition came to involve a direct attack on the traditional groups (1963:154). The goals of the rulers frequently did include an effective derogation of the powers of the aristocracies in their societies and a subversion of the social relations in which those powers were embedded. By, as it were, 'taking the point of view' of the rulers Eisenstadt seems to me to achieve here an understanding appreciably more subtle and more substantial than that of Anderson; a significant dimension of structuring is added. In terms of the rulers' understandings and intentions the historical bureaucratic empires, including those of absolutist Europe, *were* on-slaughts on feudal and other types of noble power. Subjec-tively, that was an essential feature of their conditions of existence. But, as Eisenstadt adds (1963:136), 'all these policies were replete with contradictions'.

The regimes could only exist as onslaughts on traditional aristocracies. Yet they could also only exist as systems entrenched in a world dominated by traditional aristocracies. Their persistence was a matter of constant, restless bureaucratic manipulation of that dilemma: the derogation of aristocratic privilege checked by the understanding that the regime's own legitimacy was tied to the legitimacy of aristocratic privilege; the encouragement of urban and commercial groups off-set by the alienation or extinction of those groups as the regimes extracted the resources which were the lifeblood of their existence. To the extent that they persisted their history was a history of endless movement in pursuit of immobility.

Yet in the terms of their common dilemma the historical bureaucratic empires achieved many different destinies. Eisenstadt's final concern is to account for the divergent histories of different sub-sets of the type. The balancing act was nowhere sustained indefinitely – if only because the essential conditions of persistence denied the regimes the means of generating the scale of resources needed to defend themselves in arms. Yet many persisted over centuries. And when they disintegrated some gave way once again to a less differentiated social and political order while others passed peacefully or violently into more elaborately differentiated systems. Initially, Eisenstadt seeks to explain these variations in terms of the predominant value-orientations of the rulers of the different empires. Some were more strongly oriented to conquest than others, some more equivocally devoted to traditional aristocratic values and legitimations, some to specifically political enterprises, some more caught up in religious missions, some more involved in economic and commercial ventures and so forth. And certainly these variations did relate to the ways in which the regimes in question succeeded or failed in managing the overall process of political struggle, the degree to which they exhausted free floating resources or fostered them, succumbed to aristocratic opposition or circumvented it, held or lost the crucial balance. But, once again it turns out that Eisenstadt is not in fact proposing a voluntarist, idealist or culturalist explanation. The value orientations in terms of which the rulers subjectively patterned their particular versions of the common balancing act, although an indispensable element of the explanatory work of historical sociology, are not treated as independent variables or as factors simply given in themselves in this or that society. Rather they are themselves seen as related to and decisively influenced by the levels and forms of social and political differentiation in the different societies at the point when the regimes were institutionalised. In other words, values are seen as related to power; the different value orientations of the rulers have to do with the conditions of possibility created by variously differentiated relationships and resources. They enact the state of the struggle and the rulers' position within it (1963:254): 'the same conditions that were most directly connected with the development of free-floating resources and activities also constituted a major determinant of the chief groups' political orientations'. And once again Eisenstadt proceeds to identify the possible destinies of the regimes (that is, to explain their actual destinies) in terms of a series of hypotheses strictly specified on the basis of the key terms of his theory.

In sum, Eisenstadt, manages to construct a tightly organised framework of analysis which permits the formulation of a sequence of theoretically controlled hypotheses and the appraisal of those hypotheses in the light of a wide range of empirical evidence itself properly contained by his initial classification and definition of terms. The exercise is set at a fairly high level of abstraction, but not so high that we cannot locate the categories in terms of actual historical instances quite comfortably, nor so high that the hypotheses generated fail to explain quite specific variations in the actual historical world. Studies such as *Lineages of the Absolutist State* can be sheltered quite satisfactorily under its umbrella. On the other hand it is not so down to earth as to permit as many variations as there happen to be cases – it is not a mere formalised listing – nor so down to earth as to preclude consideration of all relevant cases within the terms of the initial theorised conceptions of the phenomena to be studied. In these respects it seems to me to be a rather superior example of comparative historical sociology. It integrates meaning and structure in the process of historical structuring in a way that recognises the explanatory significance of both. And its theoretical pivot is a strongly persuasive conception of contradiction – the particular contradiction of commitments and purposes embodied in the political process of the historical bureaucratic empires in this instance – as the essential matter of history and the essential problem of historical sociology. It is at every point both responsive to historical evidence – although I have not here made any attempt to follow Eisenstadt in that respect – and coherently governed by theory. Consider, for example, the question of what is taken for granted. He quite correctly notes that 'any comparative analysis must stop somewhere and treat certain conditions as *given for the sake of this analysis*' (Eisenstadt, 1963). But in his case what is taken as given is no more and no less than the theoretical premise of his whole argument – the fact of a certain level of structural differentiation. That is a very different matter from taking as given whatever 'early' empirical circumstances happen to present themselves in different cases within the field of study. Here theory quite properly precludes historical regression. And finally, it manages to combine a sense of historical sociology as centrally concerned with the problem of historically located structuring with a fairly exceptional understanding that the historical process of structuring, although requiring the passage of time, it is not necessarily a process of change.

Conclusion

The four studies I have discussed in this chapter are by no means the only or the best available examples of this type of historical sociology, or even of this type of historical sociology concerned with the particular problem of the formation of states. They do, however, exemplify both the difficulties and the promise of long-range comparative historical sociology rather well. They suggest the need to accommodate interesting problems to some sort of principled conception of method and to accommodate formal canons of method to the empirical awkwardness of significant problems. They demonstrate the need for substantial historical scholarship as well as the need to impose theory ruthlessly, albeit conditionally, on the mass of available historical evidence. They indicate the hazards of indiscriminate formalisation as well as the need for some controlled formal terms of reference. Taken together they seem to point to the prospect of a successful mediation of history and theory – they begin to realise the sort of agenda for historical sociology drawn up by Theda Skocpol (whose *States and Social Revolutions* is itself an outstandingly successful exercise in long-range comparative history in a related field):

> It needs to be stressed that comparative historical analysis is no substitute for theory. Indeed, it can be applied only with the indispensable aid of theoretical concepts and hypotheses. For the comparative method alone cannot define the phenomena to be studied. It cannot select appropriate units of analysis or say which historical cases should be studied. All of these must come from the macro-sociological imagination ... Still, comparative historical analysis does provide a valuable check, or anchor, for theoretical speculation. It encourages one to spell out the actual causal arguments suggested by grand theoretical perspectives, and to combine diverse arguments if necessary in order to remain faithful to the ultimate objective – which is, of course, the actual illumination of causal regularities across sets of historical cases. Whatever the sources of theoretical inspiration, comparative history succeeds only if it convincingly fulfills this goal. And when it *is* successfully employed comparative historical analysis serves as an ideal strategy for mediating between theory and history. (1979:39).

At their best these studies move towards that sort of success. In doing so they perhaps also suggest that Max Weber's celebrated divorce of history and sociology was perhaps premature, indeed, possibly not a necessary separation at all:

> It has continually been assumed as obvious that the science of sociology seeks to formulate type concepts and generalised uniformities of empirical process. This distinguishes it from history which is oriented to the causal explanation and analysis of individual actions, structures and personalities possessing cultural significance. The empirical material which underlies the concepts of sociology consists to a very large extent, though by no means exclusively, of the same concrete processes of action as are dealt with by historians. Among the various bases on which its concepts are formulated and its generalisations worked out is an attempt to justify its important claim to be able to make a contribution to the causal explanation of some culturally important phenomenon. As in the case of every generalising science the abstract character of the concepts of sociology is responsible for the fact that compared

with actual historical reality they are relatively lacking in fullness of concrete content. To compensate for this disadvantage sociological analysis can offer a greater precision of concepts (1968: i, 19, 20).

In the light of the studies discussed in this chapter I would be inclined to argue that here as in so many other respects Weber was being excessively pessimistic. The estrangement of 'fullness of concrete content' and 'precision of concepts' is manifestly a real danger in long-range historical sociology. Over-ambitious attempts to reconcile them can result in conceptual muddle and empirical arbitrariness, or *vice versa*, as we have seen. On the other hand the analysis of historical structuring as the structuring of contradiction in studies such as *Lineages of the Absolutist State* and *The Political Systems of Empires* surely does achieve both conceptual precision and empirical fullness? In their different ways such works suggest that, Weber notwithstanding, one can in fact both have one's historical cake and eat it sociologically.

7

Explaining events: a problem
of method

If the historian has a special object of study it is surely events. Of course, the practice of history is now so varied, there is so much overlap between the sort of work sociologists do and the sort of work historians do, that it is perhaps no longer possible and probably no longer very desirable to worry about formal distinctions and boundaries between the disciplines. Yet there is a sense in which sociology, in its great raid on both science and commonsense in search of an intellectual identity, either ignored or felt impelled to reject events as a possible object of analysis. It was largely this absence of events from sociological accounts of the world that Weber had in mind when he spoke of the subject as 'relatively lacking in fullness of concrete content'. And conversely, events do seem to provide the distinctive matter in terms of which historians construct their reality. The field is almost always specified as a course of events. And even when it is the course rather than the separate events that is being examined it is clear that the idea of a course is arrived at only by way of the idea of events. Philosophers of history commonly present the peculiarity of history in just these terms. Thus (Mandelbaum, 1938):

> History is differentiated from knowledge in the physical sciences in being a descriptive narration of a particular series of events which has taken place; in consisting not in the formulation of laws of which the particular case is an instance, but in the description of the events in their actual determining relationships to each other; in seeing events as the producers and products of change.

Admittedly quite an array of historians – sociographers of the past such as the Cambridge Group for the History of Population and Social Structure (Laslett, 1965), groups such as the History Workshop concerned to 'recover the texture of daily life in the past' as part of a people's history (Samuel, 1980), that wing of the *Annales* school which has followed Braudel in seeking the design of the *longue durée* (Braudel, 1980), those who have tried to elucidate the states of mind, ideologies, cosmologies (*mentalités*) of individuals or communities in pursuit of the meanings of historical existence (Darnton, 1978) – now see their work as a matter of reconstructing or reconstituting the moments or epochs of the past with little or no reference to particular events. I shall discuss their work in chapter 10. Here I would only say that their professed indifference to events often strikes me as misleading; often, indeed it is among other things really a prolonged and roundabout attempt to explain events more adequately. Even *The Mediterranean and the Mediterranean World in the Age of Philip II*, often cited as the decisive manifesto and demonstration of structural history as opposed to the history of events, is in fact an effort, splendidly accomplished, to establish a many-sided explanatory dialectic *one* strand of which is unavoidably that of events (Braudel, 1973:900–903). Little of this body of work therefore seems to me seriously to qualify the general importance of the event in historical analysis. The question is whether the centrality of events in historical analysis represents – as has often been argued – a gulf of principle between history and sociology which historical sociology cannot hope to bridge.

An event is a portentous outcome; it is a transformation device between past and future; it has eventuated from the past and it signifies for the future. It is not just a happening there to be narrated but a happening to which cultural significance has successfully been assigned. And its identity and significance are established primarily in terms of its location in time, in relation to a course or chain of other happenings. Both their internal design and their assigned significance mark events as in the first instance matters of sequence, of the organisation and meaning of action in time. Events, indeed, are our principal points of access to the structuring of social action in time. And once we allow that the structuring of social action in time is an essential concern of the sociologist we cannot properly eliminate events from our field of enquiry or drop the concept of the event from our modest stock of analytical tools. It is not just that the concept of the event, and thus of an eventful history, is the best means we have of seeing our experience in time as something more than a meaningless flux. Events, the conceptualisation of history as eventful, are more specifically an indispensable prism through which social structure and process may be seen. Structure and process, say class or industrialisation, are not directly observable but are inferred from the observation of events (or conditions). Events themselves are of course in turn inferred from the observation of action. But the event is, as it were, a primary construct, relatively full of empirical content, mediating action and structure. Through the strike and the war we perceive classes and nation states. In this sense at least Ernest Gellner is quite right when he insists that (1956) 'the problem of explanation in history is also the problem of the nature of sociology.' Because it is concerned with structuring sociology must be able to explain events.

Structuring, the reciprocal flow of action and structure, is manifold and endless. To understand it we must somehow break into it, somehow construct moments or episodes within it which our analytical resources can manage. The event is such a construct – and it is an especially apt construct because it preserves just that balance of agency and social order which so many of the constructs of both history and sociology upset. What I am *not* proposing is the substitution of a one-sided historical and action-oriented perspective for a one-sided sociological and structure-oriented perspective. An event is a moment of becoming at which action and structure meet. The designation of a happening as an event indicates that the meeting has been judged peculiarly forceful, perhaps peculiarly transparent: the Archduke has been assassinated, the Shah deposed, the pickets arrested – becoming is crystallised in a moment of being. And as Durkheim, even Durkheim, well understood, 'structure ... is encountered in becoming, and one cannot illustrate it except by pursuing this process of becoming' (1933:323). The event is a point of entry to the process. For sociologists to abandon the explanation of events as beyond the scope of their discipline is in effect to renounce a major option for resolving the problematic which should most concern them: the problematic of structuring.

However, the concept of the event is not altogether straightforward. In seeming to take the Norman Conquest or the Gettysburg Address or the Depression for granted as significant happenings historians do less than justice to the complexity of their distinctive object of study. Three complexities in particular demand attention here: there is the problem of detail, the problem of concreteness and the problem of uniqueness. Most of the arguments about the inability of sociology to account for events and the peculiar capacity of history to do so have their roots buried in a conception of the nature of events which sees them as detailed, concrete and unique (Gardiner, 1961). So it is important to establish how far these are really the defining characteristics of events and, to the extent that they are, how far that constitutes an insuperable barrier to sociological explanation.

The problem of detail is really the heart of the matter. In one sense the whole point of an event is that it is constituted by its details; it is a specific, bounded happening to be studied, elucidated and explained in terms of other specific, bounded happenings that precede, surround and compose it. Yet the claim, often made by those who insist on the principled distinction between history and sociology, that it is the historical commitment to detail in the study of events that marks historical knowledge off as something essentially unlike sociological knowledge is really not tenable. On examination it turns out that events, however detailed, are constructed not observed. The point was well made by Weber in 1905 (1949:169–70):

When it is said that history seeks to understand the concrete morality of an event in its individuality causally, what is obviously not meant by this ... is that it is to reproduce and explain causally the concrete reality of an event in the totality of its individual qualities. To do the latter would be not only actually impossible, it would be a task which is meaningless in principle. Rather, history is exclusively concerned with the causal explanation of those elements and aspects of the events in question which are of

general significance and hence of historical interest from general
standpoints, exactly in the same way as the judge's deliberations
take into account not the total individualised course of the events
of the case but rather those components of the events which are
pertinent for subsumption under the legal norms.

In other words, both in constructing an event as an object of
study and in accounting for it the historian *selects* significant
detail from the plethora of available detail. To that extent the
logic of historical work is indistinguishable from the logic of
the work of the judge, or of the sociologist. In all three cases it is
the criteria in terms of which one selects detail not the
perspicacity with which one observes detail that gives the work
its force and validity. In this sense the difference between
history and sociology is a difference of rhetoric not a difference
of logic. The historian uses a rhetoric of close presentation
(seeking to persuade in terms of a dense texture of detail) while
the sociologist uses a rhetoric of perspective (seeking to
persuade in terms of the elegant patterning of connections seen
from a distance). But the logic in terms of which objects to be
explained are identified and related to their proposed contexts,
causes and effects is not necessarily different as a result of the
difference of rhetoric. In both cases knowledge is achieved by
abstraction. In both cases detail is what is selected as evidence
not what is given by the world. In each case, to adapt a further
comment of Weber (1949:111): our real problem is ... by which
logical operations do we acquire the insight, and how can we
demonstratively establish, that a given causal relationship
exists between the effects that interest us and certain elements
among the infinity of surrounding details. And at the very least
one must answer, with Weber, 'obviously not by the simple
observation of the course of events.'
    However, if the requirement to respect detail does not
distinguish historical from sociological work, surely the
concreteness with which the historian's events are specified
does? The sociologist approaching, say, the French Revolution,
will be interested in such problems as the general relations of
estates and classes, the extent to which the particular episode
exemplifies a general process of revolution, the possibility of
discerning a broad movement of thwarted expectations,

relative or absolute deprivation and so forth. The historian, by contrast, will be concerned with the machinations of Danton or Robespierre, the antagonism of peasant, seigneur and curé in a village in the Rouergue, the background and beliefs of the Jacobins of Toulouse, the state of mind of murderers in the Rhone Department in 1794 and other such empirically solid matters. The historian's Revolution surely has a palpable flesh (and blood) which the sociologist's Revolution is surely denied? Actually, although it is true that most historians work closer to the ground than most sociologists in rendering accounts of past events, the difference is once again a difference of scope and style rather than of kind. Concreteness in this respect is in the eye of the beholder and not inherent in some special order of reality which only the historian can grasp. To begin with one should note that concrete in this context does not mean natural or empirically given. Neither the historian nor the sociologist is interested in explaining natural events – say, sunrises. Both are interested in explaining constructed events – say, *The Sunne Rising* for John Donne, or calendars; meanings abstracted from the flow of events and made significant. And in that respect concreteness is not an issue: Donne's poem and the social organisation of time are the same sort of fact and present the same problems of explanation. Secondly, concreteness as a special quality of historical work cannot be held to mean any particular degree of empirical solidity or definition. The battle of Hastings was an event but so was the Norman conquest. And so was the rise of capitalism. It is the type of event chosen and constructed for investigation and not some underlying property of historical reality that determines the level of concreteness appropriate to any given historical or sociological explanation. Events are defined not by any measure of detail, specificity or concreteness within the chronology of happenings but by their significance as markers of transition. As something to be explained the challenge of an event is not a matter of grasping its concreteness but of apprehending, at an appropriate level of concreteness, the transition it signifies.

The distinction sometimes proposed between history and sociology in terms of the uniqueness of events as the special subject-matter of the historian can be dealt with in much the same way. It is not that events are not unique. It is that there is nothing in the nature of their uniqueness that removes them from the reach of sociological explanation. A stronger version of the argument, advanced by Max Weber, would hold that, uniqueness notwithstanding, the task of explaining events adequately (in terms of their meaning and thereby in terms of their causes) imposes a common methodology on sociologist and historian alike. The historian may of course choose not to be interested in meaning or cause, may claim to wish to do no more than discover and present the 'facts'. It does not follow from that that the facts historians discover, or construct, are intrinsically resistant to a generalising causal analysis. On the contrary, it could be held that what historians are doing in describing events and elaborating their complex inner design is simply taking the first, essential, step in an exercise that is the exercise of sociological explanation: they are constructing explainable objects of explanation. The fact that they do not themselves choose to take any further steps along that path is a matter of style or temperament not of possibility. Indeed, one could go on, the very concept of an event invites one to travel the path of causal explanation just because it plainly refers not to something that is mysteriously 'there', in all its uniqueness, in nature but to action which has eventuated within a context historically constructed and bounded. Thus, for Weber at least, insofar as historians do interest themselves in meaning and causality they are impelled, however reluctantly and un-selfconsciously, into the world of classification, generalisation, conditions and interconnections which the sociologist normally inhabits. Thus (1968:21), 'in working out a concrete causal explanation of individual events the procedure of the historian is essentially the same' as that of the sociologist.

In practice, as we shall see, many historians contrive to avoid this fate, or at least to avoid recognising that it has overtaken them by clinging to the method of narrative – that is, by burying the principles of explanation that underpin their work beneath the rhetoric of a story. But it is not necessary either to believe that because that is what many historians do that it is all they could do in studying events, or to follow Weber to the point of insisting that all honest historians ought to admit that they are sociologists beneath the skin. The cobbler to his last, the historian to his narrative, is an acceptable division of labour. All that must be maintained is that the uniqueness of events, far from being an intractable essence defying sociological analysis, is in fact one of the distinctive, constructed properties of the historian's world which makes it properly susceptible to sociological explanation. What is unique about an event is the conjunction of elements it embodies. It does not follow that the process of conjoining is an enigma which only the esoteric, empathic skills of the historian can tease out. On the contrary, the analysis of process exacts reference to the general rather than to the particular.

Consider, for example, Fritz Stern's *Gold and Iron* (1980), a study of the relationship between Bismarck and the banker Gerson Bleichröder which was widely acclaimed as a masterpiece of historical writing when it was first published. Stern's primary source is the Bleichröder family papers and in particular Gerson Bleichröder's correspondence with Bismarck, other leading German politicians and the Rothschilds. His immediate focus of attention is the story of the increasingly close entanglement of the two men, of the way in which Bleichröder through his role as Rothschild agent in Berlin came to be Bismarck's personal banker, his financial adviser on both personal and governmental issues and eventually a powerful, and well-rewarded, instrument of and influence on policy at the highest levels. But every page of the story is rich in larger resonances. There is the theme of finance and power, of how the interests of capital and the interests of authoritarian government came together to override constitutional liberalism in the building of the Reich. There is the theme of arrogance and submissiveness, of the fawning dependence with which Bleichröder climbed to the pinnacles of status and influence in a society where deference to authority was an axiomatic medium of social intercourse. There is the theme of German and Jew, the patronising tolerance of the Junker for the serviceable Jew, the indiscriminate eagerness of the aspiring Jew to outdo every German in devotion to a regime which never offered to do more than treat Jews with contempt. There is of course the terrible unfolding of that theme in the bemused destruction of the Bleichröders' position and fortune two generations later on. And cutting across much of this there is the theme of the peculiar German 'cult of friendship', a cultural imperative of German society which made possible historically significant relationships such as that of Bismarck and Bleichröder even in the teeth of so many other imperatives of the culture and the impossibility of friendship they entailed for a German Jew however successful in the world of German Gentiles. There is, again, the theme of individual and society, of the extraordinary personal successes of both Bismarck and Bleichröder counterpointing the calamitous outcome of the world they built for both state and capital, both German and Jew. And encompassing the whole is the theme of the complex dialectic of a much larger history in which great collective destinies are worked-out by human agents wresting the opportunities, contradictions and constraints of a given historical moment to their own ends. Here is a characteristic passage from Stern's commentary (1980:461):

> Bleichröder's success was swift and extraordinary, as was Germany's. It was brittle, as was Germany's. The career of Gerson Bleichröder mirrored some of the fundamental processes of the two worlds he belonged to, one by birth, the other by desperate desire. He was a Jew by birth, a German by choice. For years he thought he could combine both worlds, that a private and loosening association with the Jewish world would not be incompatible with a public and ever greater role in the German world. In fact his middle years described the moment of the least troubled amalgamation of German and Jewish society; his declining years marked the first organised repudiation of that amalgamation and his very success was taken as a warrant for repudiation.

Clearly, Stern's exceptional ability to evoke such resonance, to tap the general meaning of the particular, within the mountains of pettiness and trivia that made up the day-to-day relationships of his two central figures, is what largely accounts for the dramatic success of his book.

And where is the boundary between history and sociology in all that? The role and treatment of events in Stern's study provides the answer. The book is in fact organised rather obviously in terms of events – thus mirroring of course the way in which most of us organise the world. Successive chapters bring the Bismarck-Bleichröder relationship to the point of successive great events: the war with Denmark, the war with Austria, the war with France, The Congress of Berlin, the dismissal of Bismarck and so forth. And the point of this form of presentation is quite clear. The great events mark decisive conjunctions of action and structure; they are transparent moments of structuring at which human agency encounters social possibility and can be seen most clearly as simultaneously determined and determining. Time after time the analysis of the event reveals the meaning and interweaving of the general and the particular, of interests, states, cultures, rules and structured opportunity with individual understandings, capacities, motivations and more or less considered and deliberate action. *Gold and Iron* is a great work of history because it is a work that unmasks the appalling ironies of individual action in society. Thus, the peak of Bleichröder's success was his ennoblement as a Prussian baron, the first Jew of direct descent to achieve such standing. Yet (1980:168):

> He owed his unique position to the threatened plight of his fellow aristocrats. It was general knowledge at the time ... that Bleichröder and Hansemann were ennobled because they had undertaken to salvage the fortunes of Prussian Junkers who had been caught in the collapse of Dr. Strousberg's railway project in Rumania. Bleichröder worked hard indeed to extricate Prussian nobility from the unanticipated consequences of their capitalist appetites. Certainly that was the main reason for William's willingness to suspend ancient prejudice. But between being formally admitted to court society and being an accepted part of it, there was world of anguished difference.

And again (1980:107–8):

> Bleichröder's rise after 1866 illustrates dramatically the interlocking nature of Germany's social order. It was Bleichröder's simultaneous success in different realms – in the banking world, in Bismarck's world, in the world of European finance and of the Rothschilds, in the tightly ordered world of the Prussian court – that gave him the pre-eminence. He helped to bring these worlds closer together, and his success in one realm reinforced his claim in another. But for Bleichröder, as for European financiers generally,

wealth was not enough: in a traditional-hierarchical society, it was status and public acceptance that mattered. Bleichröder's spreading importance symbolized the triumph of capitalism, and yet Bleichröder's story also demonstrates the limits and travails entailed in that triumph.

The terms of analysis in such passages explode any suggestion that the uniqueness of events places them beyond the grasp of a generalising social analysis. On the contrary it is precisely through the unravelling of the uniqueness of events that larger resonances are achieved without vulgarising or losing contact with the experienced lives of the protagonists. It is difficult to think of any other object of study which would be so conducive to this integration of stories about individuals and the analysis of social structure. The integration occurs in the moment of structuring and it is in just that moment that the uniqueness of an event is caught.

Insofar, then, as sociology is concerned with the process of structuring as its primary problematic the (detailed, concrete, unique) nature of events makes them both available and necessary objects of sociological investigation. The adequate 'unpacking' of an event requires meticulous attention to both action and structure and, if the connection between them is to be seized, precludes a one-sided assertion of the predominance of either. The more extensive the event one chooses to examine the more evident the need for two-sidedness is; it is much more evident in studies of events such as the rise of capitalism than in studies of events such as the Austro-Prussian war. But there is no mysterious cut-off point at which events become so unique, detailed or concrete that they either lose their two-sidedness or elude the explanatory powers of the historical sociologist. Nor, in practice is there any way in which the disciplines of history and sociology can be sensibly differentiated in terms of the scale of the events with which they choose to deal. Some sociologists find worthwhile work in the ethnography of a cock-fight (Geertz, 1971): others in theorising the whole experience of Islamic society (Gellner, 1981). Some historians address themselves powerfully to the assassination of Henri IV (Mousnier, 1964), others to the long term 'waning' of the Mediterranean world (Braudel, 1973). What is perhaps more important, in terms of the possibility of historical sociology, is the extent to which, again in practice whatever may be said in principle, historians and sociologists seem to converge on a shared mode of explanation when dealing with events. In the rest of this chapter I shall explore that practical denouement; it suggests that the drama of the wedge driven between the disciplines by events should be read as something of a farce.

Revolutionary events: towards a common practice

Revolutions, riots, rebellions and protests have always been a slightly difficult subject-matter for sociologists precisely because of their event-like qualities. The irreducible specificity of incident they involve, the gross cultural and institutional differences between the settings in which revolutionary events occur have seemed to many writers to place adequate explanation of revolutions beyond the reach of strictly sociological work; there is a stock examination question which holds that 'there is no sociology of revolution, only the history of revolutions', and the thesis it asserts has been a commonplace of the literature for years. Similar criticisms are voiced by certain Marxists for whom the inability of sociology to achieve an explanation of revolution is central to a much larger critique of the discipline. Thus Blackburn (1969) points to the failure of some well known sociological accounts of revolution to apprehend the idea of contradiction or to find room for the conscious and deliberate element in revolutionary events, and he sees this failure as bound up with the more general 'drift of much bourgeois social theory ... to undermine the idea that men can ever transform society.' More generally, it has been held that while sociologists can of course talk not wholly meaninglessly about *categories* of events – in this context, say peasant wars or coups d'état or bourgeois revolutions – their very ability to talk in such terms, the language talking in such terms forces them to use, precludes their having anything of value to contribute to an understanding of any particular event within the category. And conversely, sociological theorists, insisting on the superior significance of questions couched in terms of categories of events, have deplored the naive empiricism which, they claim, has led historians to insist on the non-comparability of events formally grouped within given categories, say the category of revolution. So it is worth looking in a little detail at some work on both sides of this supposed divide to see just how far the claimed differences are indeed entailed by the objects of study (categories of events as distinct from particular events), or by incompatible types of explanation, and how far they are merely artefacts of a disciplinary self-interest, or myopia, which has encouraged some historians and some sociologists to insist inappropriately on the exclusive competence of their own particular trade.

As a sample of relevant historical work I shall consider all the articles on social and political protest which appeared in 25 consecutive issues of a single historical journal, *Past & Present*, between 1966 and 1973. There were 43 such articles and although they ranged over many cultures, periods and types of conflict they did display a certain coherence of interest. They were plainly tied to a cluster of debates among historians occurring at the time both in *Past & Present* and in a wider literature. To see just what arguments the authors of the articles were trying to advance or rebut called for a number of excursions into this surrounding literature and in particular into an extensive controversy over the nature of peasant revolts, tied particularly to studies of the peasant 'furies' of the 17th century, in which the work of Professors Mandrou, Mousnier and Porchnev provided a central point of reference. Sociological work on revolution and protest has never displayed quite this concentration and continuity of interest so my discussion of what sociologists have done about revolutionary events is drawn less systematically from a reading of the most enthusiastically acclaimed books published in the field between 1970 and 1979 –from Gurr's *Why Men Rebel* (1970), greeted by Coser as 'the most important book that has been published on social violence in a good number of years', to Skocpol's *States and Social Revolutions* (1979), hailed by Dunn as 'simply the best piece of political sociology I have ever read.' What I want to suggest is that, looking at these two bodies of literature one cannot but be impressed by a remarkable intellectual convergence between them – a convergence dictated, so far as I can see, by a cumulative understanding on both sides as to just what would be involved in providing an adequate explanation of the object to be explained – revolutionary events.

In a much-discussed paper, 'Ideal Types and Historical Explanation', J. W. N. Watkins (1953) has argued that there are three alternative ways in which historians can construct explanations: colligation, explanation in detail and explanation in principle. My 43 articles on protest provide examples of each of these procedures as does the work of Professor Mousnier. Colligation involves 'explaining an event by tracing its intrinsic relations to other events and locating it in its historical context.' The difficulty here of course is to reach agreement on what is meant by the term intrinsic. But what is aimed at would take the form of a 'significant narrative', satisfying in terms of canons of narrative style on the one hand and of an implicit consonance on the other with the reader's taken-for-granted sense of how the world works. It would seem to be what Oakeshott (1933) had in mind when he ruled that: 'The relation between events is always other events, and it is established in history by a full relation *of* the events.' It is the traditional mode of historical writing and it depends for its success on a substantial lack of dissent both as to what happened in the past and as to the meaning of what happened. Mousnier's treatment of the revolt of the Cossack Stenka Razin in 1667 is a good example of this sort of historical work (1971:153–232). After some discussion of the endemic state of revolt and banditry among the Cossacks faced with an expanding Russian state, famine, epidemics, loss of access to the Black Sea and the Caspian and more or less continuous piracy and looting Razin appears on the scene (1971:219):

In 1667 he got together some new Cossacks, runaway peasants, escaped serfs, some craftsmen and petty merchants and marched on Azov and the Black Sea. He was driven off by the Turks. He then went back up the Don and established himself in the marshes at the elbow of this river, not far from the Volga. From this base he attacked all the ships sailing up or down the Volga, the tsar's treasure barge, the patriarch's own ship, the corn barges of the rich Moscow merchant Shorin ... Then in June, 1667, he appeared before Astrakhan ... At the beginning of 1668 he ... In September, 1669 (he) reappeared on the Don after various adventures ... During the winter of 1669–1670 partisans flocked to his camp ... He prepared a fresh campaign, that of 1670, which unleashed the great peasant revolt.

And so on. The story is action-packed and meaning and causality appear to inhere in the 'simple' presentation of the action. In a chaotic and oppressive world Razin's protest was initially but one among many. He succeeded because he succeeded; each victory brought him new followers and an enhanced aura of success. And he failed because he failed; each defeat lost him support and diminished his reputation. Event led to event up to the vast insurrection of the Volga peasants in the autumn of 1670 and then from Razin's first defeat when he first met a large and properly trained army to his capture, 'a half-crazy bandit' on an island in the Don, and execution in June 1671. The form of presentation and explanation is particularly effective in this instance because the point Mousnier wishes to make is that the rebellion really had no point. The message of the tale is that Razin provided a focus for a peasant 'fury', violent, superstitious and ineffectual. Thus (1971:229): 'After Stenka Razin's revolt the former state of affairs was restored. This revolt changed nothing.' The blunt conclusion seems to follow unavoidably from the historian's artless narrative.

Had we no other histories of 17th-century Russia and no other treatments of the revolt of Stenka Razin Mousnier's colligation might have worked very well. It is not so much that the basic story can be told differently, although it can, as that the events can be assigned quite different causes and significance. For example the theme of class war, of feudal reaction in the making of the Russian state and of class differentiation among the Cossacks, one issue among many for Mousnier, can be given central explanatory importance. And if it is, the whole episode looks very different – as does the larger meaning of the episode for our understanding of peasant protest. And at this sort of point the explanatory power of colligation collapses. Its success as explanation depends wholly on a closed consensus of meaning between historians and their audience. Once that is challenged even the most traditional historian tends to seek other strategies of explanation. Of course, such historians will put up a fight. They will tend to cling to colligation. Their first response to doubt or disagreement will probably be to try to do that sort of work better. To tell an even more detailed, self-contained, unselfconscious and supposedly self-explanatory story. But sooner or later they will begin to concede that colligation alone cannot yield a sufficient explanation of past events. They will begin to smuggle other types of explanation into their work. Indeed, in practice, most convincing and respected historical writing combines different types of strategy of explanation from the outset. Much of the cogency of Mousnier's treatment of the pointless fury of the revolt of Stenka Razin derives from a general model, half explicit and half implicit in his work as a whole, of peasant protest in general as a matter of pointless furies – in other words from a largely concealed explanation in principle. And that capacity to combine in practice strategies of explanation held to be alternative in principle seems to be an important key to the success of much of the best historical writing.

Explanation in principle is held to stand at the opposite end of a continuum of possible strategies from colligation and involves treating events as though they were instances of 'pure', theoretically derived, types of events governed by strong internal logical necessities. Explanation in this procedure consists in revealing the 'illogicalities' of actual events or situations and treating them as conditions or causes of the actual outcomes insofar as these depart from those anticipated by the type case. More generally, as Weber put it (1949:74), explanation in principle is a matter of making plain 'the relationship between the logical structure of a conceptual system ... and what is immediately given in empirical reality.' The conceptual system may be more or less formally defined and explicitly differentiated from one's discussion of 'empirical reality' – once again, historical practice tends to be less tidy than the philosophers of history would have it. And the model one uses may be more or less generalised: Gurr, for example (1970), attempts to account for all rebellion in terms of a model of the dynamics of relative deprivation, whereas Skocpol

(1979) seeks only to account for the French, Russian and Chinese revolutions in terms of a relatively specific conception of the economic and international crises of peasant societies, and Lefebvre (1947) aimed to explain only the French revolution by reference to a highly specific model of differential class responses to economic pressure within a narrowly defined type of socio-political system. It is important to stress that all these exercises are nevertheless attempts at explanation in principle and that the degree of abstraction or generalisation involved in different versions of the strategy does *not* alter in any fundamental way the type of explanation that is being attempted – although it will certainly alter the capacity of different versions of the strategy to grip particular instances of the universe of 'immediately given' phenomena which is, as it were, 'up for explanation'. Whatever level of generality is invoked the explanatory design is the same: 'empirical reality' is to be accounted for by way of a demonstration of some relationship, of fit or deviation, between the chronological order of events in the 'immediately given' historical world and a conception of logical or meaningful relationships within a formal model of social process in the mind of the historian.

One of the best known examples of an explanation in principle in modern historical writing is the explanation of what happened in France at the end of the 18th century as a bourgeois revolution. By the hundred and fiftieth anniversary of the storming of the Bastille substantial agreement seemed to have been reached – and not just among Marxists – that the French revolution was to be explained as a triumphant bourgeois overthrow of feudal power. The course of events, the contexts of action, the observed and reported relationships of actors to one another all semed to make sense in terms of a conception of bourgeois revolution with almost uncanny precision. Admittedly, there were in fact several different models of what bourgeois revolutions were and of how they happened. Some authorities, such as Soboul (1962), envisaged a strict unfolding of the 'contradiction between the relations of production and the character of productive forces'; others, such as Lefebvre (1954), saw the revolution as the qualitative outcome of a long quantitative 'social and economic evolution which has made the bourgeoisie the mistress of the world'; yet others, such as Forster (1960) and Dovier (1964), saw it in terms of a much shorter-run process, a response to a specific 'seigneurial reaction', a tightening of feudal exploitation and a closing-off of channels of upward social mobility, in the 18th century. But one way or another the task of explaining the French revolution seemed to have been firmly bound to the question of the nature of bourgeois revolution as a type of social action. As late as 1962 Cobban could assert that 'historians are generally agreed that the revolution was a bourgeois revolution' (1964), that, as Soboul had put it ten years earlier (1953), 'the essential cause of the revolution was the power of a bourgeoisie arrived at its maturity and confronted by a decadent aristocracy holding tenaciously to its privileges.' It seemed that it only remained to fill in the details.

In fact, however, Cobban's remark was mischievous. The lectures in which it was made were themselves a major onslaught on the credibility of the received consensus about the French revolution. Ten years later the consensus had dissolved and it was possible for Colin Lucas, reviewing what had happened in a useful essay in *Past & Present*, 'Nobles, Bourgeois and the Origins of the French Revolution', to look back to what already seemed a remote period, 'once upon a time,' when 'the historians of the French revolution laboured fraternally in the vineyards of the past ... united in simple yet satisfying beliefs', and to contrast it with a present in which research had 'brought into question the whole scheme of the revolution as the product of a conflict between nobles and bourgeois' (1973:24). But it was not just empirical research that had done the damage. When an explanation in principle fails it is likely to do so on two counts. It will be found conceptually as well as empirically defective. The empirical draughts in the system will be traced to conceptual cracks in its structure; just as those draughts in turn will themselves open up new cracks. Similarly any repair work attempted by those who remain attached to the system and prefer not to move house will have to be of two kinds: the conceptual design of the explanation must be refined, and new empirical evidence must be absorbed. As Lucas makes clear this is just how the debate on the explanation of the French revolution proceeded.

Cobban himself (1964) had been mainly concerned to expose what he saw as a conceptual flaw in the old explanation – although he did so largely by invoking awkward empirical evidence. He challenged the equation, necessary in at least the simpler forms of the explanation of the French revolution as a bourgeois revolution, between the plainly bourgeois nature of the protagonists in many crucial revolutionary events and the forces of advancing capitalism. Rather, he suggested, these bourgeois persons might best be identified as members of a declining group of venal office holders, petty merchants and small landowners who were protesting not for capitalism but actually *against* its encroachments on their accustomed status, privileges and income. In other words the analytical categories of the model were too clumsy to handle the explanatory task at issue. Once the concept of the bourgeoisie was separated from that of capitalism a quite different, but no less principled, explanation of the French revolution became possible, one that absorbed the relevant evidence much more satisfactorily (1964:172):

> I have tried to show that the social developments of the revolution are capable of a very different and even an entirely contrary interpretation, that it was not wholly a revolution for, but largely one against, the penetration of an embryo capitalism into French society. Considered as such it largely achieved its ends ... The misunderstanding was facilitated by the ambiguities implicit in the idea of the bourgeoisie. The bourgeois of the theory are a class of capitalists, industrial entrepreneurs and financiers of big business; those of the French Revolution were landowners, *rentiers* and officials, including in their fish-pond a few big fish, many of moderate size and a host of minnows, who all knew that they swam in the same element, and that without the pervasive influence of social hierarchy and the maintenance of individual and family property rights against any interference by the state, their way of life, confined, unchanging, conservative, repetitive, would come to an end. The revolution was theirs, and for them at least it was a wholly successful revolution.

Such reinterpretations opened up fundamental questions about just who the bourgeoisie of the French revolution were and whether they were at all the sort of people who could have enacted the sort of bourgeois revolution which their actions were held, in principle, to have achieved. And if the bourgeois were not capitalist how feudal were the nobility? Into that gap poured a deluge of further doubts, an enormous quantity of meticulous empirical work on French social structure and relationships and also a great deal of increasingly sophisticated theoretical re-construction. The recent history of the French revolution is not just the history of an explanation in principle collapsing in the face of a mass of difficult evidence and awkward questions. It is equally clearly a history of very determined efforts to make sense of such evidence and answer such questions on the basis of alternative, revised, subtler and more carefully formulated explanations in principle. What emerges most clearly from the review of the debate by Lucas is that the overall movement of the discussion has not been towards meaninglessness, or even towards a rediscovery of the charms of colligation, but towards the elaboration and critical appraisal of new and competing explanations in principle.

Three features of this movement demand attention here: the refinement of categories; the balancing of explanatory scope and empirical detail; and a growing readiness to take the subjective meanings of the past seriously. The first two of these are, not surprisingly, closely related. The formulation of explanatory models using more sharply defined and differentiated categories of social analysis has been bound up with a wish to accommodate important variations in social relationships as demonstrated by empirical research without being swept away by the tide of detail – to acknowledge the separability of class and status in a society of estates, for example, which made it possible in pre-revolutionary France for capitalism to come to the countryside 'in a feudal mask' (to use Barrington Moore's phrase), or more generally for the effective alignment of interest to be as Lucas puts it: 'not the distinction between the privileged and the Third Estate, (but rather) between those for whom manual labour provided their livelihood and those for whom it did not' (1973:93), without being engulfed in and baffled by the minutiae of successive studies of every Department, town and village. So today we find that explanations in principle of the French revolution abound, but that they employ categories of analysis which discriminate among the elements and interests, conditions and relationships of French society far more finely and far more effectively than the old antithesis of nobles and bourgeois was ever able to do. And hand in hand with that development has necessarily gone some readiness to sacrifice the breadth of reference of the old model of bourgeois revolution in order to come to terms with what might be called the *specific diversity* of the revolution in France. Explanation in principle has to refer events to a general conception of a social process. But such conceptions must both order and respect the diversity of what is 'immediately given in empirical reality', if they are to sustain satisfying explanations. In the face of debate what should ensue therefore, and what has ensued in the debate on the French revolution, is a balancing and accommodation of theory and evidence by way of models which are at once more complex in their conceptual structure and more specific in their empirical reference. Lucas traces the discrediting of the 'bourgeois-versus-nobles' explanation of the French revolution, but his review also indicates the possible emergence of several alternative explanations in principle and the probable special cogency of one of them which, eight years later, does indeed seem to have gained very wide acceptance. At this stage in the, no doubt, continuing debate the old model of a direct bourgeois onslaught on feudalism has been widely replaced not by a celebration of detail and anecdote but by a much more complicated (but equally principled) sense of the nature of both political revolution and long-term historical change in which the opening-up of opportunities for capitalism in France after 1789 is seen as an ironic and unintended outcome of a distinct type of social crisis in which peasants and governments matter at least as much as nobles and bourgeois, in which relationships between such groups are typically ambiguous and in which effects are typically produced indirectly. More of that shortly. For the moment what is important is that explanation in principle can survive the onslaught of facts by this sort of modification.

The third feature of the debate which I want to stress is the shift of attention towards greater interest in the subjective worlds of those involved in the revolution. Plainly, one strand of Cobban's critique of Soboul was already that the term bourgeois imposed modern meanings on past actors in a quite unwarranted way. As the debate continued it became increasingly clear that historians had to know what the world of 1789 meant to those who lived in it – that, for example, a crucial part of any answer to the question whether the attack on seigneurial dues and privileges was a bourgeois move against feudalism had to involve knowing not only who the protagonists were but what seigneurial dues and privileges meant to them as distinct from their meaning, in principle, to us. Similarly, the re-interpretation proposed by Lucas rests firmly on the claim that subjectively status considerations rather than class interests mediated the relations of nobles and bourgeoisie. And in general it has come to be agreed that any explanation in principle that involves conceptions of structured social relationships has to be grounded empirically in knowledge of what different structural locations and relations actually meant to those assigned to them. This development marks not only a major move towards the third type of explanation discussed by Watkins, explanation in detail, but also in my view a major move towards common ground with contemporary sociology – at least in the study of revolutionary events. In fact as we shall see most practical explanation in both history and sociology tends to be a tightly constructed melange of explanation in principle and explanation in detail with a more or less generous measure of colligation stirred in as well.

Watkins (1953) sees explanation in principle, the attempt to clarify events by locating them in terms of the structure of an abstract model of the logic of events, as bound to resort in the face of controversy to explanation in detail. I think he is right about that (certainly, the debate on the French revolution suggests that he is), just as he is also right to concede that explanations in detail tend, when challenged, to be defended by more or less explicit appeals to explanations in principle. In other words the two strategies of explanation appear to need each other. But I also think that Watkins' own conception of what an explanation in detail is, is needlessly narrow. He defines explanation in detail as a matter of accounting for an event or situation by way of a confrontation between the logic of a model and observation of 'the specific dispositions, beliefs and relationships of actual people' (1953:37). A lot depends here on what one means by the term specific and on how one claims to validate the reliability of observations of dispositions, beliefs and relationships. But the narrowing in Watkins's analysis occurs not so much in his definition of explanation in detail as in his subsequent discussion which virtually eliminates relationships from consideration and absorbs beliefs and dispositions into a composite category which he calls personality: and which he holds to be immune, in principle, from explanations in principle. Although this may have been a necessary move in terms of Watkins's ulterior purpose of defending methodological individualism against sociology it is hard to see any other justification for it. And it certainly seems to misrepresent what historians appear actually to do. For most commonly in actual historical debates it is relationships (understood as social constructs) and *typical* rather than specific dispositions and beliefs, let alone personality, that have proved to be the type of detail to which explanatory arguments have turned. What we certainly do not find is any sort of widespread retreat to explanation in terms of the specific beliefs and dispositions of individual persons as though these were some sort of given, fundamental and pre-social reality. I shall come back to the question of whether personality has to be regarded as beyond the scope of sociological explanation in the next two chapters. What matters for the moment is simply that in the distinctive amalgamation of explanation in principle and explanation in detail which I would call practical historical explanation the kind of detail that is used to ground, confront and sustain or modify explanations in principle is a matter of relationships (of how, say, the bourgeoisie and nobility interacted with one another) and of the typical dispositions of categories of persons (say, respectable Frenchmen living in towns, the poverty-stricken *hobereaux*, the professional groups, and so forth). The personalities of actual persons may contribute much to the story but rarely provide the decisive explanatory detail.

Two articles in *Past & Present* by M. E. James may serve to illustrate the mode of work, practical historical explanation, which, rather than the individualistic form of explanation in detail advocated by Watkins, seems to me to characterise contemporary historical writing. These two articles (James 1970 and 1973), both concerned with rebellions in 16th-century England, seem at first sight to come nearer to attempting explanation in terms of the dispositions and beliefs of particular individuals than any others in my *Past & Present* sample: certainly they are both full of matter describing the actions, inclinations, motives and understandings of individual persons. Yet in both cases James makes it quite clear that an explanation in terms of that sort of detail is just what he would not regard as adequate. Thus, the problem of the Lincolnshire Rebellion of 1536 is not just that of why Lord Hussey, Bishop Mackerell and the rest joined a host of commoners in armed uprising. The issue is not just to explain how the event happened but to make clear *what sort of event it was* and thence its meaning as a moment in a larger process of historical change. And it is precisely these additional tasks, tasks which historians routinely treat as part of their job, which make the individualistic form of explanation in detail inadequate. A central puzzle of the Lincolnshire rising, James suggests, is the way in which the rebels insisted throughout on their own loyalty and obedience to the king; what then, 'was the meaning ... of a rebellion whose participants took such a curious stance?' (1970:6) The answer is found not in the personalities of the rebels but in the nature of the problem of dissent in the Tudor state. The delusions of the rebels are evidence not of their disordered brains but of a peculiar structural dilemma of the transition from feudal politics to absolute monarchy, the problem of 'how dissidence might be expressed within a context of obedience, parliament having still not established itself as an effective and sufficient vehicle' (1970:31). The event reveals the conjunction of action and structure within the larger historical process. That is the reality it contains that makes it worth explaining. And the explanation turns *in equal measure* on identification of the relationships and dispositions of categories of participants, narration of the enactment of those relationships and dispositions by particular persons, and a coherent theorisation of the process of structural change within which action had meaning. Explanation in detail, colligation and explanation in principle are all in play here and the success of the article is largely a result of the way the author uses the strengths of each to make good the weaknesses of the others.

The power of this practical conjunction of theoretically distinct modes of explanation can be seen even more clearly in the progress of debates between historians. An article by J.H. Salmon, 'Venal Office and Popular Sedition in France' (1967) (*Past & Present*, 37), is particularly interesting here because it traces a sustained argument about the proper interpretation of a particular set of illegal outbursts; it has the further advantage of bringing us back to the work of Professor Mousnier. The explanation of the violent peasant risings which occurred throughout France in the 1630s and 1640s was for a long time treated as no more than a narrative problem; it was, as it were, in the nature of the rural poor to perpetrate outrages; all the historian had to do was to tell the dreadful story. Then, in 1937, Georges Pagès, ended the happy days of colligation by proposing a systematic relationship between the peasant furies and the extension of royal fiscal administration to provincial France (1937:95). This idea was taken up vigorously by Pagès's pupil Mousnier as the basis of an explanation in detail (in my sense of that term, not that of Watkins) governing a massive study of venal office first published in 1945. Mousnier (1945) argued that attempts by the state to overcome the system of private property in office produced by venality by introducing direct administration created a situation in which venal office-holders found common cause with the peasants in resisting the state and that it was specifically on the basis of this unaccustomed leadership that the peasant furies exploded when and where they did. It was a good argument and impressively documented. Unhappily it was faced only a few years later with a quite different interpretation rooted in an exceptionally coherent explanation in principle. In 1948 the Russian historian Boris Porchnev published a thoroughly scholarly Marxist analysis of the very same movements examined by Mousnier. Porchnev (1963) saw the decisive movement of French history in the 17th century in terms of the emergence of bourgeois or proto-bourgeois interests within the shell of a feudal society with a consequent intensification of the exploitation of the peasantry. In this situation the peasants responded with a revolutionism which was at once spontaneous and indiscriminate in attacking feudal and bourgeois power alike. The furies are to be understood as a class war of the peasants against an unnatural alliance of feudal and bourgeois interests whose own natural antagonisms have been held in check precisely by a collusion in mutual exploitation of the peasantry.

So what 'really happened' in Dijon in 1630? Or in Périgord in 1637? Was it an alliance of feudatories and peasants against a bourgeois state? Or a premature revolution of peasants against an alliance of feudal and bourgeois exploiters? It naturally became imperative to study Dijon and Périgord and all the other sites of revolutionary events in this period even more closely. And the pupils of both Mousnier and Porchnev found themselves assigned to just that task. However, the important thing that happened in this debate was not the intensification of minute empirical research. It was the attempt by Mousnier and his pupils to incorporate their explanation in detail into the framework of a non-Marxist explanation in principle. And it was the attempt of Marxist historians after Porchnev to build into Porchnev's model an explanation in detail which would both accommodate awkward empirical details and make the explanation as a whole adequate on the level of meaning: to build bridges between the categories of the model and the categories of understanding of 17th-century France. As the debate proceeded the congruity of the styles of explanation on either side became steadily more apparent. Neither side has tried to settle the dispute on the basis of claims about the peculiar dispositions, beliefs or personalities of particular persons: nor in terms of the necessarily compelling logic of a theory of history. Both sides have sought instead to explain the events in question in terms of an increasingly close-knit package of theory and evidence, theorising social process and adducing evidence about the typical dispositions of typical actors in typical relationships, and in a more or less flexible way inviting theory and evidence to interrogate one another. On both sides there had been a progressive re-casting of the conceptual scheme in order to accommodate new evidence, especially evidence bearing on the problem of subjective meaning; but at the same time we can trace a progressive scepticism in the appraisal of evidence as the modified conceptual schemes have been judged on each side to be sounder, subtler, more satisfactory bases of explanation. Both the tendentiousness of conceptual schemes and the unreliability of facts have been discovered as the interrogation proceeded.

By 1960 it was possible for Mandrou (1965) to identify considerable common ground between the revised positions of Mousnier and Porchnev, a convergence confirmed by the Soviet historian A. D. Lublinskaya in 1966 (Salmon, 1967:31). And where differences remained – which was above all in what Salmon (1967:30) calls the 'broad sociological interpretations' which provided their 'highly generalized explanations of the last centuries of the ancient régime' – they persisted because both schools were committed to the same overall *mode* of explanation; one in which the *relationship* between evidence and a general model of historical process was all important. Thus, while Porchnev sought empirically to 'take all facets of the problem, including Mousnier's work, into consideration' (1967:32), Mousnier was increasingly concerned to elaborate a theoretical framework of comparable scope to Marxism to sustain his initially fairly un-selfconscious reading of the events of the 1630s. His *Peasant Uprisings*, first published in 1967, was a major attempt to develop a general model of pre-modern societies as 'societies of orders' (as distinct from societies of classes), based on a system of estates which, while strongly resistant to revolution as a result of the way in which the consciousness of estates legitimated hierarchy, were conversely especially prone to revolts as a means chosen in the absence of institutional links between estates to ameliorate the conditions of life of the lower estates. A specific feature of such societies (echoing the argument of his earlier studies) was held to be the attempt of central government to extend its own power by side-stepping the system of estates and imposing its own universalistic controls and exactions – an attempt which typically precipitated what in a society of classes would be highly improbable alliances between diverse groups in the social hierarchy in rebellious resistance to the state. An important merit of this piece of theorisation was held to be that, unlike class theory, it permitted an explanation adequate on the level of meaning of revolutionary events in pre-modern societies. Ironically, a major criticism of *Peasant Uprisings* (advanced for example by Gately, Moote and Wills (1971), in their article on 'Seventeenth Century Peasant "Furies"' in *Past & Present*) has been that while Mousnier's categories of analysis are indeed well grounded in the actual world of 17th-century France they are no more adequate than the categories of class analysis when it comes to explaining events, as Mousnier tried to do, in the very different worlds of Russia and China in the same period.

Mousnier himself has moved further towards elaborating a systematic explanation in principle as well as encouraging a steadily larger body of empirical research on particular 17th-century rebellions. His next major book, *Social Hierarchies* (1973), was in every formal sense immediately recognisable as a work of sociology, setting out a general theory of the forms and causes of stratification, specifying and filling out the model of a society of orders and aiming to demonstrate again, mainly with reference to France, Russia and China, the superior cogency of that model as a basis for explanations in principle – a cogency held to derive from the surer grounding of the model in the detailed meanings and relationships of actual historical worlds. Although written only at the end of a long series of substantive studies *Social Hierarchies* plainly has to be regarded as integral and in some senses as prior to Mousnier's work as a whole. In effect it brings into the open an element of his strategy of explanation which had been essential but half-submerged in each of his earlier attempts to account for revolutionary events. Those explanations had always presumed a theory of inequality. Defending them in the face of controversy had required both a firmer grasp of detail and a progressively more explicit and elaborate formulation of theory. And so far as I can see this type of movement, from explanation in principle towards a mode of practical historical explanation which is effectively a marriage of the two, is typical of what happens in the course of arguments between contemporary historians. And it seems to me that in this marriage, which is of course a moving relationship not a static condition, practical historical explanation – the sort of thing historians come to when they are put on the spot – does no more than recognise the force of what Edward Thompson (1978:231) has called 'historical logic'.

By 'historical logic' I mean a ... method of enquiry appropriate to historical materials, designed as far as possible to test hypotheses as to structure, causation, etc., and to eliminate self-confirming procedures ('instances', 'illustrations'). The disciplined historical discourse of ... proof consists in a dialogue between concept and evidence, a dialogue conducted by successive hypotheses, on the one hand, and empirical research on the other. The interrogator is historical logic; the interrogative a hypothesis (for example, as to the way different phenomena acted upon each other); the respondent is the evidence, with its determinate properties. And it is ... this logic which constitutes the discipline's ultimate court of appeal; *not*, please note, 'the evidence ... but the evidence interrogated thus.'

Plainly these explanations have some heuristic value. They point to certain types of relationship and interaction for which one would be well-advised to look in trying to explain any 'given act of political violence'. And since an explanation is in the end no more than that which satisfies the curiosity one cannot rule out the possibility that some enquirers will be satisfied with an account of, say, the 'general crisis' of the 17th century or the revolutions of 1848 that goes no further than to confirm the presence in those settings of appropriate measures of relative deprivation, loyalty of coercive forces and so forth. But the historical sociologist, that is to say an enquirer who sees the problem of structuring as the central problem of social analysis and who accepts that structuring must be explained in concrete historical as well as in abstract sociological terms will quite quickly be left in the lurch by the sort of theory advanced in *Why Men Rebel* (Gurr, 1970). How is the gap to be filled?

In practice sociologists have moved towards a mode of explanation strikingly similar to practical historical explanation. The movement has been halting and often reluctant but nevertheless definite. Thus, most sociological attempts at an explanation of revolution in general adopt a form of analysis that is, ambiguously, at once logical *and* chronological. The ambiguity is itself an important step forward. The ten stage 'theory of revolutionary behaviour' proposed by Schwartz (1970), or the more sophisticated seven stage model proposed by Smelser (1963b) are evidently attempts to provide, at one and the same time, statements of the necessary conditions for revolution and of their probable historical phasing. Smelser's *Theory of Collective Behaviour* is particularly interesting in this respect because the 'value-added' logic of explanation he borrows from economics in fact can only make sense as a chronology. Iron ore cannot have the value of steel until after a complex processing – steel cannot have the value of an automobile *before* the process of manufacturing has occurred. If 'value-added' is anything more than a metaphor for Smelser formal sociology has here turned into a theory of historical sequence. Widely disparaged by historians, Smelser's theorisation of revolution is nevertheless a thoroughly historical, albeit highly generalised, attempt to treat events as a working out of structural potentialities. On the other hand, Smelser's analysis gains in concreteness only at the price of losing in generality of coverage; he can explain revolutions only by not simultaneously explaining other kinds of political violence – to which, presumably, other value-added logics (and chronologies) apply. And just as Smelser's highly generalised theory of revolution is only one among a number of ways in which revolution could be explained under the umbrella of Gurr's still more general explanation of political violence, so it is possible for many explanations of particular types of revolution and revolutionary event to flourish within the framework provided by Smelser. There is, in other words a ladder of possible modes of explanation from the very concrete to the very abstract and the problem of historical sociology is not to decide which is right – it makes no sense to proclaim one rung on a ladder more 'correct' than the others – but to find that mid-point from which the very concrete and the very abstract can most easily be reached. It is not clear to me how one could discover that point in principle. But in practice it is likely to be found through a *style* of work which contrives to perch on several different rungs simultaneously – for sociologists no less than for historians. Recent studies suggest at least three different ways in which that feat of acrobatics can be accomplished.

Eric Wolf's *Peasant Wars of the Twentieth Century* (1971) is the most conventional – though not the least persuasive for that. To begin with he drastically limits the range of events about which he wishes to generalise – to a single type of event, rebellions, in which the prime mover is a single type of agent, peasants, in a single type of setting, agrarian societies contaminated by the encroachment of capitalist industrialism. He proceeds by way of a colligation of the histories of six such events. But in fact his narrative is very carefully organised to direct attention to both common and divergent general features of the six cases; to both the historically insurmountable differences of each of the events and the considerable degree to which each can be understood as an instance of a single type of event occurring within a single type of historical milieu. At least in form the similarity between Wolf's *Peasant Wars* and Mousnier's *Peasant Uprisings* is very striking in this respect. In both cases the explanatory argument advances on two levels. The explanation of how the events happened (a) is in the stories of the events, but the design of the stories collectively and cumulatively permits (b) a larger explanation of the meaning of that type of event in a context of more general historical predicaments and processes. (a) provides the basis for (b), just as (b) makes sense of (a) and binds the whole into a larger explanatory exercise. The two levels of analysis are evident in Wolf's study in the two quite different types of conclusion at which he is able to arrive. On the one hand, for example (1971:292), 'it is the very attempt of the middle peasant to remain traditional which makes him revolutionary'. On the other hand (on level (b) as it were), 'the peasant is an agent of forces larger than himself, forces produced by a disordered present' (1971:301). Or again (1971:301), 'the peasants rise to redress wrong; but the inequities against which they rebel are but, in turn, parochial manifestations of great social dislocations ... rebellion issues easily into revolution, massive movements to transform the social structure as a whole ... and when the war is over, society will have changed and the peasantry with it.'

So once again we must ask, where is the difference from sociology? Sociologists have persistently chosen to write about and claimed to explain revolutionary events. Is their logic or discourse of proof in any way different from that of the historian? Again, what matters is not so much the explanatory pretensions and ideologies from which they start out as the practical modes of explanation to which they turn when their initial claims are challenged. The issue of the relationship of history and sociology should be resolved, I am arguing, not on the basis of the legislative proposals and fiats of philosophers of history or meta-sociological theorists, but in the light of what working sociologists and historians actually do when they want to explain something – say, revolutionary events.

The methodological compulsions of sociologists incline them to begin with explanation in principle almost as fastidiously as historians tend to begin with colligation. An obvious recent example to work on revolutionary events is T. R. Gurr's *Why Men Rebel*. Quite deliberately Gurr (1970: 357) decided to sacrifice 'explanation of any given act of political violence' to the requirements of 'logical coherence, parsimony and elegance' in the formulation of an integrated system of general and abstract propositions about the causes of political violence as a whole. In effect, he was hoping to identify something like the Highest Common Factor of available knowledge of political violence in general. Whether the particular theory he elaborates achieves that aim or not he is certainly right to claim that our knowledge at that level of generality is severely limited and necessarily highly abstract. Any such theorisation in other words would have to be a statement of principles very remote from actual events. So the issue that arises for historical sociology is to decide how far such statements of principle enhance or advance the under-standing of particular processes of social structuring – in this instance as crystallised in given acts of political violence.

The heart of Gurr's model of political violence is the idea of relative deprivation. And he makes it quite clear at the outset that for the purpose of his theory even this idea must be voided of all specific social structural or relational content. For Gurr relative deprivation is not (as it was for Merton (1957), Hyman (1942), Runciman (1966)) a social comparison process at all – it is simply not having as much of something as you think you might have. In its most rudimentary form his theory of rebellion is that people (or as he prefers to say, men) rebel when they do not get as much of any value as they feel they could have: 'The potential for collective violence varies strongly with the intensity and scope of relative deprivation among members of a collectivity' (1970:360). The theory is elaborated in a further eighty-one hypotheses and corollaries and yet, although many of these are a good deal narrower in their terms of reference, the exercise as a whole remains firmly at the level of abstracted truisms: thus, (1970:364), 'Regime coercive control varies strongly with the loyalty of coercive forces to the regime', or (1970:365), 'Dissident institutional support varies strongly with the proportion of a population belonging to dissident-oriented organizations.' Sceptics might find the distinction between analysis and idiocy hard to discern in such propositions. Yet scepticism could well be unjustified: it is quite likely that these platitudes do summarise all that we know about *all* political violence; that Gurr has got it right in the sense that no particular study of political violence will ever invalidate his theory of political violence in general. The real question is not whether such theories are right or wrong, insightful or ridiculous, but whether the elaboration of analytical complexes of this sort is of any help in the explanation of historically located events or categories of events such as the French revolution or the peasant furies of the 17th century. What can a profoundly a-historical model of social process do for our understanding of processes which are quintessentially historical?

The issue of redressing wrong also provides the focus for the much more ambitious attempt to straddle levels of explanation made by Barrington Moore Jr in *Injustice* (1978). Moore's book is much more formally a confrontation of explanation in principle and explanation in detail. Part One is an 'explicitly ahistorical' explanation of the nature of injustice and moral outrage and of the conditions under which people accept or resist unjust situations. Part Two, by contrast, is a specifically historical examination of the ways in which the German working class both accepted and resisted injustices between 1848 and 1933. And the book ends with a sustained attempt to draw these materials together in a wide-ranging analysis of the relations between social structures and moral condemnation. In the underlying theory of revolt moral condemnation, the dismantling of legitimacy and the articulation of protest, is the decisive lever of action and the historical studies document the extraordinary difficulty that most people have most of the time in arriving at a state of moral outrage let alone in proceeding thence to revolutionary action: 'I strongly suspect', Moore remarks at one stage (1978:218) 'that doing nothing remains the real form of mass action in the main historical crises since the sixteenth century.' The originality and great value of the book lie in the way working class autobiographies, estate and factory records, censuses and official inquiries are all used to tease out a sense of the overwhelming difficulty of breaking the bounds of what Moore calls 'inevitability', the stifling, ingrained rightness of an established order. But when it comes to an explanation of how on rare occasions, in revolutionary events, inevitability *is* broken what is striking about *Injustice* is how closely its line of explanation resembles and, as it were, merely fleshes out, that of highly abstracted sociological explanations in principle such as that found in *Theory of Collective Behaviour* or even in *Why Men Rebel*. For example, Moore is much concerned with the problem of the 'undermining of the prevailing system of beliefs that confers legitimacy ... upon the existing social order' (1978:81) and sees that undermining as a 'main process' involved in the building of radical opposition. Although he uses terms such as 'the infusion of iron into the human soul' to try to get to grips with this process the substance of his analysis, both in detail and in general, precisely echoes Smelser's more abstract treatment of the crucial transformations effected by 'value-oriented generalised beliefs' in the making of revolutionary events. At many other points his analyses of 'the rejection of suffering' whether in general or among the German working classes in 1848 and 1918 simply give specific content to Gurr's hypotheses about the dynamics of relative deprivation. None of this belittles the stature of *Injustice*. My point is simply that the explanation of revolutionary events is a collaborative enterprise: that the links Moore builds between what happened in 1848 and 'innate human nature' or between what happened in 1918 and the 'prerequisites for social and moral transformation' are also links or perhaps I should say building-blocks, in a pyramid of explanation which includes the most abstracted explanation in principle, say that of Gurr, as well as the most densely-woven colligation, say, with reference to 1848, Namier's (1945) *Revolution of the Intellectuals* (my point is of course that the best colligations are always actually covert explanations in principle). It is the wholeness of the pyramid as a collaborative enterprise that is important. But that is not to deny that at the present state of our knowledge works which appear to claim only a modest elevation, mediating explanation in detail and no more than a mildly generalised explanation in principle, works such as those of Wolf and Moore, do seem to provide more satisfaction than those that operate at the extremes. I want only to argue that our present satisfaction with such works should not lead us to believe that they are in any qualitative or essential way unlike works which are either very much more generalised or very much more detailed. Sociologists and historians have both for the time being evolved a 'middle range' idiom of practical explanation which reflects the extent to which what they now know permits them to connect the general and the particular. Our interest should surely be in consolidating that middle ground rather than in waging war on the inhabitants of the remote frontiers.

A particularly helpful example of the possibilities of consolidation is provided by Theda Skocpol (1979) in *States and Social Revolutions*. Like Wolf, Skocpol restricts her interest to a particular type of revolution, albeit a type constituted by the three great successful revolutions of modern world history, the French, the Russian and the Chinese. They constitute a type, and manifestly a type of enormous historical significance, not because of their success but, she argues, because they are all susceptible to the same practical explanation – an explanation cast not at the level of relative deprivation and not at the level of who did what and to whom but in terms of historically located social structuring. One impressive feature of Skocpol's study, and again it is one that confirms my sense of the collaborative pyramid of social analysis, is that although she has herself done no new historical research she is meticulously aware of and responsive to the researches of professional historians. She synthesises and generalises from the best, the most particular and the most diverse that historians had by 1979 been able to tell us about the three events in question. And in doing so she generates an interpretation and explanation which persuasively unites particular events in a unified category without dissolving their concrete historical meaning in the thin air of over-generalised abstractions. More precisely, her explanation of the three revolutions seizes on the fact of the historically specific conjunction in each of the countries at the moment of revolution of causes in themselves necessary but not sufficient to cause revolution. The chronic peasant insurrections of 'rentier agrarian' societies (which is itself subjected to detailed explanation) provides a crucial momentum for revolution. However, it crops into revolution only in conjunction with separately determined international crises of the regime, 'national and international developments quite independent of the peasantry' (1979:117):

> This political factor interacted with the structurally given insurrectionary potential of the peasantry to produce the full-blown social-revolutionary situation that neither cause alone could have produced. It was the breakdown of the concerted repressive capacity of a previously unified and centralised state that finally created conditions directly or ultimately favourable to *widespread* and *irreversible* peasant revolts against landlords ... The conjunctural result was social revolution.

Once again we are in an explanatory world that is recognisably also that of Gurr and Smelser. But the limitation of scope makes it also the world of Mousnier or Cobban, of the close meshing of explanation in principle and explanation in detail. Skocpol herself is exceptionally clear (for a sociologist) about the advantages and indeed the necessity of such a limitation. The satisfactory practical explanation of categories of events can be achieved only by restricting one's categories to events not burdened with 'significantly different ... histories'. Unless one does that one is driven in search of explanation into the stratosphere of unprofitable (albeit possibly quite correct) abstraction. Thus, she firmly refuses to generalise her own analysis (1979:288):

> One cannot mechanically extend the specific causal arguments that have been developed for France, Russia and China into a 'general theory of revolutions' applicable to all other modern social revolutions. There are two important reasons why such a strategy would be fruitless. In the first place, the causes of revolutions (whether of individual cases, or sets of similar cases) necessarily vary according to the historical and international circumstances of

the countries involved. 'We do not know any universal principles of historical change,' C. Wright Mills once wisely wrote, because 'the mechanisms of change ... vary with the social structure we are examining ... Just as there is a variety of social structures, there is a variety of principles of historical change.' And, in the second place, patterns of revolutionary causation and out-comes are necessarily affected by world-historical changes in the fundamental structures and bases of state power as such. The likelihood and the forms of revolutions tend to change over world time, because, as Mills also noted ... 'historical change *is* change of social structures, of the relations among their component parts'.

At such a point the historical and the sociological explanation of events surely merge in a common recognition of practicality, a common language, a cooperative enterprise.

8

The historical sociology of individuals: identity and the problem of generations

Thus far I have argued that, sociologically, society must be understood as a process constructed historically by individuals who are constructed historically by society. But because my attention has been directed to large-scale social formations and developments the place of the individual in that process has remained rather elusive, even obscure. In this chapter I want to redress the balance and make the problem of the individual in historical sociology my main concern. Unforunately, that involves a very considerable difficulty – nothing less than the sustained rejection of one of the most profoundly taken-for-granted axioms of commonsense knowledge Western civilisation has produced. Properly to appreciate the historical and sociological relationship of individual and society we have, in my view, to make a determined effort to un-think dualism; to escape from the seductive clutches of the belief that the individual has a being distinct from that of society or, conversely, that society and the individual constitute separate realities. We have to try to convince ourselves that what we call individual and society are in fact aspects or phases of a unified human reality and not essentially distinct, let alone opposed, entities. Personally, although I find the call to abandon dualism (a call social scientists have been making to each other since the time of Marx) quite comprehensible, sensible and persuasive in principle, I must admit to finding it almost impossible to accomplish in practice. The weight of two and a half millennia of treating dualism as the obvious basis for effective thought is remarkably oppressive.

The unity of self and society

Dualism, the understanding of reality as a dichotomy of subject and object, meaning and structure, consciousness and being, self and society, really has been a stupendously powerful tool of thought, rightly celebrated as an indispensable source of the peculiar capacity of the western mind for scientific, technical and economic innovation. The ability to conceive of the individual as standing outside society and nature, an autonomous thinking agent acting on them, was an invaluable resource in the formation of that calculating rationality which Weber placed at the heart of the making of capitalism. The history of western science is in one aspect the history of an increasingly un-selfconscious assertion of the adequacy and accuracy of dualistic accounts of man and nature. Most conspicuously, the triumphant dismantling of feudal power throughout Europe and North America from the 17th to the 19th centuries proceeded under the banner of social and political theories which in all their different varieties were radically individualistic. They were theories which proclaimed the peculiar and inalienable reality, and rights, of the individual as against the social. Indeed, in their extreme form those theories and the popular beliefs associated with them abolished dualism by denying all independent reality to society, perceiving it as nothing but an artefact created by the only real agents and subjects in nature apart from the deity, human individuals; as God made His world so did individuals make theirs. The really revolutionary contribution of early sociology, entering this thought-world of rampant individualism, was to rediscover the reality of the social as something more than a by-product of the conventions, contracts and covenants made by individuals. But this of course served only to renew and aggravate the problem of dualism. Early sociology reconstructed the classical problem of dualism, the two realities, individual and society, and then set out to solve it in new ways. Durkheim's first great work, *The Division of Labour in Society* is appropriately above all an attempt to solve a problem constructed in terms of the antithesis of individual and society; its achievement is to solve a problem which exists only because it has been constructed in those terms.

For all that, a tool of thought, however heuristically useful the account of reality it makes possible, should not be mistaken for a reliable description of reality. And regrettably that is just what has almost always happened in this particular case. Self-consciousness, that cardinal and endlessly creative instrument of reflection, hardens into an 'objectified' consciousness of self, a sense of the self as an autonomous reality outside society. Our understanding of the ecology of thinking, of the fact that it occurs in individual brains gives rise to a serious misunderstanding of the nature of thought, of the fact that it is a participation in the social. It is this illusion of the individual as a separate reality, an entity in contradistinction to society, and the consequent sense of the problem of 'the individual and society' as being a problem of identifying a relationship between distinct realities, that have strenuously to be unthought if a sociologically sensible understanding of the individual is to be achieved. In the place of the famous assertion of Descartes, 'I think, therefore I am', we must force ourselves to see the truth of the more modest claim, 'I think, therefore I think I am', with all that that implies. Such a stripping away of received assumptions is extremely hard to accomplish. Marx for one (1959:109) concluded that it could not be done – not as a mere exercise in thought, that is: 'subjectivism and objectivism, spiritualism and materialism, activity and suffering, only lose their antithetical character and thus their existence as such antitheses in the social condition; ... the resolution of *theoretical* antitheses is possible only in a *practical* way ... their resolution is therefore by no means merely a problem of knowledge but a real problem of life'. Left to themselves our normal categories of thought resist the work we need to do. Even Durkheim, the most determinedly sociologistic of sociologists could get no further than to postulate the duality of human nature, seeing the individual as possessing both a social consciousness and an individual (strictly private) consciousness and finding some sort of meeting-point or integration of distinct realities in that dualism (1960:331). Post-Freudian social psychology proceeds in much the same way of course, towards a fusion of individual and social imperatives in the adult personality. So, too, does much research concerned with the socialisation of children, viewing the personality, identity or self eventually achieved by the individual as some sort of balance, intersection or more or less stable integration of social and individual forces, requirements or attributes. Throughout this literature the ulterior, governing conception is that of the individual as a reality distinct from and counterpoised to the reality of society – hence the possibility of (and the need for) analysis in terms of balance, intersection, fusion and so forth.

Understandable as such analysis is, it is also in some respects a severe obstacle to understanding. A variety of attempts to achieve a more unified account of the social world of individuals have resulted, those developed within symbolic interactionism and phenomenology being the most familiar to sociologists. But one way round the obstacle, which is indeed implicit in almost all studies of personality and socialisation, remains curiously unexplored. That is the possibility of building seriously upon the common observation that individuality, like society, is and can only be constructed historically – that socially organised time is the common medium in which social structure and identity generate each other. As a statement of principle such an idea is hardly new; it was plainly advanced by Anselm Strauss in 1950, and less plainly perhaps by G. H. Mead in 1934. As Strauss (1977:764) put it: 'Identities imply not merely personal histories but also social histories ... individuals hold memberships in groups that are themselves products of the past. If you wish to understand persons – their development and their relations with significant others – you must be prepared to view them as embedded in historical context.' When, in *The Social Construction of Reality* Berger and Luckmann direct our attention to the phenomenon of 'identity types', 'social products *tout court*' (1967:195), or when in *Identity: Youth and Crisis* Erik Erikson (1968:160) allows that the decisive episode in identity formation has to be understood in terms of 'the community's ways of identifying the individual' the same invitation to develop a historical sociology of the individual that will collapse the problem of 'individual and society' is being advanced. This chapter will try to accept that invitation.

The most remarkable recent attempt to contain the social and the individual within a unified scheme of sociological analysis is probably that made by Norbert Elias (1978b). In *The Civilising Process* Elias gives us both a principled critique of the dualism of conventional social analysis and, by way of a minutely documented case study of the 'history of manners', a thoroughly substantiated presentation of an alternative theoretical position. Just because his work offers us such an exceptionally bold and direct assault on the theoretical credentials of dualism coupled with a powerful empirical demonstration of an alternative it must command attention as a crucial point of reference in this debate. But its particular importance to me is that the alternative Elias outlines is specifically and unalterably historical; in place of the sterile pursuit of the formal interrelation of individual and society he proposes the historical analysis of what he calls 'human figurations'. Examination of that proposal seems an obvious, even compelling, point of departure for my own discussion.

In the year 1280, for example, it was taken for granted that people ate with their hands often from a common dish, blew their noses in their hands or if at table on the tablecloth, spat and belched as the spirit moved them, shared their beds with casual visitors, broke wind, emptied their bowels and bladders in the presence of others and took great delight in mutilating the bodies of those they had overcome in battle. In Paris even four centuries later, 'it was one of the festive pleasures of Midsummer Day to burn alive one or two dozen cats' (1978b:203). All these activities were at the time quite compatible with what would have been regarded as normal 'civilised' life, had the concept of civilised life existed. But of course it did not. What Elias traces is the prolonged elaboration of a pattern of living understood as civilised and involving profound redefinitions of 'normal' and 'proper' behaviour, the building of powerful psychological and institutional barriers to the old indiscriminate enactment of feeling (both enthusiasm and aggression) and, as a concomitant of that, the establishment of increasingly well-policed social distance between the civilised and the uncivilised members of society. The civilising process in other words was, in his argument, simultaneously and symbiotically a way of life for individuals, a distinctive 'structure of affects' in his own term, *and* a social system; it was a unified working-out of meaning-

and-structure. He shows, in a set of very detailed studies of personal manners and social stratification, just how impossible it is to split or disentangle the meaning-and-structure pair if one seriously wishes to understand either. The piecing-together of a new type of individuals with new standards of decorum and repugnance entrenched in this sensibility was, concomitantly and concurrently, the piecing-together of new modes of social control, new institutions, new conceptions of the nature of the social world and new ways of enacting and enforcing those conceptions. New types and styles of human social relationships were formed and were articulated in new standards of behaviour and new patterns of behaviour.

The process manifested itself in the appearance of both new types of individual and new types of society. That is to say, from one point of view the changes in question, achieved through the ever more meticulous and ever more explicit regulation of affects (whether that meant war, justice or table manners), were a matter of the creation of a new kind of 'typical' human individual – an individual whose emotional life was more closely bounded and controlled by feelings of revulsion and shame, delicacy and propriety of a quite novel sort and for whom public and private life had become separate spheres of existence in a way not understood at all in earlier centuries. The 'civilised' individual understood very well that some things were 'not done' in public, some only in the privacy of an intimate milieu and some only in complete isolation. From another point of view the same historical record marks the creation of a new kind of society, a dramatically more differentiated as well as a more controlled social order, a world in which 'classes' are separated and distinguished from one another, not least in terms of public standards of refined and coarse, respectable and disreputable behaviour, and in which the sphere of civilised life is quite strictly dissociated from that of the 'lower', and coarser, strata; the coarse and disreputable being also quite strictly stigmatised, ostracised and repressed. But, and this is the essence of the argument, each of these points of view is in fact partial and incomplete. In effect, the process of civilisation is one which, both as the history of a more stratified society and as the history of more emotionally disciplined individuals, can only be fully understood as a single, continuous and tightly-meshed experience. Both patterns, the individual and the social emerge within the same relating and interweaving of action in time.

The shared world of knight and peasant, of immediately expressed aggression and delight, in which bodily functions and sexuality, violence and starvation were alike 'on stage', accepted features of the public texture of daily life and personal experience, gives way to the tightly defined worlds of court, town and country with their minute discriminations and exclusions, the eviction of the realities of body, feeling and suffering from the constrained, stylised circle of civilised existence, not only in reality but also in art – hence the tirades of Frederick the Great against 'the abominable works of Shakespeare'. This was a substantial and ascertainable historical change. But it was not a change, Elias argues, that can be grasped or understood by a sociology that separates individual and society. The creation of the civilised individual *was* the creation of the stratified society, the creation of the stratified society *was* the creation of the civilised individual. The object of analysis of sociology is a continuously re-patterned social dance, the changing figurations of which are nothing but the dancers in action within the relationships of their dance.

Elias himself uses the metaphor of the dance to help draw out his meaning and render the idea of figurations and 'figurational change' as alternatives to the more conventional objects of study easier to apprehend (1978b:262):

> The image of the mobile figurations of independent people on a dance floor perhaps makes it easier to imagine states, cities, families and also capitalist, communist and feudal systems as figurations. By using this concept we can eliminate the antithesis, resting finally on different values and ideals, immanent today in the use of the words 'individual' and 'society'. One can certainly speak of a dance in general, but no one will imagine a dance as a structure outside the individual or as a mere abstraction. The same dance figurations can certainly be danced by different people; but without a plurality of reciprocally oriented and dependent individuals, there is no dance. Like every other social figuration a dance figuration is relatively independent of the specific individuals forming it here and now, but not of individuals as such. It would be absurd to say that dances are mental constructions abstracted from observations

of individuals considered separately. The same applies to all other figurations.

But while the metaphor of the dance does seem to help emphasise the need for the sociologist to try to understand social systems as historically produced figurations of interdependent individuals it is not, I think, quite satisfactory as a guide to an understanding of individuals. A better image from that point of view might be that of a game without rules – or rather, in which the only rule is that the players must go on playing. Dances after all are rule-governed as to both form and content. It would be only reasonable to say of an individual sitting eating an apple on a dance floor where others were doing the polka that he was not dancing. But the involvement of individuals in the social is closer and more creative than that. The image of the game without rules emphasises those properties. That is to say, if we can envisage a game in which both the objects of play and the rules of play, the number and disposition of the players, the very sense of what the game is about are all alterable within the framework of the rule that everyone is a player and must go on playing, we shall approach a more balanced sense of the part played by individuals in the historical production of social figurations.

A regular feature of such a game would surely be the attempts of different players or groups of players to change the objects and rules and conduct of the game in response to the moves of others and to suit their own various purposes. If we fail to make progress by kicking the ball, let's try picking it up and running with it, or changing its shape, or insisting that the purpose of the game is not to score goals but to run elegantly. Thus, one of the developments Elias traces is the elaboration in 18th-century Germany of a conception of culture and cultivation as an alternative human ideal to that civilisation. The German princely courts had closed the doors of civilisation to the German bourgeoisie, literally refusing contact with them. Proclamation of the ideal of the cultured crystallised the 'polemic of the stratum of German middle class intelligentsia against the etiquette of the ruling courtly upper class' (1978b:9). It changed the rules of the game affirming not only the presence in the game of the bourgeoisie but also the value as winning cards in the game of those qualities of sentiment and sensibility which the civilised individual spurned. At the same time, reflecting the actual structures of power in German society, the state of play as it were, the peculiarly German conception of the cultured individual is one with no political content at all. The new bourgeois individual in pursuit of *Kultur* made and lived in a world of morality, virtue and emotion, of nature, spirit and freedom (specifically, freedom from the 'unnatural' world of power). Culture was all 'thoughts, feelings – nothing which was able in any sense to lead to concrete political action' (1978b:8); not an attempt to beat the princes at their own game, but an attempt to expand the definition of what the game was about. Unlike a dance a game without rules allows individuals that sort of historical opportunity. The game is only what the players are playing at a given moment – a fleeting pattern of rule-making projects.

On the other hand, what the players are playing from moment to moment is not just a game some of them are trying to change and others to preserve. It is also the game as it was inherited by the whole set of contemporary players. The repudiation of civilisation presupposes the existence of civilisation. And in this sense individuals must also be seen as products of the figurations they produce. Plainly, it is very difficult to find words to express the idea of the unity of individual and society adequately in a language constructed to express the idea of their separation. The metaphor of the game without rules may be as close as one can come in general terms. But even getting that close surely does emphasise the extent to which sociological explanation of individuals no less than of society has to be historical. Description of course can be abstracted from time. If one's object of study is the 'state of play' one can indeed make a map of the network of inter-dependencies within and making-up a particular figuration at a chosen moment. But to *explain* the distinctive features of such a map, analysis of the course of the game up to that moment becomes essential – precisely because the map does not present a structure independent of the lives of individuals nor an aggregate of individuals free of the interdependencies of the social game. Figuration is a useful word because it does mean at one and the same time a pattern and a process of patterning, insists on patterning as the key to the pattern. As Elias puts it (1978b:261):

> The network of interdependencies among human beings is what binds them together. Such interdependencies are the nexus of what is here called the figuration, a structure of mutually oriented and dependent people. Since people are more or less dependent on each other first by nature and then through social learning, through education, socialisation and socially generated reciprocal needs, they exist ... only as pluralities, only in figurations. That is why ... it is not particularly fruitful to conceive of men in the image of individual man. It is more appropriate to envisage an image of numerous interdependent people forming figurations. Seen from this basic standpoint the rift in the traditional image of man disappears.

And that traditional image itself provides an interesting final example of difficulty in understanding human social interdependence because we tend to see the individual as an essentially closed system; we think of individuality as located within the person just as the brain is located within the skull – there is, as it were, a wall of self between the individual and others. Scientifically this image of the individual is of course quite unwarranted; whatever version of the familiar image we prefer – identity, superego, character – the essence of individuality is manifestly not 'there' in the individual in the way the heart is in the rib cage. The cogency the grip of our traditional idea of the individual derives, Elias argues, not at all from observation but from its plausibility as one more figurational feature of the process of civilisation. It is the self-image appropriate to the social relations of civilisation as they have been produced in six hundred years of the civilising process. Socially, the essence of 'civilisation' is social distance; at the level of behaviour it is etiquette; psychologically it is self-control. The making of the civilised individual meant especially a 'particularly strong shift in individual self-control – above all, in self-control acting independently of external agents as a self activating automatism' (1978b:257). Individuals learned to impose 'reason' and 'conscience' on their affects and those controls then came to be seen – indeed they functioned as – an invisible wall, the wall of self, between the individual and the 'outside' world. The more refined and socially differentiated individual of the civilising process is also the individual who has learned to isolate himself in his mind's eye not only from others but from the emotional inner man, distance from self matches distance from others, control of others mirrors control of self. The apogee of the process, realised in late 17th century France in what Turnell (1947) has aptly termed 'the classical moment' (aptly, because the figuration begins to be dissolved as soon as it has been achieved), is the human ideal envisaged in the heroes and heroines of Corneille and Racine. Triumphantly, it is Corneille's version (Turnell, 1947:22) of the emperor Augustus: 'Je suis maître de moi comme de l'univers; Je le suis, je veux l'être'. And tragically, it is the endless princes and princesses of Racine who simply cannot master themselves: 'Moi, régner! Moi, ranger un Etat sous ma loi, Quand ma faible raison ne règne plus sur moi, lorsque j'ai de mes sens abandonné l'empire' (Turnell, 1947:194). The endless conjunction of social power and power over the encapsulated estranged self in this literature is quite extraordinary – a fleeting crystallisation of the figuration in its purest form. Classical French drama gives us above all the distinctive predicament of civilisation: a stark division of power in society and individual alike; society and individual as objects equally to be ruled by the knowing, willing subject; and then the recurrent pathos of rebellion as the repressed orders, peasants or the emotional self break the bounds of control: 'Je crains de me connaître, en l'état où je suis', the individual recoils in horror from herself.

Elias does not use these examples but they make his point if anything even more strongly than those he does use (1978b:258):

If we now ask again what really gives rise to the concept of the individual as encapsulated 'inside' himself, severed from every-thing existing outside ... we can now see the direction in which the answer must be sought. The firmer, more comprehensive and uniform restraint of the affects characteristic of [the] civilisation shift, together with the increased internal compulsions that ... prevent all spontaneous impulses from manifesting themselves directly ... these are what are experienced as the capsule, the invisible wall dividing the 'inner world' of the individual from the 'external world', the 'individual' from 'society'. What is encapsulated are the restricted instinctual and affective impulses denied direct access to the motor apparatus. They appear in self-perception as what is hidden from all others, and often as the true self, the core of individuality.

The individual has been perceptually re-made as a reality hidden from public view. Socially the civilising process distances people from one another by stratification; psychologically it achieves the same effect by encapsulating the self. Conversely, the type of social analysis advocated by Norbert Elias and historical sociology in general, would then have to be understood as one among a number of modern efforts – of which the assault on received sexual repressions is perhaps the most far-reaching and important – to destroy 'civilisation' (at least insofar as civilisation means the withdrawal of the individual from society). Certainly it is a very serious attempt to play the game without rules on new lines, to shape a new figuration.

Whether many of us are yet mentally prepared or willing to play the game according to the new rules proposed by Elias is perhaps a moot point. No doubt most of us feel that we have a lot to lose by doing so: a private self 'in here' to treasure, a society 'out there' to fight, accept or defend. Yet the knowledge we have accumulated about the making of individuals, and about the thoroughly historical nature of that process, seems to me to make the case for thinking ourselves out of our conventional ways of describing and living the relationship of individual and society altogether compelling. That knowledge exists on two levels, although the cut-off point between them is not perhaps entirely clear. We know about the construction of individuals in general – the distinctive 'identity types', 'mentalities' or 'social character' of whole pluralities of individuals in different periods and milieux. And we also know about the construction of individuals in particular – the careers, life-histories and identities of selected concrete individuals, usually 'great' men or women of course but by analogy thought of as models for more 'ordinary' individuals too, if only we could get close enough to them. I shall try to suggest that at both levels our knowledge of individuality impels the perspective of historical sociology.

I suspect that many sociologists would now concede the argument in its weak form, as an argument about aggregate individuality, while resisting it in the strong form in which it is applied to individuals in particular. Indeed it could be urged that the work of Elias itself justifies a recasting of our understanding of individuals in general (giving us a surer basis for accounting for the social character of 20th-century Texans or 17th-century Frenchmen) only at the price of recognising that the sociologist can say nothing of value about particular individuals, the specific identities of Lyndon Johnson or Pascal. That seems to be what is involved in the distinction proposed by Berger and Luckmann (1967:190) between 'identity types' and 'identity'. Do we not gain our understanding of the 'sociogenesis' of types of individuality at the expense of having to admit that explanation of the peculiar individuality of the person who eats apples during the polka, of Luther or Lenin, is really beyond the scope of sociology? Is not the sociology of figurations really left with the same residual problem of the individual that faced, and flawed, Durkheim's attempt to advance a sociology of social facts – individual action in general is absorbed into the field of sociological knowledge, but only in a way that surrenders a crucial, and inviolably individual, area of experience and action, the inner life of meaning of particular individuals, to the biographer or the psychologist as somehow either inaccessible or irrelevant to sociology? It seems to me that this is just what Elias, unlike Durkheim, is *not* prepared to concede. On the contrary, if the figurational alternative to conventional dualistic social analysis has any merit it must surely be the merit of *not* leaving us with any sort of residual 'problem of the individual', but of offering instead a comprehensive, unified field of human social enquiry. And from this point of view it is the firmly historical conception of the field that is all-important. Elias himself does not perhaps give this aspect of figurational sociology its full due. What attracts his attention is not the task of accounting for personal action (in the singular) within this or that figuration, but rather the task of revealing the integration of personal action (in the plural) and social relationships (or structure) in the historical movement from one figuration to another. Properly to complement his own work we need therefore to turn to studies more directly concerned with the former problem: studies of individual identities and personal moral careers. And since the problem is hardly raised in any very acute form by identities and careers that fall within the 'normal' range of variation (as we might call it) for a particular period or setting, or by individuals whose mentality and activity engage undramatically, even predictably, in the figuring-out of a relatively stable social dance, it is the explanation of the eccentric, unexpected, innovating or deviant identity and career that is the crucially important test for figurational sociology. We might call this 'the Dracula problem' in historical sociology – the problem of accounting for figurational freaks. The easier problem, of explaining patterns of 'normal' identity could then, taking a cue from Talcott Parsons, be termed 'the problem of the Barbarians' – of the social taming of the annual invading horde of infant savages. I will deal with the easier problem first, saving the harder for the next chapter.

The problem of generations

From the perspective of historical sociology the problem of the Barbarians is best thought-of as a problem of generations. The idea of the succession of generations emphasises both the historical location and the historical continuity of the process with which we are concerned. The problem of generations, in turn, is a problem of the mutual phasing of two different calendars: the calendar of the life-cycle of the individual and the calendar of historical experience. Distinct patterns of social character or identity types, the 'classical moment' or the 'post-War generation', flow into distinct figurations of social action in the space created by the articulation of these two types of time. 'The youth of today' as Erikson (1967:247) puts it, 'is not the youth of twenty years ago'; new life-histories are constantly being lived in relation to new world-histories; the successive barbarian hordes invade successively different social empires and therefore conquer or settle them in different ways; the pattern of generations – the flow of noticeably different types of common identity – emerges.

There is in fact little disagreement about all this among sociologists – although emphasis on the specifically generational nature of the making of social character is not as common as it might be. Few voices are raised against the claim that 'normal' identities, that is to say identities that fall within the range of what is conventionally characteristic of their own time, can be adequately understood as participants in the particular historical figuration within which the individuals concerned are born. Berger and Luckmann, for example (notwithstanding their old-fashioned insistence on the unhelpful distinction between 'subjective' and 'objective' realities) rule quite categorically that 'identity is formed by social processes', and that 'once crystallised it is maintained, modified or even reshaped by social relations' (1967:196). And again, more generally, 'societies have histories in the course of which specific identities emerge'. And Erving Goffmann, a much closer and sharper-eyed observer of social interaction, claims still more emphatically that the self 'can be seen as something that resides in the arrangements prevailing in a social system for its members' (1968:154). Indeed, it seems that whatever particular theory of the dynamics of identity-formation is favoured – whether it is held to be a matter of 'significant others', the 'super-ego', 'ego-identity', 'the generalised other' or the 'institutional self' – there is a considerable consensus about the extent to which the process must be seen as a matter of a specifically historical entry into some specific historical figuration – an interweaving of personal and collective histories. In this double sense identity formation *en masse* is seen as a historically located historical sequence.

Two examples of the way such arguments usually proceed may serve to illustrate the way in which analyses of identity-formation typically close-off, even eliminate, the problem (or rather the non-problem) of the individual and society. The first is Stanley Elkins's now famous treatment of the 'Sambo' problem in the history of North American slavery (1959:81-139), the second Erik Erikson's equally well-known account of the making of the identity of modern 'youth' (1968). Of course, the substance of both studies has proved highly controversial. But what I am concerned with is not whether their specific claims and conclusions are right or wrong but simply the manner in which their arguments are advanced and the implication of that type of argument for our understanding of the historical nature of individuality.

Elkins begins with the proposition that the North American plantation slave displayed by the 19th century a distinct type of personality distilled in the stereotype, Sambo: 'Sambo, the typical plantation slave was docile but irresponsible, loyal but lazy, humble but chronically given to lying and stealing, exasperating in his unpredictability but lovable for his childlike innocence and dependence' (1959:82). Childishness is indeed the essence of the characterisation. There can of course be no doubt that this characterisation of the slave did really exist; it is purveyed in endless white accounts of blacks throughout the period. Whether the characterisation accurately represented a black reality is quite a different matter. Elkins – who has now (1975) retreated from many of the claims made in the original version of his book – simply took it for granted that a 'special type' of personality corresponding 'in its major outlines' to Sambo, did indeed exist on the plantations (1959:90). He then set himself the problem of explaining how such a typical identity could have come into being. His answer is still worth considering, not only because it exemplifies a method of analysis of central importance to historical sociology, but because after twenty years of debate, and despite the onslaughts of Gutman (1976), Fogel and Engerman (1974), Genovese (1974) and many others, the essential thesis advanced in *Slavery* does seem to have grasped a vital kernel of truth. It apprehends the dialectical unity of identity as a historical construct.

Three possible explanations, current at the time *Slavery* was written, for the formation of a plantation identity type approximating that indicated in the image of Sambo are examined by Elkins. One argument (1959:89) stressed the African background of the slaves – seeing childishness as an extension of their 'primitive' cultural origins. Another emphasised the impact on personality of the authoritarian institution of slavery. And a third was focused much more narrowly on the specific relationships of plantation life in North America. The first view Elkins finds unacceptable in the light of a mass of evidence about the cultural diversity of the backgrounds from which the slaves were grabbed; and in particular evidence of the relatively sophisticated, stable, disciplined and heroic nature of many of the African cultures concerned; evidence, in sum, 'of the utter absence of any particular African type – least of all of anything resembling Sambo'. The second explanation, seeing the childlike personality and feckless way of life as products of slavery as such, Elkins also rejects on the simple but decisive ground that nothing approaching the Sambo type of personality seems to have emerged in the great majority of slave systems for which we have evidence; specifically, he emphasises the contrast between North American slaves and those drawn from very similar origins into slavery in the South American colonies of Spain and Portugal; Latin American slavery was very plainly not associated with the patterns of slave personality manifested in North America even though recruitment was from essentially the same African territories. We are left, then, with the possibility that Sambo was a specific product of the North American plantation; that somehow in those particular conditions an identity type not foreshadowed in African culture or consequent upon slavery itself was necessarily assembled.

Elkins approaches that possibility (1959:135) by way of a close comparison between the institutions and relationships of plantation slavery in North America and those of slavery in the Spanish American colonies, drawing out a powerful contrast between a firmly closed and simplified world of master and slave on the one hand and a relatively open and complex world involving the slave in many relationships over and above that with the master on the other. Sambo, he argues, was the joint creation of master and slave within a uniquely sealed relationship of power and powerlessness. Reminding ourselves once again that the substance of his argument has been ferociously attacked in recent years and that Elkins himself has allowed (1975) that his original analysis overlooked much of slave family life, religion and culture, the main lines of his interpretation can be summarised as turning on the 'uncontrolled' nature of capitalism in North America and the resulting insulation of the possibilities of slave identity within the confines of the master-slave relationship. The critical feature of the North American pattern in this view was the lack of any institutional counterweight to slavery, and hence the possibility of the power of the owners being used to push the process of enslavement to a legal and relational extreme: to create a condition of 'pure slavery' not possible elsewhere. In Latin America by contrast, plantation agriculture and the master-slave relationship developed in the setting of a rich and pre-existing diversity of institutions: master and slave could act on one another only in a context of restraints and opportunities created by other, older and compelling relationships – above all those of the church and the legal and administrative world of the Imperial monarchies in Europe. Both civil government and the Church had demands to make of master and slave which were incompatible with full enslavement. Feudal law administered by the civil authorities blocked the reduction of the slave to the status of a chattel since it could find no place for the idea of property in persons. As all persons in a given territory were bound in moral obligations of allegiance to the monarch no person could conceivably be the mere property of another; like all other statuses in feudal law slavery was a finely defined and conditional status, terminable and carrying rights as well as duties – rights to acquire property and to buy or earn freedom among others. The state in other words required the slave to be a person separable from his master. So did the church. While accepting the condition of slavery the Roman church imposed on the masters a recognition that slaves, like themselve, had roles, and souls, as Christians. The life of the slave along with that of all other Christians had to involve baptism, Christian burial, Christian responsibility for sin and Christian solemnization of marriage and family life. In all these respects the slave was not exempted from religious responsibilities by the condition of slavery. And conversely he had an existence as a religious being which was essentially independent of his existence as a slave. In such a setting the slave could enter the social dance in a variety of different ways; neither his life chances not his identity could be contained within the confines of a single relationship.

In the North American case virtually the whole of this larger environment of relationships, requirements and possibilities was missing. In effect, North American slavery was developed in an institutional vacuum. The white settlement of North America was of course bound up with a strenuous rejection of both feudal law and catholic religion, a dramatic reconstruction of economic and political relations on the basis of private property and the rights of the 'possessive' individual. In these circumstances slave owners were able to develop their property, including their property in their slaves, with regard to nothing but their interests as staple producers in a competitive market. They were able, in effect, to maximise the efficiency of the exploitation of slave labour. A crucial feature of such a maximisation was the elimination of all sense of the separability of the slave as a person from the servile state. Elkins emphasises four particular ways in which masters proceeded to wage war on the moral, psychological, cultural and social as well as the legal possibility of the independent existence of the slaves. The laws of property were invoked and perfected to give masters as absolute a property in their slaves as in their household goods; the chattel status of the slaves was fixed unalterably; the children of slaves, like lambs and calves were simply new property – 'the father of a slave is unknown to our law'. In accordance with this definition of slaves as property the masters quickly developed absolute rights of discipline as well; charges that a master had murdered a slave could be dismissed on the ground that it was inconceivable that a man should destroy his own property; for their part slaves having no legal existence as persons could of course seek no redress in the courts against their masters excesses. Nor, as property, could they enter into the civil, social or legal relationships of persons in their private lives: the marriage and family relationships, which of course slaves made, had no standing in law and were not allowed to stand in the way of masters disposing of individual slaves in any way that suited their economic interests – as one Southern judge ruled, 'the contract of marriage not being recognised among slaves, none of its consequences follow'; and just as family relationships gave slaves no defensible area of private rights and responsibilities so work, saving and accumulation could give them no rights of property or way of earning their freedom; manifestly it was absurd to suggest that property could have rights of property –

'a slave is in absolute bondage', 'slaves have no legal rights in things, real or personal; but whatever they may acquire, belongs in point of law, to their masters' (1959:59). And finally, even in the most personal of all matters it was established that the slave did not really exist as a person; the fragile and fragmented Protestant churches mounted no effective resistance to the claim that the slave as a Christian was still decisively and wholly a slave; conversion to Christianity in no way modified the condition of the slave as property; unlike the Spanish who, however rapaciously, invaded America under the banner of a zealous Christian mission, the colonists of North America were all too ready to admit that they 'went not to those parts to save souls, or propagate religion, but to get Money'; getting money ended up by subjecting even the soul of a slave to the property rights of the master.

In all these ways, then, North American slavery was a quite unparalleled exercise in subjection. As Elkins puts it (1959:49) 'with the full development of the plantation there was nothing so far as the slave's interests were concerned, to prevent unmitigated capitalism becoming unmitigated slavery'. Within that structure of domination and subjection individual slaves, not as the children of black fathers but as the property of white masters, had to grow up, live and sustain an identity. To exist at all a slave had to recognise that the terms of existence were defined with overwhelming power and effectiveness by the will and interests of the masters. What, in that setting, could slaves be as individuals? Certainly, as Elkins's critics have pointed out, the social system was not totally closed. A rudimentary black culture could be shaped. Heroic but usually suicidal protests could be made. One could run away to visit one's 'wife' or 'parents' or simply to ramble living-off the countryside. About 5% of the slave population seem to have attemped such denials of the logic of enslavement in its peculiar North American version. And about 10% were employed in occupations which gave them access to a relatively open world quite unlike that of the great mass of field hands – as carters, waggoners, boatmen, a town craftsman or house-servant rather than a plantation labourer. But these were the minor imperfections of a nearly-perfected structure of power. Although a few escaped through such loopholes the balance of evidence still suggests that for the vast majority self could be created only within the terms of a relationship created and closed around them by the masters.

Elkins's argument (1959:128) is that it was the closure rather than the brutality of this system that explains the emergence of Sambo as a plantation identity type for the slave. With all other versions of self, including those contained within the African past, denied, invalidated and systematically penalised, the slave identity expected by the masters confronted the slave with extraordinary clarity and force – almost, one might say in Weberian terms with the necessity of a fate. The slave could not be an adult in the sense of claiming the rights and responsibilities of an autonomous person; attempts to live like that were fraught with disaster; the very idea of such an existence was, so far as possible, rendered invisible. Conversely the slave was cogently invited to be a child. It was an offer that could hardly be refused. In relation to their masters slaves could in effect be either objects or children. The possibility of being a child in relation to the master as parent was made highly visible – the only perception of the social dance the slave was allowed to have that permitted any participatory human activity at all. And certain positive rewards were attached to the acceptance of childishness. Within the role of child the slave won a modicum of freedom to manoeuvre, to 'play' irresponsibly (which could include not working, absconding and in various subtle and complex ways denying the seriousness of slavery) and be judged 'only childish'. More positively still wholehearted childishness could win the the benevolent affirmation of one's personal worth from masters who, after all, preferred, other things being equal, to be seen by their peers as 'using their people well'. For indeed being a child, for a good 'performance' in the required role, slaves were offered the 'sweet applause' of recognition, even love, within the only relationship they could count on having and from which they could not seriously hope to escape. Sambo, the slave child in relation to the master parent, was in other words an identity implicit within the master-slave relationship in its North American form. Given the distinctive closure of that relationship its profound inhumanity could, for both parties, perhaps only be humanised at all in terms of the parent-child construct. In those circumstances the bringing to life of the possibility of Sambo as an actual typical identity was a work of collaboration between slaves and masters – the working-out of primitively human identities for both within the framework of the inhuman conditions created by the power of the latter. Both had, as it were, an 'interest' in Sambo as something better than raw slavery; a gratifying legitimation of oppression for the masters it was also a tiny basis for both freedom of action and a social confirmation of personal existence (that is, an identity) for the slaves.

Such an analysis is fraught with difficulties which I do not propose to explore. Those who have pointed out that Elkins's initial presentation did not adequately acknowledge the creativity of the slaves within the constraints of the master-slave system are certainly correct. On the other hand all efforts to recognise that creativity have ended up also confirming the extent to which for the great mass of plantation slaves individuality was indeed made by slaves and masters alike within the compelling confines of a figuration which no black person newly entering the dance could either ignore or escape. That being so, some general points of importance for my argument plainly emerge. The first is of course that what Elkins is describing is in all respects a specifically *historical* predicament; that sort of slavery and that sort of moral translation of it into a vile parody of family life could only have come into being in uniquely particular historical cirumstances. The conditions of possibility for the creation of Sambo were very particular and could have been realised only on the basis of very particular conjunctions of factors in time; explanation of the pattern of the figuration demands an extremely precise previous patterning. Sambo cannot be understood except as the way some particular people learned to dance and had to dance given their inescapable connection with particular dancing-partners at a particular moment in the unfolding of the dance as a whole. Less fancifully we can say that Sambo was the identity of a particular black generation – using generation here in the sociological sense to refer to a cycle of historical experience. While the 'peculiar institution' lasted, a continuity of experience for blacks was ensured; successive biological generations grew up within the same existential terms of reference; unable to change those terms of reference they constituted a single sociological generation – a succession of biological lives lived within the same historical world making and re-making the same typical identity.

Secondly, it must be recognised that Elkins powerfully demonstrates the nature of individuality as a work of social cooperation. No doubt the mutuality of the self and the social appears most readily in highly simplified and above all closed and insulated relationships. It is there that one can see most clearly the extent to which the sense of self is a distillation of personal explorations and the affirmations and denials of others. Yet curiously, although that is what Elkins reveals – the typical identity of a social generation, pieced-together within a particular and historically defined relationship – he himself slightly misses the point of his own evidence. His final emphasis (1959:125) is placed quite squarely on the institutional 'side' of the process he has described, rather than on the mutuality and unity of institutions and identities. Thus, he presents the identity type of the slave as Sambo as in effect a rather mechanical product of the role imposed on slaves by their masters. Given the extreme 'clarity' of the role in a closed situation where no other roles were available or endorsed, his argument seems to be that the slave had passively to become the sort of person the role required. There is, he suggests, 'an extent to which we can say that personality is actually made up of the roles which the individual plays' – so that where only the role of perpetual child is offered the person becomes a perpetual child. Yet surely this fails to grasp the sense in which slaves actively *took* the role of child and within its confines created through their identities a social nexus which both gave them some important freedoms and constrained their masters (masters exploit their slaves but fathers love their children). One disadvantge of studying identity and individuality within relatively simple, closed social settings is evident here: such cases reveal the historical-social nature of the construction of self with peculiar force; but they simultaneously tend dangerously to represent the social as a reality separated from the individual by stressing the monolithic, unambiguous and exigent way in which institutionally prescribed roles are forced upon the individual, demanding performances which the individual must supply.

No doubt the extreme, closed and total predicaments studied by Elkins in *Slavery* (1959), Goffman in *Asylums* (1968) and Bettelheim in *The Informed Heart* (1960) do have something of that one-sidedness – although in each case one could also insist on the ways in which the apparently imposed identity of the less powerful is also a relationship which inhibits and shapes the more powerful. But the characteristic feature of the world discovered by the individual is of course the very opposite of that: figurations are typically multiple, manifold, diverse, blurred, above all ambiguous – not least because they are continuously changing in time. And to that extent the roles (ways of dancing) preferred to individuals by others are themselves typically conditional, inconsistent, even contradictory. The individual thus enters a world which not only has been made but remains to be re-made. G. H. Mead understood this feature of the unity of self and society very clearly when he wrote (1934:203): 'For the individual the world is always a task to be accomplished. It is not simply there by chance, as something that just happens. It is there because one realises it as a field for one's endeavours. It is a world, a real thing, just to the extent that one constructs it, that one organises it for one's action'. The categories of role analysis – even if one emphasises role *taking* – seem to have difficulty in grasping this element of active individual construction in the shaping of social worlds. Role analysis in the manner in which it is attempted by Elkins serves well to highlight the extent to which the individual can only be what is possible within some specifically constructed historical world. But it does so by playing down the extent to which individuals, thus constrained, construct and reconstruct such historical worlds by exploiting the distinctive ambiguities of interaction.

To draw-out fully this dimension of individuality – of the way individuals constitute historical figurations and are historically constituted by them – a more flexible perspective than that of role theory seems to be called-for. We need a perspective which can allow for the fact that identities are assembled through the meshing-together of two types of historically organised time: the life history and the history of societies. It is here that Erik Erikson's studies of the process of identity-formation are so helpful. Erikson is perhaps the most sociological of psychoanalysts. More than any other of the heirs of Freud he has built on Freud's shrewd but undeveloped insight that the ground plan of personality is to be found in the way the growing individual 'is required to exchange pleasure for value in the eyes of others' as the matrix of self. His successive writings, *Young Man Luther* (1958), *Childhood and Society* (1963) and *Identity: Youth and Crisis* (1968) in particular, provide an elaborate documentation of the ways in which 'value in the eyes of others' is at once the constant general determinant of identity and a determinant which is constantly, historically, variable in the forms of identity it determines: 'the identity problem itself changes with the historical period'. His analysis of the identity troubles of 'youth' in the 1960's is thus simultaneously an exercise in revealing the workings of an invariant process of identity-formation through socially organised sequences of interaction, and a demonstration of the irreducibly specific historical location of any given identity-type such as that of modern youth. It is difficult in a brief summary to do justice to the fluid two-sidedness of his work – but I shall try.

A few statements of his general position may help at the outset. The problem of identity is elusive, he suggests (1968:22) just because in tackling it 'we deal with a process located in the core of the individual and yet also in the core of his communal culture, a process which establishes, in fact, the identity of those two identities'. And again (1968:23) 'the process ... is always changing and developing: it is a process of increasing differentiation, and it becomes ever more inclusive as the individual grows aware of a widening circle of others significant to him, from the maternal person to mankind ... it does not end until [the] power of mutual affirmation wanes'. And yet again (1968:23) 'in discussing identity ... we cannot separate personal growth and communal change, nor can we separate ... the identity crisis in individual life and contemporary crises in historical development because the two help to define each other and are truly relative to each other'. In such a perspective identity is clearly neither a psychic shield placed between the individual and society nor an iron cage of role-requirements clamped around the individual by the social. Rather, it is the self-consciousness at successive moments in the individual's life-history of the participation of that life-history in a social history, and vice-versa. The modes of this mutual involvement which Erikson sees as decisive are exploration, affirmation and denial. The individual explores the environment in diverse ways and these exploratory actions are made meaningful by the affirmations or denials called-forth from others; new exploratory action springs from what has previously been affirmed or denied; the pattern of past exploration, affirmation and denial is the shell within which new explorations of the present take shape. Identity is a moment in this continuous dialectic. Each stage of the life cycle is a matter of trying out what one has been allowed to make of oneself hitherto in the setting of what will now be affirmed or denied. Thus, in adolescence (1968:159):

> Identity formation arises from the selective repudiation and mutual assimilation of the childhood identifications and their absorption in a new configuration which in turn is dependent on the process by which a society ... identifies the young individual, recognising him as somebody who had to become the way he is, and who, being what he is, is taken for granted. The community, often not without some initial mistrust, gives such recognition with a display of surprise and pleasure in making the acquaintance of a newly emerging individual. For the community in turn feels 'recognised' by the individual who cares to ask for recognition.

So community and individual identify one another in a process of mutual scrutiny and recognition. But while that is an invariant property of identity formation, and while in adolescence another invariant is the 'problem' of establishing an occupational and sexual self, that is, an existence as an 'adult' rather than as a 'child', the particular way in which the two-sided identification of an adult occurs varies endlessly. More precisely, it varies historically as configurations change 'in the light of events'. The attempt to secure recognition as a 'Bright Young Thing', so successful in the 1920s, only secures repudiation as a 'silly idiot' twenty years later in a world re-created by economic depression and international war. Thus, addressing the problem of explaining the phenomenon of the emergence of 'youth' as a distinct, marked-out, phase of the life cycle in advanced capitalist societies in the 1960s, a phase characterised by widespread identity-confusion moreover, Erikson seizes at once on the specifically historical context of that phenomenon. At that moment, for reasons which he does not explore, adolescence had come to be organised as a distinct biographical episode, a period of time out, of extended social exploration free of requirements to be anything in particular. Given that context, the context of a 'psycho-social moratorium' in which the individual is offered time and space to try out roles, relationships, identities, occupations and life-styles, identity-confusion becomes the inescapable hazard of the passage through personal and social time. Social play, youth culture and ideological attachments are created as the distinctive means of navigating the passage through chaos. But for those whose play evokes no emphatic affirmation of any particular experimentally tried self, who do not bring to the experiment a sense of direction accrued from past affirmations and denials, the passage becomes an odyssey without destination. Mixed-up youth is the unavoidable counterpart of the creation of youth as an episode of uncharted personal exploration. One cultural counterpart of the creation of a society founded on private property and market relationships in which individuals as workers are forced to be free to sell their labour power is the social organisation of adolescence as a stage of personal history in which one is similarly forced to be free to hunt for an identity that is affirmed both by what one has been in the past and by what others encourage one to become now. But there is a collective process of becoming, too. When first discovered the extended psycho-social moratorium typical of advanced capitalist societies evokes dismay; a certain anxious uncertainty is the characteristic disposition of youth, coupled with a rather frantic and flailing exploration of all possibilities; being neither an adult nor a child is experienced as a painful problem. But a mere ten years later the same stage of the life cycle becomes a site for more positive action and construction; the past history of youth, the spectacle of the unhappy generation of one's predecessors as it were, forms part of the world in which youth now makes itself socially; strong sub-societies of the young are formed; being neither an adult nor a child is now experienced as a resource for being something creatively different; a resource, too, for protest against the conditions of both childhood and adulthood. A new generation emerges which creates new identities and demands recognition of them. Grudgingly or readily, and with whatever conditions or regrets, recognition is won and as the young enter the adult world that adult world is accordingly changed; now the setting for adolescence in future is itself changed; new guidelines for exploration and new boundaries of possible affirmation and denial have been marked out; navigating the psycho-social moratorium becomes relatively easier and as crisis was replaced by protest so protest is succeeded by a more or less institutionalised world of youth which adolescents take in their stride. Until something happens to recast the terms of action and affirmation anew, that is.

Within this process identities, identity-types and generations take shape, and so shape the possibilities for generations, identity-types and identities in the future. The specific crisis of youth examined by Erikson is, as he sees it, only understandable as a conjunction of histories of this sort. The transition from child to adult always confronts the individual with the problem of both reconciling what one is about to become and reconciling what one is to oneself with what one is to others within a given system of socially specified possibilities. The degree of complexity and ambiguity surrounding these problems is, however, *historically* variable. The psycho-social moratorium provides a setting for the resolution of such problems in all cultures; but its specific nature, duration, range and internal possibilities are also historically variable (1968:157).

> Each society and each culture institutionalises a certain moratorium for the majority of its young people. For the most part, these moratoria coincide with apprenticeships and adventures that are in line with the society's values. The moratorium may be a time for horse-stealing and vision-quests, a time for *Wanderschaft* or work 'out West' or 'down under', a time for 'lost youth' or academic life, a time for self-sacrifice or for pranks – and today, often a time for patienthood or delinquency.

The way the moratorium is organised, the way adolescence as

a span of the life cycle is institutionalised, varies enormously. It may be a matter of a literal moment, of a rite of passage, some ceremonial, magical or ritual event effecting an instant transition fron one strongly defined identity to another. Coming-of-age parties and graduation ceremonies are no doubt residual versions of a type of transition possible only in extremely unambiguous societies and experienced as a leap from one clearly specified state of being to another. At another extreme it may be a matter of a diffuse, protracted wandering through a misty landscape in which both where one has been and where one is going can be at best dimly glimpsed. Or it may be mapped in terms of a commercial or political youth culture, constructed from within on the basis of fashion, youth movements and ideological commitments or of hedonistic refusal of commitment. In general it will be more protracted and diffuse to the degree that the possibilities for personal becoming are themselves differentiated and indeterminate and the future of any given individual to that extent unpredictable on the basis of knowledge of what he or she has been until now – most diffuse, protracted and problematic, therefore, for 'able' adolescents in affluent market societies. To the extent that the transition is specified in terms of a sharply limited range of adult possibilities a narrow range of identity types is perpetuated; successive biological generations constitute a single sociological generation. And to the extent that the possibilities of adulthood are diversified and experimentation in adolescence and youth is grasped, permitted or required as the mode of transition new identity types can be constructed and new sociological generations forged out of the entry of youth into adult life. Structural differentiation makes for faster history.

But sociological generations are not made ad lib. New styles of identity can be made only within the specific historically constructed possibilities of the world entered by any given biological generation. If a new sociological generation is to emerge, a new configuration of social action, the attempt of individuals to construct identity must coincide with major and palpable historical experiences in relation to which new meanings can be assembled. Creativity feeds on experience not will. Biological age gives individuals distinctive problems and distinctive resources for solving those problems. The social organisation of the life cycle creates moments of more or less acute exploration – searching the environment to create a unity of meaning between the self and others. But it is historical events that seem to provide the crucial opportunities for constructing new versions of such meanings. Such opportunities are seized, in turn, most avidly and imaginatively by those who are most actively in the market for such meanings (identities). Hence the peculiar connection of youth (a span of biological history) and generations (a span of social history). And the more the overall configuration of a society leaves the mode of entry of new individuals open to negotiation the more likely it is that those individuals will put together a sense of themselves as being historically unlike their predecessors; will make something culturally or politically of their distinctiveness as youth. Such attempts create the world of youth as a stage of life history. But sometimes such attempts also seize on historical experience, of war, revolution, crisis or liberation for example, as the cornerstone for a new account of the configuration of society as a whole. An age group located at such a moment in history can create a new social generation. Life history and world history coalesce to transform each other. Identity is made within that double construction of time.

Sociologically, then, a generation is that span of time within which identity is assembled on the basis of an unchanged system of meanings and possibilities. A sociological generation can thus encompass many biological generations. The whole history of many traditional societies can represent no more than one sociological generation. We are told that there were fourteen generations from the time of Kind David to the Babylonian Captivity; but there was only a single sociological generation. The example is apt because it brings out the importance of great historical events and experiences in the making of sociological generations. Some examples from political sociology may be helpful here. Tables correlating voting preferences with age have long been a standard feature of psephological studies and were at first widely used to support generalisations about supposed relationships between stage in the life cycle and political disposition – the radicalism of youth, the conservatism of old age and so forth.

Unfortunately the evidence for such direct relationships almost always turned out, when subjected to close scrutiny, to be at best unreliable and at worst quite inadequate. In *Floating Voters and The Floating Vote*, for example, Hans Daudt (1961) went a long way towards completely discrediting the whole set of claims about the relationship of age to party loyalty put forward in the best known British and American voting studies of the 1950s and early 1960s. What then remained to make sense of the patterns of preference that the surveys had undoubtedly mapped, was the possibility that the linkages might be a matter of generations rather than of age as such. The notion of 'significant historical experiences' was introduced, as an intervening variable in effect, to account for age-linked distributions of political allegiance which generalisations about the political meaning of age itself could not explain. Thus, British studies of the 1950s found widespread and consistent differences between the attitudes and loyalties of people over the age of 65 and all those under that age. Leaving aside the question of the extent to which 65 had emerged as a significant age only because the questionnaires had been pre-coded to make it significant, it seemed clear that the very oldest members of the electorate had some special sense of what British politics were about not shared by their juniors. An explanation was offered in terms of the idea of political generations. The argument was that for reasons more or less loosely tied to 'historical experiences' people born after 1900 had learned to see and interpret their political environment in ways that were sharply at odds with those of their predecessors. The period when such people began to vote coincided, it was noted, with the sweeping redefinition of British politics achieved by the Great War and the effective establishment of the Labour Party. People over 65 in the 1950s would perforce have developed their political loyalties and understandings well before these changes occurred. Thus (Benney *et al.*, 1956), 'a man of Mr. Churchill's age who [in 1951] had lived in Greenwich all his life would have reached middle age and voted in four general elections before he ever had a chance to vote for a Labour candidate'. Perhaps a generational shift of meaning had occurred.

More ambitiously one of the most famous American

studies of the same period sought to account for a dramatic age-linked shift in the relationship between social class and party allegiance in very similar terms, finding in the historical experience of the Slump and Depression of the 1930s a context for a generational discovery of the political significance of class (Berelson *et al.*, 1954).

> A whole political generation may have been developing for whom the socio-economic problems of their youth served as bases for permanent political norms ... Presumably an age generation can be transformed by political events and social conditions ... a generation that retains its allegiances and norms while succeeding generations are moving in another direction.

And Rudolf Heberle in one of the first textbooks of political sociology (1951) developed the same idea even more generally, emphasising both the connection and the difference between biological and sociological generations; sociologically he suggested 'a generation consists of contemporaries of approximately the same age' but for whom age is established not by the calendar of years but by a calendar of events and experiences (1951:119):

> A social generation cannot be defined in biological terms and in terms of definite age groups, but has to be defined in terms of common and joint experiences, sentiments and ideas. 'A generation is thus a new way of feeling and understanding of life, which is opposed to the former way or at least different from it'. A generation is a phenomenon of collective mentality and morality. [The members] of a generation feel themselves linked by a community of standpoints, of beliefs and wishes.

Political movements and social interests are constructed, Heberle went on to argue, within the shell of generations formed in response to 'decisive, politically relevant experiences'. A social generation consists in this view of people of approximately the same historical age who have shared certain politically relevant experiences and created a new world of politics on the basis of those experiences. The most compelling example he offers is perhaps that of the wholesale reconstruction of politics in Germany after the defeat of 1918, noting in particular the way in which the new meanings were created by those who were themselves young. Thus (1951:121):

> The Nazi movement in Germany was led by men and women who were born between 1885 and 1900 or who were between 18 and 33 years old when the catastrophe of 1918 occurred. The war and its aftermath thus became the experience which was decisive for the formation of their political views. Regardless of which party they chose, their political thinking differed in many respects from that of the pre-war generation. Those who were only boys when the war began received their first notions of politics from the post-war internal troubles and [came] to think of political action in terms of conflict and combat rather than in terms of consensus and compromise.

Such a generation, a construction of historical time, may last for ten years or for a thousand. In this particular case it lasted of course until a new decisive experience – defeat in 1944 – made nonsense of the earlier system of meanings.

Heberle completed his analysis (1951:122) by trying to spell out just what a 'decisive politically relevant experience' might be, and was not altogether successful in doing so. Decisiveness seems to be something of an elusive quality determined very much in the eye of the beholder. The value of his approach is not so much in settling that question therefore, as in the bridge he builds between biological generations and historical or social generations. In the manner of Elkins and Erikson but with a much stronger historical emphasis, he points to the possibility and desirability of understanding historical change as a process embedded in the coming-together of personal and social time, and conversely of understanding the typical identities of social generations as historical creations.

Of course, to get this far is only a beginning. All sorts of problems remain. For example, the translation of historical experience into new meanings and new patterns of identity does not have to be a dramatic response to single, momentous events. It can also be achieved gradually by way of a slow accretion of quite mundane experiences. In such circumstances the cut-off points between generations tend to remain obscure; one can see that at a given time a new identity type has been established but cannot fix the point at which its establishment began. Thus, in *The Lonely Crowd* David Riesman (1950) identified three broad types of social character, tradition-directed, inner-directed and other-directed, emerging to prominence in sequence in European and North American history. But he recognised the coming-into-being of each type as a matter of a gradual discovery of new personal styles in the face of new opportunities and constraints pieced together through successive biological generations. By the 1950s one could perhaps see that the other-directed type, a type guided by the approval or disapproval of others rather than by the demands of conscience which had no less decisively guided the inner-directed type, had become a normal identity in the United States. But pockets of both inner-directed and tradition-directed types remained. Neither in time nor space could the generational pattern be given clear boundaries. The same problem is apparent in Richard Sennett's *The Fall of Public Man* (1977). Sennett traces a profound reorganisation of identity from an essentially public to an essentially 'narcissistic' mode between the 18th century and the present. The change seems undeniable, but again it has been brought about piecemeal; there are no sudden discontinuities in the face of calamitous events but a prolonged always exploratory, increasingly affirmed move away from the involvement of individuality in the public domain. As it proceeds the consequences for identity are slowly revealed. At some late point it becomes clear that a new type of individual exists. Thus, the identification of the contexts of experience and the significant sequences of experience within which generations of historically located identity-types are constructed is not always going to be as easy to achieve as studies of plantation slavery, Nazism or modern youth might suggest. The process is in fact more of a process and less of an event-bounded series of stages than those studies imply. Generations with their distinct identity-types appear, but the roots from which they have grown ramify deeply within sequences of past identity-formation. Wide-ranging and minutely detailed studies like *The Fall of Public Man* or Edward Thompson's *The Making of the English Working Class* are needed to bring those sequences to light.

Then again, the process of reconstructing identity (that is, of changing society) is not evenly diffused through whole societies. Some groups or categories of people are more exposed to experiences that deny past identities and affirm the possibility of new ones than others. Some are relatively free to explore the possible meanings of their experience and attempt to construct new social worlds on that basis; some are so placed as to be impelled towards such explorations; others are relatively unfree in that respect. Here we encounter the problem which Karl Mannheim (1952) faced in introducing the concept of 'generation units'. History provides resources to be used in the process of identity-formation. Some age-sets within a society, that of youth for example, are more likely than others to make use of such resources creatively. But within any given age-set some will experience historical events more acutely than others or be able to respond to them more vigorously; they will be more directly caught up in events or more capable of giving historical experience historical significance. And where such minorities have opportunities for mutual communication, association and organisation they can become the makers of history, key agents in articulating a new sense of historical location, a new pattern of generations. The young men who made up the 'class of 1938' in the Egyptian Military Academy, haunted by their sense of Egyptian national history as a record of humiliation and finally shamed by defeat in Palestine into overthrowing the monarchy in order to 'renew history' are a good example of such a group. The students who sustained the 'May Events' in France in 1968 are another. Lewis Feuer's *The Conflict of Generations* (1969) is in effect a massive study of such groups, minorities within an age-set, placed in some privileged site, enabled by their location to translate personal concerns into public issues, to link life history and world history by building new generational patterns on the basis of historical experience. But as Mannheim pointed out the important characteristic of such generation units is that their location and effectiveness in a social system cannot be explained adequately on the basis of age alone. Age is a necessary but not a sufficient condition for their existence. Other factors such as class, religion, race, occupation, institutional setting, in short all the conventional categories of social-structural analysis, must be introduced to explain their unique ability to make something of historical experiences. In other words, the study of generations brings to light consequential differentiations *within* generations as well as between them. Far from exempting us from the study of social structure any attempt to grapple with the problem of the historical formation of identity forces us in just that direction. The emergence of generation units and their capacity or inability to reconstruct identity can only be explained in those terms. Here as elsewhere historical sociology means more work, not less.

At the same time it holds out the prospect of more fruitful work, grounded in a recognition of the fact (which it has been the main object of this chapter to demonstrate) that the process of identity formation and the process of social reproduction are one and the same. Insofar as we can understand personal identity and social structure not as distinct states of being but as elements of a single process of becoming, historical sociology is freed from the spurious dualism which puts knowledge of the individual beyond the reach of social science. But the bases for such an understanding are to be found not in general assertions of its desirability but in the empirical study of the 'becoming' of identities and societies. Thus, the further study of the Germans who became Nazis has tended increasingly to isolate a highly specific generation unit within the biological generation that grew up in the face of economic collapse and the defeat of an invincible empire. The work of Abel (1966) and Merkl (1975) in particular has located the Nazis as not just young in 1918 and therefore experiencing economic and political chaos as a peculiarly acute loss of direction in terms of their own careers and selves, but more narrowly, the children of working class or lower middle class families imbued with a strong sense of the values of hard work, patriotism and obedience – a distinct moral earnestness, as Barrington Moore (1978) puts it, giving rise in the face of collapse to a distinct moral outrage. More narrowly still, they had behind them the experience of life in the trenches, a life of togetherness, solidarity, discipline and honour, and of the shocking return to a civilian society that seemed only to deny and discredit the life of the trenches. As one of the autobiographies collected by Abel and cited by Barrington Moore (1978:413) records:

Troops were once again returning to the Fatherland, yet a disgusting sight met their eyes. Beardless boys, dissolute deserters and whores tore off the shoulder bands of our front-line fighters and spat upon their field gray uniforms ... People who never saw a battle field, who had never heard the whine of a bullet, openly insulted men who through four and a half years had defied the world in arms ... For the first time I began to feel a burning hatred for this human scum that trod everything pure and clean underfoot.

From all this came not just a diffuse resentment but a sharply defined call for a reconstructed 'people's community' modelled on the comradeship of the trenches and envisaging a reaffirmation of inherited values in the face of the immoral disorder of the post-war world – as they saw it. The generation unit thus turned the wide-ranging confusion and discontent of its age group into a very specific reconstruction of history based on the idealisation of their experience of comradeship in armed struggle. The explanation of the Nazi movement has to be found in a particular historical conjunction of four things: some specifically German cultural themes, the life histories of a particular biological generation, class structure, and war.

In making themselves within the terms of that conjunction the early Nazis found a way of re-making history. The young are not usually so lucky. A more familiar experience is that documented by Paul Willis in *Learning to Labour* (1977): the experience of working class boys discovering school as a system of power implacably hostile to their own values, understandings and culture, creating their own world – 'the counter-school culture' – in opposition to the demands of that system, enthusiastically embracing manual work as a triumphant expression of their opposition, insight and rejection only to find that in doing so they have committed themselves to the destiny the school system had in store for them all along, that they have embraced their own repression. In Willis's terms their relatively free cultural production is also the reproduction of the social structure that condemns them to unfreedom. Of course Willis was not the first to observe this paradox of the normal socialisation process of class societies. It is the central insight of a very large body of work on the social entrances of the young from which the contributions of the Centre for

Contemporary Cultural Studies (1976, 1979), Stanley Cohen (1973), Firestone (1957), Rainwater (1965) and especially the exceptionally perceptive early essay of Albert Cohen, *Delinquent Boys* (1955) might be singled-out as landmarks. Indeed, the paradox was widely understood by sensitive lay observers long before socialisation, identity-formation or social reproduction had been identified as problems for academic analysis. Thus, in *Across the Bridges*, a study of working class life in South London written in 1910, Alexander Patterson had already noticed the final effects of the social process traced in *Learning to Labour* – the loss of personal momentum that comes with the discovery that the leap into work, the individual's life-asserting protest, is in fact a leap into a living death, the life-denying normal condition of one's class (Patterson, 1910:134):

> After the first two weeks, working days are very drab. Little demand is made on intelligence, initiative or imagination in the wharves, tanneries, or food-stuff factories of South London. Work grows so monotonous that its very monotony no longer occasions comment. The boy never thinks of his work as a feature of his life; it lies at the back of his mind as an unmentioned necessity ... a dull thing of which nothing can be predicted, and no conversation can live which begins from this starting-point.

Only a little while later (1910:205):

> When school, games and marriage are well behind him, the ordinary workman by the water's edge slips into his groove and will be likely to stay there till the end of his days. Occasions for romance and excitement have passed ... At thirty a man has given up playing games, making love to his wife, reading books, or building castles in the air. He is dangerously contented with his daily work. Early rising no longer vexes his sleepy soul, for it is an instinct now to roll out of bed and light the gas; he no longer shivers as he turns into the dark wet street. Boys turn up their collars, put hands in pockets, and scutter along the streets not a little aggrieved that the hour is so early and they a little late. But the older man lights a pipe and trudges with heavy feet at a slow, even pace, with no signs of worry or animation in his face, his thoughts inscrutable.

A social world has been re-made; the barbarians have been agents of their own taming. They were never really barbarians at all of course – only a little loosely placed in the figuration. Individually they become workers to defy the alien culture of the school; in so doing they perpetuate the collective fate of their class; they renew the class structure, choosing to be what that structure requires them to be.

In sum, accepting the perspective of historical sociology on the problem of the individual and society, affirming the historical unity of personal identities and social configurations, the fusion of subject and object as states of being in a single two-sided process of becoming, merely gives us new problems to explore. It closes off one, increasingly sterile, line of debate but simultaneously it opens up a new agenda for research. Studying the social character of the Yurok Indians, Erik Erikson (1943) remarked that 'systems of child training... represent unconscious attempts at creating out of human raw material that configuration of attitudes which is ... the optimum under the tribe's particular natural conditions and economic-historic necessities'. As David Riesman (1950:5) commented, 'from "economic-historic necessities" to "systems of child training" is a long jump'. It is that jump however, or rather the long series of jumps involved in detailed studies of the dynamics of social reproduction and identity formation, the synthesis of society and the self, that the historical sociology of the individual impels one to attempt. Can we trace the incremental processes of social and individual becoming that eventually reveal the existence of new generations? Can we locate generation units and can we account for the ability of some groups within an age-set to perform that vanguard function in historical change and the inability of others? Can we trace the dynamics of social reproduction in ethnographies of personal identity-formation? I have argued that such work can indeed be done and that in doing it a specifically historical sociology could hope to overcome the otherwise daunting but essentially spurious 'problem' of the individual and society. As the understanding of personal identity as a crystallisation of the historical world of the individual and the historical worlds of others comes to be accepted the problem of trying to account for particular identity types in particular historical settings thus reappears in new, and to my mind much more promising, forms: a new programme of research tasks opens up.

And over and above all that there remains the problem of whether treating individuality as a matter of identity-formation and identity-formation in turn as a matter of social reproduction and both as the Janus faces of historically formed figurations can provide us with adequate explanations, not only of the typical identities of whole groups or populations – as I have argued in this chapter – but more narrowly of those exceptional and extraordinary individuals whose lives seem to transcend the limits of possibility set for their peers and contemporaries – the Dracula problem. Can historical sociology encompass the individual in that sense, too?

9

The historical sociology of individuals:
monsters and heroes:
careers and contingencies

The problem of accounting sociologically for the individual in particular is really only a more precise version of the problem of accounting for individuals in general. The solution in both cases lies in treating the problem historically – as a problem of understanding processes of becoming rather than states of being. Treated in that way Lenin and Luther, the Sun King and Shakespeare no more elude or defy sociological explanation than do Russian proletarians in 1900, German knights and peasants and princes in 1500, French aristocrats in 1700 or any other figuration of individuals en masse. Getting close enough to the interactional detail of the biographies of single individuals may indeed preclude a fully adequate explanation of, say, the difference between Shakespeare and Marlowe, Jonson, Middleton, Marston or Webster, or of why W. Shakespeare, born at Stratford upon Avon in April 1564 and dying there in April 1616, should have been William Shakespeare, as distinct from an explanation of the vigour and character of the English theatre in that generation. But the difficulty is essentially a technical one, not a difficulty of principle; a matter of the degree of knowledge we need, not of its nature. In principle the wall of self around the great individual collapses in the face of historical sociology just as does that around anyone else once we force ourselves to see social reality as process rather than order, structuring rather than structure, becoming not being.

The field of sociology in which emphasis has been placed most strongly on becoming rather than being is of course that of the sociology of deviance. While the ultimate reasons for this distinctive emphasis may be dubious – probably having a good deal to do with a fairly naive liberal assumption (or hope) that individuals could not just be bad and that the problem of explaining badness had therefore to be one of explaining how they sometimes became bad – there can be no doubt that the results of that emphasis have been remarkably impressive. By any standard the sociology of deviance is one of the most dynamic, sophisticated and cogent strands of modern social analysis. Knowledge accumulates, debates proliferate but are also resolved, the relationship between theory and empirical inquiry is manifestly fluid and fruitful. And most of this really does seem to be linked to the fact that the problems of the field are typically defined as problems of social becoming. Yet there is an obvious sense in which deviance is only a particular (morally stigmatised) kind of individual variation on collective themes. Could not any other type of variation – saintliness, greatness, creativity, wisdom, indeed whatever is peculiarly individual about any selected individual – be explained in much the same way? Could not the strategies developed to account for becoming deviant account equally effectively for becoming a hero, or a genius? Sociologists of deviance themselves have often claimed as much. However they have narrowed their explicit concerns to the study of crime and delinquency, implicitly they have defined their field as embracing all forms of human non-conformity. In that respect R. K. Merton (1957) represented the sociology of deviance very fairly when, in a still enormously influential essay, he proposed that criminal deviance might be studied as a specific variant within the larger social process of 'innovation'. Merton's own paradigm for the study of 'social structure and anomie' may have been swallowed up in the hungry advance of the sociology of deviance towards more refined and complex analysis of the processes of deviation, but his general sense that in principle the study of those processes also offered a key to the understanding of other forms of social becoming remains assertively alive. However, the important issue from my point of view is not so much that explanations of becoming deviant are also implicitly explanations of other kinds of social becoming, as that the structure of such explanations, as they have emerged in the sociology of deviance, is firmly historical.

They are explanations centred on the idea of temporally organised sequence. The crucial explanatory concepts refer to successions of action and reaction and of personal and social change in time: socialization, drift, the formation of subcultures, affiliation, the deviant career, signification. In all the varieties of the sociology of deviance deviants are explained in terms of their histories.

The common perspective that has come to dominate the field is well summarised by Edwin Lemert in writing of 'Deviation as a Process' (1967:50)

> The most general process by which status and role transitions take place is socialization. As it has been applied to the study of deviants the concept has been further circumscribed to designate such processes as criminalization, prisonization, 'sophistication', 'hardening', pauperization, addiction, conversion, radicalization, professionalization and 'mortification of self'. All of these speak in varying degrees of a personal progression of differentiation in which the individual acquires: (1) morally inferior status (2) special knowledge and skills; (3) an integral attitude or 'world view'; and (4) a distinctive self-image based upon but not necessarily coterminous with his image reflected in interaction with others.

Lemert himself is inclined to reject the more strongly deterministic or tendentious versions of this common approach and criticises both those explanations which envisage a 'natural history' of deviation and those which stress the idea of a 'deviant career' as a pre-determined 'course to be run'. But even while he emphasizes the extent to which the 'flux and pluralism' of social interaction make 'the delineation of fixed sequences or stages through which persons move from less to more serious deviance ... difficult or impossible' to achieve, he remains firmly and unambiguously within the historical perspective as a whole. His concern is to emphasize the open-endedness of the history of deviation, the extent to which it is beset by contingencies and shaped by either creativity or drift, not at all to challenge the fundamental idea that the explanation of deviance has to be historical. As seriously as any of the writers he criticises Lemert seeks to identify the forms that characterise the process of becoming deviant (forms of drift and discovery rather than of the deviant career so far as he is concerned), and to specify the interactions, junctures and episodes that mark the decisive passages in the life history of individuals enacting that process. Thus, his own best-known contribution to the study of deviance (1951:75) is probably the introduction of the concept of 'secondary' deviation – a concept designed precisely to identify the crucial passage from one state of being to another achieved in sequences of interaction between the deviant and others. Secondary deviation is a response to a response, a matter of what the individual makes of what a significant social audience has made of what it took the individual to have been or to have done in the first place. Or as Lemert puts it (1967:40) 'secondary deviation refers to a special class of socially defined responses which people make to problems created by the societal reaction to their deviance'. It points to a sequential move the individual makes towards a more considered deviant practice or existence following the perception of oneself as someone who has been perceived as deviant by others. Such action-reaction sequences give the individual distinctive problems, 'essentially moral problems which revolve around stigmatization, punishments, segregation and social control'. Reaction invests action with meaning; subsequent action reacts to that investment. More narrowly, secondary deviation 'concerns processes which create, maintain or intensify stigma; it presumes that stigma may be unsuccessfully contained and lead to repetition of deviance similar or related to that which orginally initiated stigmatization' (1967:41). The sequences of action and response and action implied in such a concept may be both very swift and very ramified; but that does not at all belie the fact that the reference is essentially to sequences, to historical process. The idea of secondary deviation is specifically a device of historical interpretation. 'When a person begins to employ his deviant behaviour or a role based upon it as a means of defence, attack or adjustment to the overt and covert problems created by the consequent societal reaction to him, his deviation is secondary' (1951:76). The problem of explanation thus becomes one that calls for 'detailed formulation of the processes by which societies create moral problems for deviants, define and punish or reward the individual deviant's attempts to deal with such problems in a configuration of general life problems' – and presumably for detailed analysis, too, of the ways such individuals live through such processes.

And explanations of that kind are of course exactly what we find through the most distinctive and distinguished modern contributions to the sociology of deviance – in the work of Becker (1963), Young (1969) and Kitsuse (1962) as in that of Goffman (1968), Cohen (1955) and Matza (1969). In the most famous programmatic statement of this style of analysis Howard Becker is very explicit in asserting the necessity of a sequential, historical, conception of the problem to be explained – that is, of problems of becoming. Thus (1963:23)

> We need a model which takes into account the fact that patterns of behaviour develop in orderly sequence. In accounting for an individual's use of marihuana ... we must deal with a sequence of steps, of changes in the individual's behaviour and perspectives, in order to understand the phenomenon. Each step requires explanation, and what may operate as a cause at one step in the sequence may be of negligible importance at another step. We need for example, one kind of explanation of how a person comes to be in a situation where marihuana is easily available to him, and another kind of explanation of why, given the fact of its availability, he is willing to experiment with it in the first place. And we need still another explanation of why, having experimented with it, he continues to use it. In a sense each explanation constitutes a necessary cause of the behaviour. That is, no one could become a confirmed marihuana user without going through each step ... The explanation of each step is thus part of the explanation of the resulting behaviour. Yet the variables which account for each step may not, taken separately, distinguish between users and nonusers.

Becker goes on to advocate the use in this context of just that conception of the 'deviant career' about which Lemert is so sceptical. He does so, however, in a rather peculiar way. Unlike the career of the surgeon or the bureaucrat the deviant career, like that envisaged for the mental patient by Goffman, is decisively a career of contingencies. Where advancement in the straight career is primarily a matter of movement through standardized, institutionally prescribed stages in a formally ordered sequence, progress in a deviant career is seen, by almost all of those who have used the concept, as a question of the negotiation of contingencies. At the same time these are career contingences, contingent not in the sense of being merely adventitious random occurrences but in the sense of being incident upon distinctive patters of interaction. They are significant conjunctures of uncertain outcome, decisive moments at which the career is framed and structured one way or another. Emphasising the importance of contingencies in the deviant career is not therefore to reduce the process of becoming to a record of chance happenings. Rather, what is being stressed is the way in which the process is organised in terms of sequences of characteristic but not pre-determined interactions, probable but not prescribed episodes of action and response in which the individual moves or is moved from one status to another. We are talking not about a chapter of accidents but about what Lemert calls 'the typical contingencies' of particular courses of interaction.

Thus Goffman (1968) can readily allow that the career of the mental patient is riddled with contingencies without at all having to qualify his claim that 'the self occurs within the confines of an institutional system'. The contingencies in question may be a matter of 'socio-economic status, visibility of the offence, proximity to a mental hospital' or perhaps especially of changes in the circumstances if kin, friends or neighbours which lead them to regard the pre-patient as more troublesome than they had previously thought, as perhaps a suitable case for treatment. Yet the point about such contingencies is that they are specific to the career. They select quite systematically the sorts of people who are likely to have careers as mental patients or they are the sorts of things that are systematically likely to happen to people who have such careers. They are significant as contingencies because they are occasions specifically for becoming, or not becoming, a mental patient, for the next step in the career. Within the process of social becoming structure and contingency lock together. It is accordingly as anything but a rhetorical flourish that Goffman suggests that, 'in the degree that the "mentally ill" outside hospitals numerically approach or surpass those inside hospitals, one could say that mental patients distinctively suffer not from mental illness, but from contingencies'. Becker invites us to accept a very similar conclusion in the case of marihuana users. For both Becker and Goffman, indeed, the whole value of the concept of the deviant career seems to lie in the unique way in which as a model of social process it unites contingency and structure, revealing the process of becoming deviant as a matter, almost, of the social organisation of contingencies. The individual embarks on a course of (deviant) action which in certain (contingent) circumstances is likely to evoke certain (stigmatising) responses; the responses in turn give the individual certain problems which in certain (contingent) circumstances are likely to be solved in certain (more deviant) ways which in turn evoke responses which ... and so on until the match of social definition and self-definition is firmly established. The problem is to identify the certain circumstances, responses and problems – the pattern of contingency and socialisation. And here the concept permits a useful distinction between what might be called formal and informal career contingencies in the deviant career. Consider the case of apprehension. Apprehension is a typical and formal contingency for the criminal deviant in the sense that it is an institutionally organised response to criminal action. Yet apprehension does not of course automatically follow criminal action in the way promotion in a straight career may automatically follow the passing of examinations. Who is apprehended, and still more the question of what they and others make of the fact of apprehension, is governed not by the incidence of criminal facts but by a host of further and informal contingencies: the competence and resources of the deviant, the resources and policies of the police, the social class, ethnic and sexual characteristics of deviants and perhaps still more their previous life-history insofar as it is or is not constructed as a criminal record. In all these ways informal contingencies mediate the probability and the significance of the formal contingency; but the informal contingencies are themselves systematic probabilities of a structured social world.

What is insisted upon, then, is that becoming deviant is not a matter of personal or social pathology, social disorganisation, deprivation, broken homes, viciousness, bad company or chance but of a negotiated passage to a possible identity, a *sequence* of action and reaction, labelling and learning in the face of both organised power and organised opportunity, probable constraint and probable contingency. Whether one sees the individual as forced on towards deviance by the exigent demands of powerful others that a deviant identity be acknowledged, or as creatively seizing opportunities for personal self-definition implicit in the confused reponses of others to one's actions, or (Lemert, 1967:51) as merely 'drifting into deviance by specific actions rather than by informed choices', the underlying perspective is the same. The individual becomes deviant on the basis of contingently but not at all randomly ordered sequences of interaction. It is a view aptly summarised by Rubington and Weinberg (1968:204) in their image of a 'corridor of deviation':

> Suppose we think of deviance as an interactive process taking place in the corridor of a building. There is a front and a rear to the building and there are offices off the corridor on both of its sides ... each portion of the corridor has openings at the front, the rear and along both sides ... as entrances or exits. The following diagram indicates the possible flow of deviance through the corridor. Traffic flows north, south, east and west in this corridor. The dotted lines represent the symbolic boundaries marking a person's progress through the corridor. These boundaries, though unseen by all of course, are quite real in their effects. And they are maintained by sentries, some visible, some unseen. Social typing, for example, steers people through the corridor. Defining agents work at each of these symbolic boundaries. And ... agents speed certain candidates along the corridor and usher others out the side doors or back to where they started from. At each stage of the traffic flow the person walking through this corridor is responding to his own actions in terms of the symbols by which others define him, as person and as actor. Who these others are, his relationship to them, and their symbolic definitions are important in affecting the next steps he will take. To a very great extent, it is the actions of these others that create and sustain the deviant career. In addition the visibility, the frequency, the exposure, the severity of reacting others, and the particular form of deviance shape the flow, and direction and pace of traffic up and down the corridor.

The metaphor is similar to that of the 'betrayal funnel' through which Goffman (1968:130) sees the prospective mental patient passing on the way to hospitalisation and to Becker's more general conception of the contingency-riddled deviant career: biography realises social process.

The Deviance Corridor

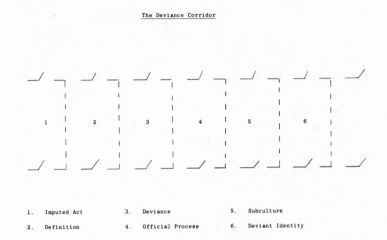

1.	Imputed Act	3.	Deviance	5.	Subculture
2.	Definition	4.	Official Process	6.	Deviant Identity

Two analytical ideas are common to all these approaches to the study of deviance. First, they all stress the two-sidedness of the process of becoming as both public and private life. In taking up the concept of the career as a tool for understanding how people become deviant Becker explicitly follows Everett Hughes in emphasising the double reference of the idea (1963:33): 'objectively ... a series of statuses and clearly defined offices ... typical sequences of position, achievement, responsibility, and even of adventure', and 'subjectively ... the moving perspective in which the person sees his life as a whole and interprets the meaning of his various attributes, actions, and the things which happen to him'. And Goffman opens his analysis of the moral career of the mental patient in just the same way (1968:119): his reference is to 'such changes over time as are basic and common to the members of a social category although occurring independently to each of them'; and the special merit of the career perspective in exploring such changes is found in 'the way it allows one to move back and forth between the personal and the public, between the self and its significant society'. And secondly, closely related to the two-sided reference of the concept, is an awareness that the process of becoming deviant has both an analytical logic – the sequence of stages that in principle must be passed through – and an empirical chronology – the actual biographies of those who become deviant. The process can be specified both as a formally ordered progression, such as the corridor of deviation, and as an actual history, the movement through the corridor of individual deviants. Both types of sequence must be examined if adequate explanation is to be achieved. But the vitally important point is that while processes of social becoming have this doubly historical character – and so can be described either logically or chronologically – the relationship between the logic and the chronology is not fixed. Or to put it another way, the logic of becoming requires *some* sort of chronological realisation but within the terms of that requirement many actual chronologies are permitted. We might, for example, encounter individuals who enter Rubington and Weinberg's corridor of deviation not at the front entrance but in, say, portion 5 (having been, in effect, born into a deviant sub-culture), are then caught up by the official process of apprehension, arraignment and punishment on the basis of police policies towards all perceived members of the sub-culture and proceed only thereafter to actual deviant acts as an available, perhaps the only available, way of life for them having been stigmatised, and so finally double-back through the corridor towards a deviant identity. The actual history constitutes a loop in the logical sequence not a direct progression through it. But the loop of action, interaction and commitment is nevertheless one that occurs within the sequential structure of the logic of the corridor of deviation. Both the conception of logical sequence and that of empirical chronology are needed if we are to understand how individuals become deviant – or perhaps anything else.

The example is in fact not fanciful. It is one that we can find enacted in many actual biographies. Thus Victor Serge, in *Memoirs of a Revolutionary* (1963), describes very vividly the dovetailing of logic and chronology in his own life-history – the convergence of a social system progressively dooming individuals such as Serge to be revolutionary, and of individuals progressively deciding that they had to be revolutionary in such a social sytem. Yet the individual journeys were very erratic, full of sudden spurts and delays, punctuated by many detours and diversions. Only in retrospect could the character of the journey as a powerfully organised social process be discerned. Serge himself, born in the 'deviant sub-culture' of a world of revolutionary exiles, of heroic aspirations and disabling insecurity, indignation and hunger, made a rapid start (1963:2): 'On the walls of our humble and makeshift lodgings there were always the portraits of men who had been hanged. The conversations of grown-ups dealt with trials, executions, escapes ... with great ideas incessantly argued over and with the latest books about those ideas'. By the age of twelve he had discovered the meaning of life in the formula: 'Thou shalt think, thou shalt struggle, thou shalt be hungry'. But then followed a period of protracted wandering, uncertainty and exploration; friendships and separations; learning and working (1963:8): 'I became a photographer's apprentice, and after that an office boy, a draughtsman and, almost, a central-heating technician'. From these experiences came the slow piecing-together of an inner condition of helpless rage, the feeling of being trapped in 'a world without escape', in which 'there was nothing for it but to fight for an impossible escape' (1963:1) In the gulf between ideals and experience 'Life displayed itself to us in various aspects of a rather degrading captivity' (1963:9). And at that point Victor Serge knew he had to fight back but not how to do so. Contemplating 'the anxious emigre existence' of his father in endless 'close combat with the money-lenders', he concluded, 'I want to fight back as you yourself have fought, as everyone must fight throughout life. I can see quite clearly that you have been beaten. I shall try to have more strength or better luck' (1963:8). But as yet he could give such conclusions only limited practical application; he decided 'not to become a student'. At this stage material conditions, the social world of his parents with its symbolism of fighting back as a moral pivot of existence, the tangible sense of personal reality and achievement that then sprang from the experience of actually fighting back and association through friendship with the comparable experiences of others of his generation seem to have been the decisive precipitants of his 'career'.

In the *Memoirs* Serge himself stresses particularly the importance of his early friendships in consolidating his sense of enraged imprisonment. But what strikes the reader is the extent to which he appears to have chosen friends who might have been carefully selected for just that purpose. At the very least a dramatic elective affinity seems to have guided him. His friends were not drawn in any random or representative way from his generation or even from those in similar objective circumstances to himself. Rather, he appears to have sought out others whose response to such circumstances echoed or complemented his own. A group of friends was formed within which a common predicament could be defined and a common reaction to that predicament collectively affirmed. He found the friends who could help him solve his particular problems. Such friends were available because his problems were in fact the problems of his society from the point of view of whole categories of its members. His friendships helped him to construct and make explicit the world, and the self, that made best sense of what he had already become. Collectively they launched themselves on the common career to which that world most persuasively invited them (1963:9):

> 'What will become of us in twenty years' time?' we asked ourselves one evening. Thirty years have passed now. Raymond was guillotined: 'Anarchist Gangster' (so the newspapers) ... I came across Jean again in Brussels, a worker and trade-union organiser, still a fighter for liberty after ten years in gaol. Luce had died of tuberculosis, naturally. For my part, I have undergone a little over ten years of various forms of captivity, agitated in seven countries and written twenty books. I own nothing. On several occasions a Press with a vast circulation has hurled filth at me because I spoke the truth ... Those were the only roads possible for us.

Yet the friendships themselves and the social construction they made possible were but a clarifying moment in the process of becoming. Affiliation with such a highly probable group of peers made possible a dramatic sharpening of the most probable account of what each subjectively had experienced – the account of life as a struggle inside a trap (1963:12): 'Where could we go, what could become of us with this need for the absolute, this yearning for battle, this blind desire, against all obstacles, to escape from the city and the life from which there was no escape?'

In the event, the opportunity for escape was provided by the experience of arrest, trial and imprisonment. Brutal practical involvement with the imprisoning society in its most directly authoritative forms provided a bridge from metaphor to reality, from the idea of anarchistic protest within a trap to the practice of revolution. Slowly Serge and his friends had moved towards the enactment of the ideas they had helped each other to articulate (1963:11): 'ideas were our salvation ... gradually we entered into battle'. By way of marches and demonstrations, anarchist communes, conspiratorial projects, skirmishes with the police, street battles, the arrest, execution or suicide of others they took up and displayed an active, visible existence as militants – albeit militants still in the cause of hopelessness: 'a positive explosion of despair was building up in us'. As they made themselves visible they ensured the obvious consequence of visibility: they became 'known' to the police and in due course, although not in any way as a direct result of anything they in particular had done, they were swept into the arms of the law. The arrests were at once casual and inevitable, out of the blue and only to be expected: 'One morning a group of enormous police officers burst into our lodgings ...' (1963:38). The trials that followed were concerned not so much to prove and punish specific criminal offences as to confirm the entry of accusers and accused into a definite, acknowledged relationship to one another (1963:37)

> My examination was short and pointless, since I was actually accused of no offence ... The prosecution had intended to unearth (for the benefit of the public) an authentically novelettish conspiracy, assigning me to the role of its 'theoretician', but had to abandon this project after the second session. I had believed that I would manage to be acquitted, but now understood that in such an atmosphere the acquittal of a young Russian, and a militant at that, was impossible, despite the entire clarity of the facts of the case ... I found this justice nauseating; it was fundamentally more criminal than the worst criminals. This was incontestably obvious; it was just that I was an enemy.

Serge was sentenced to five years of solitary confinement. He had, in an irrefutable sense, become a revolutionary. Prison opened the doors of identity and forced him through them, confirming irresistibly that the world he had with increasing self-consciousness always sought to construct did indeed exist and was unavoidably the world in which he had to live.

It is from such biographies that the social process of becoming, immanent in even the most eccentric individual lives, must be reconstructed. Individuals *are* their biographies. And insofar as a biography is fully and honestly recorded what it reveals is some historically-located history of self-construction – a moral career in fact. The setting of the biography is this or that historically given system of probabilities or life chances. The biography realises some life chances within that system and perforce abandons others. It does so by progressively narrowing and specifying the meaning of self through sequential, historically ordered interaction. The logic of becoming is realised in the chronology of interaction. It is, paradoxically, by taking the point of view of the subject in the study of becoming that one sees most clearly the extent to which becoming is a socially structured process. Viewing Victor Serge's life as a whole one can say that he became one of the people he, having been born in a particular situation at a particular historical moment, could have been. But as we follow the record of his experience and action year by year it is more and more legitimate to say that historically (within the setting of his own life history) he was what he had to become. The patterning of biography is in fact at once historically shaped and historically constructed. The destiny of Victor Serge was shaped by the experience of his parents – the consequence of the assassination of Tsar Alexander II – and by the specifically anarchist account of radicalism achieved in France in the 1880s. The heroism and defeat of the anarchism of the 1880s gave the generation of 1900 a possible understanding of the world that was both distinctively anarchistic and distinctively despairing. Emile Henry, Ravachol and the other anarchist martyrs of the previous generation had bombed and killed believing that they might somehow also change the world. Bonnot, Libertad and the rest of the militants who defined protest in the generation of Victor Serge received their predecessors' anarchist account of the world but knew in advance that their own actions were doomed. They were in Serge's own term 'desperadoes', victims of 'an utter frustration'. They constructed their historically unique (monstrous) radicalism within the confines of that historically unique (and monstrous) predicament.

The individuality of even the most peculiar individual may, then, be understood sociologically once individuality itself is recognised as a matter of historically located historical processes. The patterning of eccentric lives is itself eccentric, but nonetheless patterned. The routine sequences of a moral career appear to organise the destinies of heroes and villains, geniuses and buffoons no less than they do those of mental patients or dance-band musicians – once we choose to look for them. If we think otherwise it is often because we have failed to acknowledge the degree to which the career of any particular hero or villain, genius or buffoon is located within a particular matrix of historical meanings and life chances. The studies by Abel (1966) and Merkl (1975) of the autobiographies of 581 early Nazis – outstanding evidence of the extent to which personal outrage and innovation are patterned by socially ordered series of experiences – were discussed in this connection in the last chapter. Here I would simply suggest that exactly the same sort of analysis can be applied just as successfully to single individuals. The Nazis were not distinctively workers or peasants, petty-bourgeois or industrialists; they were people whose biographies embodied and enacted a distinctive sequential dialectic of disillusionment and expectation; who became Nazis in the course of living that dialectic – which itself could only have been lived by them at that time. And the essentially historical mode of explanation that allows us to understand them collectively will also allow us to understand them singly; to account for Hitler in particular as well as for the Nazis in general. In attempting to understand Hitler or Calvin or Napoleon or Lenin we are at least at the outset attempting to understand spectacularly successful versions of the career of the Nazi, the Protestant, the revolutionary soldier and the Bolshevik, not some inaccessibly individual departure from them. And the analysis of any career – surgeon, prostitute, marihuana-user or revolutionary – is at root an analysis of the conditions governing recruitment to it, exclusion from it and especially success or failure within it.

There are really five steps to my argument here and it may be helpful to identify them formally before going on. First, the individual is an abstraction from the process of individuation – of becoming individual – and individuality must be studied as such a process of becoming if it is to be fully understood. Second, processes of becoming, whether they contribute to social reproduction or to social innovation, are embedded, enacted, lived in particular conjunctions of life-history and social history, a two-dimensional time. Third, such processes are therefore aptly explained in terms of the social organisation of moral careers – a moral career is the moving point of articulation of those two types of time. Fourth, moral careers are lived by individuals but at the same time are the typical destinies of collectivities. They may be specified either as the characteristic series of experiences of categories of people or, within that framework, as the actual biographies of particular individuals. And fifth, the analysis of moral careers directs attention to the conditions that enable those who embark on them to succeed or cause them to fail, permit or impel them to make something new of the world, or allow them to do no more than dully repeat the experience of others. Hence, even the most spectacular successes (or failures) of particular individuals can be accounted for in terms of the historical location and logic of this or that moral career with a high measure of effectiveness.

Let us return to the example of revolutionaries. Most studies of revolutionary elites have ignored the life cycle of both individual revolutionaries and revolutionary movements. The age of leaders at the time when the blow is struck or power seized is often noted and it is clear that revolutionary elites tend to be significantly younger than the elites they challenge or displace. Lemert (1951) speaks of a systematically skewed age structure in this respect. It is clear, too, that the idea of youth has had a permanent place in the rhetoric of revolution. But these two clues have not commonly led students of revolution to see how persistently a process of becoming radical linked to the life cycle of the individual and to the historical timing of individual lives in the larger process of social history emerges from a scrutiny of any large number of revolutionary biographies. Yet so striking is the patterning of these biographies that the experience in question cries out to be treated, for sociological purposes, as a distinct moral career – the career of revolution. Consider a few cases. Lenin was 47 when he made his revolution in 1917; he was 23 when he first joined an overtly revolutionary organisation; he was 17 when he first identified himself as a person committed to a revolutionary purpose. Trotsky and Stalin were both much younger men; in 1917 they were both 38; but Trotsky had first joined a revolutionary organisation at the age of 23 and Stalin at 22; Stalin had first committed himself to the idea of being a revolutionary at 18, Trotsky at 17. For Bukharin, Zinoviev and Kamenev the picture is the same; respectively they were 31, 47 and 35 in 1917; they became permanent members of revolutionary movements at 24, 20 and 22; and they committed themselves to revolution at 18, 18, and 17. In more general terms, the average age of the Bolshevik leadership in 1917 was 39; but the average age at which they had first committed themselves subjectively to revolutionary action, first defined themselves socially as revolutionaries, was 17. In a famous study of the leadership of the CPSU in 1930 Davis (1930:47) found that 82% of his 163 Communist leaders had been under the age of 25 when they first joined a revolutionary movement. The median age for joining was 20; and the median age of their first publicly noted radical activity was 18. But it is not just that we are observing a patterning of life-histories in such data, a process of identity-formation abstracted from the history of society and operating in terms of its own logic. Age-patterning, but with quite different patterns, appears in revolutionary movements in different historical periods. It is not life-history but life-history in the context of some specific social history that seems to be important.

In the Russian case the double reference, to personal and social time, and to both as historically organised, is perhaps particularly apparent. And it is of course just that combination, that symbiosis even, of the personal and the public that is caught so well in the concept of the moral career, directing attention as it does to the idea of a moving encounter between institutions and identity. Moral careers may vary in the extent to which they impose on and impel the identity of those who follow them. But to the degree that a career lacks institutional support or is negatively defined in the public world it will require greater personal support, will need to be more deeply rooted in identity, if a committed and 'successful' performance is to ensue. That is perhaps why of all forms of deviance the political form, defiance – political revolution above all – seems to provide the clearest available example of the historical two-sidedness of moral careers. The career of revolution – at least in its Bolshevik version – begins with an apprenticeship which is both passionate and provisional. It is passionate because a role so lacking in social support must be bolstered by intense inner commitment, the identity of revolution; and it is provisional because like every identity that of revolution requires social affirmation if it is to be fully taken by the individual. Whether such affirmation is forthcoming or not remains a matter of social rather than of personal history, but perhaps especially of social history during that phase of personal history when identity is most open-ended: youth. If the old regime finds ways of making the identity of revolution implausible, for example by inducing despair about the prospects for revolution or by assimilating significant numbers of revolutionaries to positions in which they share the privileges, and see things with the eyes, of the elite, it will be dropped. In the face of despair it will be displaced by some other form of extremism or ended by suicide. In the face of assimilation it will be gently abandoned in favour of loyal reformism. In Britain the common modes of assimilation have long been junior Fellowships of Oxbridge colleges, editorships of radical but 'responsible' journals, promotion in parliamentary political parties, office in Trade Unions and hypergamy. By contrast a specific context for the career or revolution in Russia in the 1890s was the inability of the Tsarist regime to render revolution implausible either by repression or by assimilation. By taking revolution seriously, as it had to do given the fate of the last Tsar, the regime actively helped to make the identity of revolution a serious possibility.

When radicalism cannot be rendered implausible the commitment of self to the idea of revolution opens the door to the revolutionary career. The career itself may be long or short and may or may not culminate in actual revolution. That again will depend largely on the competence and inclusiveness of the state as a monopolist of coercion and manager of opportunity in particular societies – again, a matter of public rather than of private history. In modern Britain it is likely to be short and to end with marriage, children, home-ownership and a job teaching sociology or English; in extreme cases in bemused membership of the House of Lords. In more serious situations it may be protracted and its end may be startlingly brutal; after all we are talking about revolution, not about social criticism (Frölich, 1940:333):

> Shortly afterwards Rosa Luxemburg was led from the Hotel Eden by Lieutenant Vogel. Before the door a trooper named Runge was waiting with orders from Lieutenant Vogel and Captain Horst von Pflugk-Hartung to strike her to the ground with the butt of his carbine. He smashed her skull with two blows and she was then lifted half dead into a waiting car and accompanied by Lieutenant Vogel and a number of other officers. One of them struck her on the head with the butt of his revolver and Lieutenant Vogel killed her with a shot in the head at point-blank range. The car stopped at the Leichenstein Bridge over the Landwehr Canal and the corpse was flung from the bridge into the water.

Long or short the career of revolution presupposes a commitment of identity. In modern Britain the situations likely to evoke such a commitment are so few and far between and there are so many other options open that most apprentice radicals move early and easily to alternative careers. The prospects of the career of revolution being dim there is a large-scale retreat from it before the involvement of identity has lost its provisional character. For Rosa Luxemburg as for Lenin there was, in effect, nothing to do but to see the provisional commitment through to a whole-hearted end. Many see the case for revolution and embark on the apprenticeship; but it is an apprenticeship from which few master-craftsmen emerge. What are the distinctive encounters and sequences of experience that lead these few to the devoted practice of such a profession? The most obvious example must suffice to indicate an answer.

When Lenin was 17 his elder brother was hanged for his part in a conspiracy to blow up the Tsar (Shub, 1966:16). His father being already dead he found himself suddenly the head of his

family. A period of experimenting with different careers and
identities within the framework of a received, parentally-given,
social and moral world was abruptly ended by the demand he
now faced for responsibility, commitment and decision.
Within months he moved tentatively in many directions:
scholar, farmer and landlord, atheist, lawyer, member of the
political underground. In effect the next six years were spent in
the exploration of two alternative careers, that of lawyer and
that of revolutionary. But what he learned from these
explorations was that for him, the brother of an assassin, all
roads but one had been blocked; he had already been
effectively identified. The liberal friends of his liberal family
quietly disowned him. His academic successes were not for him
doors to further academic or vocational prospects. He was first
made to move from St. Petersburg to Kazan, then following
participation in a mild student protest and recognition as 'the
brother of the other Ulyanov', excluded from the university
altogether. Eventually his mother negotiated permission for
him to sit the law examinations and he managed both to
qualify and to secure the certificate of political loyalty that
would enable him to practise as a lawyer. At the same time he
immersed himself in revolutionary literature, associated with
many avowed revolutionaries and joined a succession of secret
revolutionary groups including, initially, one committed to
renewing the work of the People's Will, the movement to which
his brother had belonged and of which he had become a
martyr. The work that influenced him most at this time, and
which he read five times in the summer following his brother's
execution, was Chernyshevsky's great novel of revolution
What Is To Be Done? Perhaps the title itself had a special
significance for him at that time, but plainly it was the model
Chernyshevsky held out of a life ascetically dedicated to the
pursuit of revolution that, in his own words, 'Captivated' him,
'ploughed me over ... completely', gave him 'a charge for a
whole life' (Theen, 1974:38).

Being related to a terrorist, he discovered had more
meaning for those around him than being, as he also was, 'the
pride of the school'. Perhaps it was apt that traditional
authority in the form of the officials of the old regime should
have insisted on treating his ascribed status as more important

than that he had achieved. Those whose judgements were consequential for him defined him now as, on the one hand, 'a bad type', 'fully capable of unlawful and criminal demonstrations', and on the other as 'future leader of the labour movement', 'a great force' (Shub, 1966:40). Plainly he was failing disastrously in one of his possible careers and succeeding brilliantly in the other. Significant others already knew what he was. Against that background he had to decide what to become. Simple cost-benefit analysis would have pointed clearly to the wisdom of his becoming anything else. In actuality it was not cost-benefit analysis but the writings of Marx that resolved his uncertainty. Shocked and hardened by experiences which he had not yet found a way of interpreting coherently he continued to explore his environment for meaning and in so doing came, unavoidably given the intellectual milieu he had entered, upon the works of Marx. An explosion of understanding apparently followed. Through marxism he made sense of the world and of his own place in it. His sister had described the 'burning enthusiasm' with which he talked about the 'new horizons' Marx had opened for him at this juncture (Wilson, 1940:365). Intellectually at least the career of revolution now acquired a trajectory in terms of his own life which the career of law manifestly lacked. More and more of his time and energy were devoted to the clandestine theory and practice of revolution, less and less to the public pursuit of the law. The covert career gradually became overt; the overt career was gradually abandoned. In 1893 he moved to St. Petersburg, plunging into a world of oppositional groups, secret societies, terrorist factions, savage and endemic industrial struggle, discussions, agitation, the writing of pamphlets, and intense argument with the established leaders of Russian marxism, Axelrod, Martov, Plekhanov, deepening involvement in mass organisation, advocacy of overt mass revolutionary action, the forging of a few intimate personal relationships around a shared commitment to revolution, a ripening hatred not just of the established order but of all liberal compromises with it. Previously the collapse of his family and its social world had dovetailed with a crisis in his own progress along a conventional educational and occupational career line of that world. Now, effective failure in that

career line coinciding with felt success in practical revolutionary work, demonstrating his mastery of both theory and
action, and increasingly exclusive involvement in an illicit
world of close and strong relationships with other revolutionaries locked together in a definitive subjective commitment
to a counter-identity and a counter career. All that was now
needed to give that commitment the force of necessity was
public recognition – that is arrest, trial and imprisonment.
Given even a modicum of efficiency on the part of the police
and magistrates that had to follow. He was arrested on
December 20th 1895, imprisoned for two years and then exiled
to Siberia. Ulyanov had become Lenin (Wilson, 1940:375).

In his own judgement Lenin had tried to make his way in
Russian society as he found it and along a number of approved
career paths. Each time doors which had been open to liberals
such as himself and his father twenty years earlier were
slammed in his face. Progressively he had been defined, had
defined himself as engaged in the only career which as either he
or those around him saw it could make sense of such an
experience. Young Russian liberals after the assassination of
Alexander II were forcibly required either to be enemies of
society or apostates from liberalism. Those who especially
cherished liberal principles and ideas or who were in other
ways bound to liberal causes leapt, drifted or found themselves
driven towards the former option. And there they found,
unlike their predecessors in 1840 or their successors in 1940, the
ideas of Marx available to redefine their relationship to the
world. But those ideas in turn called, if seriously examined, for
certain kinds of action in society. And those kinds of action in
turn had their consequences. The patterning of Lenin's
biography in these years suggests, in other words, a social
process as well as a personal existence – a process which, following David Matza (1969), we could call the process of becoming radical and which like the process of becoming deviant
is at bottom a process of 'signification', historically located and
historically realised.

Broadly understood signification is a matter of the
production in rather cogent and consistent ways of signs
intended to define given actors in a given manner. The idea
refers simultaneously to the construction of meaning and to the

application of power. Viewed from without, what occurs is what Everett Hughes (1945) termed the creation of a 'master status trait' which 'increasingly over-shadows all auxiliary traits'; the actor is progressively treated by others as though inescapably assigned to a part they have written. Viewed from within, signification implies a situation in which the individual is called upon in a quite urgent way to reconsider identity in the face of accounts of self which, whether congenial or not, are both novel and cogent. It is a process in which the striking and substantial significance of a set of conventional signs for oneself is made real. The signified subject is caught up in a bid to impose a definition of who or what one is. One may participate in that process enthusiastically, fatalistically or with defiance, but one cannot escape it. In the process of becoming deviant signification involves an effort to establish what Matza calls a 'unity of meaning' between the actor and the authorities – an attempt to get the deviant subject seen, not least in the subject's own eyes, as he or she is seen by authority, as indeed a deviant subject. It is a matter of coming up against compelling indications of the meaning to others of what one is doing – indications which are forced upon one's consciousness to the extent that they raise profound issues of self-definition. A number of responses to such a situation may be open to the subject, but some response recognising the intentions of those who are trying to signify one, or at least understandable in terms of those intentions, is unavoidable. Moreover signification is clearly understood by Matza as a process; it has a natural history, a development logic, a phasing resulting from the powerfulness with which signifying agents apply their meanings and which leads the signified subject through a sequence of steadily less ambiguous, more strongly defined encounters both with authority and with self. For all his concern to stress the voluntaristic openness of the process of signification, Matza has no difficulty in identifying the overlapping stages of that sequence: ban, transparency, apprehension, exclusion, the display of authority, the building of identity.

Signification removes the provisional nature of the actor's involvement in a career. It is in that sense the culmination of a larger process which begins with experiences of 'affinity' and 'affiliation'. This larger process is seen by Matza as originating in the creation of an experimental and conditional connectedness between the subject and others who are accessible both physically and psychologically (with whom one thus has an affinity), and in interaction with whom one is 'converted to conduct novel for [one] but already established for [those] others' (1969:117). In the course of such conversion the subject moves from merely seeing the meaning of deviance and being willing to engage in it (the effect of affinity), to a state of being positively 'turned on' to deviance, of discovering, affiliating oneself with, and affirming deviance as the practical expression of oneself. Through affiliation (with marihuana users perhaps, or with revolutionaries) the subject comes to exist in a deviant project – 'makes up his mind literally' and puts 'an appearance of it in the world'. As yet one is perhaps one's own prime mover, 'conversion is mediated through a reconsideration of the self and its affinities ... only the context of experience can provide the terms and issues that are the very tissue with which meaning is built and disposition discovered'. But once disposition has been discovered (1969:122)

> What his mind made up is projected into the world. This is the final and deepest level of 'conceiving himself'. Being pregnant with meaning he gives birth and contributes to the flow of experience. He creates an act. Being is continued in the world. In other words, and less pompously, he takes another drag.

Or takes part in another demonstration, prints another pamphlet, plants another bomb. Up to this point, seizing the opportunities offered by affinity and affiliation, it has been the subject who has been (at least in Matza's eyes) the essential mediator of the process of becoming deviant – although of course only 'in the terms and issues provided by the concrete matters before him'. And this is perhaps especially true of those whose, as yet possibly implicit, project it is to become defiant rather than deviant – as Lenin's biography in the phase of affinity and affiliation seems to suggest. Beyond this point, however once the subject had begun to *enact* the deviant project, the process becomes considerably more two-sided. We enter the phase of signification.

Now, the capacity of organised social power in whatever form it has historically assumed, but above all in the form of the state, to create meaning and to require the subject (who is of course also in the political sense a subject) to collaborate in affirming the meaning it has created is made steadily more apparent and binding. Thus, the fact of ban does not of course deter the deviant subject from engaging in the banned activity but it does force such a subject to be that much more plainly deviant, confirming by the secretiveness of the activity in which he or she engages that a deviant project is indeed in hand, in order to do so. One is, in Matza's very apt expression (1969:146) *bedevilled* by ban in the sense of being made unavoidably aware of the badness of one's life from the point of view of the order of meanings which the state seeks to maintain. 'A main purpose of ban is to unify meaning and thus to minimize the possibility that, morally, the subject can have it both ways. Either he will be deterred or bedeviled' (1969:148). Encountering ban is something like the Fall – a necessary loss of innocence, a forced recognition of what taking a drag or taking part in a demonstration mean in terms of the way meaning is defined socially. It focuses self-consciousness, raises sharply the question of whether one is 'really' guilty or not and of how to conduct oneself in future. Without giving the individual adequate reasons for discontinuing deviance it does supply adequate reasons for continuing it in a more consciously deviant, secretive, furtive, covert way henceforth – for going underground as it were. Not to do so is to court, stupidly, the risk of apprehension. Either way, ban provides the deviant with powerful terms of identity, signifying a choice to be made about who one is in a way that cannot be ducked. It is the state's first step towards making both deviants and revolutionaries. Apprehension, the second step, increases dramatically the cogency with which such terms of identity are advanced and at the same time puts vastly more pressure on the deviant to make the 'right' choice of identity.

Before and after apprehension the process of exclusion from the situations in which non-deviant identities are 'realistically embedded' complements and affirms the deviant self-definition. Apprehension itself reveals the powerfulness with which the state is prepared to back its demand that the deviant subject accept the state's account of what he or she is. Matza's treatment of the logic of this encounter is strikingly perceptive (1969:162):

> Until apprehension the deviant subject exists in an abstract relation to authority. Real, organised authority lacks a certain substance. When it finally materializes – if it does – its appearance is likely to include some elements of surprise. Partly because he is usually taken without warning ... the deviant subject is likely to experience the shock of concrete discovery. Understood abstractly the most superficial features of authority appear of little or no account. Experienced and understood concretely, they are the most compelling features. They are what stand before the deviant subject when a figure of authority takes him by surprise. Shocked, he will rediscover what everyone claims to have known all along – that in several respects authority is terribly authoritative.

But there is more to it than that (1969:163):

> A main purpose of the entire display of authority is to convince the apprehended subject of the gravity of what he has done – to restore the *unity of meaning* that Hobbes correctly saw as basic to the kind of order imposed by Leviathan. In that unity of meaning it is not enough that the subject concur in assessing his behaviour as wrong; equally important is an attitude of gravity. The authoritative display aims at the creation of an attitude of gravity towards what he has done – within the deviant subject.

The utmost pressure is exerted to get the deviant to take himself seriously as a deviant person. Punishment renders explicit the degree to which Leviathan is itself serious about all this.

What is not controlled anywhere in this process is just how the dawning sense of the necessity of taking oneself seriously will be worked out. Matza envisage two main alternatives. In the first the subject accepts the meanings held out by society – including the idea that it is society's view of the subject that matters and, taking society seriously presumably reforms. In the second case what is noticed is rather the seriousness with which one is now treated; the assertion of gravity indicates the importance of the actor as the bearer of a deviant identity; one becomes someone worth taking seriously precisely by being what society says one is, really deviant. However, there is a third possibility not considered by Matza which appears to me to become an issue at the moment of apprehension and to separate once and for all criminal deviance from political defiance. Both of the responses envisaged by Matza involve an important measure of collaboration with the state on the part of the deviant subject – at least in going along with the moral terms in which the state seeks to assert the unity of meaning. But it is also possible to refuse to collaborate; or to refuse to collaborate beyond the point of agreeing that the encounter between oneself and the state is serious. Beyond that everything can be turned upside down. One version of such a response is indeed noted in passing by Matza – it is typically that of the bohemian or the withdrawn community of 'cultural' revolutionaries, a retreat to negation (1969:146):

> Occasionally the impact of ban may be thoroughly negated; usually it is contended or coped with. Such a negation is infrequent because wholly to negate the impact of ban at issue – making the activity guilty – requires a sustained growth of collective consciousness of the oppressive relations between the state and its subjects culminating in a sense of local autonomy or cultural separatism. Thus, an attitude of virtual innocence in the face of public ban is best viewed as culturally revolutionary and though such things happen, as in the case, say, of isolated centres of bohemian experimentation with drugs, it is best not to generalise from what is almost surely an esoteric exception. The usual fate of participants in banned activity is much more prosaic; their consciousness never expands or otherwise develops.

But in the process of becoming radical that is just what does happen; and the growth of collective consciousness culminates not just in assertions of innocence but in a more profound reversal of values – the assertion of the guiltiness of Leviathan, a true negation as opposed to mere denial. Here ban makes Leviathan the source of its own undoing, focusing and shifting the consciousness of the banned subject in such a way that the innocence of the latter is now seen as proof of the guilt of the former. This is the distinctive reply to ban of those who become radical, a reply that is outside the repertoire of those who become deviant.

The fact that ban is sometimes negated in this morally absolute and engaged way is not fortuitous; it is not simply something that some banned subjects choose to do while others choose other responses. The negation of ban seems rather to be a possibility dependent upon particular social and historical conditions. It is, for example, necessary that the political as a distinct field of action and morality should exist cognitively and morally for the subject. That is to say the possibility of defining experience as political rather than anything else – religious, moral, economic, medical or criminal – must be available; ban must be encountered in a cultural and intellectual milieu in which the strictly political character of Leviathan is separable from its more diffuse and encompassing moral existence. Again, it must be possible for the banned subject to be insulated, removed or estranged from the view of Leviathan sufficiently to engage through affiliation in the creation of new political meaning and in the deviant enactment of that meaning. Such conditions characterise certain moments in the historical experience of societies and more specifically in the historical process of state formation; they are not everywhere available but are historically located in quite definite ways.

When these and other relevant conditions are satisfied those who have more or less abstractly associated themselves with the idea of revolution, perhaps in the sense of a passionate longing for a new order, a new consciousness, a more just, complete or brotherly existence, are put into circumstances where ban (on the things that need to be done to bring the new order to birth) can be interpreted as revealing the specifically political as the immediate practical source of injustice. It is, one might say the historical task, or at least the function, of established authority in these circumstances to promote the revolutionary career, creating the world of revolution as a real thing for the revolutionary by unmasking the forcefulness of authority and bringing it decisively into the life of the apprentice radical. The process of apprehension and penalisation becomes the setting for a crucial opportunity for promotion in the career of revolution, a context in which the radical's negation of the unity of meaning demanded by Leviathan must be brought into the open or abandoned. Far from restoring that unity of meaning the trial of a radical can be used to display a hopeless disunity. It is a decisive moment at which the subjective and institutional sides of the career of revolution lock together. What happens in court is a moral translation in which the court itself becomes the accused. The system of meaning which authority successfully brings to bear on the deviant is shattered in the encounter with the defiant – or must be if the latter is to maintain identity. With apprehension one enters the critical career grade in the career of revolution; the moment at which commitment must be determined.

There is a passage in the transcript of the contempt citations in the Chicago conspiracy trial of 1970 which goes as follows (Swallow Press, 1970:154):

> *The Court*: One thing I have learned in this work, that a judge can't always please everybody.
> *Mr. Weiner (Defendant)*: You have pleased me ... I think we are ... only slowly groping our way towards a revolution. I think that you in your own inimitable style have made a real world and people must struggle in making their political revolution against a real world not a fantasy world. You have helped educate people ... as to what the real world is.

In such encounters the real world of revolution is constructed, displacing the play world of theories, ideals and debates in which the apprentice radical had hitherto existed. Arrest, trial, imprisonment, the powerful attempt to assert the reality of political crime and the powerful counter-assertion of the reality of criminal politics are forcing houses in the construction of that world. The radical is driven to an absolute edge of self-definition by them – one must opt either for the state's account of oneself or for one's own; there can be no collaboration, only surrender or defiance. And which option is chosen is itself hardly a random matter. It is closely related, rather, to the pattern of previous radicalisation and to earlier public construction of the meaning of the radical role. Or as Lemert puts it (1951:214): 'The symbolizing of primary radicalism as "radical" paves the way to the assumption of a systematic radical role. Variations in the symbolic milieu in which primary radical behaviour occurs are thus of critical importance'. In Russia in 1900 to put the matter more concretely, the collusion of radicals and the state in the symbolizing of primary radicalism quite plainly paved the way for a rush towards defiance. In 1900 virtually everything that a young member of the Russian Social Democratic Party did was illegal. 69% of the leadership of the Communist Party of the Soviet Union in 1930 had been arrested from two to eight times before 1917.

Apprehension and penalisation are, then, critical rungs on the career ladder of revolution – revolution itself being a form of social action peculiar to a particular phase or moment in the history of the state. Far from being career hazards, experiences which force the individual to recognise the incompetence or irrelevance of her or his activity, they confirm the significance and value of a radical account of the world. The police record is the revolutionary's equivalent of the curriculum vitae. Despite relative academic neglect of political trials revolutionaries themselves have always clearly seen that to be so. Even Mussolini understood the positive value of imprisonment when in 1911 he told his judges (Kirkpatrick, 1964:53):

> If you acquit me you will please me because you will restore me to my work and my society. But if you condemn me, you will do me an honour because you find yourselves in the presence not of a malefactor, not of a common delinquent, but of an asserter of ideas, of an agitator of consciences, of a soldier of a faith that commands your respect because it bears within itself the presentiments of the future and the great strength of truth.

The prosecutor gratified him immediately by declaring that this speech alone made Mussolini a dangerous man – someone who did indeed command respect in the sense of having to be taken seriously. A decisive step in a process of moral transformation had been taken. The dilemma of the prosecution in a political trial is of course just that – to impose a serious attitude on the defendant but to ensure that what is taken seriously is not the defendant's own account of the world, to ensure that the trial does not serve as the occasion for the debated status of the defendant being resolved by the attribution of moral heroism, for the monster *becoming* a hero.

Hitherto a disreputable vagrant in the ranks of the revolution, Mussolini was made into a significant figure by his trial and imprisonment. On his release he was feasted by the labour movement and hailed as 'the Duce of all revolutionary socialists in Italy' (Kirkpatrick, 1964:55). Twelve years later Hitler was to use his trial after the Munich rising in just the same way and to just the same effect (Shirer, 1960:106): 'I alone bear the responsibility', he told his judges, 'But I am not a criminal for that ... ' And he ended by appealing to history, 'for she acquits us'. Once again it was the seriousness accorded him that established his seriousness. And thirty years later we find what is probably the most convincing and moving of all versions of this common career move in the process of radicalisation – Fidel Castro's amazingly sustained and devastatingly reasoned onslaught on the court that tried him for the attack on Moncada in October 1953. On that occasion, too, the encounter, the challenge to meaning, turned a radical adventurer into a serious, and professional, revolutionary (Alexandre, 1968).

Where, then, do these brief observations on the historically organised and processual nature of some episodes in the lives, identities, careers of a few conspicuous modern heroes or monsters leave us in relation to the more general problem of the possibility of historical sociology encompassing the individual with which I began this chapter? I have tried to show that what is exceptional about the life of an exceptional individual is the location of that life in a particular historically organised milieu and the interactional patterning of the series of experiences through which individuation is then achieved – in fact, the meshing of life-history and social history in a singular fate. Individual lives are indeed unique but their uniqueness, I suggest, is not a matter of some elusively private personal factors but of the diversity of movement available to historically located individuals within historically located social worlds. Life histories are created by self and others to produce heroic or mediocre individuals through sequences of action, reaction, action in the setting of historically specific possibilities and impossibilities, opportunities and constraints. Each career is the dynamic realisation of a distinct sequence of probabilities. 'Moreover', as Karl Mannheim wrote in a quite different context, 'it is not merely dynamic but also historically conditioned. Each step in the process of change is intimately connected with the one before, since each new step makes a change in the internal order and relationships of the structure as it existed at the stage immediately before, and is not therefore entirely "out of the blue" and unconnected with the past' (Wolf, 1971:155). Mannheim was talking about the 'configuration' of the history of ideas, but his words apply equally well to the social design of the process of becoming individual.

But could it not be said that this argument still deals in categories of people rather than in particular individuals – just as Mannheim's concern was with conservatism in 19th century thought rather than with particular conservatives? Does the sort of argument I have advanced really get us beyond an understanding (to stay with the same example) of why there was a powerful revolutionary movement in Russia in 1900 and how the people who joined that movement did so and came to be a particular type of revolutionary? Is not the naming of Lenin or Victor Serge slightly spurious since all that is really explained by the rather general social processes I have discussed is the social recruitment of a type not the specific reality of those two people? Is not understanding Lenin as one among a world of revolutionaries a very different matter from understanding Lenin as the outstanding revolutionary of his time, his extraordinary single-mindedness, his appetite for work, his brilliant organisational talents, his relationship with Krupskaya, his feeling for Beethoven, his love of hunting?

Personally, I am not persuaded by such questions. The fine detail of individuation does not seem to me to be anything that is essentially or in principle unlike the broader patterning of that process. If the historical sociology of moral careers can tell us why there were revolutionaries in Russia in 1900 and why Lenin became one of them, or why those revolutionaries inclined to socialism and organisation rather than to anarchism and spontaneity, or why Lenin in particular turned towards socialism and organisation so uncompromisingly, then I see no reason why it could not also, if we so desired, be brought to bear even more closely on whatever individual variations in career performance, success, failure, deviation and so forth concerned or puzzled us. The real question is whether for the purposes of sociological analysis we would actually want or need to get that close? What matters to my mind is our capacity to explain significant individual destinies and achievements in the terms of historical sociology, in terms of the historical organisation of careers and milieux that is, not the further possibility, which nevertheless seems to be implicit in that capacity, of going on to account for everything about everyone. We can leave that possibility, and the moral and philosophical excitement it is likely to provoke, open to debate and still conclude that the individual can be eliminated as a problem for historical sociology by a determined concentration on the process of individuation. The problem of the individual can, I conclude, be made manageable in historical sociology by treating it as itself genuinely a problem of history.

10

Theory, questions and some limits
of historical sociology

A generation ago when the relationship between history and sociology was commonly discussed in terms of the contradictions and incompatibilities of 'idiographic' and 'nomethetic' sciences (Rickert, 1962), or of particularising and generalising interests (Popper, 1962), it seemed reasonable to many who hoped to make the relationship a little closer to see the problem of *rapprochement* as essentially one of discovering ways of getting a bit more theory into history or a few more facts into sociology. There was a good deal of speculation as to whether the desired union would take place on the basis of mutual attraction (Stone, 1966), a marriage of convenience (Lipset and Hofstadter, 1968; Thomas, 1966), or rape (Thompson, 1972). Although those debates have continued (Samuel and Stedman Jones, 1976; Burke, 1980; Hay, 1981), the really significant development of the past twenty years has been the publication of a solid body of theoretically self-conscious historical work which has progressively made nonsense of earlier conceptions of history as somehow, in principle, not engaged in the theoretical world of the social sciences. Social change is made by people doing new things. As the acknowledged masterpieces of the discipline of history become increasingly theoretically explicit, and as the unity of theoretical method between history and sociology becomes thereby steadily more obvious, the continued insistence of a rump of professional historians that theory is no part of their trade becomes steadily less firmly the effective basis of the 'institution' of history and steadily more plainly an ineffectual nostalgia. More important institutions are of course also dismantled in that way. A marriage may not have taken place, but some pre-marital intercourse seems to have had results – legitimate or not, the infant historical sociology is embarrassingly alive.

Historians anxious to deny responsibility for the squalling progeny tend now to appeal to the rhetorical mysteries of narrative, to the gulf between narrative and analysis, as somehow still marking the autonomy and chastity of their discipline (Elton, 1967: Stone, 1979). I have touched on this argument in an earlier chapter but must now pursue it a little further. For it seems to me that the extent to which historical sociology collapses previously cherished or taken-for-granted distinctions between history and sociology depends not so much on the mode of discourse one favours as on the type of question one is asking and the theoretical strategies (overt or latent) one adopts in pursuing answers. My argument up to this point has been that sociologists need to ask historical questions and that the distinctive subject-matter of history does not defy sociological analysis. Further, that across a very wide range of subject-matter historians and sociologists, insofar as they work within the terms of a common problematic – however loosely defined or even unperceived – already adopt common rules of explanation and common conceptions of effective analysis. Disputes over particular substantive theories or explanations have obscured the presence of interchangeable methods of explanation and shared strategies of theorising. Now, I want to develop this last point by exploring further the ways in which what I have called the problematic of structuring exacts certain theoretical strategies from sociologists and historians alike; and conversely, to emphasise that the methodological unity of history and sociology is indeed bound up with the nature of what one wants to know. To that end two types of work normally undertaken by both historians and sociologists must be distinguished at the outset. The first, whatever its particular focus of attention, is basically concerned with 'how (or why) it happened', an attempt to answer questions about even-tuation. The second, again regardless of topic, is primarily interested in 'how it was (or is)', an attempt to answer questions about what the world was or is 'really' like at a given moment then or now. In practice the two types of question do not have to be as distinct as my formulation of them suggests. But I shall argue that, clearly distinguished or not, they set distinct limits for historical sociology – and for history and sociology as separate disciplines, too.

So far as 'how it happened' questions are concerned, I have already suggested that the unity of history and sociology as historical sociology springs from the discovery by both sides of the cogency of a common strategy of explanation. The explanation of patterning or process, of individual careers or events comes to ground in a distinctive conception of causality (or structuring) as *manifold, sequential and cumulative.* Whatever refined superstructures of interpretation or mountains of contextual detail may be heaped up by particular scholars the intellectual core of historical sociology is the way in which historians and sociologists are forced towards the idea of cumulative causation. At first sight the appeal to the integrity and effectiveness of narrative might seem to be a serious challenge to this claim – even though the claim itself recognises the force of many earlier objections made by historians to some once sadly characteristic sociological styles of argument. In trying to deal with this difficulty I shall assume – not without some authority (Elton, 1967:22, 124–6; Carr, 1964:43, 100–2) – that historians, like sociologists, are concerned to demonstrate significant patterning. The question, then, is whether narrative can in principle serve as an effective vehicle for such demonstrations. And if so, do those demonstrations involve recourse, however deviously, to the procedures and strategies of explanation found in more explicit theorisations of cumulative causality? Or are they achieved on some other basis? In sum, can narrative resolve 'how it happened' puzzles, and if so does it do so in ways that are distinctly independent of the theoretical assumptions and strategies I have attributed to historical sociology? On the one hand it is suggested that firm shared methodological ground lurks beneath the surface of even the most theoretically brash sociology and even the most theoretically taciturn history (Stinchcombe, 1978) – that whatever they may think they are doing historians actually follow the same rules of argument and make the same explanatory assumptions as sociologists. But against that it is asserted that narrative is an essentially different enterprise from that of sociological explanation, demonstrating significance on altogether different terms (Gallie, 1964; Stone, 1979). The position I shall urge, somewhere between these extemes, is that while Gallie and other philosophers of history are right to insist that narrative is in principle autonomous its capacity to handle the explanatory tasks historians normally face is, also in principle, severely restricted. The argument complements and underpins the observation made in chapter 7 that in practice narrative historians tend to abandon narrative rather rapidly when the credibility of their stories is challenged.

Let me try to begin with an apparently open mind. In discussing the explanation of events I suggested that debates among historians often serve to bring to light the presence of theoretical ventures quite similar to those of sociologists demurely embedded in a great deal of historical writing. And I have drawn attention to a large and growing number of major historical works which openly examine their own theoretical strategies, attending explicitly to the integration of narrative and analysis and in that sense at least treating history and sociology as symbiotic projects: above all, there is the magnificent architectural achievement of Braudel (1973); but one would want to mention Anderson (1974), Skocpol (1979), Wallerstein (1974), Tilly (1964) and Macfarlane (1978) in even the shortest short list of such works. Yet many eminent works of history manage to avoid both these forms of analytical self-exposure. And in the light of them one must give serious consideration to the possibility that narrative, adapted as it is to the representation of the flow of action in time, might also be an apt medium, in its own peculiar ways, for the explanation of happening. We need, in other words, to look a little more closely at what is going on when historians tell stories.

Valiant, but to me finally unconvincing, efforts have been made to insist that all historical writing, insofar as it explains anything, is bound to carry within it an analytical design which on examination shows history to be necessarily a project of the same methodological order as sociology. There are major proponents of that view, notably Hempel (1942), Nagel (1952) and Murphey (1973); and perhaps those versions of it which stress the latent analytical work done by metaphor and analogy in narrative historical writing, say, White (1978) or Stinchcombe (1978), would nowadays be thought especially convincing. Without going that far, however, one can maintain three claims about the practice of historians which, while not asserting the necessity of historical sociology do seem to make quite a strong case for its possibility and desirability. First, one can observe that within the confines of an overall narrative rhetoric a good deal of explanatory work which is indeed of the same type as the explanatory work of sociologists can be and commonly is done. Secondly, one can notice (as I did in chapter 7) that beyond those limits reputable historians seriously committed to answering 'how it happened' questions commonly can and do take up non-narrative strategies of explanation without appearing to feel that they are thereby betraying their integrity as historians. And finally, one can suggest that to the extent that historians refuse to make that move serious objections can be advanced as to the ability of narrative (even by their own criteria) to sustain the sorts of explanations historians seem to wish to propose.

In other words history and sociology *can* achieve the symbiosis of historical sociology but they do not have to. First class historians such as Geoffrey Elton, with a principled dislike for analysis and particularly for analysis in terms of forces, trends and factors (1967), may in practice manage to bury analysis – up to the neck, at least – in the interstices of a consummate narrative (1963). But some historians will no doubt be more successful than Professor Elton in putting together tales signifying nothing. And no doubt some sociologists will continue to abstract structure, trends and forces from history while wilfully refusing to attend to the (irretrievably historical) process of structuring or to the activity which constitutes forces and trends. Such freaks do not impair the possibility of historical sociology. To do that it would be necessary to show that narrative can, without covertly exploiting the explanatory strategies of sociology, do all the explanatory work serious historians wish to do in talking about 'how it happened'. To the extent that narrative cannot accomplish such tasks historical sociology might be an option to be seized.

Two points seem to follow at once. First, one is bound to see that in practice the historian's attachment to narrative has had the effect of forcing reflective historians to worry about problems of analysis with which they feel, evidently, that narrative may not be able to cope, but which they also feel must be coped with by serious historians – a worry which has had the effect of leading many historians into non-narrative analytical exercises which are immediately recognisable as involving the same repertoire of questions, assumptions and theoretical designs as one finds brought to bear on historical problems by sociology, anthropology and other social sciences. And secondly, while it seems that more analytical work can indeed be done under cover of the narrative mode than appearances might suggest, under scrutiny that work also turns out to be quite akin to what we would expect social scientists facing 'how it happened' questions to attempt. In both respects it seems that what typically passes as narrative history is typically a good deal more than just narrative. In practice narrative is contained by and itself contains analysis – and the forms of analysis in question fail to distinguish narrative as an independent explanatory discourse. What is left as truly peculiar to narrative does not satisfy our curiosity. We are faced with a double contamination of narrative by analysis, constituting a slide of history towards social science which I shall call 'the Elton dilemma' – simply because few historians have recognised it more clearly and more reluctantly or struggled against it more heroically and ambiguously.

The dilemma is first experienced (Elton, 1967:173) as a matter of somehow coping with explanatory tasks apparently beyond the reach of narrative without making it too obvious that one has stopped narrating. Thus, 'to be satisfactory, and in order to avoid the charge of superficiality, historical narrative must, as it were, be thickened by the results of analysis'. Or again, in a passage in which one cannot but sense the author's struggle against, as well as his surrender to, the dilemma:

> In order that action may be understood, its setting, circumstances and springs must be made plain, and these are found not only in the psychology of individuals and crowds, but especially in the details of administration, the economy, the intellectual preoccupations of the time, and all other so called 'factors' ... It is [the historian's] task to accommodate such matters which require analytical

treatment, in such a way that the narrative seems hardly to be interrupted at all. This means that he should not treat of them as plainly separate entities, in separate chapters or sections clearly marked off. Rather they should be erratic boulders carried along in the glacier flow ... so that the reader is barely aware of the change of pace.

And yet, in exemplifying the procedure by pointing to his own practice in *Reformation Europe* (1963), he makes it clear that the dilemma is, in practice, much more acute than the image of occasional boulders in the ice flow would imply. In that context he was, for example, driven to just the device of separate chapters and sections (on 'the Age' and 'the state of Germany') which he advises against, in order to 'be satisfactory' in accounting for the impact of Martin Luther and communicating his own sense of the significance of his chosen period. The conclusion is unavoidable: 'large scale history cannot be written without some patently analytical sections which I regard as incescapable setbacks in a battle that must on balance be won' (1967:175). But what exactly is the battle about?

When we turn to the relevant chapters of *Reformation Europe* we find that the author writes in a number of important ways as though the work of accounting for what happened in Europe between 1517 and 1559 was governed by quite familiar rules of sociological method – a cross perhaps between Weber's recommendations on objectivity (1949) and those of Glaser and Strauss on the discovery of grounded theory (1967). Professor Elton may not care for trends, forces and factors, but he is quite happy with connections, conditions and causes ('causes are real'). He may not choose to speak of structure or structuring but he agrees to live with patterns and patterning. He uses the comparative method with economy, subtlety and effect to assess hypotheses and identify causal and conditional significance (most strikingly in treating the varying successes and failures of the Reformation in different parts of Europe). And he theorises the whole experience in quite the grand manner as not just a revolution but a 'necessary' revolution. We have little difficulty in 'reading' the overall message that what those forty two years were decisively about was a religious transformation decisively conditioned by political power. The question is, how much of this is actually achieved by narrative and how much by overt or covert recourse to (sociological) analysis? My own impression is that the function of narrative in this enterprise is to carry – in a highly persuasive way not accessible to intellectual scrutiny – those bits of the argument the author does not choose to make available for direct critical examination on the part of his readers.

A particularly bold example of this procedure occurs right at the outset. Even before we start reading the text itself 'happening' has been thoroughly designed for us by the mere title of the work. Two generations of European experience are signified, apparently with no questions asked, as 'Reformation' Europe. In effect fundamental analytical questions have already been both asked and answered. And we naturally (as it were) expect the text itself to open (as it does) with Luther nailing his theses to the door of the church in Wittenberg; we are already caught up in an easy surrender to a familiar tale – and to the unconsidered assumption that it is the right tale about that particular bit of the past. Before we know it were have succumbed to a piece of interpretative sociological theorising on a major scale. The 'period' itself is defined by a choice of events (Luther's theses and the Treaty of Cateau Cambresis) which are significant, or at least decisively significant, only in terms of the author's prior decision about the significance of the period. Yet it is after all quite possible and plausible to treat those years, or some overlapping block of years, in entirely different ways – outstanding historical studies have done so both implicitly (Ehrenberg, 1928) and explicitly (Wallerstein, 1974). Of course the subsequent text provides a mass of facts woven elegantly together in a reasonably complex story which seems to ground and validate the initial signification. But from the title onwards, if we attend to what is going on, the form of exposition is both doing analytical work and, *without doing the necessary analytical work*, luring the reader into accepting the author's preferred interpretation simply as a happening. It enables him both to obscure the degree to which he is theorising and to pursue the validation of his theory in a peculiarly, and to my mind improperly, privileged way, undistracted by the need to justify his own criteria of interpretation or proof. The silences of narrative are not the least of its argumentative strengths.

Its silences make narrative a superficially effective means of making theoretical points but one that is ultimately fradulent. So does its tolerance for irrelevant noice. A clever narrator will interject or weave into the texture of a story a great deal of interpretative and analytical matter which is not properly part of the story at all although vital for its persuasive allure – this is presumably what Professor Elton has in mind when he speaks of enabling the reader not to notice the change of pace. The ponderous, but plainly honest sociological paragraph is replaced by the deft rhetorical flourish. Consider the end of the very first paragraph of *Reformation Europe*:

> Certainly Luther had no thought of starting a schism in the Church. These were not the first theses he had offered for public disputation, nor did they embody necessarily revolutionary doctrines. Nevertheless, the day continues to be celebrated in Lutheran countries as the anniversary of the Reformation, and justly so. The controversy over indulgences brought together the man and the occasion; it signalled the end of the medieval Church.

Signalling is of course just what this sort of device is all about; the assertion of a connection of man, moment and meaning at that stage in the narrative is quite unwarranted by anything that has gone before in the story; it is not a summary but a daring synthetic anticipation, claiming importance and design for the tale that is to come. But before we have really registered just how much we have been told, or how far the acceptability of one view of the period has already been framed in our minds and others pushed aside, the narrative is on its ways again: 'Martin Luther (1483–1546) was born the son of a miner ...'. The narrative current flows so strongly that the erratic boulders of analysis are swept past before we have had any real chance to look at them carefully. And unfortunately, that seems to be just the point of using narrative. There is little doubt that if we were strong enough to plunge into the torrent and gather together all the boulders, and pebbles, of analysis swept along in it they could be assembled into a quite substantial analytical mass. If we could get hold of it in that way we could then go on to ask whether we liked the look of it, how firm and cohesive it really was, where it had come from and various other pertinent questions. I shall try to do something of that sort for *Reformation Europe* very shortly. But first it is necessary to insist a little on the point that an essential feature of narrative would seem to be its ability both to carry analysis and to protect analysis from the sorts of critical reading appropriate to it. W. B. Gallie (1964) puts the matter nicely:

> It is worth noticing that, once embarked on a good story, we cannot properly be said to choose to follow it. It would be far better to say that we are pulled along by it, and pulled at by something far more compelling than our intellectual presumptions and expectations. We read ... that the lovers are parted, that the child is lost in the forest, and we must hear more about them, we could almost cry out like children 'What happened to them next?' However disguised such basic feelings may become in the case of more sophisticated stories, they are always there. If they were not, if we were not following the to us irresistibly compelling thoughts and actions and feelings of other human beings, we simply wouldn't be following a story. This means that there is something arbitrary, something due to the set and structure of our basic interhuman feelings, involved in the following of any and every story. Or, in other words, following ... cannot be regarded as a purely intellectual operation, definable by reference to a specific task or problem.

Narrative history is story-telling governed by some normally quite rigorous notion of getting the story right in the light of the factual evidence, but insofar as it is still story-telling its appeal is not to any logic of theoretical reasoning but to the illogic of 'following'. The sense of connectedness and unity that commands assent is achieved by presenting a flow of events with which we allow ourselves to flow. The resulting account is acceptable because we have 'followed' it. But acceptability is not to be confused with explanation, nor empathy with judgement. And unfortunately, because they often disagree with one another historians also worry about explanation and judgement.

Perhaps we can now see just what the narrativve historian's battle is about. It is not so much a battle against analysis as a battle for an integration of narrative and analysis which can never be fully accomplished. The narrative historian starts out

from the entirely sound appreciation – which sociologists also
need to share – that 'how it happened' questions demand
answers in terms of manifold, sequential and cumulative
structuring. Narrative is far and away the best type of talk
available to us for representing the action involved in such
processes. But the rules of narrative do not permit adequate
analytical treatment of what is being represented (the
elucidation of structuring). Indeed, the persuasiveness of what
is being represented is directly threatened by such treatment.
Yet, because what is being represented is not just 'the facts',
however well researched, but an interpretative arrangement of
the facts, historians must be able to discuss the arranging they
have done. They must if challenged (and happily they almost
always are challenged) be able to abstract both the arrangement and its explanatory cogency from the story they have had
us follow. They have, despite the rules of narrative, to be able to
be rather explicit about both interconnection and structuring.
Accordingly, narrative historians grudgingly admit the need
for a modicum of analysis alongside their narrative. But their
confession is made in much the same spirit as the Jew of
Malta's confession of fornication ('but that was in another
country, and besides the wench is dead'). Just as the Jew's
confession was designed to evade the graver charge of murder,
the confession of the historians distracts us from pursuing the
charge of narrative's explanatory impotence.

An analogy suggested by Ernest Gellner (1974:122) may be
helpful at this point. He distinguishes between two ways in
which one gives an account of a game of chess. In one sense 'a
game of chess, is most emphatically, a story, a sequence of
events meaningfully connected. Moreover a precise notation
exists for telling the story, without ambiguity'. And chess
journalists, for example, write about games of chess on just
that basis. However:

> What makes the sequence of moves in ... a chess game into *one*
> game, which can ... be turned not merely into a narrative but into a
> precise and unambiguous one, is over and above the fact that the
> moves happen consecutively in one place, the fact that they
> presuppose a shared set of rules which connect one move with the
> next.

Narrative history, one could say, depends for acceptability on the historical equivalent of the rules – the conventions, understandings, legitimations and powers in terms of which people interact – being known and taken for granted and agreed by all concerned; so that, as for the chess journalist, it is simply not necessary to stop and point out why such and such a move was possible, unavoidable, a mistake or whatever – 'giving an account' of the play 'accounts for' the outcome. But unfortunately, while that is a perfectly reasonable basis on which to give accounts of games of chess it is doubly unreasonable when it comes to giving accounts of happenings in history. It is unreasonable first because the rules (or what some sociologists would call structure) are characteristically not known, agreed or taken for granted: the connection between action and structure is on the contrary one of the things that is most enigmatic and most in need of elucidation. And it is unreasonable again because in history, as distinct from chess, the rules are not fixed and given (even if unknown) but are being constantly made, remade and debated in the course of play; in a sense that is what the game is about. Gellner puts it like this:

> The rules of chess are very stable, and they are imposed on each game by a convention external to that game, a convention which is a kind of absolute and extraneous datum as far as any one game is concerned. The account of the origin of that convention and the processes by which it is sustained, is in no way part of the analysis of an individual game. Not so for the sociologist. The tacit rules or constraints limiting human behaviour are not stable, and the mechanisms which enforce them are not extraneous to the story in progress: on the contrary from the sociologist's viewpoint, they are by far the most interesting aspect of that game. The constraints, the 'rules' within which social life is played out, are themselves a consequence of the game. A 'structural' account of a society is an account of how this comes to be; how the game itself generates and sustains the limits within which it is played.

In this sort of 'self-generating' game explanations of how things happen must relate action to structure, must break with narrative and embrace analysis. Rather than the game of chess the appropriate image is the one I suggested in an earlier chapter of the game in which the only rule is that everyone plays by the existing rules until someone changes them. History and sociology alike confront the paradox of accounting for a game with mutable rules whenever they attempt to explain happening. Which is why narrative always lets the historian down. Giving an account of the play is not merely enough to account for the outcome.

One can see the problem very clearly in *Reformation Europe*. The idea of connection has a particularly prominent place in Professor Elton's armoury of explanation – not least in the absolutely proper claim (1967:126) that: 'meaningful interconnection in the particular, illuminating generalization beyond the individual case – these are the marks that distinguish the inspired and inspiring historian from the hack'. And connections are constantly being drawn or suggested in the course of *Reformation Europe*: 'Germany's position as the centre of European trade also helped greatly': 'the growth of new Churches depended largely on the effects of political alignment and power': 'a situation in which the Reformation could find succour from the political ambitions and manoeuvres of the powerful'; 'circumstances forced the reformers increasingly into the position of revolutionaries not only against ecclesiastical but also against civil rule'. And the book as a whole conveys a sustained sense of the deep connectedness of action and reaction in religion, politics and the main currents of secular intellectual life. More explicitly a number of passages argue the absence of connection between religion and various social and economic changes associated with the rise of capitalism. The difficulty, however, is that it is only in these latter passages where the author is discrediting the case for some connection he considers spurious, non-existent or unimportant that we ever get any precise idea of just what relations of connection he has in mind. For the rest the language of narrative persistently enables him both to create impressions of connectedness and to avoid saying just what any particular connection actually was; let alone what its linking value relative to that of other connections might have been. When it is particularly important to him to make the nature of a given connection, or lack of connection, quite clear narrative tends to be suspended. Thus:

It is, therefore, obvious that the state of Germany helped Luther; it helps to explain the extraordinary speed with which his ideas – assisted by the new weapon of the printing press – seized upon the imagination of a whole people. Not that these conditions – anticlericalism, nationalism, hatred of a foreign pope, social discontents, political ambitions, intellectual and spiritual turmoil – in any way form the 'causes' of either Luther or the Reformation. The situation was thoroughly disturbed, but the disturbance could have developed into anything.

We are not to impute causality; but we may think in terms of helpful conditions. Behind the surface precision of actions and events this terminology of helping, depending, finding succour and so forth maintains a maddening explanatory vagueness.

Insofar as the empirical reality of connection resides in action and events the procedure could be defended. But insofar as the binding effect of connection is a matter of the structuring of events and action in some particular ways and not others it is surely inadequate. So long as the 'business of historians' was simply in the words of W. H. Walsh (1951), 'to construct ... a *significant* narrative ... which makes us see not only the order of events but also their connections' the narrative refusal to specify causal or even conditional design or values was viable even if not entirely creditable. But once the task had become argumentative, a matter of convincing the reader that, say the link between the Reformation and the formation of states (or the politics of princes) was a consequential one while the link between the Reformation and the rise of capitalism (or the morals of entrepreneurs) was inconsequential, the analytical appraisal of connection has to become overt. In order to choose intelligently between the different significances found in the Reformation by Elton, Weber and, say, R. H. Tawney (1926) we are entitled to know just what system of connections each is really urging us to accept – from that point of view Elton's strongest criticism of Weber is perhaps not his doubtful claim that the 'facts' belie the Weber thesis but his entirely correct observation that in presenting the connection that is central to his explanation Weber is himself extremely vague: at the end of the day just what *is* the relationship between the Protestant ethic and the spirit of capitalism?

'How it happened' questions thus present difficult problems

of explanatory strategy. But they present them in equal measure to both historians and sociologists. Both have to recognise the force of Professor Elton's 'the disturbance could have developed into anything'. But both have also to recognise that three hundred pages later the connections of action and structure are going to have resulted in one thing rather than anything; and that at least in retrospect one can speak of that one thing as 'necessary'. Both, that is to say, have to proceed in terms of the idea that causality and significance reside cumulatively in the concatenation and phasing of actions and conditions. For both, in other words, the assignment involved in the explanation of historical happening is a great deal more than a matter of compiling the sort of story in which in Gellner's words (1974), happening is 'something more than contingency, something less than necessity'. Beyond that explanation is a debate between the story (or facts) and a theory of cumulative causation. In that respect Elton, Weber and Tawney are all in principle undertaking identical tasks. But what I have tried to argue is that narrative cannot cope with such a task – precisely because if knowledge and debate are to accumulate it is necessary to place one's explanatory design with all its connections and weightings of connections, assumptions of significance and inferences of structuring squarely before the reader, to allow one's work to be seen for what it is, an argument related to a theoretical design rather than a story naively accomplishing an inarticulate sense of it. In sum, in relation to 'how it happened' questions both the nature of the work to be done and the difficulties of doing it point towards the recognition of history and sociology as a common enterprise. In particular, the attempt to drive a wedge between history and sociology by appealing to narrative seems to me to fail on three counts. First, the sort of explanation that one finds skulking in the folds of narrative is characteristically of just the same sort as that attempted, however heavy-handedly, by any sociologist who understands history as structuring. The point could be elaborated by considering Dray's unravelling (1980) of the paradigms of causality involved in the debate between A. J. P. Taylor and his critics over the 'origins' of the Second World War; or by following Stinchcombe's subtle comparative analysis (1978) of the common argumentative design to be found in the work of de Tocqueville (1971), Trotsky (1934), Smelser (1959) and Bendix (1956); or in the light of Roth's careful demonstration of the parallels of theoretical strategy between Weber (1968) and Braudel (1973). Secondly, when historians reach the limits of narrative the type of analysis to which they turn is (and can only be) indistinguishable in its theoretical design from that of sociological analyses of cumulative causation. And finally, despite the efforts of Dray and Stinchcombe to persuade us that narrative can imply much of what analysis states there quickly comes a point at which the difference between accounting *for* happening and simply giving an account of it is undeniable and unbridgeable by narrative. In other words the signifying work that narrative can do when it is not serving as a vehicle for covert sociological explanation is quite inadequate as explanation, fails to convince when exposed to critical scrutiny or the challenge of alternative, more analytically articulate significations. Weber's keen and still unimpaired insight is perhaps worth recalling again here (1949:176):

> The most important phase of historical work ... namely, the establishment of the causal regress, attains ... validity only when in the event of challenge it is able to pass the test of the use of the category of objective possibility, which entails the isolation and generalisation of the causal individual components for the purpose of ascertaining the possibility of the synthesis of certain conditions into adequate causes.

Weber's clumsy language of analysis is no more able than the falsely naive language of narrative to conceal the force of the requirement here for history and sociology to get together. The sociology of happening needs the historian's sense of the complex but finally causal phasing of action. The history of happening needs sociology's sense of the remote but cogent causal weight of structure. Both need an overt, simple and self-conscious capacity both to represent and account for significant sequence which neither as yet fully possesses.

And when we turn to 'how it was' questions a similar message is delivered with still greater force. It is perhaps in this context that one sees most clearly the force of the case made and practised in different but equally cogent ways both by Marx and by Weber for historical sociology to be understood as a dialectic of theory and evidence, an enterprise in which knowledge is achieved by an intellectual estrangement from phenomena as well as by intimate contact with them. The point is important because in spite of all the philosophical and methodological arguments against them, empiricism and phenomenalism are still likely to be rampant when historians or sociologists set out to 'tell it like it was' or is. The temptation to believe that all human life is there in one's archive or interviews, finally reached by one's sophisticated research techniques, seems extraordinarily hard to resist. History and sociology must have empirical materials to reconstitute as knowledge; in the hunt for such materials it is apparently only too easy to come to see the empirically accessible as, of itself, constituting this or that 'lost' social reality. Whereas, in dealing with problems of 'how it happened' even the most committed of narrative historians will admit at least to a covert concern with formal analytical issues, with problems of theorisation and the non-phenomenal realities of structuring, what might be called a fantasy of self-evidence – or what Selbourne (1980) has termed 'the hallucination of direct encounter' – seems to take over when the problem of 'how it was' (or is) comes to be addressed.

Typically, that problem is seen, first, in terms of a need for massive detailed documentation – especially documentation of action, experience and meaning – and secondly, in terms of a need for an essentially descriptive presentation of the details thus found. Issues are therefore raised both about the extent to which appropriate detail can actually be obtained and about the extent to which descriptive presentations of such evidence can properly be thought to render social realities. Both issues have been debated exhaustively by philosophers of history and methodologists of social science. The balance of argument – accomplished from a wide variety of different positions, from Collingwood (1956) and Dray (1980) to Dunn (1978) and Hawthorn (1979), from Louch (1966) and White (1978) to Carr (1964) and Bhaskar (1979), might be thought by now to be clear enough: the hallucination of direct encounter is indeed a hallucination. Yet the search for such encounters, for a direct

descriptive representation of how it was, is renewed inde-
fatigably. Without getting too caught up in issues of principle it
is perhaps useful, therefore, to look at a few examples of what
is involved, in practice, in ventures of that sort.

Obviously, the philosophical issues cannot be wholly set
aside. My view of what 'how it was' studies accomplish in
practice is bound up with my sense of what description in
general can and cannot in principle accomplish. But having
already committed myself to a broadly dialectical, and I
suppose in Jary's sense (1981), broadly 'realist', position on the
general issue of the possibility of knowledge of the social, my
view of this particular question can be quickly anticipated and
stated: we cannot as I see it hope to recover the past (or the
present) as it was in all its empirical actuality, only to know it as
it 'must have been' from our own more or less theoretically
considered present situation. Social realities are there for the
discovering but discovering them involves analytical distance
as well as empirical access; they are not to be known by direct
representation. Social reality stands behind social appearances
not in the relation of face to veil but in the relation of process to
moment. Its apprehension is more a matter of analytical
structuring than of empirical seeing-through. And it is
therefore particularly unfortunate that in studies of 'how it
was' many authorities have looked towards an alliance of
history and sociology as a better was of seeing-through; as a
basis not for much discriminating observation but simply for
more observation, definitive observation of social reality.
Thus, Drake (1973), Lipset and Hofstadter (1968), Thernstrom
(1968), Hays (1968) Laslett (1972), Shorter (1971), Darnton
(1978), and even in attentive moments Burke (1980), all give the
impression that the convergence of history and sociology
might turn upon the ability of the observational techniques and
methods of sociology, and especially its quantitative and
ethnographic tools, to give history immediate empirical access
to past social realities. The tools of sociological research are
held by these writers to make poor history an offer of
observational intimacy which it can hardly refuse. In this they
are at one with those who, without advocating convergence,
see the peculiar value of their particular discipline in the ways
in which it, unlike other disciplines, can directly grasp and

present the realities of otherwise unknown social worlds: Samuel (1980), Stone (1979), Geertz (1973), Cobb (1970), Lazarsfeld (1968). Without in any way minimising the capacity of many modern techniques of social research (both quantitative and qualitative) to generate solid, interesting and occasionally enormous bodies of new data – a point made very plainly by Wrigley (1979) and Samuel (1981) – I shall try to suggest that the project of recovering the past as it 'really' was by way of observation – Selbourne calls it 'resurrectionism' – is, especially insofar as it is thought to be a matter of technique, essentially misconceived, not properly part of any serious argument for historical sociology. Excavation is a necessary first step, but sifting the ore from the dross and processing the ore for use are what distinguish mining from grubbing around.

The interchange of techniques is now very widely taken for granted. Historians are as likely to be versed in computing, statistical regression or the rules of ethnography as in palaeography, the organisation of archives or medieval Latin. Semiology, structuralism, understanding of the mysteries of 'thick description' or simple numeracy can be found as readily among historians as among sociologists. We are rapidly reaching a point where the disciplines will quite obviously share a common armoury of technique. But that is not what historical sociology is about – although it is something historical sociology can and should exploit. The capacity to observe, describe, reconstitute or resurrect is not to be confused with the capacity to judge, interpret, explain and make sense. Yet just such confusions abound in 'how it was' studies, compounded often by the dazzling sophistication of this or that newly found research procedure. I will take just two examples: demographic reconstitution from the quantitative side and the history of mentalities from the qualitative. And I shall suggest that the real value of both is to be found not in their (doubtful) ability to make good the assumption of direct access but in the way they have contributed indirectly to sharpening, focusing and elaborating analysis and criticism oriented to the explanation of structuring – which *is* what historical sociology is about.

Demographic reconstitution is, as both Laslett (1977) and

Le Roy Ladurie (1979) have recognised from rather different points of view, largely a creature of computer technology. The sheer data-processing capacity of the computer permits historians and sociologists alike to mobilise the evidence lurking in vast accumulations of records (of births, marriages, deaths, wills, property transactions and so forth) always known to be interesting but hitherto judged unusable. The technical breakthrough precipitated the usual uncritical euphoria – not least in Le Roy Ladurie's extraordinary proclamation (1979:14) that the historians of the future would 'be either a computer programmer or nothing at all'. But it did also genuinely permit far-reaching and dramatic increments in historical description. Whether one thinks of *The Peasants of Languedoc* (Le Roy Ladurie, 1974), with its formidable statistical locking-together of demographic and social change, of *Family Structure in Nineteenth Century Lancashire* (Anderson, 1971), meticulously manipulating small area census data both to describe family change in the course of industrialisation and to develop a complex theory of social exchange and reciprocity, of the long, imposing series of exercises in reconstitution, reconstruction and record-linkage associated with the Cambridge Group (for example, Wrigley (1973)), of Macfarlane's careful recipe (1977) for *Reconstructing Historical Communities*, the great French work of historical criminology from Quetelet (1836) and Ferri (1891) to Mandrou (1968) and Deyon (1972), of Fogel and Engerman's bombshell, *Time on the Cross* (1974), of Vovelle's exhaustive coding and processing (1973) of almost nineteen thousand wills to elucidate the meaning of death in pre-revolutionary Provence, or of any of the other familiar landmarks of the genre, it is clear beyond serious doubt that Wrigley (1979) is quite right to claim that at least in the fields of demographic history and of 'the behaviour of mankind in the mass', statistical approaches to the gathering and processing of data have permitted a radical transformation of the historian's (or the sociologist's) ability to know the past. More specifically, he is absolutely right, too, to maintain that: 'the advent of electronic computers and especially the development of methods of input and analysis well suited to large alphanumeric data sets ... offers to the current generation of scholars opportunities denied to their predecessors'. But opportunities to do what?

So far as I can see the real achievement of the new quantitative techniques has not been a definitive access to the realities of the past, not incontrovertible description, but a drastic intensification of the analytical problems involved in theorising history, a contribution to criticism. The obvious, and compelling, example is that of the fate of Peter Laslett's famous discovery (1965; 1972) of the pre-industrial 'reality' of the nuclear family. Almost as striking is Macfarlane's ingenious assertion (1978) of the non-existence of peasants. Extensive and conscientious family reconstitution led Laslett (1972:67) to a firm contention that the extended family cherished in sociological theory as the peculiar kinship mode of western Europe before capitalism had not in fact been there. And not just as a quantitative matter: 'The inescapable conclusion would seem to be that ... in all English communities so far recovered from the past, familial experience was in fact pretty well congruent with familial ideology ... and that the operative term in both was the nuclear family, the simple family household'. The initial reconstitution had revealed many small households. Laslett had inferred small families. Challenged, he had shown to his own satisfaction that household as a unit of organisation and family as a frame of meaning were one and the same – small. I am not myself convinced that his work has as yet made this all-important second step. The 'qualitative' criticisms of Berkner (1972), Flandrin (1979) and Poster (1978) remain very much in force. And powerful qualifications of even his quantitative thesis have been demanded by the work of Stone (1977) and Chaytor (1980). Chaytor, for example, whose techniques of reconstitution are quite on a par with those of the Cambridge Group, feels able to suggest that perhaps after all, 'changes did take place in the 16th and 17th centuries as Marx, Tawney and [many other earlier historians] thought they did' (1980:59). In sum, family reconstitution through the linking of data on household composition cannot dispose of profound doubts to the effect that kinship might, in the past as it does now, have meant more than household. And the plain evidence that noble and at least some commoner families lived lives quite at odds with the overall statistical picture of reconstituted households calls for appraisals and interpretations well beyond the range of the techniques of demographic reconstitution as such. At the end of the day Peter Laslett's achievement has been, not to demonstrate the reality of pre-industrial family life, but to exact a much more refined and discriminating conception of the analytical problems involved in family history, a re-working of categories not a representation of reality. He has managed, without showing us 'how it was', to convince us of the problematic nature of our concepts. And both his success in opening-up new problems of theorisation and his failure to recover the past as it was confirm the wisdom of Wrigley's judgement (1977) that 'empirical data hold little meaning unless subject to a constant dialectical exchange with a developing body of theory'.

Laslett establishes how it was *not*, not how it was. The sociological confusion of family and household occupants – that is, of kin relationships and housing arrangements – is exposed. Mobilising data about the occupants of units of accomodation demonstrates simply that households were small. That is an important finding – despite a solid residuum of evidence that (for sound theoretical reasons as Flandrin points out) they were not small everywhere. But it leaves the question of what the realities of the family (as experience, relationship and structure) really were, wide open. As Poster (1978:xi) puts it: 'While quantitative, demographic studies are needed, they cannot provide historians with a concept of the family that can pose the important questions and render the family intelligible in pre-modern and modern Europe'. The heart of the matter is that Laslett's 'facts' are already categories of a certain theorisation of family history by the time they emerge from the machine room, indeed, long before the raw data are assembled for machine processing. What they do is to destroy the credentials of the particular theorisation to which they are critically addressed. They do not, however, adequately or directly present the family to us as it 'really' was. His achievement is to have renewed the history of the family as a problem of the whole relationship of kinship to domesticity, property, inheritance, social reproduction, the relations of dependency and domination. That is actually a much more

valuable achievement than that of simply substituting a pre-
industrial nuclear family for a pre-industrial extended family
would have been. But what it contributes to our knowledge of
how it was is not so much new facts as new doubts, a more
complex sense of the relational realities standing within the
social forms directly available to empirical scrutiny. The problem of how it was runs beyond the observational techniques of
quantitative data-gathering into a distinctly theoretical terrain.

A more problematic example of the contribution of
demographic data to the critique of categories is provided by
Macfarlane (1978). *The Origins of English Individualism* may
by read as a prolonged assertion of Macfarlane's inability to
discover a peasant society in English history. The importance
of the failure is said to be that many accounts of English
industrialisation, and many explanations of why England was
the first country to industrialise, presume the existence of a
peasant society prior to industrialisation and as in some
analytically important sense the womb from which industrialism grew. Insofar as those accounts require the pre-existence
and disintegration of a peasant society, failure to find such a
society actually there, as 'how it was', would seem to threaten
the whole theorisation. That at least appears to be Macfarlane's argument. In pursuit of it he begins by constructing a
bold, unambiguous, broad definition of peasant society and
then, drawing mainly on demographic evidence, sets out to see
whether such a society, or anything very like it, can be found in
English history. Working backwards from the eighteenth
century to the thirteenth he suggests that, regress as one may,
the peasant society is never actually there, never in a
convincing sense how it was. On the contrary (1978:163), 'the
majority of ordinary people in England from at least the
thirteenth century were rampant individualists, highly mobile
both geographically and socially, economically "rational",
market-oriented and acquisitive, ego-centred in kinship and
social life'.

Macfarlane's definition, or as he rather revealingly calls it,
ideal-type of a peasant society is built up by abstraction from
studies of pre-industrial Eastern Europe by Thomas and
Znaniecki (1958), Galeski (1972) and Shanin (1972). Derived in
this way it has a good claim to be a sound account of the reality

of rural social relations among the population directly engaged in agricultural labour in Poland and Russia in, say, 1900. Macfarlane's subsequent contention is that England was never a peasant society in that sense (or at least not between 1200 and 1750), that the 'ordinary people' of England were never throughout those centuries peasants in the terms of his model. The evidence he cites is tied closely to that model and concerns such matters as: age at marriage, proportion of the population ever married, inter-generational geographical mobility, extent of wage-labour, contacts between kin – strongly emphasising the absense of collective linkages – household size and composition, the property rights and status of women, and centrally, the ownership and transfer of land, the most important single defining feature of a peasantry being family ownership of land. In all these respects he argues that social relations in the English countryside were always strikingly unlike those required by the ideal type. Peasant society was simply not how it was.

The argument gives rise to quite a number of problems: both problems of empirical detail and problems of conceptualisation. What is perhaps most important is that in both respects Macfarlane's argument appears to be essentially empiricist and quantitative rather than analytical and qualitative. His requirement for recognising a peasant society seems to be that some very large majority of the relevant population should be identifiable as peasants. Almost all of his arguments turn on attempts to demonstrate that in various ways large *numbers* of people in medieval England were not peasants. The effect of this approach is to set up a thoroughly pettifogging regression in which Macfarlane and his adversaries exchange ever-more microscopic bits of empirical evidence: Earls Colne was not peasant-like; Kibworth Harcourt (Howell, 1976) was peasant like; this village, that family, ad infinitum. On balance the state of the quantitative argument still seems to me to favour those who cling to the view of medieval England as a peasant society; but of course that misses the important point. Which is that the problem is not necessarily a quantitative one at all. Indeed, one of the most interesting things to emerge from any close reading of the controversy between Macfarlane and, say R. H. Hilton, on this question is the regularity with which Hilton entirely agrees with Macfarlane about the large numbers of people who were not peasants. He readily concedes, for example that there were large, often very large, numbers of wage labourers, craftsmen, and others who revolved around the 'solid central core' of the peasant economy as essential features of it (1973:38). As a matter of fact Hilton does hold to the view that a majority of the English rural population in, say the fourteenth century, can be identified as peasants. But again that misses the point; which is that the use of the category as an indicator of social reality is not *in* principle quantitative in Hilton's case any more than Marx or Weber when speaking of a given society as a capitalist or a slave society were proposing that a numerical majority of the population of that society would be found to be capitalists or slaves. The head count is simply not the relevant test.

But if Macfarlane's argument fails to connect with the account of how England was advanced by the writers he criticises and does so because of its quantitative and observational nature, on what alternative basis do Hilton and others rest their view that, large numbers of non-peasants notwithstanding, it makes sense to say that medieval England was in some real way a peasant society? In Hilton's case at least the answer is quite clear (1975; 1978), his claim is part of a more general thesis about the reality of the feudal mode of production. Although he does indeed refer constantly to peasants, peasant society and the peasant economy the reference is not simply or primarily to the phenomenal conditions and circumstances of medieval society, not a description of experiences but an analysis of structure, an attempt to identify the central importance – as structuring agency – of the *relationships* of peasant and non-peasant in the formation, persistence and dissolution of the feudal mode. The point (1978:6) is 'to analyse, not a self-contained "peasant economy" (which has probably never existed) but the *feudal* economy of the middle ages'. The specific reality of feudalism in this view is the relation of lordship, the nexus of a 'specific form of productive labour ... the peasant family living on its own landholding' (1973:37) and an equally distinctive mode of extracting surplus, the feudal conversion of agrarian surplus into landowner income (1978:7). It is through the relation of lordship that both peasants and lords have their distinctive historical being and significance – a conception entirely absent from Macfarlane's descriptive model of peasant society. And the construction, enforcement, struggle against, escape from the reproduction of that relation are the pertinent empirical realities in terms of which the society as a whole operated, held together and lived the hidden reality of the feudal mode of production.

The crucial consideration in such analysis is plainly not whether at any particular moment peasants made up any particular proportion or number of the population, but whether the relation of lordship (with peasants a constrained party to it) can indeed be shown to have been the operational pivot of the whole social formation. Hilton's work is a sustained argument that it can, that that is precisely how it was. And in many respects it is an argument that has little difficulty in accommodating the non-peasant features noted by Macfarlane. Both parties to the relation of lordship, the economy of petty agrarian households and the regime of feudal lords, possessed their own internal dynamism (for example – Hilton, 1978:6 – 'the self-destructive cycle of demographic expansion and impoverishment' on the one hand, and perhaps the equally self-destructive cycle of military-political expansion and impoverishment on the other). In conjunction, brought into contradictory relation with one another the whole system, for all its obsession with order, stability and tradition, became quite explosively dynamic. And when we add to that a host of further occasions for divergence, innovation and experiment resulting from the historical peculiarities of the institutionalisation of feudalism then and there in medieval England it is hardly surprising that we find a society which, around its central, defining relationship, endlessly spins-off just the sorts of deviant patterns noted by Macfarlane and so largely accepted by Hilton. But which nevertheless for centuries manages more or less brutally also to reproduce its central, defining relationship in the face of all innovation.

Yet, if Macfarlane's critique of earlier accounts of pre-modern England misses the mark insofar as its quantitative and descriptive tendencies fail to grip the analytical and relational conceptions of historical reality involved in those accounts, he does again, usefully clear some ground. The very formalism and empiricism of his approach (measuring the world against the model) highlights the extent to which the category 'peasant' has been used in far too eclectic and undiscriminating a way by others. Hilton, for example, really does seem to use the term so inclusively as to deprive it of much of its possible analytical value; it becomes almost as loose as 'country dweller', 'worker', 'poor people' or indeed, 'almost everyone except nobles, merchants and priests' on some occasions. And even when he offers an apparently close definition (as for example, 1973: 26ff) he can be ambiguous on vital matters. Is a peasant society defined by family landownership, family land-holding or family units of production, for example? And just how extended or nuclear were peasant families (indeed, does it matter)? Is it really useful or sensible to treat primogeniture and partible inheritance as minor variants of a single peasant mode? Is a peasant society with extensive marketing acceptably the same sort of thing as a peasant society with virtually no marketing? Since it is precisely on such variations that further empirical analysis of the workings of the feudal mode of production, and particularly of its dissolution in England, largely depend, Macfarlane's call for more discriminating categories, as distinct from his claim to have shown us how it was, seems very much in order. For the rest, what he has established is perhaps little more than that 'the historical process of divorcing the producer from the means of production' (Marx:1954), was much more protracted, devious and deeply rooted in the dynamic realities of the specifically English workings of the feudal mode of production than some people (non-marxist historians, for example) might have thought. I am not sure that Hilton and many of the other writers Macfarlane criticises would want to disagree with that. But a reminder that history takes time is no bad thing.

Ressurectionism – Selbourne's term strikes me as entirely apt – can proceed either in terms of masses of data (the quantitative mode) or in terms of immediacy and depth of data (a qualitative mode). But can the qualitative approach take us further than the quantitative towards knowing the past as it was? Can ethnography accomplish the lived moment of the past even if quantitative empiricism serves only to sharpen and focus our curiosity? Serious suggestions that it can have been made both within the field of the history of mentalities and from the recently renewed territory of 'people's history'.

The history of mentalities embraces a multitude of projects. Insofar as it has a common reference it would seem to be to the attempt to elucidate 'how it was' by close presentation and reading of the understandings of previously ignored, often supposedly inarticulate inhabitants of the past in their own terms of understanding. By directly recovering the experience of common people it is hoped to reveal the mental apparatus in terms of which they lived that experience and experienced their lives. Much of the work towards a people's history undertaken by the History Workshop can be treated as falling within the field of the history of mentalities therefore; indeed *History Workshop Journal* has now probably joined *Annales* as a prime sponsor of this type of work. In any event there are now plenty of studies to testify to the depth and detail with which the experience and consciousness, perhaps even the 'cosmologies', of the unknown, the oppressed, the marginal and the ordinary inhabitants of the past can indeed be resurrected: we have Cobb on *The Police and the People* (1970), an unmasked, almost physical encounter with the minds and habits of the villains of the 1790s, White on the fearful world of *Rothschild Buildings* (1980), Ginsburg's anatomy of the thought world of a sixteenth century Italian miller (1976), Le Roy Ladurie, appearing here too, to unweave the fabric of a fourteenth-century village in the Pyrenees (1978), or render the latent meanings of a festival turned riot two centuries later (1980), Keith Hopkins tracing the clouds of astrology and superstition in Imperial Rome (1978), Ariès on what was meant by childhood (1965) or death (1974) and a vast literature of local ethnographies, case studies, collective biographies and reconstructed moments.

And the agendas for the history of mentalities that have been offered from various quarters are remarkably congruent with one another in stressing a few key themes. The most disciplined versions of the programme have come from France, from Febvre (1965) to Le Goff (1974), and I shall return to them shortly. Most English-language verions could be said to be distinguished by their enthusiasm for vicarious experience rather than their discipline. Thus, Stone (1979), who appears to understand the history of mentalities as a matter of an essentially 'pictorial' mode of work which 'rambles around inside people's heads', speaks of the 'role of the study of *mentalité* in the revival of non-analytical modes of writing history'. That is perhaps an extreme statement; but certainly this type of work does seem to be widely understood both by its practitioners and by its excited audience as at last accomplishing explanation through description which really describes, as somehow, by close enough description bringing-off a direct grasp of how the past really was. Though more restrained, Samuel's appraisal (1981: xviii) of the work of the History Workshop is plainly in the same world as Stone's panegyric for a rambling impressionism:

> The main thrust of people's history in recent years has been towards the recovery of subjective experience ... reconstituting the small details of everyday life ... the shift from 'places' to 'faces' ... the enormous research ingenuity which has gone into attempting to capture the voice of the past – the cadences of vernacular speech, the tell-tale turns of phrase ... the major effort is to present historical issues as they appeared to the actors at the time; to personalise the workings of large historical forces; to draw on contemporary vocabularies; to identify the faces in the crowd.

I should say at once that the whole enterprise, described thus, strikes me as misconceived and quite utopian. It involves a double naivety about the meaning of what qualitative descriptive research can hope to resurrect. It is naive in the way it presents selected esoteric or lost moments or persons as *representing* past realities. And it is naive in the assumptions it makes about the capacity of individuals to give the historian or sociologist unreflective but accurate accounts of the meaning of their own lives – or even reflective ones. In both respects it rests on the notion that the problem of 'how it was' can be reformulated adequately as a question of how it was said to be (or lived as though it was) by certain individuals. In both respects it denies a fundamental proposition of the whole argument I have been trying to develop – that the past (like the present) can only be known in terms of some conscious effort to theorise it, and that any such effort involves a recognition of the sense in which social realities are strange, relational and not directly accessible to us – a recognition of the extent to which knowledge has to be an act of estrangement. We have a problem of knowledge just because in a quite radical sense – a sense splendidly drawn out by Marx in *The 18th Brumaire of Louis Bonaparte*, as I tried to make clear in an earlier chapter – individuals typically don't 'know' what they are doing.

The first point is made very effectively by Darnton (1978) in a discussion of the resurrectionist work of Cobb and Ariès. The trouble in Ariès's case is fairly straightforward; a dearth of appropriate evidence. The great themes in the history of consciousness in which he is interested, childhood and death, simply cannot be directly recovered at the relevant level of popular consciousness. The history of education and evidence from high art have therefore to stand in at crucial moments when the lives of ordinary people are silent. We glimpse the faces in the crowd only through the eyes of priests, moralists, educators and patrons of art, persons all themselves well-removed from the immediate existence of the crowd. Cobb, on the other hand, writes from the thick of the crowd, pointing out face after grotesque face for our intimate inspection. The problem here is that his particular vantage point is not a very good one from which to see what the crowd as a whole is doing, or even to judge its size and shape. Indeed, it seems that the crush of faces and voices can be quite misleading. Moving nimbly among a multitude of thieves and murderers, brigands, terrorists, anarchists, vagrants, prostitutes, perverts and outsiders of all sorts, Cobb brings an underworld of revolutionary France violently to life. But the method – Darnton calls it 'methodology as empathy' – tends to subvert meaning. As Darnton comments, the resurrection of the 'obscure people of the Revolution' is superbly accomplished, but it is accomplished in such a way that the Revolution itself almost disappears, 'dissolves in buzzing confusion'. We are brought face to face with 'a wild variety of individuals', but 'their stories do not lead to any general conclusions about their lives or their time'. Presumably that would not matter if what Cobb wanted us to understand was that the times were 'really' no more than a meaningless discord. But in fact he, too, has

conceptions of structure and ordered meaning and is interested
in advancing a number of quite firm interpretative arguments
about the general significance of the discord. He would have us
believe, for example, that 'the murder rate went up drastically
during the years between the Terror and the Empire' and that it
did so because many homicides were, in reality, 'a form of
political protest, a Counter-Terror'. Such an argument plainly
requires the support of more than individual case studies and
Darnton cogently points out both that Cobb's method, the
method of resurrecting mentalities, cannot provide such
support and, that if one turns to the criminal records, judicial
files and statistics from which support would have to come and
analyses them systematically Cobb's impressionism would
have to give way both to evidence of a persistent decrease in
violent crime in the period at issue and to the view that
'criminal and revolutionary violence were unrelated, that the
Bastille-storming and purse-snatching impulses had little in
common and that even seem from "below" the Revolution
took place above the heads of France's bread-and-butter
criminals'. In sum: 'Historical criminology ... has revealed
realities of behaviour and psychology that could not be
reached by Cobb's methods'. Further: 'The point is not that
Cobb was wrong (his kind of history is too subjective to be
classified as right or wrong) but that his historical impressionism does not lead anywhere'.

Although serious, such criticism is hardly fatal to the
determined resurrectionist. To begin with it is not as obvious as
Darnton claims that criminal statistics can render the meaning
of crime for criminals as distinct from its meaning for judges.
But even if it were, the resurrectionist historian or sociologist
would seem not so much to be put out of business by Darnton's
objections as invited to adopt a more sophisticated approach.
Perhaps case studies *plus* statistics would do the trick. That is
indeed just what Darnton himself appears to recommend.
Speaking of Cobb's haunting accounts of the states of mind of
refugee undercover former terrorists in the period of anti-
terror reaction he says: 'As an imaginative evocation of the
nastiness of village life it is utterly persuasive; and it would
compensate for a book full of faulty statistics ... The problem
is how to move beyond evocation by anecdote' (1978:114). And

his own solution to that problem is that 'the history of mentalités ought to ally itself with sociology' – by which he appears to understand social statistics – 'not fight it to the death' (1978:117). But we have already seen that social statistics are themselves no sure guide to historical realities. Two blind men merely compound the darkness. And it is here that my second doubt about historical impressionism also comes in. Of course case studies sensitively related to long-range and large-scale demographic and social quantification would almost certainly carry us further than either case studies or historical statistics on their own could do. But sooner or later we are still going to run up against the problem of access as a problem of epistemological principle. And when we do the point is once again simply that the reality of the past is just not 'there' waiting to be observed by the resurrectionist historian. It is to be known if at all through strenuous theoretical alienation. As well as searching for its telling detail we must withdraw from it to know it. This seems especially true if what we are most interested in is recovering the past by way of knowing the meanings of its inhabitants – meanings which insofar as they are social, implicit and situated will evade all our efforts to hear them directly, however good our ear for the vernacular. The close encounter may make the voices louder; it does not, as Hawthorn (1979) sensibly insists, make their meanings clearer. To that end we must turn back from 'their' meanings to our own and to the things we know about them which they did not know, or say, about themselves.

In the light of such difficulties it is perhaps not surprising that we should find that the distinctive effect of 'how it was' projects whether of the quantitative or of the qualitative variety is *not* to establish factual pictures which close debate and settle interpretation but on the contrary to precipitate radical criticism of received categories of interpretation and so stimulate and advance debate. Certainly we can get a good idea of household composition in 1670, or of the incidence of bastardy, primogeniture or the disinheritance of children; certainly we can see what it was like to be superstitious or fanatical, hungry or without work; we can visit the worlds of shoemakers and village priests, car workers in Coventry in 1940 or apprentices in Romans in 1580. And when we have done so the problem of putting the pieces together to make the right picture will remain. It is a task for which some sense of overall design, as distinct from the shape of the pieces, is essential. Which is why most seemingly resurrectionist studies are not in the end merely resurrectionist at all: the point of Hopkins' investigation (1978) of Roman astrology is to say something about how emperor worship worked and thence about the structuring of a world of Conquerors and Slaves; the point of White's reconstruction (1979) of the awful bohemia of Campbell road in North London, 'the worst street in North London', is to restore the lumpenproletariat both to visibility and to theoretical significance in the analysis of capitalism. And so on. The real danger of resurrectionism is not that historians and sociologists will be seduced into mere impressionism and a mass flight from theory; it is that they will encourage the belief (among themselves or others) that the theoretical work necessary to know the past can be done adequately in the very act of representation; the belief that enough facts, or intimate enough facts, will of themselves show us the theoretical reality of capitalism or feudalism, the extended family or peasant society.

It is not that we can do without detail. Detail constitutes the world to which analysis is addressed. Analysis can only work on and through detail. But one can have too much detail. Reality is always 'our' construct as well as 'theirs', and in any given construction a lot of the pieces on the table may turn out (as I think they do in Macfarlane's case against the medievalists) simply to be bits of a quite different puzzle. Where resurrectionism is omnivorous, reality tends to be parsimonious. Do we really need more studies of Louis XIV's mistresses' wigs, or Mussolini's valet's friends' hobbies to understand the reality of absolute monarchy or fascism?

As Selbourne (1980:156) puts it: 'Resurrectionism – the re-peopling of the past by archival exhumation – is in particular prone to the illusion that it is an historian-free history; that it is history which speaks for itself ... a history without a subject or knower, but only objects known or to be known'. Far from speaking for itself the reality of the past speaks only when first firmly spoken to by the historian. It is not just that the analytical and the descriptive are not 'mutually incompatible' –

as Samuel (1980:170) urges – they are thoroughly mutually interdependent. And their interdependence also demands recognition of their separate identities whether one is interested in how it happened or in how it was. Knowledge of social reality is something the analytical and the descriptive achieve by deliberate and considered collaboration. Theory is kept alive by the nourishment of constantly-renewed, theory-relevant empirical enquiries and resurrections – such as Godelier's attempt (1980) to recover the 'representations' of work or Davis's excavation (1971) of 'the real uses of popular recreation' in 16th-century France. But empirical description is itself saved from the consequences of excessive appetite only by the lean discipline of theory. Yet theory, as the editors of *History Workshop Journal* note (1978:4) 'does not spring ready-made from nowhere'. It can spring, *seemingly* ready-made from quantitative or qualitative resurrectionism; and it can spring, again *seemingly* ready-made from highly abstracted 'theoretical practice'. If it does either it is likely to prove extremely foolish when put to the test. That is the problem: theory must work on the empirical without either dominating or being dominated. At the same time, at any given moment in the course of theoretical and empirical work the empirical will be deeply contaminated by theory and theory will be deeply contaminated by the empirical. A difficult problem.

What it does is to commit the historical sociologist to a rather agile intellectual life. Specifically, we have to find a way of living with the fact of the mutual interdependence and contamination of theory and evidence without resorting to either the anti-theoretical fetishism of history-as-evidence towards which the History Workshop sometimes seemed to slide or the a-historical fetishism of theory-as-knowledge which some structuralists in their more extreme moments seem to espouse. Either retreat pulls the core, reality-apprehending, project to pieces.

By way of a conclusion, as an affirmation that the project can hold together, and as an alternative to portentous generalities, consider the work of Fernand Braudel. Braudel is of course a champion of the view that history and sociology are a single unitary enterprise: 'one single intellectual adventure, not two different sides of the same cloth but the very stuff of

that cloth itself, the entire substance of its yarn' (1980:69).
Braudel argues that position from the point of view of the
needs of historical knowledge and it is of course the position I
have tried to argue from the point of view of the needs of
sociological knowledge. But it is not just as an eminent figure
with whom I happen to agree that I cite him here. It is as a
writer whose own practical historical work (as distinct from
programmes and general reflections) has shown magnifi-
cently what a unified historical sociology would be like. His
major analytical contribution is widely thought to be the
differentiation he has established between levels or modes of
historical time: the time of conjunctures; and the time of
structure, or the *longue durée*. Thus:

> History exists at different levels. I would even go so far as to say
> three levels, but that would be only a manner of speaking and
> simplifying things too much. There are ten, a hundred levels to be
> examined, ten, a hundred different time spans. On the surface the
> history of events works itself out in the short term; it is a sort of
> micro-history. Halfway down, a history of conjunctures follows a
> broader, slower rhythm. So far that has above all been studied in
> its developments on the material plane, in economic cycles and
> intercycles ... And over and above the 'recitatif' of the conjunc-
> ture, structural history, or the history of the *longue durée*,
> inquires into whole centuries at a time. It functions along the
> border between the moving and the immobile, and because of the
> long-standing stability of its values, it appears unchanging when
> compared with all the histories which flow and work themselves
> out more swiftly, and which in the final analysis gravitate around
> it. (1980:74)

It is just that sense of history as a complex of 'planes' and
'levels', of orders of time – or as I would be inclined to say,
phases of structuring – that is worked out so powerfully in
Braudel's great study of the Mediterranean (1973). The design
of the book, and its achievement, is to display the working of
different historical times on one another: 'that dialogue
between structure and conjuncture, the moment in time and
the long or very long term' (757); 'the division of history into
the slow and fast-moving levels, structure and conjuncture'
(1242), the combination of 'structure and conjecture, the

permanent and the ephemeral, the slow-moving and the fast . . .
two aspects of reality . . . always present in everyday life which
is a constant blend of what changes and what endures' (353). It
is not that the analysis of structuring can proceed only in these
terms – indeed, in some ways I think that Braudel's terms are
unfortunate, appropriating as they do the idea of structure for
the very long term and so implying, something he plainly does
not intend, that structuring occurs only in that sort of time; we
need to be able to think of epochs, periods and moments as *all*
interacting orders of structuring. It is rather, that Braudel has
shown, conclusively I think, that the sort of conceptual
discipline and explicitness needed for the analysis of
structuring is not just compatible with thorough historical
scholarship but that it enormously invigorates it and extends
its reach towards the realities of the past. He has begun to
articulate – although he himself has not much refined or
developed – the sorts of categories and the sort of ordered sense
of the empirical complexity of time which a serious historical
sociology would need. And he has, but he is less original in this,
demonstrated that the type of interrogation of concept by
evidence and evidence by concept called for by Edward
Thompson and so many others can indeed by creatively
pursued even though concept and evidence speak different
languages. The project of historical sociology involves us in
superimposing structure on history with a view to recovering
the way history superimposes structure on us. It crystallises as
a negotiation of concept and evidence in the concrete study of
structuring. If, somewhere between Marx's great abstract
drama of commodity values and Cobb telling it as it was, an
effective analytical historical sociology is to be found, it is
works such as Braudel's *The Mediterranean* that point the way.

Bibliography

Abel, T., 1966, *The Nazi Movement: Why Hitler Came Into Power*, New York, Atherton Press.

Alexandre, M. (ed), 1968, *On Trial: Fidel Castro, Regis Debray*, London, Lorimer.

Anderson, M., 1971, *Family Structure in 19th Century Lancashire*, Cambridge, Cambridge University Press.

Anderson, P., 1964, 'The Origins of the Present Crisis', *New Left Review*, 23.

Anderson, P., 1974, *Lineages of the Absolutist State*, London, N.L.B.

Ariès, P., 1974, *Western Attitudes towards Death*, Baltimore, Johns Hopkins University Press.

Ariès, P., 1965, *Centuries of Childhood*, London, Cape.

Atkinson, A. B., 1968, *Poverty in Britain and the Reform of Social Security*, Cambridge, Cambridge University Press.

Barnes, J. A., 1971, 'Time Flies Like An Arrow', *Man*, vi, 537–52.

Becker, H., 1963, *Outsiders: Studies in the Sociology of Deviance*, Glencoe, Illinois, The Free Press.

Bell, D., 1974, *The Coming of Post-Industrial Society*, London, Heinemann.

Bendix, R., 1956, *Work and Authority in Industry*, New York, Wiley & Sons.

Bendix, R., 1964, *Nation Building and Citizenship*, New York, Wiley & Sons.

Benney, M., Gray, A. P., Pear, R. H., 1956, *How People Vote*, London, Routledge and Kegan Paul.

Berelson, B., Lazarsfeld, P. F., McPhee, W. N., 1954, *Voting*, Chicago, University of Chicago Press.

Berger, P. and Luckmann, T., 1967, *The Social Construction of Reality*, London, Allen Lane.

Berkner, L., 1972, 'The Stem Family and the Development Cycle of the Peasant Household', *American Historical Review*, 77, 398–418.

Bettelheim, B., 1960, *The Informed Heart*, Glencoe, Illinois, The Free Press.

Bhaskar, R., 1979, *The Possibility of Naturalism*, London, Harvester Press.

Blackburn, R., 1969, 'A Brief Guide to Bourgeois Ideology', in Cockburn, A. & Blackburn, R. (eds), *Student Power*, Harmondsworth, Penguin Books.

Bourdieu, P., 1973, 'Cultural Reproduction and Social Reproduction', in Brown, R. (ed), *Knowledge, Education and Cultural Change*, London, Tavistock.

Bourdieu, P., 1977, *Outline of a Theory of Practice*, Cambridge, Cambridge University Press.

Braudel, F., 1973, *The Mediterranean and the Mediterranean World in the Age of Philip II*, (2 vols.), London, Fontana.

Braudel, F., 1980, *On History*, London, Weidenfeld & Nicolson.

Buckle, T. H., 1857, *History of Civilisation in England*, London, Routledge.

Burke, P., 1980, *Sociology and History*, London, George Allen & Unwin.

Burrow, J., 1966, *Evolution and Society*, Cambridge, Cambridge University Press.

Carr, E. H., 1964, *What is History?*, London, Penguin Books.

Centre for Contemporary Cultural Studies, 1976, *Resistance Through Rituals*, (ed. S. Hall *et al.*), London, Hutchinson.

Centre for Contemporary Cultural Studies, 1979, *Working Class Culture*, (ed. J. Clarke *et al.*), London, Hutchinson.

Chaytor, M., 1980, 'Household and Kinship', *History Workshop*, 10.

Chodak, S., 1973, *Societal Developmental*, New York, Oxford University Press.

Cobb, R., 1970, *The Police and the People: French Popular Protest 1789–1820*, London, Oxford University Press.

Cobban, A., 1964, *The Social Interpretation of the French Revolution*, Cambridge University Press.

Cohen, A., 1955, *Delinquent Boys*, New York, Free Press.

Cohen, S., 1973, *Folk Devils and Moral Panics*, London, MacGibbon & Kee.

Collingwood, R. G., 1956, *The Idea of History*, Oxford, Oxford University Press.

Darnton, R., 1978, 'The History of *mentalités*', in Brown, R. H., and Lyman, S. M., (eds.), *Structure, Consciousness and History*, Cambridge, Cambridge University Press.

Daudt, H., 1961, *Floating Voters and the Floating Vote*, Leiden, Stenfert N. V.

Davies, A., 1964, 'The Origins of the French Peasant Revolution of 1789', in *History*, xlix.

Davis, J., 1930, 'A Study of One Hundred and Sixty Three Outstanding Communist Leaders', *Publications of the American Sociological Society*, 24.

Davis, N. Z., 1971, 'The Reasons of Misrule: Youth Groups and Charivaris in Sixteenth Century France', *Past and Present*, 50.

Dawe, A., 1979, 'Theories of Social Action', in Bottomore, T. and Nisbet, R. (eds.), *A History of Sociological Analysis*, 362–417, London, Heinemann.

Deyon, P., 1972, 'Delinquance et répression ... au XVIIIe siècle', cit. Darnton (1978).

Dicey, A. V., 1905, *Law and Public Opinion in England*, London, Macmillan & Co.

de Tocqueville, A., 1971, *The Ancien Regime and the French Revolution*, London, Fontana.

Dobb, M., 1946, *Studies in the Development of Capitalism*, London, Routledge & Kegan Paul.

Drake, M. (ed.), 1973, *Applied Historical Studies*, London, Methuen.

Dray, W., 1980, *Perspectives on History*, London, Routledge & Kegan Paul.

Duby, G., 1974, *The Early Growth of the European Economy: Warriors and Peasants*, London.

Dunn, T., 1978, 'Practising History and Social Science on "realist" assumptions', in Hookway, C. and Pettit, P. (eds.), *Action and Interpretation*, Cambridge, Cambridge University Press.

Durkheim, E., 1933, *The Division of Labour in Society*, New York, Macmillan.

Durkheim, E., 1938, *The Rules of Sociological Method*, Chicago, University of Chicago Press.

Durkheim, E., 1960, 'The Dualism of Human Nature and its Social Conditions', in Wolff, K. H. (ed.), *Emile Durkheim 1858–1917*, Columbus, Ohio University Press.

Ehrenberg, R., 1928, *Capital and Finance in the Age of the Renaissance*, London.

Eisenstadt, S., 1963, *The Political Systems of Empires*, Glencoe, Illinois, Free Press.

Eisenstadt, S., 1965, *Essays on Comparative Social Institutions*, New York, Wiley & Sons.

Elias, N., 1978a, *What is Sociology?*, London, Hutchinson.

Elias, N., 1978b, *The Civilising Process*, Oxford, Blackwell.

Elkins, S. M., 1959, *Slavery*, Chicago, University of Chicago Press.

Elkins, S. M., 1975, 'The Slavery Debate', *Commentary*, 1975, 10.

Elton, G. R., 1963, *Reformation Europe*, London, Fontana.

Elton, G. R., 1967, *The Practice of History*, London, Fontana.

Engels, F., 1947, *Anti-Duhring*, Moscow, Foreign Languages Publishing House.

Engels, F., 1962, 'Socialism: Utopian and Scientific' in Marx and Engels *Selected Works*, ii, 116–165, Moscow, Foreign Languages Publishing House.

Engels, F., *The Peasant War in Germany*, London, Allen & Unwin.

Erikson, E., 1943, 'Observations on the Yurok: Childhood and World Image', *University of California Publications in American Archaeology and Ethnology*, xxxv.

Erikson, E., 1958, *Young Man Luther*, New York, Norton.

Erikson, E., 1963, *Childhood and Society*, New York, Norton.

Erikson, E., 1968, *Identity: Youth and Crisis*, London, Faber and Faber.

Faunce, W. and Form, W., 1969, *Comparative Perspectives on Industrial Society*, Boston, Little, Brown & Company.

Febvre, L., 1965, *Combats pour l'histoire*, Paris, Armand Colin.

Feigl, H., and Brodbeck, M., 1953, *Readings in the Philosophy of Science*, New York, Appleton-Crofts.

Feldman, A. and Moore, W., 1969, 'Industrialisation and Industrialism: Convergence and Differentiation', in Faunce and Form (1969), 55–71.

Ferri, E., 1891, *La Sociologie criminelle*, Paris, A. Rousseau.

Feuer, L., 1969, *The Conflict of Generations*, London, Heinemann.

Firestone, H., 1957, 'Cats, Kicks and Color', *Social Problems*, 5, July.

Flandrin, J.-L., 1979, *Families in Former Times*, Cambridge, Cambridge University Press.

Fogel, R. W., and Engerman, S. L., 1974, *Time on the Cross: the Economics of American Negro Slavery*, New York, Little, Brown and Company.

Forster, R., 1960, *The Nobility of Toulouse in the Eighteenth Century*, Baltimore, Johns Hopkins University Press.

Frölich, P., 1940, *Rosa Luxemburg*, London, Gollancz.

Galeski, B., 1972, *Basic Concepts of Rural Sociology*, Manchester, Manchester University Press.

Gallie, W. B., 1964, 'What is a Story?' in *Philosophy and Historical Understanding*, London, Chatto & Windus.

Gardiner, P. (ed.), 1959, *Theories of History*, New York, Free Press.

Gardiner, P., 1961, *The Nature of Historical Explanation*, Oxford, Clarendon Press.

Gately, M. O., Moote, A. L., Wills, J. E., Jr, 1971, 'Seventeenth Century Peasant "Furies"', *Past and Present*, 51.

Geertz, C., 1971, 'Deep Play: Notes on the Balinese Cockfight' in Geertz, C. (ed.), *Myth, Symbol and Culture*, New York, Norton.

Geertz, C., 1973, *The Interpretation of Cultures*, New York, Basic Books.

Genovese, E., 1974, *Roll, Jordan, Roll: the World the Slaves Made*, New York, Knopf.

Gellner, E., 1956, 'Explanations in History', *Proceedings of the Aristotelian Society*.

Gellner, E., 1974, 'Our Current Sense of History', in *Contemporary Thought and Politics*, London, Routledge & Kegan Paul.

Gellner, E., 1981, *Muslim Society*, Cambridge, Cambridge University Press.

George, C. H., and George, K., 1961, *The Protestant Mind of the English Reformation*, London, Methuen.

Gerschenkron, A., 1957, 'Reflections on the Concept of "Prerequisites" of Modern Industrialisation', in *Scrotti in onore di G. U. Papi*, Milan.

Giddens, A., 1979, *Central Problems in Social Theory*, London, Macmillan.

Gilbert, B., 1973, *British Social Policy 1914–1939*, London, Batsford.

Ginsburg, C., 1976, *The Cheese and the Worms*, London, Routledge & Kegan Paul.

Glaser, B. G., and Strauss, A. L., 1968, *The Discovery of Grounded Theory*, London, Weidenfeld and Nicolson.

Godelier, M., 1980, 'Work and its Representations: a Research Project', *History Workshop Journal*, 10.

Goffman, E., 1968, 'The Moral Career of the Mental Patient', in *Asylums*, Harmondsworth, Penguin Books.

Goldthorpe, J. H., 1964a, 'The Development of Social Policy in England', in *Transactions of the Fifth World Congress of Sociology*, Vol. IV, International Sociological Association.

Goldthorpe, J. H., 1964b, 'Social Stratification in Industrial Society', in P. Halmos (ed.), *The Development of Industrial Societies*, Keele, University of Keele.

Gouldner, A. W., 1970, *The Coming Crisis of Western Sociology*, London, Heinemann.

Green, R. W., 1959, *Protestantism and Capitalism: the Weber Thesis and its Critics*, Boston, D. C. Heath & Company.

Gurr, T. R., 1970, *Why Men Rebel*, Princeton, Princeton University Press.

Gutman, H., 1976, *The Invisible Fact: Afro-Americans and their Families*, New York, Pantheon.

Hawthorn, G., 1979, 'Characterising the History of Social Theory', *Sociology*, 14, 3.

Hay, C., 1981, 'History, Sociology and Theory', in *Transactions of the Annual Conference of the British Sociological Association, 1980*, London, British Sociological Association.

Hays, S. P., 1968, 'New Possibilities for American Political History', in Lipset and Hofstadter (1968).

Heberle, R., 1951, *Social Movements*, New York, Appleton-Century-Crofts.

Hempel, C. G., 1942, 'The Function of Causal Laws in History', *Journal of Philosophy*.

Hilton, R., 1973, *Bond Men Made Free*, London, Temple Smith.

Hilton, R., 1974, Review of Duby (1974), *New Left Review*, 83.

Hilton, R., 1975, *English Peasantry in the Later Middle Ages*, Oxford, Oxford University Press.

Hilton, R. (ed.), 1976, *The Transition from Feudalism to Capitalism*, London, NLB.

Hilton, R. H., 1978, 'Agrarian Class Structure and Economic Development', *Past and Present*, 80.

Hirst, P. Q., 1976, *Social Evolution and Sociological Categories*, London, Allen & Unwin.

History Workshop Journal, 6, 1978, 'Editorial: History and Theory'.

Hobsbawm, E. J., 1980, 'The Revival of Narrative: Some Comments', *Past and Present*, 86.

Hopkins, K., 1978, *Conquerors and Slaves*, Cambridge, Cambridge University Press.

Howell, C., 1976, 'Peasant inheritance customs in the Midlands, 1280–1700', in Goddy, J., *et al.* (eds.), *Family and Inheritance*, Cambridge, Cambridge University Press.

Hughes, E. C., 1945, 'Dilemmas and Contradictions of Status', *American Journal of Sociology*, 50, 353–359.

Hyman, H. H., 1942, 'The Psychology of Status' in *Archives of Psychology*, 269.

James, M. E., 1970, 'Obedience and Dissent in Henrician England', *Past and Present*, 48.

James, M. E., 1973, 'The Concept of Order and the Northern Rising of 1569', *Past and Present*, 60.

Jary, D., 1981, 'The New Realism in British Sociological Theory', in *Transactions of the Annual Conference of the British Sociological Association, 1980*, London, B.S.A. Publications.

Johnson, R., 1979, 'Three Problematics: Elements of a Theory of Working Class Culture' in J. Clarke, C. Critcher and R. Johnson (eds.), *Working Class Culture*, London, Hutchinson.

Kerr, C., Dunlop, T., Harbison, F., Myers, C., 1960, *Industrialism and Industrial Man*, Cambridge, Mass., Harvard University Press.

Kirkpatrick, I., 1964, *Mussolini: study of a Demagogue*, London, Odhams.

Kitsuse, J. I., 1962, 'Societal Reaction to Deviant Behaviour', *Social Problems*, 9, 3, 247–256.

Laslett, P., 1965, *The World We Have Lost*, London, Methuen.

Laslett, P., 1972, *Household and Family in Past Time*, Cambridge, Cambridge University Press.

Laslett, P., 1977, *Family and Illicit Love in Earlier Generations*, Cambridge, Cambridge University Press.

Lazarsfeld, P. F., 1968, 'The Historian and the Pollster', in Lipset and Hofstadter (1968).

Lefebvre, G., 1947, *The Coming of the French Revolution*, Princeton, Princeton University Press.

Lefebvre, G., 1954, *Études sur la Révolution Française*, Paris.

Le Goff, J., 1974, 'Les mentalités: une histoire ambiguë', in Le Goff, J., and Nora, P., *Faire de l'histoire*, Paris.

Lemert, E., 1951, *Social Pathology*, New York, McGraw-Hill.

Lemert, E., 1967, *Human Deviance, Social Problems and Social Control*, Englewood Cliffs, New Jersey, Prentice-Hall.

Le Roy Ladurie, E., 1974, *The Peasants of Languedoc*, Urbana, University of Illinois Press.

Le Roy Ladurie, E., 1978, *Montaillou: Cathars and Catholics in a French Village 1294–1324*, London, Scolar Press.

Le Roy Ladurie, E., 1979, *The Territory of the Historian*, Hassocks, Harvester Press.

Le Roy Ladurie, E., 1980, *Carnival: a Peoples' Uprising at Romans, 1579–1580*, London, Scolar Press.

Levy, M. J., Jr, 1952, *The Structure of Society*, Princeton, The Princeton University Press.

Lipset, S. M., and Hofstadter, R., 1968, *History and Sociology: Methods*, New York, Basic Books.

Lipset, S. M., and Rokkan, S., 1967, *Party Systems and Voter Alignments*, New York, Free Press.

Lockwood, D., 1958, *The Blackcoated Worker*, London, Allen & Unwin.

Loewith, K., 1970, 'Weber's Interpretation of the Bourgeois – Capitalistic World in Terms of the Guiding Principle of "Rationalisation"', in Wrong (1970).

Louch, A. R., 1966, *Explanation and Human Action*, Oxford, Blackwell.

Lucas, C., 1973, 'Nobles, Bourgeois and the Origins of the French Revolution', *Past and Present*, 60.

Macfarlane, A., 1977, *Reconstructing Historical Communities*, Cambridge, Cambridge University Press.

Macfarlane, A., 1978, *The Origins of English Individualism*, Oxford, Blackwell.

Maine, H. J. S., 1954, *Ancient Law*, Oxford, Oxford University Press.

Mallet, S., 1975, *The New Working Class*, London, Spokesman.

Mandelbaum, M., 1938, *The Problem of Historical Knowledge*, New York.

Mandrou, R., 1968, *Magistrats et sorciers en France au XVIIe siècle*, Paris.

Mandrou, R., 1965, *Classes et luttes des classes en France*, Florence, Casa D'editrice G. d'Anna.

Mannheim, K., 1952, 'The Problem of Generations', in *Essays on the Sociology of Knowledge*, pp. 276–320, London, Routledge and Kegan Paul.

Marsh, R. M., 1967, *Comparative Sociology*, New York, Harcourt, Brace.

Marshall, T. H., 1970, *Social Policy*, London, Hutchinson.

Marx, K., 1959, *Economic and Philosophical Manuscripts of 1844*, London, Lawrence and Wishart.

Marx, K., 1962, 'The Class Struggles in France', in *Selected Works*, i, 139–242.

Marx, K. and Engels, F., 1962, *Selected Works*, (2 vols.), Moscow, Foreign Languages Publishing House.

Marx, K., 1962, 'The 18th Brumaire of Louis Bonaparte', in Karl Marx and Frederick Engels, *Selected Works*, Vol. I, 247–344, Moscow, Foreign Languages Publishing House.

Marx, K. and Engels, F., 1965, *The German Ideology*, London, Lawrence & Wishart.

Marx, K., 1970, *Capital: a Critique of Political Economy* (3 vols.), London, Lawrence & Wishart.

Matza, D., 1969, *Becoming Deviant*, Englewood Cliffs, New Jersey, Prentice Hall.

Med, G. H., 1934, *Mind, Self and Society*, Chicago, University of Chicago Press.

Merkl, P. H., 1975, *Political Violence Under the Swastika*, Princeton, Princeton University Press.

Merton, R. K., 1957, *Social Theory and Social Structure*, Glencoe, Illinois, Free Press.

Mill, J. S., 1843, *A System of Logic*, London, Longmans, Green.

Mills, C. W., 1959, *The Sociological Imagination*, New York, Oxford University Press.

Moore, B. Jr, 1966, *Social Origins of Dictatorship and Democracy*, Boston, Beacon Press.

Moore, B. Jr, 1978, *Injustice: the Social Bases of Obedience and Revolt*, London, Macmillan.

Mousnier, R., 1945, *La Vénalité des Offices*, Rouen, Maugard.

Mousnier, R., 1964, *The Assassination of Henri IV*, London, Faber & Faber.

Mousnier, R., 1971, *Peasant Uprisings in 17th Century France, Russia and China*, London, George Allen & Unwin.

Mousnier, R., 1973, *Social Hierarchies*, London, Croom Helm.

Murphey, M. G., 1973, *Our Knowledge of the Historical Past*, Indianapolis, Bobbs Merrill.

Nadel, S. F., 1951, *The Foundations of Social Anthropology*, New York, The Free Press.

Nagel, E., 1952, 'The Logic of Historical Analysis', *Scientific Monthly*.

Namier, L. B., 1945, *1848: The Revolution of the Intellectuals*, London.

Neale, R. S., 1981, *Class in English History, 1680–1850*, Oxford, Blackwell.

Oakeshott, M., 1933, *Experience and its Modes*, Cambridge, Cambridge University Press.

Nisbet, R., 1969, *Social Change and History*, New York, Oxford University Press.

Pagès, G., 1937, 'Autour du "Grand Orage"', *Revue Historique*, clxxix.

346   *Historical Sociology*

Parkin, F., 1972, *Class Inequality and Political Order*, London, Paladin.
Parkin, F., 1974, 'Strategies of Social Closure in Class Formation', in F. Parkin, (ed.), *The Social Analysis of Class Structure*, London, Tavistock.
Parsons, T., 1937, *The Structure of Social Action*, Glencoe, Illinois, The Free Press.
Parsons, T., 1949, 'The Social Structure of the Family', in R. Anshen (ed.), *The Family: Its Function and Destiny*, 276–305, New York, Harper & Row.
Parsons, T., 1951, *The Social System*, Glencoe, Illinois, The Free Press.
Parsons, T., 1960, 'Some Reflections on the Institutional Framework of Economic Development', in *Structure & Process in Modern Society*, Glencoe, Illinois, The Free Press.
Parsons, T., 1966, *Societies: Evolutionary and Comparative Perspectives*, Englewood Cliffs, New Jersey, Prentice-Hall.
Parsons, T., 1971, *The System of Modern Societies*, Englewood Cliffs, New Jersey, Prentice-Hall.
Patterson, A., 1910, *Across the Bridges*, London, Edward Arnold.
Pirenne, H., 1936, *Economic and Social History of Mediaeval Europe*, London, Routledge & Kegan Paul.
Pirenne, H., 1939, *Les villes et les institutions urbaines* (2 vols.), Brussels, Librairie Félix Alcan.
Popper, K., 1959, *The Poverty of Historicism*, London, Routledge & Kegan Paul.
Popper, K., 1962, *The Open Society and its Enemies*, London, Routledge & Kegan Paul.
Porchnev, B., 1963, *Les Soulèvements Populaires en France*, Paris.
Poster, M., 1978, *Critical Theory of the Family*, London, Pluto Press.
Quetelet, A., 1836, *Sur l'homme et le développement de ses facultés*, Paris, Bachelier.
Radcliffe-Brown, A. R., 1951, 'The Comparative Method in Social Anthropology', in *The Journal of the Royal Anthropologial Institute*, 81.

Rainwater, L., 1965, 'Crucible of Identity: the Negro Lower Class Family', in T. Parsons and K. Clark (eds.), *The Negro American*, Boston, Beacon Press.

Rickert, H., 1962, *Science and History*, Princeton, N.J., Van Nostrand.

Riesman, D., Glazer, N., Denney, R., 1950, *The Lonely Crowd*, New Haven, Yale University Press.

Roth, G., 1979, 'Duration and Rationalization: Fernand Braudel and Max Weber', in Roth, G., and Schlechter, W., *Max Weber's Vision of History*, Berkeley, University of California Press.

Rubington, E. and Weinberg, M. S., 1968, *Deviance: the Interactionist Perspective*, New York, Macmillan.

Runciman, W. G., 1966, *Relative Deprivation and Social Justice*, London, Routledge and Kegan Paul.

Salmon, J. H., 1967, 'Venal Office and Popular Sedition in France', *Past and Present*, 37.

Samuel, R., 1980, 'History Workshop Methods', *History Workshop*, 9.

Samuel, R., (ed.), 1981, *People's History and Socialist Theory*, London, Routledge and Kegan Paul.

Samuel, R. and Stedman Jones, G., 1976, 'Sociology and History', *History Workshop*, I.

Samuelsson, K., 1961, *Religion and Economic Action*, London, Routledge and Kegan Paul.

Schwartz, D. C., 1970, 'A Theory of Revolutionary Behaviour', in J. C. Davies (ed.), *When Men Rebel and Why*, New York, Free Press.

Selbourne, D., 1980, 'On the Methods of the History Workshop', in *History Workshop*, 9.

Sennett, R., 1977, *The Fall of Public Man*, Cambridge, Cambridge University Press.

Sennett, R. and Cobb, J., 1977, *The Hidden Injuries of Class*, Cambridge, Cambridge University Press.

Serge, V., 1963, *Memoirs of a Revolutionary*, Oxford, Oxford University Press.

Shanin, T., 1972, *The Awkward Class*, Oxford, Clarendon Press.

Shils, E. A., 1975, *Center and Periphery*, Chicago, University of Chicago Press.

Shirer, W., 1960, *The Rise and Fall of the Third Reich*, London, Secker & Warburg.

Shub, D., 1966, *Lenin*, Harmondsworth, Penguin Books.

Shorter, E., 1971, *The Historian and the Computer*, Toronto, Toronto University Press.

Skocpol, T., 1979, *States and Social Revolutions*, Cambridge, Cambridge University Press.

Smelser, N. J., 1959, *Social Change and the Industrial Revolution*, London, Routledge & Kegan Paul.

Smelser, N. J., 1963a, 'Mechanisms of Change and Adjustment to Change', in B. E. Hoselitz and W. E. Moore (eds.), *Industrialization and Society*, Paris, Unesco/Mouton.

Smelser, N. J., 1963b, *Theory of Collective Behaviour*, New York, Free Press.

Smelser, N. J., 1968, *Essays in Sociological Explanation*, Englewood Cliffs, N.J., Prentice-Hall.

Soboul, A., 1953, 'Classes & Class Struggles during the French Revolution', *Science and Society*, xvii.

Soboul, A., 1962, *Précis d'histoire de la Révolution française*, Paris.

Spencer, H., 1961, *The Study of Sociology*, Ann Arbor, University of Michigan.

Stedman Jones, G., 1976, 'From Historical Sociology to Theoretic History', *British Journal of Sociology*, xxvii, 295–305.

Stern, F., 1980, *Gold and Iron*, London, Allen & Unwin.

Stinchcombe, A. L., 1968, *Constructing Social Theories*, New York, Harcourt, Brace.

Stinchcombe, A. L., 1978, *Theoretical Methods in Social History*, New York, Academic Press.

Stone, L., 1966, letter, *Times Literary Supplement*, 21.4.66.

Stone, L., 1977, *The Family, Sex and Marriage in England, 1500–1800*, London, Weidenfeld & Nicolson.

Stone, L., 1979, 'The Revival of Narrative', *Past and Present*, 85.

Strauss, A., 1977, *Mirrors and Masks: the Search for Identity*, London, Martin Robertson.

Swallow Press, 1970, *Contempt: transcript of the Contempt Citations, Sentences and Responses of the Chicago Conspiracy, 10*, Chicago: Swallow Press.

Tawney, R. H., 1926, *Religion and the Rise of Capitalism*, London, John Murray.

Theen, R. H. W., 1974, *Lenin*, London, Quartet Books.

Thernstrom, S., 1968, 'Quantitative Methods in History', in Lipset and Hofstadter (1968).

Thomas, K., 1966, 'The Tools and the Job', *Times Literary Supplement*, 7.4.66.

Thomas, W. I. and Znaniecki, F., 1958, *The Polish Peasant in Europe and America*, New York, Dover Books.

Thompson, E. P., 1963, *The Making of the English Working Class*, London, Gollancz.

Thompson, E. P., 1965, 'Peculiarities of the English', in R. Miliband and J. Saville (eds.), *The Socialist Register*, 1965, London, Merlin Press.

Thompson, E. P., 1972, Review of K. Thomas, *Religion and the Decline of Magic, Midland History*, 1, 3.

Thompson, E. P., 1978, *The Poverty of Theory*, London, Merlin Press.

Tilly, C., 1964, *The Vendée*, London, Edward Arnold.

Titmuss, R. M., 1958, *Essays on the Welfare State*, London, George Allen & Unwin.

Toennies, F., 1955, *Community and Association*, (translated by C. Loomis), London, Routledge & Kegan Paul.

Trotsky, L., 1934, *The History of the Russian Revolution*, London, Gollancz.

Turnell, M., 1947, *The Classical Moment*, London, Hamish Hamilton.

Vovelle, M., 1973, *Piété baroque et déchristianisation*, Paris, Plon.

Wallerstein, I., 1974, *The Modern World System*, New York, Academic Press.

Walsh, W. H., 1951, *An Introduction to Philosophy of History*, London, Hutchinson.

Watkins, J. W. N., 1953, 'Ideal Types and Historical Explanation', in J. Feigl and M. Brodbeck (eds.), *Readings in the Philosophy of Science*, New York (1953).

Weber, M., 1930, *The Protestant Ethic and the Spirit of Capitalism*, translated by T. Parsons, London, George Allen & Unwin.

Weber, M., 1949, *The Methodology of the Social Sciences*, translated and edited by E. Shils and F. Finch, New York, Free Press.

Weber, M., 1961, *General Economic History*, translated by F. Knight, New York, Collier- Macmillan.

Weber, M., 1968, *Economy and Society*, edited by G. Roth & C. Wittich, New York, Bedminster Press.

Weber, M., 1976, 'Social Causes of the Decline of Ancient Civilisation', in *The Agrarian Sociology of Ancient Civilisations*, translated by R. I. Frank, London, NLB.

Westergaard, T. and Resler, H., 1975, *Class in a Capitalist Society*, London, Heinemann.

White, H., 1978, *Tropics of Discourse*, Baltimore, Johns Hopkins Hopkins University Press.

White, J., 1979, 'Campbell Bunk: a Lumpen Community in London Between the Wars', *History Workshop Journal*, 8.

White, J., 1980, *Rothschild Buildings*, London, Routledge & Kegan Paul.

Willis, P., 1977, *Learning to Labour*, Farnborough, Saxon House.

Wilson, E., 1940, *To the Finland Station*, New York, Harcourt, Brace.

Wolf, E. R., 1971, *Peasant Wars of the Twentieth Century*, London, Faber & Faber.

Wolf, K. H., 1971, *From Karl Mannheim*, New York, Oxford University Press.

Wrigley, E. A., 1977, 'Reflections on the History of the Family', *Daedalus*.

Wrigley, E. A., 1979, 'Historical data and historical research', London, Social Science Research Council.

Wrong, D., 1970, *Max Weber*, Englewood Cliffs, New Jersey, Prentice-Hall.

Young, Jack, 1971, 'The role of the police as amplifiers of deviancy, negotiators of reality and translators of fantasy. Some consequences of our present system of drug control as seen in Notting Hill', in S. Cohen (ed.), *Images of Deviance*, Harmondsworth, Middlesex, Penguin.

Index

ADS 0711

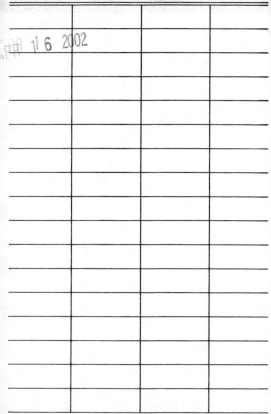

DATE DUE

APR 16 2002			